LOVING
EACH OTHER

LOVING EACH OTHER

For Better and For Best

Gary Smalley

INSPIRATIONAL PRESS
New York

First Inspirational Press edition published in 1993.

Inspirational Press
A division of BBS Publishing Corporation
450 Raritan Center Parkway
Edison, NJ 08837

Inspirational Press is a registered trademark of BBS Publishing Corporation.

Published by arrangement with Zondervan Publishing House.

Distributed by World Publishing
Nashville, TN 37214
www.worldpublishing.com

Library of Congress Control Number: 92-76130

ISBN: 0-88486-345-X

Printed in the United States of America.

Contents

The Joy of Committed Love

REVISED EDITION

To the number one woman in my life,
Norma Jean,
and to our children,
Kari, Greg, and Michael

Contents

Introduction

Fulfilling marriages don't just happen. They are built on proven principles essential to the development of any warm and loving relationship. Whether you and your loved one are about to be married or have been married a few years or many, the principles in this book, a combination of my two previous volumes, *If Only He Knew* and *For Better or for Best*, will help you strengthen your relationship in a practical, every day way.

From the outset, let me admit that I don't think men and women are alike. They have different needs and different emotional responses to certain behavior and situations. Of course, men and women share the universal need to be loved and accepted just as they are, though the expression of this universal need is different for a man than it is for a woman. Thus the structure of this volume.

The first section, *If Only He Knew*, is written for men. We need to understand how to love our wives; many times we don't. Even those of us who think we're good husbands will find in reading this section that we have treated our wives cavalierly, flippantly, callously. But don't despair. I know these things because I have acted that way toward my wife. I developed my marital principles first to help myself and my marriage, then to help others who were experiencing the same small frustrations and irritations that make a marriage mediocre or bad. It is comforting to know that other people have experienced the same problems you have.

The second half of this volume, *For Better or for Best*, deals with the women's side of a marital relationship. Women, too, need to know and understand their husbands. They need to learn how to encourage their husbands to better marriages. Here I present principles to women to help them motivate their husbands to change, to listen, and to become more sensitive. The methods most women use are counterproductive at best. These practical principles work; my wife has used them throughout our marriage.

As you begin to put these principles into practice, remember one thing, though. Changes do not happen overnight. It takes work and consistency, but every day, every month, every year as you continue in this course, you will see reflected in your spouse's face the joy of committed love.

Part I

Marriage Building Principles for the Husband

1

How to Drive
Your Wife Away
Without Even Trying

"You husbands
likewise,
live
with your wives
in an
understanding
way."
1 Peter 3:7

AT THE OTHER end of the phone a quivering voice said, "You've got to help me. She has a court order against me." George was coming to me for help after his relationship with his wife was already in shreds. "We've been married over twenty years, and she won't even let me back in the house. I can't believe she would treat me this way after all I've done for her. Can you help us get back together?"

Before I answered his question, I wanted to talk to his wife. "There's no way you can talk to Barbara," he said. "She wouldn't talk to you. The moment you say you're representing me in any way, she'll hang up on you."

"I've never been turned down by a wife yet," I assured him, "so we might as well see if this will be the first time. Would you give me her phone number?"

To be honest, as grim as things sounded, I did wonder if she would be the first wife not willing to talk to me about her marital strife. But my doubts were unfounded—she was more than anxious to discuss their problems.

"What would it take for you to be willing to let your husband back into your life? What would have to happen before you would try to rebuild a marriage relationship with him?" Those were the same questions I had asked many wives who claimed they didn't want their husbands back.

Her response was typical. "I can't possibly answer that

9

question. He's the worst husband in the world, so I wouldn't think of taking him back. I can't stand his personality or his offensive habits any more." The court order would take care of him, she told me. "Just keep him away!"

I gently asked her if she could tell me the things he had done to offend her. When I heard her response, I said, "It sounds like he hasn't been a very sensitive and gentle husband, has he?"

Once again I asked her to stretch her imagination and think about what changes would be necessary before she would take him back.

There was plenty of room for improvement, she told me. First, he was too domineering and critical of her. Second, he tried to control her every move with a possessive grip. Third, he trampled her sense of self-worth with constant ridicule. And fourth, although he always had time for business and other interests, he seldom took time to listen to her. On top of all that, he spied on her and didn't give her any freedom.

"Don't get any ideas, though," she told me at the end of our conversation. "Because no matter what, I won't stop the divorce."

When I relayed these complaints to George, I knew I had touched some sensitive spots. He defended himself and accused her. I let him rant for a while before asking, "Do you want your wife back?"

"Yes, I'd do anything to get her back," he said.

"Good. I'm always willing to work with someone ready to readjust his life. But if you're not totally serious, let me know now. I don't like to play games." Again he committed himself to change, but his commitment didn't last beyond my next statement. "We're going to have to work on your domineering and possessive nature. It shows you don't genuinely love your wife."

He fumed and spouted, defended and fought so much I began to wonder if he really would commit himself to the necessary changes.

"I've never met a more belligerent, stubborn man in my entire life!" I exclaimed.

Suddenly subdued, he responded, "That's not my nature. I'm usually rather submissive inside. Maybe I'm putting up a front because I'm really not a pushy person. I feel like people run all over me."

"I don't think you and I are talking about the same person," I responded. "If I were your wife, I'm not sure I could bear up emotionally under your domineering personality."

That stopped him long enough for him to give our conversation some serious thought. After talking to his friends and even praying that God would help him understand, he returned to my office, able to confess his faults and ready to change.

"If you really want to love your wife, then you need to begin right now, at the divorce trial," I said. Now that we were on the subject, he mentioned that he needed to get a lawyer because she had one.

"No," I cautioned him. "If you want to win her back, you need to forget about a lawyer this time." (I don't always recommend this, but based on their personal background, I felt he would stand a better chance of regaining her love without legal counsel.)

"You're crazy," he said. "They'll take me to the cleaners."

Feeling somewhat defenseless, he reluctantly agreed to forfeit legal counsel.

Two of his friends and I waited in the courthouse for the closed-room session to end. He came running out of the courtroom bellowing. "She wants 20% of my retirement . . . 20%! No way I'm gonna do that!"

Once again I asked him, "Do you want your wife back?" Again, he nodded yes! "Then give her 25%." I reminded him that *now* was the time to respect her and treat her sensitively. Later, he emerged from the courtroom a divorced man, but not for long. . . .

Several months later I ran into him at the grocery store. "My wife and I remarried," he said triumphantly. "I thought you were crazy when you first told me the things I should do for my wife . . . there was no way I would ever be able to do them," he continued. "It took sheer will power at first. I only did them because you said that God rewards those who seek Him and follow His ways. But you know, it's really amazing. After doing them for three months, I actually enjoy them."

He continued to give examples of the new ways he was treating his wife. Like the time she took a business trip and he wrote her a note telling her how much he wished he could be with her. Inserted in the note were extra money and directions on how to reach her destination.

George has finally realized that his wife is a special person who needs tender treatment, almost as if her forehead were stamped "Very Important—Handle With Care"!

He has discovered the secret to renewing any strained relationship—honor. This is discussed further in chapter 3; before we discuss rebuilding a failing marriage, let's examine two major reasons marriages fail.

1. Men and women enter marriage with "storybook" expectations and limited training.

I once asked a college girl what kind of man she would like to marry. "I'd like for him to be able to tell jokes, sing and dance, and stay home at night."

"You don't want a husband," I told her. "You want a television set."

Her visions of a husband reveal one of the most common reasons marriages fail. We marry with unrealistic expectations and few, if any, caring skills. In fact, most of us are rather fuzzy when it comes to our mates' real needs.

Isn't it ironic that a plumber's license requires four years of training, but a marriage license requires nothing but two willing bodies and sometimes a blood test? Since most of us bounce through the educational corridors without any basic communication courses, many men marry with absolutely no knowledge of how to build a meaningful relationship. In short, most men have no idea how to love their wives in a way that makes both of them happy.

Recently I asked five divorced women, individually, "If your husband began treating you in a consistently loving manner, would you take him back?"

"Of course I would," each replied. But, unfortunately, none had hope that her husband would ever be like that.

Because I knew one of the men personally, I had to concur with his wife's hopelessness. If he were willing to try, he could win her back. Unfortunately, he wasn't interested in learning.

"What he doesn't realize is that a lot of women are as responsive as puppies," one woman explained to me. "If he'd come back and treat me with tenderness, gentleness, and understanding, I'd take him back tomorrow."

How sad that we men don't know how to win our wives back or even how to keep from losing them. How can we win their affection, their respect, their love and cooperation when *we don't even know where to begin?* Instead of trying to learn what it takes to mend a cracked marriage, most of us would rather jump on the divorce bandwagon.

We violate the relationship laws inherent in marriage, and then we wonder why it all goes sour. But we wouldn't wonder if the law of aerodynamics sent a one-winged airplane plummeting to the earth.

Imagine yourself an aerospace engineer working for NASA. Your job is to put several men on the moon, but something goes wrong halfway through their flight. You wouldn't dream of walking out on the entire project because something went wrong. Instead, you and the other engineers would put your heads together, insert data into the computer, and . . . *voilà!* You would work night and day to try to discover the problem and make all the vital adjustments to get that spacecraft back on course or help the men return to earth. If the project had failed altogether, you still wouldn't forsake it. You would study what happened and modify it to avoid similar problems in the future.

> Like the spacecraft, your marriage is subject to laws that determine its success or failure. If any of these laws are violated, you and your wife are locked into orbits, destined to crash. However, if during the marriage you recognize which law or principle you are violating and make the necessary adjustments, your marriage will stay on the right course.

2. *Men and women lack understanding about the general differences between men and women.*

I would venture to say that most marital difficulties center around one fact—men and women are TOTALLY different. The differences (emotional, mental, and physical) are so extreme that without a *concentrated effort* to understand them, it is nearly impossible to have a happy marriage. A famous psychiatrist once said, "After thirty years of studying women, I ask myself, 'What is it that they really want?'" If this was his conclusion, just imagine how little we know about our wives.

You may already be aware of some of the differences. Many, however, will come as a complete surprise. Did you know, for instance, that virtually every cell in a man's body has a chromosome makeup entirely different from those in a woman's body? How about this next one? Dr. James Dobson says there is strong evidence indicating that the "seat" of the emotions in a man's brain is wired differently than in a woman's. By virtue of these two differences alone, men and women are miles apart emotionally and physically. Let's examine some of the differences between men and women.

MENTAL/EMOTIONAL DIFFERENCES

1. Women tend to be more *personal* than men. Women have a deeper interest in people and feelings—building relationships— while men tend to be more preoccupied with practicalities that can

be understood through logical deduction. Men tend to be more conquer oriented—competing for dominance—hence, their strong interest in sports such as football and boxing.

Why would a woman be less interested in a boxing match? Because close, loving relationships are usually not developed in the ring! Also, watch what happens during many family vacations. He is challenged by the goal of driving four hundred miles a day, while she wants to stop now and then to drink coffee and relax and relate. He thinks that's a waste of time because it would interfere with his goal.

Men tend to be less desirous and knowledgeable in building intimate relationships, both with women and with others. For example, women are usually the ones who buy marriage books. They are usually the ones who develop the initial interest in knowing God and attending church. When a man realizes that his wife is more naturally motivated to nurture relationships, he can relax and accept these tendencies and *choose* to develop a better marriage and better relationships with his children.

As a husband, do you realize that your wife's natural ability for developing relationships can actually *help* you fulfill the two greatest commandments taught by Christ—loving God and loving others (Matt. 22:36–40)? Jesus said that if we obey these two commandments, we are fulfilling *all* the commandments. Think of it! Your wife has the God-given drive and ability to help you build meaningful relationships in both these areas. God knew you needed special help because He stated, "It is not good for the man to be alone; I will make him a helper [and completer] suitable for him" (Gen. 2:18). If you let her, your wife can open up a whole new and complete world of communication and deeper relationships.

2. Women become an intimate part of their surroundings. Dr. Cecil Osborne, in his book *The Art of Understanding Your Mate*, said women become *an intimate part of* the people they know and the things that surround them; they enter into a kind of "oneness" with their environment. Though a man relates to people and situations, he usually doesn't allow his identity to become entwined with them. He somehow remains apart. That's why a woman, viewing her house as an extension of herself, can be hurt when it's criticized by others. A man may not realize it, but when he yells at the kids for something they did, his words affect her deeply as well.

Women tend to find their identity in close relationships, while men gain their identity through vocations.

3. Women often need more time to adjust to change. Because of a woman's *emotional identity* with people and places around her, she needs more time to adjust to change that may affect her

relationships. A man can logically deduce the benefits of a change and get "psyched-up" for it in a matter of minutes. Not so with a woman. Since she focuses on immediate consequences of relocating, for example, she needs time to overcome the initial adjustment before warming up to the advantages of it.

4. Women tend to express their hostility *verbally* whereas men tend to be more *physically* violent.

PHYSICAL DIFFERENCES

Dr. Paul Popenoe, founder of the American Institute of Family Relations in Los Angeles, dedicated his most productive years to the research of biological differences between the sexes. Some of his findings are listed below.

- Woman has greater constitutional vitality, perhaps because of her unique chromosome makeup. Normally, female outlives male by four to eight years in the U.S.
- Woman's metabolism is normally lower than man's.
- Man and woman differ in skeletal structure, woman having a shorter head, broader face, less protruding chin, shorter legs, and longer trunk.
- Woman has larger kidneys, liver, stomach, and appendix than man, but smaller lungs.
- Woman has several unique and important functions: menstruation, pregnancy, lactation. Woman's hormones are of a different type and more numerous than man's.
- Woman's thyroid is larger and more active. It enlarges during pregnancy and menstruation; makes woman more prone to goiter; provides resistance to cold; is associated with her smooth-skinned, relatively hairless body and thin layer of subcutaneous fat.
- Woman's blood contains more water and 20 percent fewer red cells. Since the red cells supply oxygen to the body cells, woman tires more easily and is more prone to faint. Her constitutional vitality is, therefore, limited to "life span." (When the working day in British factories was increased from ten to twelve hours under wartime conditions, accidents increased 150 percent among women but not at all among men.)
- On the average, man possesses 50 percent more brute strength than woman (40 percent of a man's body weight is muscle; 23 percent of a woman's).
- Woman's heart beats more rapidly (average 80 beats per

minute vs. 72 for man). Woman's blood pressure (10 points lower than man's) varies from minute to minute, but she has less tendency toward high blood pressure—at least until after menopause.

- Woman's vital capacity or breathing power is significantly lower than man's.
- Woman withstands high temperatures better than man because her metabolism slows down less.

SEXUAL DIFFERENCES

A woman's sexual drive tends to be related to her menstrual cycle, while a man's drive is fairly constant. The hormone testosterone is a major factor in stimulating a man's sexual desire.

A woman is stimulated more by touch and romantic words. She is far more attracted by a man's personality, while the man is stimulated by sight. A man is usually less discriminating about those to whom he is physically attracted.

While a man needs little or no preparation for sex, a woman often needs hours of emotional and mental preparation. Harsh or abusive treatment can easily remove her desire for sexual intimacy for days at a time. When a woman's emotions have been trampled by her husband, she is often repulsed by his advances. Many women have told me they feel like prostitutes when they're forced to make love while feeling resentment toward their husbands. However, a man may not be AWARE of what he is putting his wife through if she feels he is forcing sex upon her.

These basic differences, which usually surface soon after the wedding, are the source of many conflicts in marriage. From the start, the woman has a greater intuitive awareness of how to develop a loving relationship. Because of her sensitivity, she is initially more considerate of his feelings and enthusiastic about developing a meaningful, multilevel relationship: that is, she knows how to build something more than a sexual marathon; she wants to be a lover, a best friend, a fan, a homemaker, and an appreciated partner. The man, on the other hand, does not generally have her instinctive awareness of what the relationship should be. He doesn't know how to encourage and love his wife or treat her in a way that meets her deepest needs.

Since he doesn't have an understanding of these vital areas through intuition, he must rely *solely* upon the knowledge and skills he has acquired *prior* to marriage. Unfortunately, our educational system does not require a training program for a husband-to-be. His only education may be the example he observed in his home. For many of us, that example may have been insufficient. We enter marriage knowing everything about sex and very little about genuine, unselfish love.

I am not saying men are more selfish than women. I'm simply saying that at the outset of a marriage most men are not as equipped to express unselfish love or as desirous of nurturing marriage into a loving and lasting relationship as women are.

INTUITIVE DIFFERENCES

Norman was planning to invest more than $50,000 in a business opportunity that was a "sure thing." He had scrutinized it from every angle and had logically deduced that it couldn't miss. After signing a contract and delivering a check to the other party, he decided to tell his wife about the investment.

Upon hearing a few of the details, she immediately felt uneasy about the deal. Norman sensed her uneasiness and became angry, asking why she felt that way. She couldn't give a logical reason because she didn't have one. All she knew was that it just didn't "sit right." Norman gave in, went back to the other party, and asked for a refund. "You're crazy!" the man told him as he returned Norman's money. A short time later, ALL of the organizers and investors were indicted by the federal government. His wife's intuition had not only saved him $50,000, but it may have kept Norman out of jail.

What exactly is this "woman's intuition"? It's not something mystical. According to a Stanford University research team led by neuropsychologists McGuinness and Tribran, women do catch subliminal messages faster and more accurately than men. Since this intuition is based on an unconscious mental process, many women aren't able to give specific explanations for the way they feel. They simply perceive or "feel" something about a situation or person, while men tend to follow a logical analysis of circumstances or people.

Now that you know several reasons why men and women cannot understand their respective differences without great effort, I hope you will have more hope, patience, and tolerance as you endeavor to strengthen and deepen your relationship with your wife. With this in mind, let's look at some of the serious consequences of allowing a poor marriage to continue in its downhill slide.

SERIOUS CONSEQUENCES OF A POOR MARRIAGE

First, a woman who is not properly loved by her husband can develop any number of serious physical ailments needing thousands of dollars' worth of treatment, according to Dr. Ed Wheat, a noted Christian physician.

Second, every aspect of a woman's emotional and physical existence is dependent on the romantic love she receives from her husband, says Dr. James Dobson. So, husbands, if *you* feel locked out of your bedroom, listen closely. According to Dr. Dobson, when a man learns to love his wife in the way she needs to be loved, she will respond to him physically in a way he never dreamed possible.

Third, a husband's lack of love for his wife can drastically affect their children's emotional development, according to John Drescher in his book, *Seven Things Children Need.*

Fourth, a disrespectful wife and rebellious children are more likely to be found in the home of a man who does not know how to lovingly support his family.

Fifth, when a man settles for a poor marriage, he is forfeiting his reputation before all the world. He is saying, "I don't care what I promised at the marriage altar; I'm not going to try any longer." By refusing to love his wife as he should, he is telling those around him that he is self-centered and unreliable.

Sixth, the son of an unloving husband will probably learn many of the wrong ways to treat his future wife by modeling after his father. Unloving parents simply can't keep their problems to themselves. They are bound to affect their children's future relationships.

And seventh, improper love increases the possibility of mental illness requiring psychiatric treatment of family members. Echoing what the Bible said centuries ago, Dr. Nathan Ackerman in an article in *Family Weekly*, said mental illness is passed on within a family, transmitted from generation to generation. In that same article, Dr. Salvador Minuchin, a psychiatrist, said family members often get caught in a groove of mental illness by putting undue stress on each other.

THE HARDEST DECISION YOU MAY EVER MAKE

I am not trying to force you into the "perfect husband" mold. I don't know *any* perfect husbands. However, I do know some who are learning how to respond to their wives' special needs.

What I do want to do is to help you learn how to love your wife more effectively and consistently. At first you may feel like you're learning to walk all over again. Weeks, months, or even a year may pass before you reach your goal of consistent loving behavior. After you learn to make progress, you will gain confidence. Soon you will be right in the midst of the kind of marriage you never thought possible.

Remember—you may feel it's impossible to change lifelong habits, but it's not. It usually takes from thirty to sixty days to change a habit. So I hope you will decide to try to change yours. For some men it may take the accountability of a small group or the support of a pastor. However, I know from experience that the rewards are well worth the effort.

The Secret to a Fulfilling Marriage

Persistence!! Sometimes in the middle of a conflict with Norma I really want to give up. But that's only how I felt. Often I'm tired, run down, under too much stress—consequently, the future looks bleak. That's when I rely upon knowledge, not feelings. I act upon what *will* strengthen our relationship, and in a few days I see the results. In fact, I usually feel better the next day and have renewed desire to work on our marriage. So *I never give up.* I keep acting on what I've learned from the Bible are the secrets of lasting relationships.

I act on those secrets no matter how I feel. I've tried to expand and illustrate those secrets throughout this book.

Remember, *you* are the one who gains when you strive to have a loving relationship with your wife. My wife has told me dozens of times that when I treat her right I'm the one who wins. My loving care motivates her to do extra things for me, to respond gladly to my needs and desires, but this has never been my main motivation. The strongest motivation for me has been the *challenge* and *rewards* of living my life as outlined in Scripture. For me, it's following the two greatest teachings of Christ—to know and love God and to know and love people (Matt. 22:36–40). All the joy and fulfillment I have desired in this life have come from these two relationships—with God and with others (Eph. 3:19–20; John 15:11–13). These relationships are so important that I have added to my own life another motivation— perhaps the best motivation for me. I allow a few other couples to hold me accountable for loving my wife and children. They have the freedom to ask me how we're doing, as a couple and as a family, and I know they love me enough to lift me up when I fall. And I always try to remember that love is a *choice.* I choose to care about my relationships. That same choice leading to great rewards can be yours.

My wife and I have committed the remaining years of our lives to the study of skills needed to rebuild meaningful relationships. I have personally interviewed hundreds of women about what actions of their husbands tear down or build up their marriages. Basically, this book is a summary of my findings. (Even now, we're in the process of researching and discovering what it takes to motivate men relationally and why men tend to resist growth in this area. Our goal once we isolate these key factors is to call 100,000 men, nationwide, to an all-out commitment to their families.)

Your wife may be a career woman without children or a busy homemaker and mother of three. Whatever the case, I believe you can *customize* the general principles in this book to build a more fulfilling relationship with her.

Before reading the next chapter, take this short quiz to rate how stable your marriage is at this moment. Then, when you have pinpointed your weak and strong points, use the chapters that follow to take steps necessary to strengthen your relationship. Some of the ideas for this checklist are from Dr. George Larson, a psychologist who has done extensive work helping people develop good relationships. He believes, as I do, that good relationships don't just happen. They evolve and are sustained only when people know what they want and how to get it.

Answer YES or NO to each question, then check your score below:

1. Do you make your wife feel good about herself? (yes _____ no _____)
2. Do you value the same things in your wife that you value in yourself? (yes _____ no _____)
3. Does your face spontaneously break into a smile when you see your wife? (yes _____ no _____)
4. When you leave the house, does your wife have a sense of well-being, having been nourished by your company? (yes _____ no _____)
5. Can you and your wife tell each other honestly what you really want instead of using manipulation or games? (yes _____ no _____)
6. Can your wife get angry at you without your thinking less of her? (yes _____ no _____)
7. Can you accept your wife as she is instead of having several plans to redo her? (yes _____ no _____)
8. Is your behavior consistent with your words? (yes _____ no _____)
9. Do your actions show you really care for your wife? (yes _____ no _____)
10. Can you feel comfortable with your wife when she's wearing old clothes? (yes _____ no _____)
11. Do you enjoy introducing your wife to your friends or acquaintances? (yes _____ no _____)

12. Are you able to share with your wife your moments of weakness, failure, disappointment? (yes _____ no _____)
13. Would your wife say you are a good listener? (yes _____ no _____)
14. Do you trust your wife to solve her own problems? (yes _____ no _____)
15. Do you admit to your wife you have problems and need her comfort? (yes _____ no _____)
16. Do you believe you could live a full and happy life without your wife? (yes _____ no _____)
17. Do you encourage your wife to develop her full potential as a woman? (yes _____ no _____)
18 Are you able to learn from your wife and value what she says? (yes _____ no _____)
19. If your wife were to die tomorrow, would you be very happy you had the chance to meet her and to marry her? (yes _____ no _____)
20. Does your wife feel she's more important than anyone or anything else in your life other than God? (yes _____ no _____)
21. Do you believe you know at least five of your wife's major needs and how to meet those needs in a skillful way? (yes _____ no _____)
22. Do you know what your wife needs when she's under stress or when she's discouraged? (yes _____ no _____)
23. When you offend your wife, do you usually admit you were wrong and seek her forgiveness? (yes _____ no _____)
24. Would your wife say you praise her at least once a day? (yes _____ no _____)
25. Would your wife say you are open to her correction? (yes _____ no _____)
26. Would your wife say you are a protector, that you know what her limitations are as a woman? (yes _____ no _____)
27. Would your wife say you usually consider her feelings and ideas whenever making a decision that affects the family or her? (yes _____ no _____)
28. Would your wife say you enjoy being with her and sharing many of life's experiences with her? (yes _____ no _____)
29. Would your wife say you are a good example of what you would like her to be? (yes _____ no _____)
30. Would you say you create interest in her when you share things you consider important? (yes _____ no _____)

If you answered "yes" to *10 or less* questions, then your relationship is in major need of overhaul.

If you answered "yes" to *11–19* of the questions, your relationship needs improvement.

If you answered "yes" to *20 or more*, then you're probably on your way to a good, lasting relationship.

FOR PERSONAL REFLECTION

1. What two main responsibilities are required of every husband? 1 Peter 3:7.
2. What is the biblical requirement to love and what do these verses have in common? John 15:13; 1 Corinthians 13:5; Philippians 2:3–8.
3. What do we gain from loving others? John 15:11; Galatians 5:13–14; Ephesians 3:19–20.

2

Where Have All
The Feelings Gone?

"But
the greatest
of these
is
love."
1 Corinthians 13:13

"I DON'T LOVE you any more," Sandi said casually, shocking Jim out of his intense interest in a baseball game on TV. "I want to leave you, and I'm taking Jamey with me," she added. Jim whirled around in his chair, wondering if he had heard correctly.

Since Sandi and Jim believed themselves to be sensible, educated adults, they separated calmly and agreed on a settlement without dispute. Jim, in his "maturity," even helped Sandi pack. Then he calmly watched as she and his daughter left his house for good. But he wasn't calm on the inside. He couldn't keep food down for the next month, and it wasn't long before he developed shingles and boils. His physical problems were only symptoms of a much deeper problem—a lack of *knowledge* and *interest* in building a lasting marriage relationship.

Fortunately, Jim was able to win his wife back with genuine love. It took a year, but Sandi was finally convinced by the changes in Jim that their marriage deserved another try. Jim got a second chance at his marriage. Unfortunately, not all men do.

Just what did Jim learn about love during a year of separation from Sandi? He learned that a successful marriage, like any other worthwhile endeavor, takes time and study.

Who would think of allowing an untrained man to climb into the cockpit of an airplane and tinker with the gauges? Or who would allow a novice to service the engines of a modern jet? Yet we expect men to build strong, loving relationships without any education at all. A man must be "educated": He first must discover the essentials of genuine love, then practice them until his skills are sharp and natural. Soon his awkwardness will give way to masterful ability.

Remember the couple I mentioned in the first chapter? By the time George finally asked me how he could win his wife's love back, she had already obtained a court order to keep him away from the house. The divorce was pending, although he desperately wanted to salvage their marriage of many years. I can remember telling him, "It'll be difficult. But I assure you, as long as she isn't in love with another man, what I'm going to share with you will work."

At first, he felt awkward using the techniques I shared with him. He had to begin at zero and slowly learn to talk to Barbara, to be tender, and to care about and understand her feelings. He didn't know her special needs, that she longed for comfort and not lectures when discouraged. But in time, he DID learn and he DID win back his wife. He said he couldn't believe the gestures that once felt so awkward were now an enjoyable part of his life.

"It's just not worth it," one husband said when I told him how to save his marriage. "Don't you see, I don't like her any more. She bugs me, and I don't even want to make the effort to build what you're talking about. I just want out."

"What's the matter between the two of you?" I asked, trying to find out why his love for her had vanished. "Why can't you extend yourself toward her and try to build a loving relationship? Why don't you want to?"

"Well," he confided, "several things she has done have hurt me so much that I just can't try any more."

The next day at lunch he named seven things his wife had done, and continued to do, that made him feel like leaving. To his amazement, we were able to trace each area he hated in his wife to an area he saw lacking in his own life. Once he understood this, he asked, "What kind of man would I be to dump her when I'm contributing to the way she is?"

A marital relationship that endures and becomes more fulfilling for both the husband and the wife is no accident. Only hard work makes a marriage more fulfilling five, ten, fifteen, or twenty years after the honeymoon. I enjoy my wife's company more than ever, and I'm looking forward to a deeper relationship in later years.

THE THREE ESSENTIAL KINDS OF LOVE

Nearly every man enters marriage believing his love for his mate will never fade. Yet in the U.S., for every two marriages, there is one divorce. Why? Because we have believed in Hollywood's version of love. But it doesn't take long to discover that mere passion, which revolves around sexual gratification, is not sufficient, in itself, to establish a lasting relationship. Unfortunately, too many couples begin their marriages thinking this type of love is all they need.

There are at least three kinds of love, each totally unique. Of the three—companionship, passion, and genuine love—I believe only the latter provides an adequate foundation for a secure relationship. If a relationship lacks genuine love, it will most likely deteriorate. One of the most exciting virtues of *genuine love* is that it can be developed within your character without the help of affectionate feelings. Before we look at genuine love, let's first consider the other two types of love.

Companionship

Here we're talking about the "I like you" feelings we have toward the opposite sex—the kind of love that pleasantly stimulates all five senses. She smells good, feels good, sounds good, and looks good. She is pleasant company because she makes you feel happy. You love her like you "love pizza" or you "love country and western music."

Many relationships begin with this type of love. We all notice attractive features in others. Soon we find ourselves enjoying the parts of their lives that make us feel good.

Though this love is the foundation for many marriages, it doesn't always withstand the pressure of time. After two or three years, the wife changes her lifestyle and hairdo while her husband opts for a new cologne and different political views. The older they get, the more they change.

We all change to some degree each year. The danger arises when we base our love on changeable characteristics we found attractive on the companionship level. Our feelings grow colder and colder until we finally wonder what we ever liked about our mates in the first place. So we're off to look for someone new to love. It's easy to see why *companionship love* has trouble maturing and lasting over the years.

Passion

Passion works harder on the emotions than companionship. It's the type of love that keeps the heart working overtime: "Hey, you really turn me on!" The Greeks called it eros—a sensual and physical form of love that often produces ardent physical involvement before and after marriage. Eros love heightens our senses and stimulates our bodies and minds. It's the kind of love that hungers for the other person to stimulate and satisfy our sexual urges. This love is certainly found in marriage, but if passion exists without genuine love, usually lust gives way to disgust and repulsion, somewhat as it did with King David's son Amnon who hated Tamar after he raped her (2 Sam. 13:15).

Genuine Love

Genuine love is completely different. It means, "I see a need in you. Let me have the privilege of meeting it." Instead of taking for itself, genuine love gives to others. It motivates us to help others reach their full potential in life.

Most importantly, genuine love has no qualifications. It doesn't say, "I'll be your friend if you'll be mine." Nor does it say, "I want you to be my girlfriend because you are beautiful and I want people to see us together"; nor, "I want to be your friend because your family is rich." This love does not seek to gain, but only to give. Don't you remember those junior-high crushes when you said, "Well, I'll like her if she likes me, but if she gives me a bad time, I'm dumping her." Genuine love has no such "fine print."

THE LOWEST LEVEL OF MATURITY

The ability to love in a selfless way is dependent upon your level of maturity. The emotions listed below are typical of immature love. Check the ones characteristic of your life.

- ☐ *Jealousy* is caused by a fear of losing something or someone we value because it or they meet our needs.
- ☐ *Envy* springs from a desire to possess what someone else has. We imagine that if we gain what he or she has, then we'll be happy.
- ☐ *Anger* results from the inner turmoil and frustration we feel when we cannot control people or circumstances. We cannot have what we believe will make us happy or our goals are blocked.
- ☐ *Loneliness* results from a dependence on other people for our happiness.
- ☐ *Fear* results when we imagine or perceive that our needs or goals will not be met.

If you want to continue this exercise, you should make a list of incidents that have triggered each emotion you checked. Then ask yourself, "Why did I feel the emotion? Was I focusing on what I could *get* out of life or what I might *lose* in life?"

All these emotions are characteristic of immature love—a desire to use other people for personal happiness, a hunger for pleasure without regard for the cost. This same immaturity is behind the *abuse* of alcohol, drugs, and sex and the weakening of all our relationships.

THE HIGHEST LEVEL OF MATURITY

I believe the more we help others achieve their full potential in life, the closer we are to maturity. Demonstrating a selfless desire for others to gain is the strongest base for building lasting relationships. How can you go wrong when you develop a love that is primarily concerned with discovering what builds a deep and lasting marriage and how to identify your wife's specific needs and then you look for creative ways to meet them?

LEARNING TO DEVELOP A LASTING, MATURE LOVE

What do you think is the major stumbling block for most husbands in developing a lasting love for their mates? I have found that it is failing to meet a woman's needs from *her viewpoint.*

When Anna told me she felt unloved in special areas, Mike was dumbfounded. "What do you mean?" he asked her.

"Well, for years you have been a great husband and a very helpful person, and you've done a lot of nice things for me," she explained gently. "But sometimes you do things I don't need. I'd appreciate it if you'd find out what is important to *me.*"

A man's brilliant idea can backfire. Like the time I decided to have our house painted as a special surprise for my wife. What was special to me wasn't so special to her. Although she appreciated the paint job, she would have much rather had a new kitchen floor. When I realized that, I stopped my projects long enough to buy her a new kitchen floor. Then we made a list of priorities from her point of view. They were quite different from mine!

Doing things for others *our* way is a selfish, immature form of love. My heart goes out to those wives who have received pool tables for Christmas, tickets for a trip to the fishing swamps of Louisiana, or invitations to the Motorman's Ball.

If you've never done so, find out what *your wife* needs to feel fulfilled as a woman. Then look for special ways to fulfill her needs. At first she may not believe your caring attitude will last. Don't despair. It takes a long time to develop a sturdy relationship.

Many wives are cautious at first when they see their mates becoming more caring. Like the husband who heard a lecture on love and marriage and surprised his wife with a box of candy and a dozen roses. "Oh, this is terrible," she said, weeping. "The baby cut his finger, I burned your dinner when I couldn't get rid of the vacuum cleaner salesman, the sink is stopped up . . . and now *you* come home drunk!"

Don't be surprised if your wife doesn't understand your actions at first. It took at least two years before mine would admit that I really was changing. Now she knows I am committed to spending the rest of my life developing our relationship and meeting her needs.

Learning how to love your wife in a mature way is like raising a productive vegetable garden. If you have ever tried it, you will appreciate the comparison. Our first year in Texas we decided to grow a vegetable garden. After we dug a small plot, I dumped nearly half a bag of fertilizer on it and let it sit for three months to be sure I'd have a lush garden. But something went wrong. When the carrots came up, they were a little brown around the edges. All the tomatoes began to rot on the bottom before they ripened, so we had to pick them while they were green. None of our beans survived above the half-foot level, and our cucumbers bit the dust.

I was truly puzzled until an expert gardener told me I had "burned" my vegetables with too much fertilizer. My intentions were good, but my knowledge was limited. A husband can fail in much the same way if he doesn't know exactly how much of each "love ingredient" his wife needs. In fact, this book was written to give you some very specific guidelines for "growing" a stronger marriage.

I've seen many marriage relationships that looked just like my garden does now: full of weeds and overrun with bermuda grass— neglected. I've often thought how great it would be if vegetables could talk. If only the beans could have said, "Hey, you up there! You put way too much fertilizer in this garden, and we're having a tough time. The chemicals are killing us, and if you don't do something about it, we're all going to die." If my vegetables could talk, I could have the world's greatest garden. Fortunately, my wife can talk. I can ask her just *what* she needs, *how much* she needs, and *when* she needs it.

(Wives, if you are reading this, let me assure you that we as husbands generally *do not* know what you need. So we ask you to help us learn by telling us your needs in a gentle, loving way. Let us know when we aren't meeting your needs—but not in a critical way that could cause us to lose interest.)

Since understanding and meeting your wife's needs is a golden key to a fulfilling marriage, the rest of this book deals with that subject.

Your wife's needs.

I believe a woman needs to be in harmony with her husband through a deep, intimate relationship. She needs comradeship, harmony, and a feeling of togetherness.

To satisfy your wife, I believe you need to make a dedicated effort to meet each of her needs explained below and expanded in later chapters.

1. Your wife needs to feel that she is very valuable in your life, more important than your mother, your children, your friends, your secretary, and your job.
2. When your wife is stressed out and hurting, she needs to know that you are willing to share an intimate moment of comfort without demanding explanations or giving lectures.
3. She needs open or unobstructed communication.
4. She needs to be praised so she can feel a valuable part of your life.
5. She needs to feel free to help you without fearing retaliation and anger.
6. She needs to know that you will defend and protect her.
7. She needs to know that her opinion is so valuable that you will discuss decisions with her, and act only after carefully evaluating her advice.
8. She needs to share her life with you in every area—home, family, and outside interests.
9. She needs you to be the kind of man her son can follow and her daughter would want to marry.
10. She needs to be tenderly held often, just to be near you, apart from times of sexual intimacy.

When her needs are met, a woman gains security and glows with a sense of well-being. Some of her glow will rub off on you, especially if you are responsible for it in the first place.

THREE SAFEGUARDS IN READING THE REST OF THIS BOOK

I hope you will practice these "safeguards" with each chapter you read, since the ideas I put forth are general in nature.

First, discuss each chapter with your wife to see where she agrees and disagrees. Think of her as a flower. All flowers are beautiful, but each needs a specific amount of sunlight, nutrients, and water to flourish. You need to discover who she really is, especially as she changes from year to year.

Second, after she has shared her unique needs, rephrase them in your own words until *she* says you have picked up her meaning. It is your responsibility to find out what your wife means when she says, "You said you'd be back in a *little while.*" A little while might mean thirty minutes to her and two hours to you.

Third, it is important to remember how much you both differ as male and female. In general, a wife is naturally more sensitive and more aware of relationships than her husband. Try to understand that she will probably feel, see, and hear more than you. When your wife says something to you, allow it to sink in. Make an extra effort to understand your relationship as she sees it.

100 WAYS

The rest of this chapter is devoted to showing you one hundred ways you can love your wife *her way.* Discuss this list with your wife. Ask her to check the ones that are meaningful to her, and then arrange them in order of importance to her. Use the list as a basis for learning her views. I know your relationship will be greatly strengthened as you learn how to use these suggestions:

1. Communicate with her; never close her out.
2. Regard her as important.
3. Do everything you can to understand her feelings.
4. Be interested in her friends.
5. Ask her opinion frequently.
6. Value what she says.
7. Let her feel your approval and affection.
8. Protect her on a daily basis.
9. Be gentle and tender with her.
10. Develop a sense of humor.
11. Avoid sudden major changes without discussion and without giving her time to adjust.
12. Learn to respond openly and verbally when she wants to communicate.
13. Comfort her when she is down emotionally. For instance, put your arms around her and silently hold her for a few seconds without lectures or put-downs.
14. Be interested in what she feels is important in life.
15. Correct her gently and tenderly.
16. Allow her to teach you without putting up your defenses.
17. Make special time available to her and your children.
18. Be trustworthy.
19. Compliment her often.
20. Be creative when you express your love, either in words or actions.

21. Have specific family goals for each year.
22. Let her buy things she considers necessary.
23. Be forgiving when she offends you.
24. Show her you need her.
25. Accept her the way she is; discover her uniqueness as special.
26. Admit your mistakes; don't be afraid to be humble.
27. Lead your family in their spiritual relationship with God.
28. Allow your wife to fail; discuss what went wrong, after you have comforted her.
29. Rub her feet or neck after a hard day.
30. Take time for the two of you to sit and talk calmly.
31. Go on romantic outings.
32. Write her a letter occasionally, telling her how much you love her.
33. Surprise her with a card or flowers.
34. Express how much you appreciate her.
35. Tell her how proud you are of her.
36. Give advice in a loving way when she asks for it.
37. Defend her to others.
38. Prefer her over others.
39. Do not expect her to do activities beyond her emotional or physical capabilities.
40. Pray for her to enjoy God's best in life.
41. Take time to notice what she has done for you and the family.
42. Brag about her to other people behind her back.
43. Share your thoughts and feelings with her.
44. Tell her about your job if she is interested.
45. Take time to see how she spends her day, at work or at home.
46. Learn to enjoy what she enjoys.
47. Take care of the kids before dinner.
48. Help straighten up the house before mealtime.
49. Let her take a bubble bath while you do the dishes.
50. Understand her physical limitations if you have several children.
51. Discipline the children in love, not anger.
52. Help her finish her goals—hobbies or education.
53. Treat her as if God had stamped on her forehead, "Handle with care."
54. Get rid of habits that annoy her.
55. Be gentle and thoughtful to her relatives.
56. Do not compare her relatives with yours in a negative way.
57. Thank her for things she has done without expecting anything in return.
58. Do not expect a band to play whenever you help with the housecleaning.

59. Make sure she understands everything you are planning to do.
60. Do little things for her—an unexpected kiss, coffee in bed.
61. Treat her as an intellectual equal.
62. Find out if she wants to be treated as physically weaker.
63. Discover her fears in life.
64. See what you can do to eliminate her fears.
65. Discover her sexual needs.
66. Ask if she wants to discuss how you can meet her sexual needs.
67. Find out what makes her insecure.
68. Plan your future together.
69. Do not quarrel over words, but try to find hidden meanings.
70. Practice common courtesies like holding the door for her, pouring her coffee.
71. Ask if you offend her sexually in any way.
72. Ask if she is jealous of anyone.
73. See if she is uncomfortable about the way money is spent.
74. Take her on dates now and then.
75. Hold her hand in public.
76. Put your arm around her in front of friends.
77. Tell her you love her—often.
78. Remember anniversaries, birthdays, and other special occasions.
79. Learn to enjoy shopping.
80. Teach her to hunt and fish or whatever you enjoy doing.
81. Give her a special gift from time to time.
82. Share the responsibilities around the house.
83. Do not belittle her feminine characteristics.
84. Let her express herself freely, without fear of being called stupid or illogical.
85. Carefully choose your words, especially when angry.
86. Do not criticize her in front of others.
87. Do not let her see you become excited about the physical features of another woman if that bothers her.
88. Be sensitive to other people.
89. Let your family know you want to spend special time with them.
90. Fix dinner for her from time to time.
91. Be sympathetic when she is sick.
92. Call her when you are going to be late.
93. Do not disagree with her in front of the children.
94. Take her out to dinner and for weekend getaways.
95. Do the "little things" she needs from time to time.
96. Give her special time to be alone or with her friends.
97. Buy her what she considers an intimate gift.
98. Read a book she recommends to you.

99. Give her an engraved plaque assuring her of your lasting love.
100. Write her a poem about how special she is.

If your wife persistently reacts negatively to you, it may be because she perceives a threat to one or both of two important areas: 1) her security 2) her established relationships.

FOR PERSONAL REFLECTION

1. Who did Jesus say would be the greatest in His kingdom? Matthew 20:25–28.
2. If we desire to renew our minds and to think like Christ, we need to consider these:
- What were His thoughts? Philippians 2:5–8.
- What were Paul's thoughts on the same subject? Philippians 2:17, 22, 25.
3. If a husband is to love his wife as Christ loved the church, how does Christ love the church? Ephesians 5:25–27, 29.

3

If Your Wife
Doesn't Win First Place,
You Lose!

*"For where
your treasure is,
there will
your heart
be also."
Matthew 6:21*

RECENTLY I HAD opportunity to interview some of the married members of a popular cheerleading squad on an NFL football team. I found that they face many of the same problems other married women do. One cheerleader said her greatest disappointment is knowing she is not the most important person in her husband's life.

"Even our dog is more important to him than I am," she said. "He comes home and plays with the dog and then it's more of a when's-dinner-going-to-be-ready? attitude," she sighed.

A woman's sparkling affection toward her husband is diminished when he begins to prefer other activities or people over her. Many times he is not even aware of the way his misplaced priorities damage her and their relationship. For a marriage to flourish, a wife desperately needs to know she has a very special place in her husband's heart. In fact, her husband's relationship with God should be the only priority above his relationship with her.

Many husbands are shocked when their wives leave them "for no reason" after twenty or even thirty years of marriage. They feel they provided everything their wives could have possibly needed—a nice home, a good car, enough money to raise the children. Yet that wasn't enough. Why? A woman needs much more than things.

I have met creative businessmen who make large sums of money with their business skills and who keep their employees satisfied with respect and an awareness of their needs. Isn't it ironic that such intelligent men can go home at night and not even know how to apply the same principles to their wives? Could it be that their most important accomplishments are over at 5:00 P.M.?

Without meaning to, a husband can communicate nonverbally that other people or activities are more important to him than his wife. Haven't you heard of golf widows? Whether it is golf or tennis, club activities or community leadership, your wife and your marital happiness will suffer if most of your time and efforts are directed toward some other interest, with only cold leftovers for her. A wife can feel less important just by comparing the amount of time her husband spends with her to the time he spends elsewhere. Women notice how our eyes light up and our entire personalities change as we become excited about fishing or hunting or other activities. If your wife doesn't sense that same excitement in you when you're with her, she has a gnawing sense of failure because she feels she isn't as attractive to you as are your activities or friends. This can be devastating to a woman's sense of personal worth and security.

My own wife graphically illustrated this very important concept to me during our fifth year of marriage. I arrived home for lunch to find her standing quietly at the kitchen sink, not even interested in talking when I tried to make conversation. In a moment of insight, I perceived that I was in hot water. I remembered her coolness toward me during the previous few days, which I had mistakenly attributed to some sort of "hormonal change."

"Is there anything wrong between us?" I asked her.

"It doesn't matter. You wouldn't understand anyway," she answered.

"Funny thing, I'm losing my desire to go back to work right now. I can see there are some real problems here. Wouldn't you like to talk about it? I'm not sure what I'm doing wrong."

"Even if I told you, either you wouldn't understand or you wouldn't change, so what's the use? Let's don't talk about it. It's too painful. It discourages me and disappoints me when you say you're going to do something and then you don't."

But I gently resisted, telling her that I wished she would share it with me, that I just didn't understand. Finally, she was able to verbalize what actions during the past five years had driven a wedge between us and were causing me to violate an important biblical principle.

"You'd really rather be at work, or with your friends, or counseling people than spending time with me," she said.

I asked her to explain.

"If someone calls you when we have plans, you're liable to say,

'Let me check with my wife and see if I can't postpone our plans.' I just can't believe you would do that to me over and over again."

I explained how it was easier for me to turn her down than to say no to other people.

"What about when I cook a special dinner, sometimes even with candlelight? You'll come home or call and say you've had to make other plans. You go off somewhere with other people as if I didn't even exist, as if it didn't even mean anything that I've gone to extra-special effort for you."

She continued, "I don't care any more. I don't even want to do these special things for you. I've been disappointed so many times that I just can't handle it emotionally."

She made me realize that although I always had time for someone in need of counseling, I made little effort to spend meaningful time with her. When I did spend time with her, she said, I didn't have the same concentration or excitement about being with her.

I listened as she revealed her innermost feelings for several hours. I really didn't know what to do, and I wasn't sure I'd be able to change. But I could understand her complaints. I had neglected her and offended her with my unloving ways. However, when I agreed with her, she was unresponsive, and I could tell she was no longer expecting anything from our relationship.

She helped me discover that I was ignoring the biblical principle found in 1 Peter 3:7, and since then I've come to realize that it's the cornerstone of all relationships! *Grant her honor.* Honor basically means to attach high value, worth, or importance to a person or thing. Norma felt less important than my vocation and activities. Without realizing it, I was not honoring her as the most important person in my life, second only to my relationship with Christ.

"Could you forgive me for the way I've treated you?" I asked. "I'm willing to change. I'll really plan on changing."

"Sure, I've heard that song before," she said skeptically.

I didn't know how long it would take for me to reform. But I knew the next time someone called right before dinner I would have to ask, "Is this an emergency, or can we work it out tomorrow?" I had to show her I really meant business about valuing her and meeting her needs *first.*

I *wanted* to tell her she was the most important person in my life. I really *wanted* to feel that way. At first I didn't have those feelings, but I *wanted* to have them. As I tried to make her more important to me than anyone else, I soon began to *feel* she was top priority.

41

Feelings *follow* thoughts and actions. In other words, the warm inner feeling I have for Norma began to burn *after* I placed the "queen's crown" upon her head. (I shouldn't have been surprised because in Matthew 6 we're told that what we "treasure" or "value" is what we'll have feelings for.)

My pride was broken, my ego bruised, and my feelings wounded in numerous falls from marital harmony during the first two years of living these principles. Because I tried so hard to make it work, Norma finally believed I was earnest in my endeavor to change. But it took two years to convince her—and it may take you that long to convince your wife.

I learned from Norma and other wives that women need to see effort and not hear mere promises. Give your wife time to watch you climb the mountain if she doesn't believe what you say initially. Show her you are learning to scale the cliffs and hurdle the crevices. The more *consistently* loving we are as husbands, the more trustworthy we become to our wives. Soon they will join us as we climb hand-over-hand toward the goal of a loving marriage.

The most important way I've ever expressed my love to Norma was when I finally attached a high value to her, when I decided that next to my relationship with God and His Word, she is worth more to me than anything on this earth—and she knows it.

THE EVIDENCE WIVES NEED
BEFORE THEY WILL BELIEVE THEIR HUSBANDS

Wives need proof of change over a consistent period of time in at least three areas before they will believe their husbands' commitment.

Careful Listening Without Justification or Argument

Can you imagine a husband being able to justify everything he ever did to hurt his wife? Wayne thought he could. He and his wife couldn't talk for more than fifteen minutes before falling into a heated argument. Inevitably, through his logical deductions, the argument ended up being her fault.

Finally, Wayne told Cathy he really wanted to change, and to love her. A few hours later she suggested a quiet little vacation, just for the two of them to get reacquainted. "Couldn't we just take a week's vacation?" she asked.

"Are you kidding?" he replied, crushing her hopes for better understanding. "You mean you want me to pay rent here at the apartment and then pay for a motel too? That's double rent!"

The topic developed into a fight that led to more fights as the months went by, until their relationship deteriorated and she finally left. He had refused to listen to her needs without arguing and lost her as a result. Tragically, even today, several years later, he still doesn't understand what ended their relationship.

It is often difficult for a man to converse with his wife without challenging the meaning of various words she uses to explain how she feels inside. If a husband can *overlook the actual words* his wife uses to express herself and instead actively pursue *what she means*, fewer arguments will take place. One man I know finds it almost impossible to do this. When his wife uses phrases like "You *never* do this," or "You *always* do that," he will inevitably say, "Now, dear, I don't *always* do that," or "Did I do it yesterday?" Or he begins to analyze her statement to prove its fallacy. In ten minutes, they're off on another hot discussion. It is essential in communication to *look past the surface words* to the real meaning behind the words.

There is no meaning in a word. Meaning is in people.

Everyone has his or her own definition for a given word. We attach meanings to words based on our own unique experiences. So when we attempt to communicate with another person, we use words we believe will accurately convey our thoughts. For instance, in this book I may use words that you enjoy or words that irritate you. You might even be indifferent to my words because you have another frame of reference or because my definitions might be different from yours. That is why I try to illustrate all the important points I make, probing for our common point of reference.

If we can stop justifying our actions and quit arguing about the words our wives use, we can get down to the heart of the matter. We can try rephrasing our wives' statements until they say we have grasped their meaning. "Is this what you're saying, dear?" or "Is this what I'm hearing?" At all cost, avoid sarcastic questions like, "Is this what you're having trouble saying?" A budding relationship between husband and wife can be stunted by an attitude of male superiority.

Quickness to Admit Error

Countless wives and children have told me how their family relationships were weakened because of a husband's or father's unwillingness to admit his errors. Though husbands sometimes think admission of error reveals their weaknesses, the opposite is true. Just think back through your own life to the times when someone admitted his or her offense to you. Chances are, your respect for him or her increased, not decreased.

A friend of mine told me about the time he made a racially derogatory statement to an associate during the day. The man was offended; however, the situation was not discussed. My friend drove away feeling somewhat uneasy and guilty for what he had said. Before he reached home, he turned around and drove back to confront the man.

Walking into the room, he said, "A few minutes ago I said something very offensive to you. I know it was wrong, and I have come back to ask if you could forgive me for what I said."

The man nearly fell over. Of course he forgave him, and I'm sure his respect for my friend doubled. A humble admission of wrong produces positive results. When a husband admits he has hurt his wife, she feels better just knowing he understands. His admission of wrong can produce a much stronger marriage. Not only that, it demonstrates that he is a wise man because the Scriptures tell us only the wise seek correction.

Patience When She Is Reluctant to Believe He's Changed

What if you've been doing everything within your power to let your wife know she has first place in your life, and she still doesn't believe you've changed? Do you throw up your arms in disgust? Or do you gently persuade her over a period of time? I hope you choose the latter. Her initial respect for you wasn't lost overnight, and it can't be regained in a day. Show her that no matter how long it takes, you want to earn her respect.

TWO REASONS WHY A WIFE
CAN BECOME LESS IMPORTANT TO HER HUSBAND

What causes a man to come home after work, pick up his young son, and kiss and cuddle him without even greeting his wife? How can a husband walk straight to the garage to begin a project without even acknowledging his arrival to his wife as he passes by her in the kitchen? *Why* does a man *lose* affection and enthusiasm for his wife after marriage? I think there are two major reasons.

1. A man will pursue and charm a woman with words or flowers or whatever he needs to do to *win* her. But after the wedding, he feels he has conquered her. She is his, so he doesn't have to maintain the same level of enthusiasm and creativity as he did before they married. She is his emotionally and legally. The husband may say to himself, "I have my wife. Now I need to conquer my business . . .

become a better hunter . . . begin a family. . . ." Each frontier is viewed as a new conquest, a new experience.

2. Almost anything is sweet to a starving man, but when he's full, even honey nauseates him (Prov. 27:7). In a very real sense, a man is filled up when he marries because his wife is now a part of him. He believes he has experienced knowing her in every way—spiritually, emotionally, mentally, and physically. He may feel there is nothing left to know about her. He is satisfied and, therefore, has a tendency to look for other potential "frontiers."

HOW TO GAIN YOUR WIFE'S LOVE AND MORE

If it came down to an evening with your friends or a night with your wife, she needs to know you would choose her company just because you enjoy being with her. In the same way, if it came to the children or her, she needs to know she would be your choice. She needs to know she's Number One. When she is satisfied that she's in first place in your life, she will encourage you to do the other things you like doing. For example, I am taking six weeks away from my wife and children to write this book. Several years ago my wife would have been crushed at the mere suggestion of such a long separation. Yet today she is as enthusiastic about it as I am because she knows I will be able to fulfill *our* dream of writing our inner convictions about marriage. More importantly, she knows I would rather be with her than with my typewriter and editor.

Putting your wife in the Number One slot just below God doesn't shackle you to the house; instead, it frees you of the dread of going home.

"Why don't you let me go to the meeting alone tonight so you can go to the basketball game?" Mary said. Her husband was pleasantly shocked. Not so long ago they had had misunderstandings about his insatiable appetite for basketball. In fact, they were thinking about separating because he did not have the knowledge or skills he needed to treat Mary right, and she did not have the emotional strength to continue living with him or loving him. Today he regularly puts her before his work, his activities, etc. And Mary is now free to encourage his outside interests, knowing she's at the top of his list.

My wife also encourages me to enjoy my interests in hunting and fishing because she feels secure in her position of importance. If an emergency arose, she knows my first commitment would be to taking care of her or the children, not to my recreational enjoyment.

> The more important a woman feels she is to her husband, the more she encourages him to do the activities she knows he enjoys.

Do you wonder whether your wife feels she is more important to you than other people or things in your life? Complete the following exercise, and I think you will find out.

First, list your favorite spare-time activities.

_____

_____

_____

_____

_____

What is an enjoyable after-work activity for you?

Monday _____

Tuesday _____

Wednesday _____

Thursday _____

Friday _____

Saturday _____

Sunday _____

Where do you enjoy taking your vacations?

_____

_____

_____

Now, look back over these three lists and ask yourself, *"Is there anything on the lists I would rather do than be with my wife?"* Probably so. And if so, chances are you have already "communicated" to your wife that she is not as important to you as your activities, even though you have never uttered those words. Since a woman has tremendous perception, she knows where your heart is, even when you haven't said a word. But that doesn't mean it's too late to adjust your priorities.

YOUR WIFE'S "RADAR" CAN DETECT YOUR SINCERITY

What a man values, he takes good care of. Or as Christ said, "Where your treasure is, there will your heart be also" (Matt. 6:21). If your hobby is fishing, you probably hesitate to loan out your best rod and reel. If you enjoy hunting, you probably know how to carefully oil and polish guns. Based on the amount of time you spend on each activity, your wife can sense which is most important to you. If she doesn't feel that you are as careful with her as you are with your other interests, she will know she is not as important. That feeling shatters her self-worth and can result in physical as well as emotional problems. The emotions she struggles with now may surface years later in the form of serious and expensive physical problems.

However, some husbands feel threatened by the thought of giving their wives special treatment, fearing they will lose out with their friends, career, or hobbies. They falsely believe if they give up other activities for the sake of being with their wives, they will give them up forever. Remember, when a wife feels she is the most important, she gets excited about her husband being able to do the things he wants to do. But don't try and deceive her! Simply telling her she's first so she'll let you out to do what you want doesn't work. In fact, if she finds out you've tried to manipulate her, you may be faced with major problems concerning her trust in you and her own feelings of worth.

HOW I GAINED MY WIFE'S LOVE AND EVERYTHING ELSE

After ten years of marriage, I felt I was finally becoming a success at my work. I was privileged to speak regularly for various organizations in our city and throughout the country. My wife and I had a beautiful home and two children. What more could a man want? Then from my point of view, a tragedy occurred in my marriage. Norma became pregnant with our third child. I was not enthusiastic. If anything, I was depressed, realizing our youngest had only been out of diapers for two years. I was just starting to enjoy my children, and the thought of another little baby around the house was almost overwhelming, particularly when the doctor had told us specifically that we couldn't have any more children.

Although I tried to be nice to Norma, I couldn't hide my disappointment. I was afraid I might not be able to travel as much and would be forced to take a less prestigious position in the company.

My work load increased as the months passed, and I warned my wife I would not be able to help her with the children because of job demands. Even on the day our son was born, I worried about the added hardships he would add to my vocational dreams.

Norma's health suffered during the first year after our son's birth because of the long night hours and the responsibility of taking care of two other small children. Our baby had to have surgery and was often sick, adding to her burden. How insensitive I was during that year! Whenever the baby would cry at night or need special attention, I would quickly remind Norma he was her child. She had wanted another baby, not I.

A year passed in this way before Norma finally said to me, "I can't take it any more. I wish I had the emotional and physical strength to take care of the kids, discipline and train them, but I just can't do it with an absentee father."

She wasn't demanding. She wasn't angry. She was simply stating the facts. She had had it. I could see the *urgency* and *calmness* in her facial expressions and realized that she desperately needed my help. I faced a major decision. Should I go to my boss and ask for a different job in the company? Ask for a job that would allow me more time at home? It was a struggle because I knew I could get a less prestigious and less lucrative job. I felt I would have to sacrifice some of my career goals. Inwardly, I felt resentment toward my son and my wife for being weak. But I gave in. In nervousness and embarrassment, I approached my boss to explain I needed more time at home because of the children. "Is there any possibility that I could have a different job that would allow me to stay home more?"

My boss graciously cooperated by giving me another job. But to me the new job was a demotion. I was asked to do some things that only a few weeks earlier I had been training my subordinates to do. What a blow, which did nothing but fuel my resentment!

I was devastated for a while, but soon I became interested in home life. I actually looked forward to five o'clock. My family and I began doing more things together, like camping and other special activities. Before long, a deeper love blossomed within both Norma and me. Norma began to feel more physically alert which, in turn, made her more cheerful and outgoing. She changed some habits I disliked without any pressure from me. My "big" career sacrifice seemed smaller every day in comparison to the richer relationship we were developing.

Within a few months, my boss gave me a new position in the company that I liked much better than the one I had given up. By this time, Norma was so secure with me that she had no resentment toward my new job or any necessary travel that went with it. I gave in and gave up at first, but I won in the long run. That's almost exactly how Christ explains the principle of exchange in Mark 8:34–37.

Even to this day, if I ask our son Michael, "Why are you so important to Dad?" he'll say, "Because I brought you back to Mama and the family."

THE INCREDIBLE RESULTS
OF MAKING YOUR WIFE FEEL IMPORTANT

One morning Sandy was so sexually responsive to Rick that he was stunned and surprised by her excitement. How did Rick motivate her? With one very simple statement. He was getting ready for work that morning, running a little late, when he heard Sandy complaining of a growing headache and neckache.

"Let me rub your neck," he offered.

"No, you don't have time," she replied. "You've got to get to work."

His usual response would have been, "Yeah, you're right. I don't want to be late. But I hope you feel better. Take an aspirin."

On this particular morning he said, "I tell you what. I'd rather be with you any day. Let me rub your neck." As he gently massaged her tense muscles, he continued, *"Work can wait . . . you're more important to me."* She was so thrilled with his attitude and so encouraged by his sensitivity and gentleness that she said she could hardly resist giving herself to him in every way.

We men are not aware of the effect we have on our wives by being gentle and tender, showing our unshakable devotion.

Do you want a more enjoyable marriage? It's possible. And it all starts by loving your wife more than any person or any activity.

Here are a few questions you can ask your wife to open up a discussion concerning her real feelings about the place she shares in your life:

1. Do you feel you are the most important person in my life?
2. Are there any activities in my life you feel are more important to me than you are?
3. Are there any special ways you believe I could better communicate how important you are to me?

Remember, the more you do to build a valuable, healthy relationship, the better you'll feel about your marriage. If you change any of your activities because you want to enrich your relationship, at first you may feel you're giving up your favorite pastime. But in the long run, you'll not only gain a better marriage, but a greater freedom to enjoy other areas of life. Today I wouldn't trade my deep friendship with Norma for anything on this earth. I am finding that the more important a man's wife is to him, the more she encourages him to enjoy life.

How a military officer loved his wife out of a mental hospital.

The psychiatrist had prescribed that his wife be admitted to the local mental hospital. He was stunned and challenged, but had no idea how to help her. He sought counsel from the chaplain and learned he should allow his wife to sit in his lap and share her true feelings about him.

He followed this advice with great difficulty because it hurt to hear the things she said he was doing to weaken their marriage. As she was talking, the telephone rang, and he felt "saved by the bell." She was angry because she thought he would probably not return. But she overheard one statement he made that not only kept her from a breakdown but prompted her to slip into a nightgown and actually desire to arouse him (something she had not done in years). After the call, she calmly snuggled back into his lap.

What had he said to his commanding officer?

He simply said, "Sir, could someone else take that assignment tonight? I'm in the middle of a very important time with my wife. It's serious, and I really don't want to leave at this point." That military officer had begun to prove to his wife that she was of high value to him. As a result, her mental condition stabilized, and she never had to go to the hospital.

FOR PERSONAL REFLECTION

1. What is the basic meaning of the word "honor"? 1 Peter 3:7.
2. How can your emotional feelings for your mate grow? Matthew 6:21.

4

Your Wife Needs Your Shoulder, Not Your Mouth

*"Put on
a heart of
compassion,
kindness,
humility,
gentleness and patience."
Colossians 3:12*

AS I PULLED into the driveway, I heard a sickening thump under the tire. Only a few seconds earlier our cat had been running expectantly toward our car to welcome us home.

"Watch out for Puff," Norma said.

"Oh, he'll get out of the way," I replied.

I hadn't been driving fast. *How fast can you pull into a driveway?* I thought.

"Oh, no!" I whispered. "Can someone get me out of this mess?" My family thought it was just another one of my jokes about wanting to get rid of our two cats.

Our oldest son jumped out of the car, looked underneath, and fell to the ground screaming. Our daughter began sobbing, and our youngest son woke up from his nap to join the chorus. Bedlam set in. They all started accusing me of purposely killing the cat. In fact, I was accused of things that would have put me in jail for years. How I regretted the times I had joked about it.

Puff was the kitten of our other cat. We all loved the mother cat, but they loved Puff much more. We had kept the kitten because of his "puffy" hernia. His stomach grew larger and larger until finally I had to give in and take him to a veterinarian to have the hernia repaired. But the operation was a failure. A few months later I had to take him back for another operation. And I didn't even want the cat in the first place! I told my family, "This cat sure is costing me a lot." I was saying

53

things some men typically say, blind to the hurt I was causing my family.

Now that I had run over the cat, I was under attack. When they started screaming at me, I wanted to yell back. But the things Norma had shared with me in the past about herself and our children strangled the words. "Don't talk. Just hold me or hold the kids whenever there's a tragedy," she had said.

They were making so much racket in the front yard that I knew the neighbors were going to think I was killing them. I was so embarrassed and crushed that I herded them all into the house. Then I put my arm around Kari and hugged her. But as I hugged Greg, I could tell he didn't want me to touch him. I tried to put my arm around Norma, but she gave me one of those familiar looks a woman saves for times when her husband bombs out.

"This is what you always wanted, isn't it?" she asked. "You wanted him dead." With that, she marched into the bedroom and closed the door.

But I still didn't say anything. I didn't get angry, although I felt my family misunderstood me. I knew that raising my voice wouldn't help. Since Michael didn't want me to touch him either, Greg and I went out to the driveway to get Puff and bury him. We took him to our little burial ground where Peter, our rabbit, rests. Greg was still sobbing, "Dad, life will never be the same." Greg loved that cat just about as much as you can love anything. As Greg and I buried him, I prayed, and Greg concluded the funeral service.

I felt nauseous as I went back inside. There stood twelve-year-old Kari comforting five-year-old Michael. "Michael, it was Puff's time to go. It was Puff's time."

When Greg was getting ready for bed, I went to his room and held him. His eyes red, he asked, "Dad, what am I going to do when I come home from school? What am I going to do, dad? Puff won't be there to jump into my arms." And like Greg, I had tears streaming down my cheeks.

Courageous little Kari was standing in the hall after putting Michael to bed. "Well, Dad, it's all over," she said. "It was Puff's time. I tell you what, Dad, I think we can eat those donuts now." (We had bought donuts and milk after church, planning a quiet family snack.)

"Kari, you can if you want, but I just wouldn't be able to eat. I just can't eat tonight," I told her.

Opening the door to our bedroom, I wondered if my wife was ready to face me yet. She had told me many times in the past, "Don't demand anything. Wait until I am able to respond to you."

I got down on my knees next to her, gently touching her hand, and asked, "How are you feeling?"

"I'm feeling better. I know you didn't mean to murder Puff," she said.

I could have reacted to her statement in anger but I only said, "That's okay. I understand. You know all those things I said when I was joking about Puff? I really feel bad about them. You can rest assured I'll never joke about things like that again. Would it make you feel better if we made Angel an 'inside' cat from now on?"

From time to time for a few weeks, I would say to Norma, "You know, I really do feel bad that you don't have Puff around to jump up into your arms." She would put her head down on my shoulder and say, "Yeah, I know, I feel bad too." Through that painful experience, I learned more about comforting my wife than I could have in years of troublefree existence.

Let your wife teach you how you can best meet her needs during a crisis or when she's discouraged and losing energy.

Probably the most important lesson my wife taught me on how to comfort her was when she told me in a calm way that she could not handle my busy work schedule along with the pressures of the children and the home. *By coming to me without threats to explain her limitations,* she touched something within me. I was eager to comfort her. I don't know if she stirred my protective manly feelings or what, but when she told me she couldn't take the pressure I was putting on her and that she might be close to a collapse, I was motivated to relieve her of that pressure.

I have found that this nonthreatening approach works even in a father-daughter relationship. A university graduate student came to me because of a poor relationship with her father. Financially, he had been very generous to her, but she needed his love and gentleness much more than she needed his money. I tried to work with her father, explaining what I had learned about women. "Comfort her," I suggested. "Be tender and gentle. Don't lecture her." But he couldn't grasp it, although he is a very skillful and intelligent lawyer, quite successful in his profession. (I have noticed that my lawyer friends have a difficult time being tender and loving without lecturing. They have been inculcated with the need for logical expression.)

"I tried to take my life last week," this young woman told me. "I just cannot handle the emotional pressure I'm under with my father."

"You've got choices," I said.

"What?"

"You can respond to your father in a way that you and I know will bring healing to your life."

"I'm not able to do that," she said wearily.

"Okay, then you can call your father and say to him, 'Daddy, I love you. I wish that I could spend more time with you, but, Daddy, I feel like I just can't handle seeing you right now. I can't emotionally handle the way you treat me—your lectures, your insensitivity, and your harshness. As much as I wish I could, as much as I wish I were stronger, I just can't handle it right now!' "

This girl has unique needs and qualities. Nobody could tell her she needed to be stronger. She is who she is. To tell her to be what she can't be is like saying to the sun, "Don't come up tomorrow." It's reality!

Happily, her father was motivated to change, thinking, *I must really be insensitive. My own daughter can't handle my presence. She can't even handle a phone call from me.*

> Many men don't realize that tender love through a gentle touch and listening ear is all a woman needs at times— just a comforting hug, a loving statement like, "I understand. You're hurting, aren't you? You're feeling under a lot of pressure, aren't you?" Listening to her talk without making critical comments or offering quick solutions is important.

GIVE HER YOUR SHOULDER, NOT YOUR MOUTH

Your goal should be to become a gentle, loving, and tender husband who does not lecture. Lectures during stressful times only create more stress. This was a new concept to me because I wasn't fortunate enough to have a father who knew how to be tender to his wife. I wasn't aware of my wife's needs for tenderness until a few years ago. No one had ever told me that one of a woman's greatest needs is tenderness and a husband who will listen instead of lecture, and even if someone had, I don't think I would have understood. (I should have been able to figure it out, though, because when I am down, I like people to be gentle and comforting to me.)

I'll never forget what one woman told me: "If my husband would only put his arms around me and hold me, without lecturing me, when I am feeling blue!" But Lecture #734 would begin as he told her she would feel better if she took an aspirin . . . if she were more organized . . . if she wouldn't wear herself down so much . . . if she would discipline the children better. . . .

"Have you ever told him what you need?" I asked.

"Are you kidding? I'd be embarrassed," she laughed. "Come on, you're kidding."

"No. He probably doesn't know what to do. He doesn't know

you need to be held instead of lectured. Why don't you tell him during a calm conversation some day?"

"That does kind of make sense to me. A lot of times when I am down and crying and all upset, he'll ask, 'What do you want me to do?' I just flare up and say, 'If I have to tell you what to do, it would wreck the whole idea.'"

As a husband, I recommend that you ask your wife when and how you need to hold her when she needs to be comforted. Ask her what circumstances prompt her to seek your gentle caring arms and touch. You can't dream them up on your own. We just can't perceive the deep feelings of other people. We've got to draw them out and then *practice, practice, practice* the skills of meeting our wives' needs.

The first time I ever tried to ski, I rode a rope pulley to the top of a small hill. The hill looked a lot bigger from the top than it did from the bottom.

I thought, *No way am I gonna go down this hill.* So I sat down on the back of my skis and scooted all the way down.

Even if you have to scoot instead of ski your way through the skills in this chapter at first, remember that you'll eventually be able to get to your feet. This book is certainly not an exhaustive marriage manual, but it is a start. Believe me, if you practice what is written here, you and your wife can have a more loving marriage.

When I was first learning the art of comforting my wife, we had an experience that took every ounce of self-control I could muster. But I came through a stronger man, encouraged by my new-found strength. I want you to imagine yourself in my situation. How would you have reacted?

I had bought a dumpy-looking boat for $400 because we wanted to do more things together as a family. That same night my son and I decided to take it for a quick trip to the lake, only five minutes from our house, just to see how it ran. Because of my inexperience as a boater, the wind blew the boat back to the bank the first time I put it in. I got wet and frustrated trying to push it out again. After an irritating ten minutes trying to start the cantankerous thing, the boat wouldn't go faster than ten miles an hour. Something was obviously wrong. I was quite a way from the shore before I realized I had better get back in case the motor stalled.

Then—"Dad, the boat's sinking!" Greg cried. I looked behind me and saw the foot of water that had gurgled in. The previous owner had taken the plug out the last time it had rained but had forgotten to tell me. With the hull full of water, I couldn't find the hole for the plug. Luckily we didn't sink. I put the boat back on the trailer, determined to take it back first thing in the morning. I was a little embarrassed to have the dumpy-looking thing parked in front of my house anyway.

A boat dealer told me it would take $150 to fix the engine's broken seal, so I returned it to the owner who had promised me I could have my money back if I didn't like it.

When I left home early that morning, I had agreed to be back by eleven o'clock so Norma could go shopping. Retrieving my money took longer than I had planned, and I arrived home an hour-and-a-half late. In the meantime, Norma had decided to take our minimotor home to the grocery store. Trying to turn it around in the driveway, she accidentally drove too close to the house and sheared off a section of the roof. As the roof fell, it put a huge dent in the front of the motor home.

When I pulled into the driveway at 12:30, I saw part of the roof lying in the driveway next to the dented motor home. I just laughed out loud, more out of desperation than humor.

I wanted to say to my wife, "Oh, no, $500 at least to fix this. Where did you get your driver's license, at a garage sale?" I wanted to lecture her angrily and then ignore her for a while.

For once, I remembered what I was supposed to do. I told myself, "Keep your mouth shut and put your arms around her. Just hold her. Don't say anything, okay?"

However, my basic human nature told me, "Give her a lecture. Let your anger out. Express it."

My mind finally triumphed over my will. I put my arms around her and said gently, "You must feel terrible, don't you?" even though war was still raging inside me. We went into the house and sat on the couch. I let her talk her feelings out.

I held her, and after a couple of minutes I felt good because I could feel the tenderness begin to flow from me. Soon I was fine, and she was encouraged. Minutes later, a carpenter friend drove up who had already heard about the accident. We had the roof patched and painted in two hours.

It felt good not to be angry for once. I hadn't offended my wife, shouted at the kids, or diminished any of the beauty of our relationship. I could have reverted to my old excuse, "Well, I just can't keep from blowing up." Instead, I had one of those encouraging victories.

My new-found sensitivity has been tested on several occasions. Once I almost blew it on a fishing trip. I normally become completely oblivious to my family and the world when I'm near a stream, totally "submerging" myself in the exhilarating environment of fishing: the smell of the air, the tension when a fish strikes, the sound of the stream.... Oops! Back to the story.

When we pulled up in our minimotor home beside a beautiful stream, my heart was pounding. I could hardly wait to get my reel rigged up. First, I rigged the kids' reels and told them, "Look, if you get tangled up, you're on your own." (I used to get so frustrated when I was trying to fish and they were yelling, "Dad, I can't get this reeled in." I wanted to devote my entire energy to fishing on my own.)

I found the perfect spot: a nice deep hole in a pool in front of a big boulder. I threw in the lure and let it wander naturally to the bottom of the pool. It swirled around and WHAM! I got my first trout! I had nearly caught the limit when Greg came running up. I was sure he was about to jump into the stream and spook the fish. I was already upset and angry from his interruption when he said, "Dad! Kari broke her leg!"

Kari broke her leg? What a time to break her leg! I couldn't believe she would do this to me. It was hard for me to leave, but I gave the line to Greg and said, "Don't break it. Don't get it tangled up. Just keep it in there." I ran in Kari's direction, avoiding the big pool. After all, I didn't want to scare the fish.

Downstream, Kari was crying. "Daddy, I think I broke my leg."

When I looked at it, I realized it was only bruised.

"Don't touch it," I said. "It's not broken, it's just bruised. Put your leg in this cold water to soak for a few minutes."

I'm really embarrassed to tell the rest of the story, but maybe you can learn from my insensitivity. I ran back to the fishing hole and caught a few more trout before walking back to where Kari was crying. "Dad, this water is cold."

I rather roughly got her up to walk, but she couldn't. When I tried to hoist her up on the bank and couldn't, she started crying again and said, "Dad, you're so rough with me. Can't you be *tender?*" Something flashed when she said that word. It reminded me of all the times my wife and other women have told me, "What we need is tenderness and gentleness, not harshness. We don't need lectures." And I couldn't even be tender with my eleven-year-old daughter. I had already lectured Kari because I felt she was interrupting my day. "Why didn't you look first?" I had asked her.

Just who was more important anyway? Those trout or my precious daughter? It was hard for me to face, but those trout had been more important to me. I had let fishing and my own desires endanger my only daughter. I was wrong, and I should have known better!

When I came to my senses, I hung my head low and said, "Kari,

I've been so wrong to be harsh with you. I really feel bad. Would you forgive me?"

"Yeah, I'll forgive you, Dad."

"Kari, you are more important to me than any fish, and I want you to know that. I was so carried away by this activity today that I really hurt you, didn't I?"

We just held each other for a while, and then she looked up into my eyes and asked gently, "Dad, did you use deodorant today?"

HELPING YOUR WIFE OVERCOME DEPRESSION

Both men and women experience stress daily. Some days are worse than others—like the day I ran over Puff. Psychologists tell us that stressful experiences and prolonged anger affect our mind, our emotions, and our body. The amount of stress we experience in each of these areas can mean the difference between happiness or depression. Positive input in any *one* area has been proven to have beneficial effects on all the other areas. If a husband is tender with his wife, for example, he lifts her emotions and, in turn, helps her in other dimensions of her life.

According to Dr. Jerry Day, a clinical psychologist from Tucson, Arizona, if a wife has at least four of the following symptoms she could be diagnosed as depressed. As a husband, you need to know these signs in order to be able to comfort your wife more effectively. Let's not forget that a major destroyer of any relationship is hurt and anger held inside.

General Symptoms of Depression

1. Sadness
2. Hopelessness
3. Loss of humor
4. Premature awakening
5. Early morning awakening
6. Insomnia
7. Feeling better as the day wears on
8. Loss of sexual interest
9. Loss of appetite and weight
10. Sharp increase of appetite and weight gain
11. Vague physical complaints
12. Sense of personal loss (death of a close relative, loss of job, etc.)
13. Poor concentration and memory
14. Deep sighing or moaning

Should you detect these symptoms in your wife, you should comfort her first with statements like, "Honey, I'm not sure I know how you feel, but I really want to. And I want to help you work through whatever it is that is discouraging you." Then use the information below as a guideline to *help her* out of depression.

Remember, if your wife is depressed, it may or may not be something you've contributed to—but it is always your responsibility to help.

1. If your wife has at least four of the above symptoms, encourage her to have a complete physical examination. Her symptoms might be caused by a hormone or vitamin deficiency or by a physical illness.

2. Avoid lecturing her. Arguing with her only makes her feel you don't understand. But sending her a card or flowers can lift her emotionally. Help your children do something special for her. For example, you can go down to the store and buy a small roll of shelf paper. Roll it out and on it paste magazine pictures that depict things you appreciate about her. With brightly colored pens, write affectionate words all over the banner. Roll it up with a pretty bow and present it to her as a family. Your thoughtful gesture will affect her emotions and *help* lift her out of the darkness.

3. Listen to your wife with the "third ear." In other words, listen for her emotional message. What is she trying to say? Can you understand the meaning behind her words? Try saying something like, "I don't know why this terrible thing has happened to you, but I can really see that it has deeply upset you." By saying those words, you will allow her time to gain physical strength through your understanding.

4. Help her feel better by "blocking" her symptoms. Dr. Day explained this concept to me as follows: Whenever actors are on stage, they have to overdo and exaggerate to communicate a thought to the audience. Though they feel they are exaggerating, the audience perceives their behavior as normal. Dr. Day believes it is important for you to exaggerate your wife's problem so she will really believe you understand how badly she feels. She will receive your statements as normal, though you may feel you have overdone it.

For example, suggest a very hard project for her. It can be something physically exhausting like jogging, or something else that requires fierce mental effort. Tell her, "Maybe you ought to do something serious to get over this." Many times this shocks a depressed person into reality. They come away feeling, "Things aren't that bad."

When things seem hopeless, though, a depressed person often feels like sleeping the day away. Nothing could be worse. Help your wife get up and go out, even if you have to go shopping with her. My wife sometimes feels like hiding under the blanket when she's down or feeling blue, even though she knows she will feel better if she gets up and goes to an exercise class or becomes vigorously involved in an activity.

5. Another helpful therapy for depression is writing down our thoughts. A certain "washing of the soul" occurs when we record our thoughts while in depression, Dr. Day says. Buy your wife a notebook and encourage her to write down the ways you or others have hurt her.

Better yet, encourage her to write down the benefits that will enter her life as a result of the depressing things that have happened to her. She may resist at first, saying she can't think of a single benefit. You may need to come up with at least one benefit for her before she can get started. The more benefits she uncovers, the better she will feel. Most women who do this exercise end up telling me, "Things really aren't so bad." In fact, this is so important that I've written an entire book to help people find value in troubled times. *Joy That Lasts* can assist you in helping your wife actually find benefit in trials and gain a whole new perspective on anger, worry, fear, hurt feelings, and guilt.

Even when your wife can't take time to write down her feelings, you can help her avoid negative thinking. Gently steer her away from the two words, "If only." Those words, one psychiatrist said, have kept more people in depression than any others. "If only I hadn't . . . if only I would . . . if only he had. . . ." Those two words can tear up a person emotionally, mentally, and physically.

6. During stressful times, encourage your wife to relax her muscles. I practice regularly an exercise recommended by Dr. Day. I can personally testify that this ten-minute relaxing technique has, at times, made me feel like I've just had four hours of deep sleep. It renews creativity and strength.

Allow your body's natural relaxing mechanism to work: relax in a chair or on a bed, take several deep breaths, tighten every muscle in your body for as long as you can hold one deep breath, and then exhale. Visualize your muscles relaxing, and then don't move a muscle for the remainder of the ten minutes.

7. Gain a firm commitment from your wife to begin and continue a vigorous physical exercise program. Norma has joined a women's health club just to have a place to exercise when she feels discouraged. Physical exercise helps a person mentally and emotionally. Those who work with depressed people say it is one of the most important areas of therapy.

8. Part of being wise is discerning when we need help as well. If your wife gets and stays depressed for longer than three weeks, you need to think seriously about calling your pastor or a Christian counselor to help you make a difference in your loved one's life.

How Does Your Wife Need to Be Comforted?

Why not ask her to help you understand how and when she needs comfort? Encourage her to be patient with you until you master the skill of tenderly comforting her.

FOR PERSONAL REFLECTION

1. Is it natural to be comforting and gentle during tension or a crisis? Colossians 3:8–14; 4:6.
2. Do you understand your wife's needs during a crisis? 1 Peter 3:7. Write out her response to this question, too.

5

Climbing Out Of Marriage's Deepest Pit

*"It is inevitable
that stumbling blocks
should come,
but
woe to him
through whom
they come!"
Luke 17:1*

IT WAS 4:00 P.M. on Valentine's Day when I remembered my basketball game. I reached for the phone to call Norma, my bride of less than a year.

"Honey, I forgot to tell you I have a basketball game tonight. We're supposed to be there about 7:00. I'll pick you up about 6:30."

Silence hung heavily on the line before she answered, "But this is Valentine's Day."

"Yeah, I know, but I need to be there tonight because I promised the team. I don't want to let them down."

"But I have a special dinner prepared with candles and—"

"Can you hold it off until tomorrow?" She didn't answer, so I continued. (What I was about to say caused a great deal of damage in our relationship. Like many young husbands, I didn't have the slightest hint of how deeply this would wound her.) "Honey, you know how important it is for a wife to submit to her husband. I really need to be there tonight, and if we're going to start off with good habits in the early part of our marriage, now is the time to begin. If I'm going to be the leader of this family, I need to make the decision."

"Ice" perfectly describes the reception I received when I picked her up. It was easy to see I had severely offended her, but I figured she had to learn to be submissive sometime, and we might as well start now.

The lifeless expression on her face grew worse as the evening wore on. When we returned home after the game, I noticed that the table was all set up for a special dinner—candles, our best dishes, and pretty napkins. She still wasn't speaking to me the next day, so I rushed to the florist to gather a variety of flowers, which I put in various spots all over the house. That warmed her up a little. Then I gave her a giant card with a hand on the front that could be turned thumbs up or thumbs down. "Which way is it?" I asked her. She turned it thumbs up. I never said whether I was right or wrong, only that I felt badly about the night before. And so began a history of offenses I never knew how to clear up with her.

Had someone not shared with me later the secret of developing a lasting and intimate relationship, we might have joined the millions who seek divorce each year.

> End every day with a clean slate—no offenses between
> the two of you.

Couples often ask me, "Where have we gone wrong?" "Why don't we feel romantic toward each other?" "How come we argue so much?" "Why do we avoid touching each other?" These problems are not primarily attributable to incompatibility, sexual problems, financial pressure, or any other surface issues. They are a direct result of *accumulated offenses*. If a husband and wife can understand how to maintain harmony by immediately working to clear up every hurtful offense between them, they can climb out of such common problems and even marriage's deepest pit—divorce.

HOW DID I GET DOWN HERE ANYWAY?

When a man treats his wife carelessly, she is usually offended far deeper than he realizes. She begins to close him out, and if he continues to hurt her feelings, she will separate herself from him mentally, emotionally, and physically. In other words, she doesn't want any contact in any way with him. Haven't you noticed how your wife clams up after you have insulted her? She not only avoids conversation, but also avoids being touched. *A wife simply will not respond to her husband when he continually hurts her feelings without "clearing the slate"—draining away her anger.*

Some people justify their reactions by saying, "But he/she hurt my feelings." There's no such thing as hurt feelings, according to psychologist Dr. Henry Brandt. He says, "Let's call hurt feelings what they really are—anger." It isn't right for your wife to react in anger, but that's not the point of this book. Our goal as husbands should be to adjust our behavior so our wives won't have to react in anger.

To understand why your wife naturally "clams up" when you offend her, imagine yourself the proud owner of a new car. When you first drive that classy model into your driveway, every part of you says, "I love it." You love the smell, the feel, the look. Because you love the car, you polish it until it sparkles. You devote special time and care to it. However, a month later when the engine starts knocking, or the oil leaks, or the gleaming paint job suffers a few scratches, or the windshield wipers quit right in the middle of a rain storm, you become irritated with this "lemon" that you've bought. Soon you can think of seventy-two reasons to get rid of it. As long as it treats you right, you like it. But as soon as it starts to fall apart, you wish you'd never bought it, and soon you don't even want to be near it.

The same thing can happen with a job. Did you ever quit because you weren't happy with the boss or working conditions? I remember how much I loved one job until the boss offended me deeply. At that moment, my mind became tangled in a web of reasons to leave. Although I knew what was going on inside me, I couldn't seem to control my emotions. They had changed, and I wasn't as fond of the work as I had been. I eventually didn't want to show up or have anything to do with that job.

We tend to follow a natural pattern when we've been offended. Mentally, we are more alert to the flaws of the offender. Emotionally, we feel estranged. Physically, we avoid that person. And spiritually, we close out the person (Prov. 15:13).

I have watched my wife go through this process many times. When I played basketball that Valentine's evening instead of going home to her romantic candlelight dinner, she was so angry that she didn't want to talk to me. She didn't want to touch me or have me touch her. Have you ever put your arm around your wife after provoking her and felt her tighten up? You may have criticized her when that happened. But you need to accept the responsibility for her coldness and say, "I understand how you feel, and I don't blame you for not wanting me near you right now. What I did was wrong, and I ask your forgiveness." If your wife does not want you to touch her, if she has lost some of that romantic "spark" she once had for you, or if she is plotting ways to get away from you even for short periods of time, *you can be sure you have offended her and possibly "closed" her spirit.* (In my book, *The Key to Your Child's Heart,* I talk in detail about what "closes" a person's spirit and specific ways in which we can "reopen" it.)

A not-so-funny thing happened on the way to a party one evening. Norma teasingly said she planned to play a joke on the company president, a joke that would have embarrassed me. I couldn't believe she would consider such a thing, and I said, "Norma, you can't do that. I'm not going tonight if you really plan on doing it."

I stopped the car and with harshness and impatience yelled, "I would be too embarrassed to go there." She kidded around with me a little more and admitted she really wasn't serious, but my persistent harshness was too much for her (Prov. 15:4). Because I was so abusive, she began to cry. Realizing I had done the wrong thing, I tried to make it right. The more I talked, the worse it grew. At the party, whenever I glanced at her, she looked away. She was thinking of all the reasons her husband wasn't such a "great catch" anymore. It took days for me to reestablish harmony.

What does a man have to do to clear up offenses against his wife? How can he maintain harmony with her?

> Harmony can be defined as the absence of unsettled offenses between the two of you.

When a real harmony and oneness exist between you and your wife, the two of you will want to relax and spend time talking. Your wife will be more agreeable. She will feel emotionally and physically attracted to you. But when you have offended her, she will probably *resist* you and *argue* with you.

Wives are often accused of being strong-willed and rebellious when, in reality, they're simply responding to their husbands' thoughtless abuses. They are sometimes accused of wrecking marriages because they have lost affectionate or romantic love for their husbands. Of course, husbands seldom realize that their insensitive behavior is what ushered the affection out the door.

It doesn't make much sense to withhold the necessary elements a plant needs (like air, water, soil, etc.) and then blame the plant for not thriving. However, many a man has labeled his wife sexually frigid for not wanting to be touched or have sex. But wives have often told me that when a woman is mistreated, she feels like a prostitute having physical relations with her husband. Sex is more than just physical—it involves every part of us. A woman must first know she is valued as a person and be in harmony with her husband before she can give herself freely in sex. She has to feel romantic love before *wholeheartedly* entering the sexual union in marriage. Without harmony, the sexual relationship between husband and wife will most certainly deteriorate.

Have you ever known the futility of trying to reach a woman mentally, emotionally, and physically after offending her?

Mark tried to reach out to Laurie, his estranged wife, but she wanted no part of him. He kept saying to her, "I miss you so much. I want to be near you. I love you." But she was *closed* to him emotionally. "Don't you see how you're hurting our daughter?" he said. "Don't you see what kind of reputation we're going to have by being separated?" He tried to appeal to her mentally, but she wouldn't listen. He had already gone too far—he had offended her too often and too severely—so her spirit completely shut him out of her life.

I asked him, "Are you willing to forgo touching Laurie for the time being, to forgo wondering if she will ever again have emotional feelings for you, to forgo trying to reason with her mentally? Will you concentrate on clearing up your past offenses?

"If you will accept my counsel and reestablish a harmony with Laurie, she will mentally open up to you again. She'll gain new romantic love for you. Finally, she will desire to be near you again.

"This is the reality of life," I advised Mark. "In cases where a woman has fallen in love with another man or has been *severely* mistreated, it may take longer to win her back."

A man often becomes disgusted when his wife doesn't sparkle with romance any more, not realizing that he killed that sparkle with his hurtful ways.

What steps can a man take to rebuild a harmonious relationship with his wife?

FIVE WAYS TO LOVINGLY DRAIN ANGER
FROM YOUR WIFE AND GAIN
A LASTING AND LOVING RELATIONSHIP

1. *Endeavor to understand the ways you have hurt or offended your wife.* To help you avoid hurting your mate, I have included a list of ways a husband commonly offends his wife. (This list is on pages 82 to 86.) In the past, perhaps you haven't realized how deeply your actions were hurting her.

Ken and Sharon's story is a good example of how a man's insensitivity damaged a marriage. After eight years of marriage and three children, Sharon's once-petite figure was a little on the chubby side. Since Ken couldn't understand why she had not regained her slender figure after the birth of their third child, he found a number of "creative" ways to point out the extra poundage to Sharon. He tried to make her lose weight by lecturing, demanding, and bribing. He even threatened to cancel their vacation unless she lost weight. But nothing worked. She seemed powerless to comply.

Ken's continually critical, harsh attitude wounded Sharon. As a result, she slowly began to close him out of her life. She shut him out emotionally, and resisted when he demanded sex, excusing herself because of headaches or fatigue. His occasional jabs, "Do you realize you had two desserts for dinner tonight?" and his overbearing personality continually pressured her, making her more nervous and increasing her desire to eat. Ken was totally unaware of what he was doing to her. There was no way he could really understand her. "If you want to lose weight," he said, "you just decide to do it!"

Since Sharon had little or no interest in pleasing Ken, she might have been subconsciously punishing him by staying overweight. Quite by accident, Ken did one thing that finally motivated Sharon to lose weight. He called her long distance while on a business trip and said, "Honey, as I've been away from you and the kids these past few days, I've had a lot of time to think. I know I've never been able to face it before, but I've been judgmental and offensive to each of you. In fact, I can see now that *I've* been the one out of control. In many ways, my crummy attitude is worse than anything you've done to me.

"What I plan to do is to stop pestering you about losing weight, and to spend the rest of my life focusing on how I can work on being a better friend and husband. I want to concentrate on learning how to love you for who you are, not criticizing you for not measuring up to my standards. I want you to know that you're free from demands from me to change and that I love you just the way you are."

After a few stunned seconds, Sharon responded, "You know, every time you demanded that I lose weight, your attitude made me want to run to the refrigerator and eat everything in it! I never had any desire to please you in this area. But now that you say I'm free to do whatever I want and I sense you mean it, I actually have a greater desire to lose weight"—which she did by losing over seventy pounds in the next few months.

When Ken began to recognize that his criticism was wounding his wife, he was on the path to a restored relationship.

2. *Admit the fact that you've participated in weakening your marriage.* Men, what you're about to read may be very difficult for you to believe or even accept. I want you to keep in mind that this whole book, *If Only He Knew,* is directed to *you.* It's not intended for a woman to read, and it doesn't specifically apply to what she needs to do to restore or rebuild a relationship. Steve Scott and I took the time to write an entire book for her, *For Better or for Best,* to point out areas where her attitudes and actions can serve to strengthen or weaken your marriage.

But let's get back to the crucial point you need to consider: *If your marriage is continually under stress, is filled with strife, and is bordering on collapse, you've been participating in weakening it.*

When I first heard what you're about to read, I squirmed and fought and argued against the whole idea for at least a month. I want you to experience whatever emotions are natural to you as you read the statement in the box below. If you react strongly, I understand why. In spite of my initial opposition, I ultimately realized that there was more truth in it than I wanted to admit. You may want to react like I did and spend long hours trying to disprove it. But let's face it together.

> IF A COUPLE HAS BEEN MARRIED FOR MORE THAN FIVE YEARS, ANY PERSISTENT DISHARMONY IN THEIR MARRIAGE RELATIONSHIP IS USUALLY ATTRIBUTABLE TO THE HUSBAND'S LACK OF UNDERSTANDING AND APPLYING GENUINE LOVE.

I'm not suggesting that the husband is solely responsible for all disharmony in a marriage. Day-to-day conflicts can arise because of his wife's physical exhaustion, health problems, or overloaded schedules. On any given day, she may respond negatively to her husband due to a headache, a disturbing phone call from her father, or any number of other temporary upsets. Certainly, the husband is not to blame for these occasional problems.

Perhaps you have married a woman who believes her father or mother hated her, rejected her, or otherwise never "blessed" her. (For insight into the powerful biblical concept of "blessing" others, see my book written with John Trent, *The Blessing*, which talks about the tremendous benefit of growing up with parental love and acceptance, their "blessing," and the incredible damage that can come from living without it.) If your wife didn't receive her parents' blessing, you're probably going to experience a woman who tends to be critical, judgmental, or otherwise difficult to live with.

In situations like that, I certainly can't say that daily disharmony is all the fault of the husband. But I can say that biblically speaking, you're still responsible for the disharmony in your home. Does this sound confusing?

The Scriptures teach that the husband is charged with the responsibility of overseeing the welfare of his wife and children. In fact, Ephesians 5:23 says that he is to love his wife as Christ loved the church and actually sacrificed Himself so others might live. After five years of marriage if a husband has failed to understand or seek help for the major causes of their disharmony, he either doesn't understand what genuine love is or has chosen to ignore God's command to shepherd his family wisely.

During a lecture I was giving, one man violently reacted to this concept, saying, "When a woman gets out of line, I think you ought to knock her up against the wall!"

"Throw him out!" a woman in the meeting shouted back.

His reaction shocked me at first, but I later discovered that he and his wife were in one of those "marriage pits." Since he was trying to scare and convince his wife into believing that all the problems in their marriage were her fault, accepting any part of my statement would have destroyed his line of reasoning—and forced him to deal with the pain he had caused her and the guilt he sought so hard to repress.

I know of at least three types of men who vigorously resist accepting this concept I've shared here:

A man who is bitter over his wife leaving him. He would have to admit the failure of the marriage was at least partially his fault, and that admission is almost too much to ask of him.

A man with a close relative or friend whose wife has divorced him. "It couldn't have been my brother's fault. You never met his terrible wife." (Don't forget, though, most of what you know about that "terrible wife" you learned from your brother. He may be a great brother but a very insensitive husband.)

A man having an affair. It's just too hard for him to blame himself for a frigid or nagging wife. He feels she was enough to drive him into another woman's arms and explains away his own error and insensitivity.

I tried in vain to find an exception to this concept by asking the question, "How can this be true when. . . ?" For example, I looked at two "exceptions" I had heard about recently.

"How can this be true when my neighbor down the street is so hard to get along with that no man could live with her negative moods day after day?" and "How could you possibly blame Jim for flirting when his wife, Jane, doesn't respond to him sexually?" I soon discovered that I couldn't disprove this concept with these two types of objections. One uses a hypothetical situation, the other a second-hand example.

These two "exceptions" don't work because vital facts are missing. What was it that developed the bad attitude in our neighbor? It may have been her father or her husband or any number of causes. In any case, the husband has the biblical responsibility to find out what is causing it (even if it's him) and begin to take steps to solve it.

Hypothetical situations leave out the context of the problem. Excusing Jim's flirting behavior because his wife is sexually frigid also ignores the fact that Jim may have caused her to close her spirit, which resulted in their sexual problems. Not only that, but other people's errant behavior still doesn't give anyone a license to be irresponsible.

DOES THIS WHOLE CONCEPT SOUND ONE-SIDED?

I knew by Norma's facial expression that I had offended her one morning. I immediately said, "I understand what I just said was too harsh, and I shouldn't have said it. I would like to ask you to forgive me."

"Okay, I'll forgive you," she said.

I thought to myself, *You know, this whole thing is one-sided here. It seems like all the pressure is on me to act right. What about her?*

So I said, "Hey, how come I'm always the one that has to ask forgiveness when I do something wrong? Why don't you ask me to forgive you anymore? This is one-sided, isn't it?"

Then she looked at me and said, "I'd be happy to admit where I am wrong and seek your forgiveness *if* I have offended you."

"Well, that's just too much! What an arrogant statement. What a terribly selfish thing to say," I said. "There are lots of things you have done to offend me. I can't remember the last time you admitted you were wrong and sought my forgiveness."

"Well, what are some of my offenses?" she asked.

"Give me a minute and I'll think of a lot of them," I said.

"Well, what are they!" she asked again.

"Just a minute and I'll think of some," I said, stalling for time.

I thought and thought, but I couldn't come up with even one. I told myself, *This can't be true.* But I couldn't think of a thing she had done to offend me.

Finally I said, "But I can think of some things I'd like to see you change about yourself."

"Well, what are they?"

"Even though we've been married five years, I'm going to come up with the first exception to this thing of it being all my fault. (I was pleased with myself.) There are some times when you don't respect me and you don't honor me as a special person in your life. Sometimes your words are cutting and disrespectful . . . *now how is that my responsibility?*"

We sat down at the kitchen table and started going through each item. It took only ten minutes for us to figure out that every time she had been disrespectful to me I had either rolled out of bed grouchy or been critical of her most of the day. I hadn't earned her respect. It was amazing. All three things I had felt *she* should change were a direct result of *my* failure to love her in a genuine way. Once we talked, Norma was more than willing to apologize for her offensive reactions. She freely admitted her reactions to my behavior were wrong. But for the first time, I saw clearly how much my insensitive actions had provided a backdrop for her negative reactions!

Now I have to admit the whole episode left a bad taste in my mouth. Even today, when I'm tired or a little down, I think to myself, *This is crazy. I shouldn't even tell people this because it'll make wives run all over their husbands.* But just the opposite is true. When a man treats his wife with gentleness, when he is loving and understanding, and when he does most of the things we describe in this book, she will respond to him on every level. She'll desire intimate conversation with him, she'll feel emotional love for him, and she'll respond to him sexually. The only exception, as I mentioned before, occurs when a wife is romantically involved with another man.

In Search of an Exception

Recently, I talked with a man. After years of raising the children, his wife had reluctantly gone back to working part-time. Soon she was getting so many pats on the back for her hard work habits and positive attitude that she was asked to become a full-time employee. And that's when the problems began with her husband.

Now she was too tired to prepare him the kind of dinners he was used to having and all she wanted to do was talk about work. Finally, his anger built up to the point that he lashed out at her, "Where are your priorities, anyway? Isn't our marriage important to you any more?"

Not wanting to inflame him further, she tried to avoid the conversation with a half-hearted response that she'd try a little harder to have dinner on time. Unfortunately, that wasn't the only thing wrong, and soon their marriage had deteriorated so much that they were in my office for counseling as a last step before undertaking divorce proceedings.

When I met this couple, I asked them several questions, the same questions the husband could have asked his wife if he had known how to bring healing to their marriage. I asked them, "On a scale of 0 to 10, where has your marriage been over the past several years, overall?" He responded with a "6 or 7" and then after a long pause, she said it had been a "2, at best."

Then I asked, "Where would you two like to be?" Both of them agreed that what they had married for was to have "a 10 as often as possible, but at least an 8."

Then I asked them a key question, "What would it take to move your relationship up to an 8 and on the way to a 10?" Almost immediately, this man's wife said, "He'd have to talk to me more. . . ." But before she could finish her sentence, her husband cut her short and said, "I *do* talk to you; *you're* the one who is too tired to talk because of working all the time."

After his angry outburst, his wife's response was typical of what I have heard time and time again in counseling sessions. She said to him, "What you call conversation is really verbal abuse, and I'm tired of it. You don't want to talk to me. You just want to lecture me about all the things I'm doing wrong. Well, not everyone thinks I'm such a loser! People at work think I'm worth something. Why do you think I enjoy it there so much?"

For almost twenty years, any conversation this man had with his wife had been an opportunity for him to demand what he could have asked for nicely or to criticize another area of her character or appearance. When his wife was finally around some positive people, she blossomed like a flower—and didn't want anything to do with her insensitive husband as a result.

Fortunately, there was still a spark of love in their marriage and they were both willing to make a decision to try to make it work. After several counseling sessions, he understood and admitted for the first time that he had been offensive, angry, and a poor communicator. And even though she continues to work, now several years later, their marriage relationship has tripled in terms of mutual satisfaction.

If only he had known years ago what it took for her to want to spend time with him, he could have avoided years of unnecessary pain. He needed to realize that wisdom dwells in those people willing to be corrected and even seeking to get error out of their lives.

I realize how difficult it is for us to admit we are wrong. One night Norma and I were lying in bed when I said something obnoxious to her. She closed me out, and though I wanted to restore our relationship, I was too proud to say anything.

The words stuck in my throat. I wanted to say, "Norma, I was wrong about what I just said." I tried, but the words just wouldn't come. I decided to roll over and go to sleep, thinking it would be easier to admit my mistake in the morning. Throughout the night I woke up, feeling more and more eager to admit I was wrong and feeling worse and worse about what I had done.

By morning I could admit my mistake, and our relationship was restored. But do you realize what I had done to Norma and what many of us men are capable of doing to our wives? Not only do we offend them on the one hand, but we leave them to suffer for hours (or even weeks or months) before being willing to make things right. Over the years, hundreds of wives have told me that if their husbands had come to them earlier and dealt with problem issues, they would have been spared double the pain—feeling the hurt of the initial offense and then having to wait for restoration.

One of the quickest ways to restore your marriage is to demonstrate genuine conviction and sorrow for seeing such a valuable person as your wife treated in a dishonoring way.

3. *Express genuine sorrow to your wife whenever you offend her.* One of the most dramatic examples of the power of this particular point was shown to me by an All-Pro defensive player on an NFL championship team.

At a professional football conference where I was speaking, I walked into the coffee shop and witnessed this player and his wife in the middle of a very tense and tearful discussion. Knowing how big and powerful these athletes are—especially when they're angry—I was a little reluctant when he called me over to the table and asked if I would talk with them a few minutes.

He had been upset with his wife because she was too tired after their long airplane flight to go out with some friends after the evening meeting. Her reluctance displeased him, and he shamed her in front of the other couple. He was angry with her all night, too. Now, over breakfast, he was trying to make up and she wasn't responding.

When they walked into the coffee shop, he tried to put his arm around her, and she pulled away, embarrassing him in the process. Before they knew it, they were in the middle of another fight. That's when he called me over to the table."I don't want to spend the whole week like this. What can we do?" he said.

I encouraged him to understand how hurtful it was for her to hear his harsh put-downs in front of the other players and wives.

And he said, "Well, it was wrong of her, too. She could have stayed up for another hour. We're at a conference, and this is a place to have fun!"

Then she said, "This is so typical. He's always thinking about having fun with his friends and doesn't really care about me. I was tired from getting us packed and the kids off to my folks, and he got mad because he didn't want to go without me."

The tension level between the two of them was so high by this point that it could have reheated the coffee in front of us. Other people seated around us were painfully aware of the scene between them.

I tried something with them that I had never done before (nor since), and the immediate results amazed all of us. I asked him to pay attention to what I was about to say to her and said, "If you don't want to be upset all week, would you be willing to do something like this? For just a minute, let me pretend that I'm you."

I reached across the table, and I put my hand gently on top of hers. I looked her right in the eyes, and I said in a soft voice, "What I said to you in front of our friends last night was really wrong. I know it embarrassed you and really offended you. You're just too valuable to be treated like this. In fact, I don't even know how you put up with me like you do. You may not be able to respond right now, and I'll try and understand if you can't, but if you could, I'd love it if you forgave me. I know I don't deserve it, and I know I may blow it again. But I want you to know with all my heart that I don't want to hurt you, and I don't like living this way."

I pulled my hand away and sat back. Immediately, tears welled up in her eyes, and her facial muscles and her entire body seemed to relax.

"Do you see what's happening to your wife here?" I asked my NFL friend. As he looked at her, tears began to show in his eyes as well, and I said to him, "Can you see how your wife would respond if you would treat her with tenderness and be willing to admit the times that you're wrong?"

She immediately turned to him and said, "Yeah, but you could never do that!"

"Oh, yes I could," he said in an irritated tone of voice. Almost instantly he was feeling defensive again, and her facial muscles tightened up again.

For the next hour and a half he practiced—with his arm around her or gently holding her hand—how to speak to her and ask her forgiveness in a soft, genuine way when he had wronged her. On the football field, this fellow had spent years learning to "never give an inch." Now he began to discover that in marriage, when he wronged his wife he needed to take off the shoulder pads and admit that he was wrong. Two years later, I saw this same couple at another conference, and their marriage had never been better because of practicing this one principle.

My wife, Norma, has told me time and time again how much she appreciates seeing my genuine sorrow when I have hurt her. "How do you put up with me? How do you live with me? You deserve the medal of honor for staying with me. You deserve the purple heart. You are an amazing woman to live with such an insensitive man." Sincere words like those express my repentant spirit and soothe our relationship.

I asked one woman, "After your husband has verbally abused you, would you appreciate it if he admitted he was wrong and expressed sorrow that you were hurting? What would you do if he said, 'How do you put up with such a crumb like me, as insensitive as I am?' "

"I'd call the cops," she said.

I repeated in amazement, "You'd call the cops?"

"Yes, because I'd know that there was an imposter in the house," she replied.

I have had wives say to me, "My husband will never admit when he's wrong. He's too proud." Yet I meet husbands everywhere who are willing to admit their offenses if their wives are patient enough to help them understand *how* they have offended them.

Before we go on, let's review why each of these major steps greatly contributes to restoring harmony in the home. First, persistent disharmony is almost always reduced by you sincerely endeavoring to understand the ways you have offended your wife—literally trying to understand the depth of the hurt she has felt by your actions.

Second, you need to be willing to admit to yourself specifically what you have done to weaken your relationship. The greater your understanding of her suffering, the easier it can be for you to see what you've done wrong, and to take the third and often hardest step— expressing your sincere sorrow for your offensive actions. The more specific, the better when it comes to sharing how you have been wrong. This helps your spouse realize that you really do understand how she has suffered. And it leads to the fourth important aspect of restoring the relationship, seeking her forgiveness.

4. *Seek her forgiveness for your offensive behavior.* A woman needs a man who *understands* the *depth* of her grief after his hurtful behavior. Wives have said to me, "If only my husband knew how much I feel those words that he says so glibly and harshly. If only he knew how long they stay with me." Harsh words can stay with a woman for years.

A woman loves to hear her man say, "Will you forgive me?" And when she verbalizes, "Yes, you're forgiven," she is freer to restore her side of the relationship. However, if her husband simply says, "Oh, honey, I'm sorry," it's not always enough. He might be able to get away with it if he says it in a tender and gentle way, but a woman really needs to hear, "Will you forgive me?" That proves her husband values her half of the relationship. A flippant "I'm sorry" may mean "I'm sorry I got caught" or "I'm sorry to have to put up with your insensitivity." It usually doesn't restore the relationship to oneness and harmony.

Initially, your wife may appear unable or unwilling to grant forgiveness for any number of reasons. Perhaps she doesn't really believe you, or she thinks you really don't understand her real hurts or disappointment. She may even bluntly say, "No, I won't forgive you. . ." or "Give me some time. . ." or, "When I see a change in you, *maybe*. . . ." All of these are responses of a woman who has been deeply hurt, and all of them might tempt you to react in anger or try to verbally attack her for not forgiving you.

As hard as it may be to restrain yourself, reacting in anger to her statements can only drive her further away. Very often, a woman needs a track record of demonstrated forgiveness before emotionally feeling like granting it to her husband. She may make the decision to forgive, but it may take her some time to feel forgiving. That's why husbands need to be aware of something very unique about women.

Most women respond to a husband who genuinely and *persistently* seeks to restore their relationship. It may take an hour or several hours of "cooling off" and then coming back to talk. But like the situation of the NFL football player, a wife will usually respond positively to a man who gently and persistently asks her forgiveness. And that is why the next point is so important.

5. *Let her see your consistent and sincere efforts to correct offensive actions or words.* This is another way of saying, "Repent." For the Greeks, the word "repent" literally meant "to turn around." It means that you are to change your way of thinking or acting to the way Christ thought and acted (Luke 17:3–5).

A woman isn't impressed with a man who seeks forgiveness or admits he is wrong and then continues to hurt her year after year in the same areas. Words are nice, but they are not enough.

Attitudes, not words or actions, often harm a woman the most. When she *sees* her husband's attitudes changing, she is more willing to hope again and to be open with him and accept him into an intimate relationship. Otherwise, she'll keep him closed off for fear of being offended again.

People of the Lie

One of the most important words in the boxed statement on page 73 is the word "usually." It means that a broken relationship is not always attributable to the husband. After more than twenty years of working with couples all across the country, I have discovered only one situation that makes it more difficult and, in some very rare cases, nearly impossible for a wife to respond to her husband's genuine love when he consistently applies it.

This situation arises when a woman has had prolonged anger in her life. She has spent years being bitter and resentful toward her mom and dad or others, and as a result she has developed into a habitual liar and someone who has deep-seated feelings of inferiority.

These three deadly ingredients—unresolved resentment, habitual lying, and deep-seated inferiority, when mixed together over the years—can create what M. Scott Peck calls a "Person of the Lie." These people are unwilling to recognize or deal with the hurts they cause others, and they steadfastly refuse to admit any wrong in their own lives.

Remember, it is most unusual for a wife to be unresponsive to her husband's sincere love. Before you jump to any conclusions or say to yourself, "Now that's better. He's finally talking about *my wife*," let's look at some of the ways (more than one hundred of them) that a husband can offend his wife and can contribute to her developing anger, resentment, or other negative emotions or behavior.

When a husband recognizes that he has offended his wife in any of these ways, he needs to clear it up in order to restore the relationship. Why not ask your wife to check the ones that are true of you?

1. Ignoring her.
2. Not valuing her opinions.
3. Showing more attention to other people than her.
4. Not listening to her or not understanding what she feels is important.
5. Closing her out by not talking or listening to her (the silent treatment).
6. Being easily distracted when she's trying to talk.
7. Not scheduling special time to be with her.
8. Not being open to talk about things that you do not understand.
9. Not being open to talk about things that she does not understand.
10. Not giving her a chance to voice her opinion on decisions that affect the whole family.
11. Disciplining her by being angry or silent.
12. Making jokes about areas of her life.
13. Making sarcastic statements about her.
14. Insulting her in front of others.
15. Coming back with quick retorts.
16. Giving harsh admonitions.
17. Using careless words before you think through how they will affect her.
18. Nagging her in harshness.
19. Rebuking her before giving her a chance to explain a situation.
20. Raising your voice at her.
21. Making critical comments with no logical basis.
22. Swearing or using foul language in her presence.

23. Correcting her in public.
24. Being tactless when pointing out her weaknesses or blind spots.
25. Reminding her angrily that you warned her not to do something.
26. Having disgusted or judgmental attitudes.
27. Pressuring her when she is already feeling low or offended.
28. Lecturing her when she needs to be comforted, encouraged, or treated gently.
29. Breaking promises without any explanation or without being asked to be released from the promise.
30. Telling her how wonderful other women are and comparing her to other women.
31. Holding resentment about something she did and tried to make right.
32. Being disrespectful to her family and relatives.
33. Coercing her into an argument.
34. Correcting or punishing her in anger for something for which she's not guilty.
35. Not praising her for something she did well, even if she did it for you.
36. Treating her like a little child.
37. Being rude to her or to other people in public, like restaurant personnel or clerks.
38. Being unaware of her needs.
39. Being ungrateful.
40. Not trusting her.
41. Not approving of what she does or how she does it.
42. Not being interested in her own personal growth.
43. Being inconsistent or having double standards (doing things you won't allow her to do).
44. Not giving her advice when she really needs it and asks for it.
45. Not telling her that you love her.
46. Having prideful and arrogant attitudes in general.
47. Not giving daily encouragement.
48. Failing to include her in a conversation when you are with other people.
49. Failing to spend quantity or quality time with her when you're at a party.
50. "Talking her down"—continuing to discuss or argue a point just to prove you're right.
51. Ignoring her around the house as if she weren't a member of the family.
52. Not taking time to listen to what she believes is important as soon as you come home from work.

53. Ignoring her at social gatherings.
54. Not attending church as a family.
55. Failure to express honestly what you think her innermost feelings are.
56. Showing more excitement for work and other activities than for her.
57. Being impolite at mealtime.
58. Having sloppy manners around the house and in front of others.
59. Not inviting her out on special romantic dates from time to time (just the two of you).
60. Not helping her with the children just before mealtimes or during times of extra stress.
61. Not volunteering to help her with the dishes occasionally—or with cleaning the house.
62. Making her feel stupid when she shares an idea about your work or decisions that need to be made.
63. Making her feel unworthy for desiring certain furniture or insurance or other material needs for herself and the family.
64. Not being consistent with the children; not taking an interest in playing with them and spending quality and quantity time with them.
65. Not showing public affection for her, like holding her hand or putting your arm around her (you seem to be embarrassed to be with her).
66. Not sharing your life with her, like your ideas or your feelings (e.g., what's going on at work).
67. Not being the spiritual leader of the home.
68. Demanding that she submit to you.
69. Demanding that she be involved with you sexually when you are not in harmony.
70. Being unwilling to admit you were wrong.
71. Resisting whenever she shares one of your "blind spots."
72. Being too busy with work and activities.
73. Not showing compassion and understanding for her and the children when there is real need.
74. Not planning for the future, making her very insecure.
75. Being stingy with money, making her feel like she's being paid a salary—and not much at all.
76. Wanting to do things that embarrass her sexually.
77. Reading sexual magazines in front of her or the children.
78. Forcing her to make many of the decisions regarding the checkbook and bills.
79. Forcing her to handle bill collectors and overdue bills.

80. Not letting her lean on your gentleness and strength from time to time.
81. Not allowing her to fail—always feeling like you have to lecture her.
82. Refusing to let her be a woman.
83. Criticizing her womanly characteristics or sensitivity as being weak.
84. Spending too much money and getting the family too far into debt.
85. Not having a sense of humor and not joking about things together.
86. Not telling her how important she is to you.
87. Not sending her special love letters from time to time.
88. Forgetting special dates like anniversaries and birthdays.
89. Not defending her when somebody else is complaining or tearing her down (especially if it's one of your relatives or friends).
90. Not putting your arm around her and hugging her when she's in need of comfort.
91. Not bragging to other people about her.
92. Being dishonest.
93. Discouraging her for trying to better herself, either through education or physical fitness.
94. Continuing distasteful or harmful habits, like coming home drunk.
95. Not treating her as if "Handle With Care" were stamped on her forehead.
96. Ignoring her relatives and the people who are important to her.
97. Taking her for granted, assuming that "a woman's work is never done" around the house.
98. Not including her in future plans until the last minute.
99. Never doing little unexpected things for her.
100. Not treating her like an intellectual equal.
101. Looking at her as a weaker individual in general.
102. Being preoccupied with your own goals and needs, making her feel like she and the children do not count.
103. Threatening never to let her do something again because she made some mistake in the past.
104. Criticizing her behind her back. (This is really painful for her if she hears about your criticism from someone else.)
105. Blaming her for things in your relationship that are clearly your failure.

106. Not being aware of her physical limitations, treating her like a man by roughhousing with her or making her carry heavy objects.
107. Losing patience or getting angry with her when she can't keep up with your schedule or physical stamina.
108. Acting like you're a martyr if you go along with her opinions.
109. Sulking when she challenges your comments.
110. Joining too many organizations which exclude her and the children.
111. Failing to repair items around the house.
112. Watching too much TV and therefore neglecting her and the children.
113. Demanding that she sit and listen to your point of view when she needs to be taking care of the children's needs.
114. Insisting on lecturing her in order to convey what you believe are important points.
115. Humiliating her with words and actions, saying things like "I can't stand living in a pigpen."
116. Not taking the time to prepare her to enjoy sexual intimacy.
117. Spending money extravagantly without helping those less fortunate.
118. Avoiding family activities that the children enjoy.
119. Taking vacations that are primarily for your pleasure, like fishing or hunting, while preventing her from shopping and doing the things she enjoys doing.
120. Not letting her get away from the children just to be with friends, go shopping for special items, or have a weekend away with her friends.
121. Being unwilling to join her in the things she enjoys like shopping, going out for coffee and dessert at a restaurant, etc.
122. Not understanding the boring chores a housewife does: like picking up clothes and toys all day long, wiping runny noses, putting on and taking off muddy boots and jackets, washing and ironing, etc., etc.

CAN A WEAKENED MARRIAGE RELATIONSHIP REALLY BE TRACED TO THE HUSBAND'S LACK OF GENUINE LOVE?

I want to emphasize the fact that *only after five years* of marriage is a husband responsible for the prolonged disharmony in his marriage. When you marry a woman, you inherit the way she was treated by her father, her mother, her brothers and sisters, and even her friends. She is the sum total of her environment, her associations, and her life as a single person. Here again let's keep in mind that God called the man to be the leader in nurturing his wife and children. If he leads in offensive, harsh, angry behavior, he will reap the results in a weakened or fractured marriage. On the other hand, he can also set a positive tone, which is encouraged by many suggestions in this book.

The main problem that we men have to overcome is our *lack* of knowledge and skills to nurture (Eph. 5:28–29) our wives to a level from which we can enjoy a growing, loving, and intimate relationship with them. We, too, are the sum total of our environment, etc.

You may be thinking thoughts similar to those Mike had when he challenged me on this whole concept.

"Now wait a minute," Mike said. "That can't be true."

I assured him, "I know, it's hard to believe."

"Well, take my wife, Carol, for example," he said. "She has divorced me, but you can't tell me that the problems we had in our relationship can all be traced to my failure to love her. I just can't buy that."

To prove my point, I said, "Give me an example—something you didn't like about her—and we'll see if we can check this thing out."

"Take this one example," he said, confident that he could disprove this concept. "On our wedding night we had sexual relations. She was turned off by the whole experience and from that day on, for over twenty years, she never really enjoyed our sex life. She never initiated it. She didn't even want to be involved. It was always at my initiative.

"I felt she was more of an object that wasn't really involved in this relationship. How would I be the cause of that? On our wedding night, she changed on me!"

Mike had dated Carol for three years. So I asked how he treated her during those years.

"Well, okay," he said.

"Mike, I happen to know that it wasn't okay. You and I both know that you had a reputation of being mean and extremely insensitive to her. Do you remember some of the things you did?"

When he admitted that he did remember, I said, "You really hurt her feelings. During all those years that you dated her, did you ever clear up your offenses with her?"

"No, I didn't. I didn't know how to do it. I didn't know what to do," he said.

"Why did she marry you—to get away from her family?"

"Right."

"Then the first night she realized that sex wasn't that great. And do you know why?" I asked. "Because you two weren't in harmony. Besides this fact, did you prepare her for sex?" I explained that many women tell me they need as much as three days' preparation for sex, romantically and emotionally, before they can respond to their husbands. A woman is sort of like an iron and a man is like a light bulb. She *warms up* to the sexual expression, while he *turns on* immediately.

"Did you ever clear your conscience with her? Did you ever clear those past offenses when you were married?" I asked him.

"No, I never did." Mike had never admitted he was wrong.

"Did you criticize your wife a lot?" I asked. Mike's head sank lower and lower. He even admitted that he once told her all their problems were her fault. After a few minutes, tears appeared in his eyes because he realized how insensitive, cruel, and harsh he had been for all those years.

The chart on pages 90–93 will provide some additional illustrations to help you discover how you might have contributed to a weaker marriage relationship. (This chart was devised by Ken Nair, a marriage and family lecturer/counselor.) If you need help, you have an expert in your own home—your wife. You may be amazed at how well she remembers your unloving words and actions. However, many wives say they are afraid of their husbands, afraid to be honest for fear they'll be *rejected* or *criticized* for being illogical, too sensitive, or unforgiving.

IF YOU REACT TO THIS IDEA, YOU'RE NOT ALONE. MANY WIVES AND SINGLE WOMEN JOIN YOU

I explained this concept to an older woman whose husband had left her, after many years of marriage, for a younger woman. She resisted the idea that I could trace their broken relationship to her husband's failure.

"Oh, this is ridiculous. Everyone knows it's a fifty–fifty deal. I'm just as much responsible as he was," she argued.

"Well, I'm looking for my first exception. I would certainly appreciate it if you would explain to me where you were wrong in the relationship," I told her.

An hour later, she realized that if her husband had treated her differently, she would have responded much differently during those years. We traced everything he had accused her of to his failure to love her.

Some men (including me) have said this material is dangerous because it will make women irresponsible. They panic because they are afraid their wives will accuse them of things their wives really are guilty of in their marriage relationship. I can understand the panic. In general, the concept provokes us to rage because it reveals our irresponsibility as husbands, and we just can't take it—especially at first. Believe me, I know and understand the fight that might be going on inside you at this moment. However, if someone really thinks through this concept, it actually makes the husband and wife *more* responsible for their actions, not less.

Some single women also react negatively to this concept at first. For example, I overheard two of my editors discussing the concepts in this book; one was single and the other married.

"I just can't believe that some of the ideas in that book are good," said Debi, a twenty-five-year-old single woman. "I don't believe part of it—like women are more emotional."

"Just wait until you're married," Judy told her. "In a year and a half of marriage, my husband and I have run into many of the problems discussed in Gary's book."

"Some of the generalizations bother me, though," Debi continued. "I don't feel that women in general are more sensitive and men more logical. I don't think you're more sensitive, because I've seen you at work. I know you."

"But it's different in a marriage," Judy said. "Just the other day when my husband was reading a chapter I had edited, he said, 'Hey, I think you're letting your thoughts creep into this book!' because the example was almost an identical account of a discussion we had recently." If this section of the book doesn't do anything more than stimulate you to try and find an exception to the rule, it will be worthwhile. And if five years from now we discover hundreds of exceptions, the experience will still not have been damaging, because you and I need to become more responsible, loving partners, no matter what our wives do. That is the basis for genuine love— *doing what is right no matter what the other person does or says.*

Genuine love motivates us to build a relationship primarily for the other person's sake, and when we do that, *we* gain because we have a better relationship to enjoy.

FOR PERSONAL REFLECTION

1. What should we do if our mates offend us? Luke 17:3–4.
2. What attitude should we have when we rebuke an offender? Galatians 6:1; Proverbs 15:1.

HUSBAND'S ACTIONS

Husband's Lack of Genuine Love	Amplified
UNRELIABLE	Lets time slip by unnoticed.
UNTRUSTING AND CONDEMNING	Has an attitude of superiority in finances. Demands the control of all money. Won't let his wife know about their financial status. Feels certain his wife would bankrupt him if she were given the chance.
ANGRY AND DEMANDING	In anger, over-reacts to children and others. Doesn't like to be inconvenienced by family. Sets standards too difficult for children to meet.
INSENSITIVE AND UNKIND	Uses hurtful words to others. Uses his wife or others as his source of humor.
INATTENTIVE AND THOUGHTLESS AND UNTRUST-WORTHY	Preoccupied with personal concerns. Dismisses others' personal feelings as unrealistic or invalid—if he acknowledges them at all. Family's reputation has been damaged by his lack of consideration for others.
UNCARING AND IRRESPONSIBLE	Doesn't seem to care about his family's needs. Seems to think the only obligation he has to the family is financial.

RESULT	WIFE'S RESPONSES
Wife's Offensive Habits	Amplified
NAGGING	Repeatedly reminds her husband about things that need attention, with illustrations of his past wrongs and forgetfulness.
IMPULSIVE SPENDER	Spends money as though it were very easily obtained. Seems irresponsible with money when it comes into her possession. Uses credit cards without concern.
PERMISSIVE WITH CHILDREN	Makes excuses for children's disobedience to husband and keeps secrets from him about their conduct.
TOO EMOTIONAL	Cries often and is easily hurt. Holds on to hurts for a long time. Able to recall past offenses in detail.
DOMINATING	Answers all questions, even those directed to her husband. Makes the decisions in the home and assumes responsibility for disciplining the children.
NAGGING	Repeatedly reminds her husband about things that need attention, with illustrations of his past wrongs.

THINGS A HUSBAND DISLIKES AND
CRITICIZES IN HIS WIFE

1. She wants to be with her mother more than with him

2. She's lazy around the house

3. She's sexually frigid

4. She's sneaky

5. She's overly critical of the way he spends money

6. She avoids doing activities with him

7. She makes him feel like a nobody

8. She's afraid of speaking in front of groups

9. She yells at the kids in the morning

10. She's inflexible, always gets offended

11. She's independent

12. She's rebellious (unsubmissive)

13. She's disrespectful to him

14. She's snappy, angry

15. She reacts negatively to his friends

16. She's naggy

17. She's afraid of moving

18. She talks too much on the telephone

19. She's too lenient with the children

20. She reacts negatively to his relatives

21. She's too strict with the children

22. She's unwilling to pray with him

COMMON EVIDENCE OF THE HUSBAND'S FAILURE
TO GENUINELY LOVE HIS WIFE

1. He's overly critical and non-communicative

2. He's critical of how she keeps a house, a demanding perfectionist

3. He offends her by his harshness, is demanding, and offends the children

4. He's critical, judgmental, harsh, unyielding, insensitive to the needs of the children, stubborn, overly argumentative

5. He's irresponsible with money, extravagant

6. He's critical, not fun-loving, non-communicative, unwilling to shop or stop for a cup of coffee with her

7. He's harsh, offends her severely

8. He's critical of her grammar or speaking ability

9. He's undisciplined, neglects the training of the children, and does not help get them off to school

10. He rejects her and is overly critical of her

11. He's too possessive and critical of her

12. He has severely offended her and has not cleared it up

13. He's harsh and avoids her when with other people

14. He has severely offended her and broken promises

15. He prefers his friends over hers and defends his friends over hers

16. He doesn't assume his responsibility or is inattentive or untrustworthy

17. He makes sudden changes or is too impulsive

18. He isn't talking with her enough

19. He's too strict with the children

20. He prefers his relatives over hers

21. He's too lenient with the children

22. He has been offending her without clearing it up

6

What No Woman
Can Resist

*"Let
no unwholesome word
proceed
from your mouth,
but only
such a word
as is good
for edification."*
Ephesians 4:29

THE CRUNCH OF corn chips distracted my attention from the Saturday afternoon football game. I watched in amazement as my wife and three children began to eat their sandwiches and drink their Cokes while I sat only a couple of feet away without a bite to eat.

Why didn't she make me a sandwich? I asked myself. *I'm the sole bread winner, and I'm being ignored as if I didn't exist.* I cleared my throat loudly to catch my wife's attention. When that didn't work, I became so irritated that I walked into the kitchen, got the bread out, and made my own sandwich. When I sat back down in front of the TV, Norma didn't say a word nor did I. But I kept wondering, *If women are so sensitive, how come she didn't know I wanted a sandwich? If women are so alert, why didn't she hear me clear my throat or notice that I wasn't speaking to her? Why didn't she notice the expression of irritation on my face?*

A few days later when we were talking calmly, I said, "I've really been wondering about something, but I hesitate asking you this question. I was really intrigued the other day, and I wonder if I could ask you a personal question?" By now I had aroused her curiosity.

"Sure," she said.

"You know last Saturday when I was watching the football game and you made sandwiches for all the kids? Could I ask you why you didn't make one for me?"

"Are you serious?" she asked. She looked at me with such amazement that it really confused me.

"Sure, I'm serious. I would think that since I'm the one who earns all the money for food around here that you would have made me something to eat too."

"You know, I really can't believe that you would even ask a question like that," she said. By now, I was thinking, *Maybe I shouldn't have asked. Maybe I should know the answer.* It seemed very obvious to her, but it didn't seem obvious to me at all.

"Norma, I really don't see it. I admit I am blind in some areas," I pursued, "and I can see this is one of them. Would you mind telling me?"

"Sometimes women are accused of being stupid, but we aren't," she answered. "We don't just set ourselves up to be criticized." She seemed to think that explained why she hadn't made me a sandwich.

"I can understand that. But what does that have to do with the sandwiches?"

"Do you realize that every time I make you a sandwich, you say something critical about it? 'Norma, you didn't give me enough lettuce . . . Is this avocado ripe? You put too much mayonnaise on this. Hey, how about some butter? Well, it's a little dry'. . . .

"Maybe you've never realized it, but you have had a critical statement for every sandwich I ever made. I just wasn't up to being criticized the other day. It wasn't worth it. I don't enjoy being criticized."

I had egg all over my face because I could recall many times when I had criticized her as she handed me sandwiches. But "every" time? I wanted to say, "Come on, Norma, let's get realistic! Every time?" But instead I remembered that for a woman, "always" and "never" don't mean the same thing as they do to a man when they're spoken with emotion. Norma's tone of voice and facial expression as well as her words were telling me this was something that really bothered her. I was simply eating the fruit of my ways. I sowed criticism and reaped an empty plate. I am happy to say that after that experience I began praising every sandwich she made for me, and now she unhesitantly makes them for me.

Shortly after Marilyn left Bob, I asked her if she could recall things for which Bob had praised her. She couldn't remember a single time during their twenty-plus years of marriage. Her children confirmed it. They agreed that their mother had never served a single dinner that their father didn't criticize in at least one way. He had complained when the salt and pepper weren't on the table or when she didn't cook the meat just right. She finally reached the point where she didn't even want to be near his critical personality. She left him for another man.

"I'm kind of happy she's leaving me, because she never wants to do anything with me anyway," Bob said. "She's a party-pooper and a loner. She excludes me from her activities. Do you know she never wanted to go on a vacation with me? I've tried and I've tried, but she never wants to. I'm disgusted with her too."

We didn't discuss his marital problems until after he told me about his job change due to friction with his former boss.

"How did he treat you, Bob?" I asked.

"He'd come out to the shop where I was the foreman, and he'd look for one little thing to yell at me about in front of all my men. That really hurt me deeply. Then he would go back to his office, and I'd continue working my fingers to the bone. He'd never notice how hard I worked or even say anything positive about it. I couldn't take it any more, so I asked for a transfer."

I asked Bob, "Would you take a vacation with your boss?"

"Are you kidding? That would be the worst thing in the world," he answered.

"How about doing other activities with him?"

"No way! He's so critical he'd even ruin a trip to Hawaii!"

What I told Bob next blew open his mind to finally understand his wife. I pointed out how as a husband he was just like his boss, and his face dropped and tears came to his eyes.

"You're right. No wonder Marilyn never wanted to go anywhere with me. I never think about things she does to please me, and I'm always criticizing her in front of the children and our friends."

But it was too late. Marilyn was already in love with another man. Though Bob changed drastically and is now much more sensitive to women, his wife divorced him and remarried.

Women need praise. We should be able to understand their need because we, too, want to know that we are of value to other people. One of the ways we know we're needed is when others express appreciation for *who we are* and *what we do.*

The Scriptures remind us that our major relationships involve praise:

1. Praising God (Ps. 100:4).
2. Praising our wives (Prov. 31:28).
3. Praising others; for example, our Christian friends (Eph. 4:29).

I can vividly remember my boss saying years ago, "If only I had ten men like you, we could change the world." After that, I was so motivated I couldn't do enough for him.

Teachers know how praise motivates children. One teacher said she praised each student in her third-grade class every day, without exception. Her students were the most motivated, encouraged, and enthusiastic in the school. When my substitute high school geometry teacher praised me regularly, my "D" average climbed to an "A" in six weeks.

Knowing how significant praise can be, why do we as husbands fail to express it to our wives? Several reasons. The most common is preoccupation with our own needs, vocation, and activities. We lose sight of the positive and helpful qualities in our wives when we are preoccupied. Even worse, we fail to acknowledge our wives' helpful traits when we do notice them.

When a husband forgets his wife's need for praise, the marriage is usually on its way downhill. And if he constantly expresses the bitter instead of the sweet, his marriage will become less fulfilling every day. Criticism is devastating, especially when voiced in anger or harshness (Prov. 15:1, 4). When a husband rails against his wife for her unique feminine qualities, he conveys a lack of approval for her as a person. This automatically weakens their relationship.

Charlie Jones, in the book *Life Is Tremendous*, says we really can't enjoy life until we learn how to see and say something positive about everything. Though *none of us will ever be completely positive* about life, he says, we can be *in the process* of learning, growing, and developing toward a positive attitude.

If you develop a positive attitude, not only will others want to be around you more often, but your wife will also benefit tremendously. She will have a greater sense of worth and value, knowing you have provided the encouragement only a husband can give.

Encourage your wife and deepen your marriage relationship by following these two simple steps in learning how to praise her.

PRAISE HER (AT LEAST) ONCE A DAY

Promise yourself to tell your wife daily what you appreciate about her. Promise yourself—not her—because she might develop expectations and be hurt if you forget. Begin by learning to verbalize your thoughts of appreciation.

Here are some typical statements wives have told me they enjoy hearing:

1. "What a meal! The way you topped that casserole with sour cream and cheese.... M-m-m-m...that was delicious."

2. (This next one is great with an early-morning kiss.) "Honey, I sure love you. You're special to me."
3. While in the company of friends say, "This is *my* wife. She's the greatest!"
4. Put little notes on the refrigerator like, "I loved the way you looked last night."
5. "You're such a dedicated wife to make my lunch every day."
6. "Our kids are really blessed to have a mother like you. You take such good care of them."
7. "I don't know if I prefer the dress or what's in it better."
8. "Do I like your hairstyle? I'd like any hairstyle you have just because it's on you."
9. "I'd love to take you out tonight just to show you off."
10. "Honey, you've worked so hard. Why don't you sit down and rest for a while before dinner? I can wait."
11. "You're so special to me that I'd like to do something special for you right now. Why don't you take a bubble bath and relax. I'll do up the dishes and get the kids started on their homework."

In her book *Forever My Love*, Margaret Hardisty emphasized that women tend to approach life on an emotional plane while men approach it on a more logical, sometimes coldly objective one. Therefore, when you praise your wife, it's important to use words and actions that communicate praise *from her point of view*. Anything that is romantic or deals with building deeper relationships usually pleases wives.

BE CREATIVE WITH YOUR PRAISE

One husband won his wife back partly through creative praise. He bought 365 pieces of wrapped candy, wrote a special message on every wrapper, and then sealed them again. She opened one piece every day and read what he appreciated about her for a full year.

A woman loves to find hidden notes—in her jewelry box, the silver drawer, the medicine cabinet. . . .Search for ways to praise your wife. The possibilities are endless.

What kind of praise would you like to hear from your boss? Try a little of it on your wife. You may say, "Well, I don't need too much praise. I'm secure in my job, and I really don't need it." Then interview some of those who work with you to see how they would appreciate being praised. Some of their ideas might work with your wife. Also, ask your wife what kind of praise she likes to hear.

DON'T DRAW ATTENTION
TO HER UNATTRACTIVE FEATURES

Wrinkles, gray hair, and excess weight are definitely not on the list of possible conversation starters. Even your casual comments about them can make your wife insecure—she may fear being traded in on a "newer model." She knows divorce is just too easy and common nowadays.

One husband wrote his wife a cute poem about how much he loved her little wrinkles and how he loved caressing her "cellulose cells." His card, though softened with flowers, made her cry for hours. Men, we have to praise our wives without drawing attention to what they believe are their unattractive features.

That doesn't mean you should use insincere flattery. Have you ever been to a party where someone compliments you and you know inside he or she don't mean what they say? Sometimes a husband will casually remark, "Oh, yeah, I really like that dress." But his wife can generally detect his insincerity. Even if you don't like her dress, you can say something sincere like, "Honey, the dress isn't half as good-looking as you are."

Did you know you can even find something to praise in your wife's faults? The chart *How to Find the Positive Side of Your Wife's "Negative" Traits* can get you started on finding the positive aspects in the things you consider her "flaws."

HOW TO FIND THE POSITIVE SIDE
TO YOUR WIFE'S "NEGATIVE" TRAITS

Negative	Positive
1. Nosy	She may be very *alert* or *sociable*.
2. Touchy	She may be very *sensitive*.
3. Manipulating	She may be a very *resourceful* person with many creative ideas.
4. Stingy	She may be very *thrifty*.
5. Talkative	She may be very *expressive* and *dramatic*.
6. Flighty	She may be an *enthusiastic* person with *cheerful vitality*.
7. Too serious	She may be a very *sincere* and *earnest* person with *strong convictions*.
8. Too bold	She may have *strong convictions, uncompromising* with her own standards.
9. Rigid	She may be a *well-disciplined* person with *strong convictions*.

10. Overbearing	She may be a very *confident* person—sure of herself.
11. A dreamer	She may be very *creative* and *imaginative*.
12. Too fussy	She may be very *organized* and *efficient*.

Specific praise is far better than *general* praise. For example, "That was a great dinner" doesn't do nearly as much for her as, "The asparagus with the nutmeg sauce was fantastic. I've never had asparagus that tasted so good. I don't know how you can take plain, ordinary vegetables and turn them into such mouth-watering delights."

"You're a great mom" won't send her into orbit, but this might: "I'm really grateful that I married a woman who is so sensitive that she knows just the perfect way of making our kids feel important. They're sure lucky to have such a sensitive mother."

There is no right or wrong time to praise your wife. She'll love it when you're alone or when you're with the children and friends. Make sure you don't limit your praise to public or private times. If you only praise her in public, she might suspect you're showing off for your friends. If you only praise her in private, she may feel you're embarrassed about doing it.

Whenever you praise her, it's important that your full attention be on her. If she senses that your mind or feelings are elsewhere, your praise will be less meaningful to her.

As you learn how to praise your wife genuinely and consistently, you'll begin to see a new sparkle in her eyes and new life in your relationship.

HOW TO TALK ABOUT PRAISE WITH YOUR WIFE

1. *Learn to "prime the pump."*

Husband	What kind of praise do you really enjoy receiving from people?
Wife	Oh, I don't know. As long as it's sincere, I'll like it.
Husband	Do you feel I praise you enough?
Wife	I think so.
Husband	(priming the pump) How about last week's meals? Would you appreciate it if I let you know more often how much I enjoy your cooking?
Wife	Oh, yes, I remember I went to a lot of extra effort on two meals last week, and you didn't even mention it. . . .

Now you've got the water flowing. If you can take it, keep pumping. Show your *concern* and *understanding* by saying things like, "That must really hurt you when I don't say anything. You deserve a medal for putting up with me." Comfort her and let her get rid of some of her pent-up feelings.

2. *Look for the hidden meaning behind her words.*

Husband   Dear, remember last week when I thanked you for the meal? Did I overdo it in front of Steve and Mary?

Wife   Don't worry about it—it's okay.

Husband   Even when I said, "I'm glad we had company over; she's never cooked better"?

Wife   Oh, yeah, I did feel bad. You made it sound like I don't cook good meals for you unless we have company.

Husband   I thought you might have felt bad. Let's see, what would have been a better way to say what I meant?

A husband needs to help his wife be as honest and straightforward as possible so he can know where the relationship is strained. So many times during our early married years I asked Norma not to "beat around the bush" or "play games with me." I needed the facts in order to adjust my behavior and learn how to be a better husband. I hope you encourage your wife to be as straightforward as possible to help build a deeper, more fulfilling relationship.

FOR PERSONAL REFLECTION

1. How do we develop a general positive attitude? 1 Thessalonians 5:16–18; Romans 8:28; James 1:2–3; Hebrews 12:11, 15.
2. What does praising God show us about our relationship with Him? Psalm 100:4.

7

What Women Admire Most About Men

"Reprove
a wise man,
and he will
love you."
Proverbs 9:8

"I'M QUITTING ON Monday," Jim yelled as he blasted through the front door. Elaine greeted him quietly and listened to her husband's outburst of anger. "My boss finally did it! I'm not working for him any more," he said. Giving him time and her full attention, Elaine let Jim vent his frustration. Then when he had poured it all out, she began to help him rethink the situation. She reminded him that he could never replace the ideal working conditions or the six-figure income. Soon Jim had changed his mind. Since then, he has told me it was the best decision he ever made. Today he enjoys his job more than ever.

When Jim *honored* Elaine's advice—when he gave high value to her input—he not only made a wise vocational decision but also a wise marital decision. Her respect and admiration for him greatly increased in response to his openness.

The proverb that honor follows humility is still true today (Prov. 15:33). And even more significant is the truth that the man who regards reproof *will* be honored (Prov. 13:18). Humility is an inner attitude which is evidenced by an openness to the ideas and suggestions of others. It is the recognition that we are not all-knowing, that we can make mistakes, that we can always gain more knowledge and understanding.

The inability to accept advice from others can destroy a relationship. Read how Larry had to learn the hard way to take his wife's correction seriously.

Lynn had tried for ten years to explain to Larry how bad he made her feel, but Larry simply couldn't understand. His first problem was preferring his relatives over his wife. Whenever he and Lynn were around his family, he expected her to change her schedule to fit in with his family's. It didn't matter what she had planned. To make matters worse, Larry always took their side and defended them during arguments.

Larry also had a habit of making more commitments than he was able to fulfill—a promise here and a promise there. He was often guilty of forgetting his commitments. He didn't mean any harm. In fact, his intentions were good. He wanted so much to make people happy that he couldn't say no when asked to do something.

Year after year, Lynn tried to think of creative ways to point out these two problems to Larry, but nothing seemed to get through to him. Finally during one particularly straining visit to their hometown, Lynn broke down and cried. She openly expressed dislike for his relatives, bringing on Larry's lectures and retaliation. Neither of them could handle the emotional scene, so Larry drove the car to a parking lot. He sat there for nearly an hour, trying to understand the problem, but he simply couldn't. Larry and Lynn tried to discuss their problem once again as they began the long drive home. Lynn finally hit just the right combination of words that made sense to Larry.

"Oh, so that's why you don't like my relatives," he said. "Now I see why you don't want to move back to our hometown. When we're with my relatives, I always choose their feelings over yours. You feel second-rate. That makes sense now." Lynn was thrilled. One problem down, one to go.

But Larry remained just as blind to the second problem as he had been to the first. Though Lynn tried to tell him, he finally had to learn it from his friends through a very painful experience. Six of his buddies called a special meeting to tell him about his problem with over-commitment. They had all suffered from his neglect. Graphically, yet lovingly, they explained to Larry that his inability to say no was causing them to be resentful toward him. Larry was straining his friendship with each of them. He was so embarrassed and humiliated by this two-hour meeting that his first thought was, *Why didn't I listen to Lynn?*

His wife was relieved to see that he finally understood his second major problem. Her respect for him automatically increased because of his willingness to improve once he finally comprehended his faults. He became eager to expend the effort and study necessary to learn how to love Lynn (and others) properly.

Let's set some goals: that we as husbands decide to be wise

and open ourselves to correction (Prov. 9:8–9). That we be willing to listen to the lessons in each chapter of this book, however painful or difficult, and with our new knowledge commit ourselves to building a better marriage. A better marriage doesn't just happen. It takes serious effort channeled in the right direction. The basic principles presented in each chapter, taken one at a time, will *correct or prevent* the most serious pitfalls we face in marriage.

Some of us entered marriage with an extremely limited knowledge of how to develop a fulfilling relationship with our wives. But it's not hopeless. With a great deal of teaching and patience on their part, *we can learn*. A man needs to take an honest inventory to *assess* where he is in his marriage and be able to *admit* that he might have a long way to go. Your wife can certainly help with that inventory and suggested corrections.

IF I'M OPEN TO MY WIFE'S CORRECTION, DO I GIVE UP BEING THE LEADER?

A man may resist being open to correction from his wife because he feels it somehow negates his position as the leader of the home. If he listens to his wife's complaints or suggestions to improve their relationship and acts on them, he fears it means letting his wife make every decision or giving up control of the home.

I've noticed that almost without exception, the same man who has so much difficulty accepting correction from his wife, also struggles with accepting correction from others. Not only that, but he is usually an expert at criticizing his spouse for her many faults.

Without question, the Scriptures call the man to be the leader and head of the home. Yet like Christ, we are to lead in love—and love does not exist apart from discipline and correction. The Bible tells us that everyone whom the Lord loves, He corrects. I've found that God often uses a man's wife to point out areas in relationships he needs to grow in—correction that can actually help him to love his family and even God in a deeper, more meaningful way.

Although a man may fear that responding to suggestions from his wife might "open the flood gates" to her trying to take over the marriage, I have seen just the opposite to be true. When a woman sees her husband's willingness to accept correction—a mark of someone who wants to gain wisdom—she is more willing to follow his leadership in the home because she values him more highly.

Can you imagine the ecstatic feeling you would have if your wife volunteered the question, "How can I become a better wife?" The honor you would feel would be overwhelming. Of course, it would be absurd to expect this kind of question to come up between most husbands and wives. But just close your eyes for a moment, lean back in your chair, and picture your wife asking you such a question. It would be great, wouldn't it?

> If you want your wife to do this for you, first set the example and work on becoming a better husband. *Ask her how you can improve as a husband.*

You'll give her new hope for gaining the type of marriage she's always wanted. If she sees you are sincere, ultimately she'll become far more responsive to your needs and desires.

Do you want to be the type of husband wives complain about the most? All you need is an arrogant, all-knowing attitude and an unwillingness to admit when you're wrong. Three words produced such disgust in one wife that she said, "I get sick inside and ask myself, 'Why did I ever marry this man? What a mess I have gotten myself into.'" What were those three words? *"I'll never change."* According to Scripture, that's a very foolish statement (Prov. 12:15; 18:2).

"I'll never change," her husband repeated, "so don't try to change me and don't tell me where I need to change. If you think changing is so important, then why don't *you* change and just leave me alone. The biggest change our marriage needs is for you to keep your mouth shut!"

Wives tell me they admire and honor a husband who admits when he is wrong, especially when he openly seeks his wife's advice on how to improve. I believe a man needs to *motivate himself* to become more interested in his wife's ideas on how he can improve (Prov. 9:9). Then when he has asked her advice, he should observe the following:

LISTEN TO WHAT SHE'S REALLY SAYING

Look for the meaning behind your wife's statements. It is easier to avoid reacting solely to her words if you actively search for the meaning behind them. Have you ever said to your wife, "You're wrong.

I don't *always* do that. Don't you think you're exaggerating?" She probably didn't mean *always*, as in "every single time." That's just her way to emphasize a point. The *wise* husband looks beyond that offensive word and says, "Tell me how you're feeling right now. Tell me some of the thoughts behind what you just said. Tell me why you feel you need to use the word 'always.'" Reassure her that she does not have to explain in detail right away. Ask if she'd like to think about it for a day or two. A genuine learner does not put demands on others, forcing them to comply with his impatient desires immediately. He gives others time to feel, think, and change their words.

Many a husband has refused to listen to his wife's correction because of hang-ups over her choice of words. Words have no meaning apart from the interpretation we each place upon them. It is our responsibility in communicating with our wives to understand their *true* intentions.

A husband's tone of voice and facial expressions will reveal whether he has a sincere motivation to learn. His wife will not be as honest if she perceives that he is not really serious about learning and changing.

Chapter 10 delves more into deep communication, so I will conclude with this summary: *Avoid reacting to the words your wife uses and look for the meaning or intention behind them.*

LET HER WORDS SINK IN

Let your wife's advice sink in like a good spring rain. Hold off on responding until you have deeply received what she has said. Norma told me for years that I frowned when I said certain things to our children. She told me they felt I was angry with them, that I was rejecting them. My furrowed brow frightened them, she said. "I'm not frowning, and I'm not angry," I told her. But after I *took the time* to look in the mirror, I said, "You're right. I need to work on that. I appreciate your sharing that with me."

HOLD YOURSELF ACCOUNTABLE FOR FAILURE

When my children were very young, I used to flick them with my finger on their foreheads or arms when they misbehaved. If one of them was chewing food with his mouth open, I would reach across the table and flick him on the head and say, "Cut that out." Norma has made me aware of how this belittles and wounds our children. What a degrading action! Besides, it must hurt. It even hurts my finger.

I knew deep inside that flicking them was not right. Sometimes, right when I did it, Norma would ask, "Kari, how does that make you feel?"

Kari replied, "It always makes me feel bad when dad does it."

I finally came up with a way to break myself of this habit. I said to each of the children, "If I flick you on the head in anger or irritation, then I will pay you a dollar for each time I do it." (I thought this might work well because I don't like to give money away.) Believe me, my kids are alert enough not to let any slip by. And it's been a long time since I've flicked one of them.

Eventually, you can sometimes even laugh together about something that used to be a problem. On one occasion my son Greg came into the house eating a delicious-looking chocolate candy bar he had just bought. I asked him for a bite. *It was good.* Then Kari and Michael came in and wanted a bite too. Greg soon wished he hadn't unwrapped his candy in front of us. Little Michael didn't think Greg was too generous with the portions he doled out, so he decided to buy his own. He asked Greg where he bought it and how much it cost. Then with a longing look in his eyes, he said, "Dad, would you please flick me? I need a dollar."

SEEK HER FORGIVENESS

As I said before, a woman won't set herself up to be hurt. If you have offended her in the past, she won't be eager to share advice or correction in the present. Seek her forgiveness to reestablish the spirit of communication. Her admiration and respect for you will be strengthened and maintained by your willingness to admit your wrongs. Since chapter 5 dealt with forgiveness, review it from time to time when you need more help in this area.

RECEIVE HER ADVICE WITH GRATEFULNESS

Oh, the bounty of a grateful man—less nagging, more admiration and gentleness from his wife. When a man shows genuine gratefulness for his wife's correction, she feels a greater freedom to be more gentle the next time she corrects him. No need to nag when you have a grateful listener. A wife also admires her husband more when he is willing to thank her for her advice or correction. (The only exception is when a wife has been *deeply* hurt by her husband. Then she needs his time and patience until she is able to respond with admiration and gentleness. Don't quit trying when you're so close to success.)

Continue to look for the meaning behind what your wife says, let it sink in, and establish consequences for your failure. When you continue to thank her for helping you, you will begin to see the development of a stronger relationship.

Though the following illustration is the story of a father and son, it can be applied to a husband and wife. Jim's dad was irresponsible in many ways during his son's formative childhood and teen years. He disciplined Jim by kicking him, ridiculing him, scolding him, and slapping him. As a result, his son withdrew in spirit and, consequently, his mind and emotions also withdrew. He moved out of the house. When I explained to this father how he had crushed his son in the past, he realized he had not only damaged *their* relationship but possibly his son's future relationships.

Because he really wanted to have his son back emotionally, mentally, and physically, this father made an appointment to see his son. It took a lot of nerve, but he admitted to Jim that he was wrong and was sorry for not being the kind of father he should have been. During his confession, he mentioned all the hurtful incidents he could recall.

His son remembered these specific incidents too. "But, dad, that's not all." Then for the next few minutes he reminded his father of all the other things he had done to hurt him. Jim's father was amazed that his son still remembered it all so vividly. They wiped the slate clean. And for the first time Jim reached out to hug his dad.

When you offend your wife, she withdraws mentally, emotionally, and physically. But you can learn to draw her back. Just your willingness to learn will encourage her to respond as she becomes secure in the knowledge that you really want to change.

FOR PERSONAL REFLECTION

1. How can a husband become a wise man and increase his love for his wife? Proverbs 9:8–9.
2. What are the consequences of not listening or listening to God's reproofs? Proverbs 1:22–33.

8

If Your Wife's Not Protected, You Get Neglected

*"For no one
ever
hated his own flesh,
but nourishes and cherishes it,
just as Christ
also does the church
(emphasis mine)."*
Ephesians 5:29

DAN AND JANET had been married more than twenty years when he called me in a panic. "Janet's leaving me for another man," he said. He was crushed and bewildered. "Gary, is there anything you can do to help me?"

Dan's main problem was easily detectable when we met to talk. Let me explain why he lost her by using his hobby as an illustration.

Dan was an avid, meticulous, and knowledgeable gardener. Lush flower gardens defined the borders of his well-kept yard. Pruned trees shaded the delicate greenery from the hot summer sun. Dan knew where to plant each variety of flower so it would obtain the proper sunlight and soil. Since each plant had special needs, Dan had taken the time to research those needs so he would know exactly how much fertilizer and other nutrients they required. The results were magnificent. But while his garden was a glorious blaze of harmony in nature, his marriage was wilting from lack of attention. He entered his work and other activities with the same enthusiasm he applied to gardening, which left little time for Janet.

Dan hadn't the faintest idea what Janet's needs were. He had very little knowledge about how to protect her from the "scorching summer sun and wind." Not only did he fail to protect her, but he convinced her through his logical arguments that she should handle household responsibilities that she had said were too much for her.

117

Throughout their twenty years together Dan had failed to listen to her many, many pleadings for tender protection.

Janet was not only holding down a full-time job, but was also responsible for keeping the finances, cooking the meals, cleaning the house, and training the children. She faced many crises alone while Dan was fishing, hunting, or cultivating his posies. He could not recognize Janet's need to have a strong and gentle man to support her during times of stress, one who would protect her from some of the "dirty work" (we all need protection like this at times). She needed to be accepted and loved as a person with her own special physical limitations. When Dan repeatedly failed her, she looked elsewhere.

When a man doesn't understand his wife's limitations or explains them away as laziness, numerous misunderstandings can result. For example, a woman with several small children can be totally exhausted both physically and mentally by five in the afternoon. If her husband doesn't recognize this, he may resent her avoidance of sexual relations at ten or eleven at night when she is genuinely too tired to even think of a romantic experience with him.

Some men think that their wives will take advantage of them if they are gentle, loving, and giving. Keith was willing to gamble money to see if his wife would take advantage of him. He took his wife to a shopping center for her birthday. He told her he would like to help her buy some clothes but never mentioned the amount she could spend. Two hours and ten shops later, as his feet began to ache, Keith wondered whether this birthday outing was a good idea or not.

"Mary, how do you like this dress? It would look good on you."

"No, I don't like it."

Finally they wandered into a nice shop where Mary found a coordinated skirt, jacket, blouse, and pantsuit that she liked well enough to buy. Though the money was beginning to add up, Keith said, "Mary, look at this. Here's a dress on sale."

Mary liked the dress and tried it on.

Keith said, "Why don't you get it?"

"Keith, I shouldn't be spending any more of our money."

"Oh, no, go ahead and get it," Keith replied. "I like it. Hey, Mary, what do you think of this dress?"

"This is getting ridiculous," Mary protested. But she tried it on when Keith insisted.

At this point, he was beginning to wonder if she would buy every dress that he told her to buy. "Oh, I like this one, Mary."

"Keith, I cannot buy another dress," she said. "This is getting ridiculous. We can't afford all this."

"Ah, what difference does it make?" he asked. "You're more

118

important than money, and even if I have to work extra, I'm happy to do it." He really put the pressure on her to buy the dress.

She replied, "I'm embarrassed. I can't buy another dress. Please let's pay for these and go get something to eat."

"Come on, Mary. Would you buy just one more for me? I just want this to be a very special day for you!"

"Keith, I can't do it," she said.

"Okay, we'll pay for them. I want you to be happy and satisfied."

Keith didn't admit until some time later that he just wanted to prove that a woman well-treated will not take advantage. He praised her for her thriftiness and caution, proud of her willingness to work with him for the financial security they both desired. Now he never worries that Mary will overspend because he knows she will look for the right price and the best buy. This experience has also convinced him that Mary will not take advantage of him in other areas of their life.

I'm not advocating that you try this with your wife or in any way "test" or manipulate her. However, I have often seen what happens when a husband learns what Keith learned: When a wife is treated with tenderness and genuine love, she won't take advantage of the situation.

When the Scripture teaches that a husband is to *cherish* his wife (Eph. 5:29), it basically means to protect her, especially in the areas that cause her emotional or physical discomfort.

THREE WAYS TO PROTECT YOUR WIFE
AND HELP HER BECOME MORE FULFILLED

1. *Discover where your wife needs protection.*

First, a husband needs to discover areas in which his wife feels vulnerable. Through informal discussions and observation on your part, you can compile mental lists of the major and minor areas where she is frustrated or fearful. Driving a car is one of my wife's vulnerable areas. Because she was involved in a serious auto accident in which some good friends were killed, she is naturally very alert to any possible danger when she is driving or even riding in a car. It would only frustrate her if I did not give her the freedom to be cautious, knowing her past circumstances. She also feels vulnerable when driving long distances alone in the winter because she fears the car will break down. When we lived in Chicago, the car broke down twice, and she had to accept help from passing motorists. Both she and the children could conceivably have been hurt or abused. Since I am aware of her fear, I don't push her to drive long distances alone any more.

What about her physical limits?

Many times a man treats his wife too roughly. He is unaware that his wife's physical make-up keeps her from enjoying roughness even when being playful.

One wife told me that her husband enjoyed wrestling but didn't realize how much it had injured her in the past. He never intentionally hurt her, but she would find bruises on her arms or her body after they had wrestled on the carpet. He was rough with her in other ways too. For example, one night they were in the grocery store, and she lingered a while in the book section. Her husband was waiting for her in the parking lot with a sack of dog food and other items. When she caught up with him, he said, "No wonder you didn't hurry out here. You're not the one holding all the groceries."

"Well, all right, I'll help you," she said. He playfully threw the sack of dog food at her, hitting her in the stomach so forcefully that it left her gasping for breath. The ride home was silent. As they pulled up in the driveway, he said, "The reason I was quiet wasn't because I was mad at you. I was mad at myself for hurting you again." He wanted to make an effort to change his behavior because he realized she needed to be treated with more tenderness and more carefulness.

What about financial pressures?

A man also needs to protect his wife from unnecessary financial stress. Many wives endure a tremendous amount of pressure because of a husband's irresponsibility with finances. To compensate for overspending, a husband may force his mate to work when she would rather be home with the children. In fact, some husbands demand it, feeling "she should do her part." If a woman is home all day, her husband may expect her to handle bill payments and financial bookkeeping for the family because he wonders what she does all day anyway. He might think, *I work eight hours every day. The least she can do is pay the bills.*

If it were just a matter of bookkeeping, this would not be a problem. But when it comes to facing angry bill collectors, juggling figures in a checkbook that won't balance, coping with mounting pressures resulting from insufficient money, deciding which bill to pay first, and making phone calls to appease businesses, the burden *can* become physically and emotionally too much for some wives. The problem is magnified if the husband appears to be spending money loosely and enjoying himself.

I made this mistake in the early years of our marriage. Norma worked for a bank, and I logically concluded that anyone working for a bank would obviously be able to take care of the money at home. Since financial matters were a weak point for me at that time, I asked her if she would take that responsibility, which she graciously did for four or five years. One day, though, she came to me in tears, laid the records, the checkbook, and all the bills in my lap and said that she just couldn't handle it any more. You see, we had two checkbooks between us and only one checking account. I would write a check, hoping the money was in the bank. It was a tremendous pressure on my wife. Today I am very grateful she handed over that responsibility, because it forced me to take more responsibility for the financial well-being of our family.

What about expecting her to do all the cooking?

So many men treat their wives as objects to be used. They don't verbalize it, but they maintain the inward conviction that women should remain in the kitchen cooking or cleaning while they play golf, hunt, or watch the game on TV. Have you ever noticed during get-togethers with friends or relatives that the women are usually the ones who are expected to work in the kitchen while the men just shoot the breeze? Little girls are trained to watch for the special needs of a male family member. For instance, a mother will say, "Go ask daddy if he wants a glass of iced tea." But we seldom see little boys asked to do the same thing.

I had a real problem with role expectation during our first few years of marriage: it was Norma's job to cook and my responsibility to fix the car. I finally realized that it was okay for me to cook and clean the house, especially if Norma was needing a rest or some time alone away from all of us. We as men need to take a close look at our traditional roles and choose what is best based on genuine love and the commitment to cherish our mates.

Think of your wife's special limitations before expecting her to take on *added* responsibilities. Such forethought will avoid extra strain on your relationship and protect your wife's mental, spiritual, emotional, and physical life.

What about her need for rest?

Why is it that some men feel their wives need less sleep than they do? While the husband sleeps, the wife prepares breakfast and takes care of the children. This is certainly true where babies are involved. During our early years of marriage, when my children would cry during the night, I automatically expected my wife to get up and take care of them. And she did. Never did I feel compelled to get up and take care of the kids. Be tender and alert to her physical needs. Be the leader in taking whatever steps are needed to insure that your wife gets the rest she needs.

What about the pressure of the children?

Often my wife has said how much she appreciates the times I take charge of the kids when I come home from work. I get them out from underfoot so she is able to finish dinner peacefully. She is also grateful for the time to be alone. She likes me to take them outside to play, into another room to read, or just to talk to them about whatever topic they choose. After the meal, the children and I often clear the table and wash the dishes to let Norma have some time off. Instead of resenting her need for my help as I once did, I now look forward to helping her as often as I can.

Thoughtful, creative ideas on your part are worth much more than the time or energy they cost. They strengthen your marriage and lift your wife's spirit.

One night Jim thrilled Debbie when he asked her to let him cook dinner, set the table, and feed the children. He told her he had a gift he would give her if she let him do those things—a bottle of bath oil. While she took a leisurely bath, he took care of the household chores. It was only a small gift; it just took a bit of Jim's time. But to Debbie, it meant that he cared enough to give something extra of himself.

What about the added pressure of moving?

A move from one city to another is a major step for a woman. It requires that her husband be extra sensitive to her limitations. Many times a woman's emotional and physical endurance is depleted just from normal day-to-day routines. A move obviously adds additional stress, even when the move is welcomed.

What can cause her the most stress?

We as husbands need to be aware of the amount of stress our wives face daily. To aid your wife with stress, you must first be aware of the situations that cause her the most anxiety. To help you, we have included a list from the *Holmes-Rahe Stress Test*, which ranks items from the greatest amount of stress to the least amount of stress. The higher it is on the list, the greater the stress it produces. Check to see how much stress you and your wife are facing today. (See Holmes-Rahe Stress Test on page 126.)

If your score is 150 or less, there is a 33% chance that you will be in the hospital within two years. If it is 150–300, the chances are 51%; and 300 and above, 80%. Purpose to protect your wife in all areas where she feels fearful or vulnerable. That's the first way to show her how much you cherish her.

2. *Discover how your wife wants to be fulfilled.*

Another way to cherish your wife is to help her become fulfilled as a person. You can do this by discovering her personal goals in life and helping her reach them if possible. We all love to know that someone is pulling for us, that others are cheering when we reach a goal. It makes a woman feel worthwhile and valuable when her husband takes time to help her achieve a personal goal.

From time to time, my wife and I get together on a date, for breakfast out or just a retreat from home. During that time we list our personal goals. We commit ourselves to help each other fulfill those goals. This book is the result of a goal that my wife and I wanted to reach together. Since she was as excited about it as I was, I knew it was okay with her for me to take several weeks away from my family to work on our goal.

I feel so satisfied, knowing my wife is committed enough to sacrifice for my goals, that I get excited when I think of helping her with her goals. Since I know she wants to maintain her physical health as best she can, we decided she should join a health spa. To see that she has the opportunity to exercise regularly, I am happy to babysit sometimes so she can accomplish her personal goal of good physical health.

Sit down with your wife and ask her to name some goals. She might want to finish college, advance in her vocation, study public speaking, learn to sew, or cook some new exotic meals. Her goals may change as she discovers the real pressure or motives behind them. Maybe she says she wants to go back to school, when all she really wants is a couple of days a week away from the children. By relieving her of some of the pressure, you may help channel her energies in the right direction, helping her to reach her *real* personal goals. I believe it is our responsibility to discover our wives' goals and to understand how they want to fulfill themselves as women. Then we must let them be who they want to be by respecting their unique ambitions.

3. *Discover what personal problems your wife wants to solve.*

My wife would like to share with women how to be fulfilled in the home without outside work. Unfortunately, during our early marriage she became timid when speaking to groups, due to another one of my irresponsibilities. I used to correct her grammar or give suggestions on how to improve her teaching methods in an insensitive way. Whenever I heard her share in front of groups, I always called her attention to anything I thought was less than perfect. Little did I know that my wife's nature was so sensitive that she eventually stopped speaking in front of groups because of my criticism. It took five years of my praise and encouragement to heal the wounds I had thoughtlessly inflicted. She is speaking to groups more and more now, but is still quite nervous when I am in the audience.

Has your wife ever told you emphatically in the morning that she is going to lose weight . . . and that very same evening she's eating donuts? The harmful action you can take is to remind her sarcastically of that early-morning commitment. However, you can comfort her by saying nothing at all or by putting your arm around her to say, "I love you for who you are, not for what you decide to do." She probably feels disappointed enough about her lack of will power. Knowing she is loved *as she is* will probably boost her self-confidence and strengthen her will power.

In summary, a woman loves to build a lasting relationship with a man who cares about her enough to let her lean on him when she needs comfort. She needs a man who will understand her fears and limitations so that he can protect her. She feels important when her husband stands up and defends her in the presence of someone who is criticizing her.

Each person is unique, and the only way you can pinpoint your wife's needs is to discuss them with her. You may want to question her to see if she feels that you are protective or helpful enough in these areas:

The family finances
Raising of the children
Household needs and responsibilities
The future—insurance, a will

Her own employment and the people with whom she works
Her friends and relatives

You should also endeavor to discover how she would like to be fulfilled as a person. Ask her to explain two or three goals she has always wanted to accomplish. Then reevaluate your goals together each year.

FOR PERSONAL REFLECTION

1. Clearly define the word "cherish" as it is used in Ephesians 5:29. Ask your pastor for help, or consult a Bible commentary.
2. How does Paul encourage Christians to treat each other? How do you treat your wife? 1 Thessalonians 5:11, 14.

HOLMES-RAHE STRESS TEST

In the past 12 months, which of these have happened to you?

EVENT	VALUE	SCORE
Death of a spouse	100	___
Divorce	73	___
Marital separation	65	___
Jail term	63	___
Death of a close family member	63	___
Personal injury or illness	53	___
Marriage	50	___
Fired from work	47	___
Marital reconciliation	45	___
Retirement	45	___
Change in family member's health	44	___
Pregnancy	40	___
Sex difficulties	39	___
Addition to family	39	___
Business readjustment	39	___
Change in financial status	38	___
Death of close friend	37	___
Change in number of marital arguments	35	___
Mortgage or loan over $10,000	31	___
Foreclosure of mortgage or loan	30	___
Change in work responsibilities	29	___
Son or daughter leaving home	29	___
Trouble with in-laws	29	___
Outstanding personal achievement	28	___
Spouse begins or starts work	26	___
Starting or finishing school	26	___
Change in living conditions	25	___
Revision of personal habits	24	___
Trouble with boss	23	___
Change in work hours, conditions	20	___
Change in residence	20	___
Change in schools	20	___
Change in recreational habits	19	___
Change in church activities	19	___
Change in social activities	18	___
Mortgage or loan under $10,000	18	___
Change in sleeping habits	16	___
Change in number of family gatherings	15	___
Change in eating habits	15	___
Christmas season	13	___
Vacation	12	___
Minor violation of the law	11	___
TOTAL		___

126

9
Arguments ...
There's A
Better Way

> *"For this cause*
> *a man shall leave*
> *his father and mother,*
> *and shall* cleave
> *to his wife;*
> *and the two*
> *shall become*
> *one flesh*
> *(emphasis mine)."*
> Ephesians 5:31

A SIMPLE AGREEMENT can eliminate heated arguments between you and your wife. No, it's not a divorce!

It is an agreement that will increase the time you and your mate spend discussing important areas *without* that familiar anger and silence routine; it will also build your wife's self-respect.

When my wife and I stumbled upon this concept during a Fourth of July argument several years ago, both of our fuses were getting short. The fireworks show was dull in comparison. I wanted to vacation in Colorado in July; she wanted to go to Florida in August. Since we didn't agree on separate vacations either, the discussion became hotter and hotter with no end in sight. Sizzling, I compared her attitude to some of the more submissive single women from the office.

"You don't have a calm attitude. Besides that, you're wrong," I said.

"I have never met this 'calm woman' you talk about," she replied angrily. "If you can show me just one, I might consider following her example."

At this point, the accidental brainstorm that has helped us avoid heated discussions for several years came to me. I asked Norma if she would be willing to drop the conversation and try an experiment for just two months. If it worked, we'd use it; if not, we'd search for another solution.

"Will you not make decisions in the home that affect me and the rest of the family without my complete agreement?" I asked her. "And I won't make any decisions affecting you unless I have your full consent."

I didn't know if the experiment would work, but I did know that I was tired of arguments and futile discussions that led nowhere except to tears and angry silence. Since I worked for an organization that taught family harmony, I was desperate to achieve it in my own home. (You've heard of the plumber with leaky pipes, haven't you?)

Many things had to change if we were going to agree to agree. We had to reason together for longer periods of time. We were also forced to discover the reasons behind each other's comments. I had to search for the meaning behind Norma's words and understand her frame of reference if I hoped to convince her of my point of view. Several of our first discussions ended with the consensus that since we couldn't agree we would just wait. Amazingly enough, many "problems" seemed to solve themselves—or at least their importance seemed to diminish as the days passed.

In spite of the success of our agreement, I went back on it after two months. Hearing a growing argument between Kari and Greg at the kitchen table, I rushed in to referee just in time to see Greg shove his full plate across the table, spilling it all over Kari. I was about to take Greg upstairs for a little discipline when Norma said she disagreed.

"Well, our experiment doesn't apply in every situation," I said, stopping in my tracks. "I can't relinquish my responsibility as Greg's father just because you don't agree. I'm sorry. I'll have to overrule you this time."

After Greg and I had our "little talk," Norma greeted me coldly in the kitchen.

"Well, Norma, I had to do what I thought was right," I explained. "I wish we could agree in every situation, but it's not practical."

She replied, "I don't think you took the time to find out the facts."

"I saw all I needed to know."

But I had to admit that I didn't know what Kari had done to provoke Greg. Norma had told Kari to make sandwiches for Greg. Kari probably didn't want to do it in the first place, so when Greg didn't want the sandwiches, she tried to force them on him.

"Mom told me to make you sandwiches and you're gonna eat 'em," she said.

"You're not my boss. I don't have to eat them," Greg retorted.

And to make his point, he pushed the sandwiches away. But the table was slicker than he anticipated, and the sandwiches slid into Kari's lap.

I admitted to Greg that I was wrong and apologized. To keep such mistakes from happening in the future obtain all the legal counsel needed from within the family. After all the facts are presented, the family decides who is guilty. We also set up written "contracts" covering desired behaviors and these have been a tremendous help during our children's teenage years. (See my book, *The Key to Your Child's Heart*, for details of this powerful parenting method.)

Whenever Norma and I do not agree on something that affects the family, I have been amazed at the number of times her decision has been right. I'm not sure whether she has a hot line to heaven or what, but somehow she can sense when something is not right. Committing ourselves to agree has brought more harmony and deeper communication than anything else we practice. It has increased my wife's self-worth and eliminated pressure-packed arguments.

Constant disagreement can only weaken a marriage relationship. That's probably why Paul emphasized having oneness of spirit and mind in the church. He likened the struggle for oneness to an athlete *striving* to reach the goal (Phil. 1:27). Likewise, as husbands and wives we can learn to enter into a oneness or agreement.

As I mentioned earlier, I know some men will react strongly to having their wives share in any of the decisions that affect the family. Like battlefield generals, they demand acceptance of their orders, not input from those people the decisions will most affect.

As we'll discuss at the end of the chapter, there may be rare times of deadlock when you'll have to make the final decision that goes against your wife's or your family's feelings. However, I've found that by my slowing down, talking through major decisions with Norma and the children, and valuing their opinions and input, over the years such impassable situations have been almost nonexistent.

The rest of this chapter discusses the specific consequences of not agreeing on decisions that affect the family and ways to apply the "agreement" principle in your family.

WHAT HAPPENS WHEN YOU MAKE ALL THE DECISIONS

When a wife is left out of the decision-making process, she feels insecure, especially if the decisions involve financial security or living conditions. Her constant state of insecurity spreads like a disease to produce instability in other areas of the marriage.

Steve and Bonney had been struggling to make just enough money to put food on the table. His small business was requiring eighteen hours a day on his part, and she was putting in at least eight hours a day at the office, even though she was seven months pregnant. Steve flew East to show his business ideas to a multi-millionaire. The man was impressed and made Steve a generous offer which he accepted in less than five minutes. It was the only "reasonable" course of action.

He could hardly wait to call Bonney and tell her the great news in "logical" order so she could get as excited as he was. He told her, "First, you won't have to work anymore. Second, he's giving me 20 percent of the profits—he says I'll be a millionaire in a year. Third, you won't believe how beautiful it is back here, and he's going to pay all of the moving expenses."

Steve was shocked to hear uncontrollable weeping on the other end of the line. At first he thought she was crying for joy (I know it's hard to believe, but he actually thought that.).

As soon as Bonney caught a breath, she had a chance to ask some questions Steve considered totally ridiculous (in fact, he thought her mind had snapped). She asked questions like, "What about our parents?" and "What about our apartment—I just finished the room for the baby." With her third question, Steve, in all of his masculine "sensitivity," abruptly terminated the phone call. She had the nerve to ask if he'd forgotten she was seven months pregnant.

After giving her an hour or two to pull herself together, he called her back. She had gained her composure and agreed to move back east. She left her parents, her friends, her doctor and childbirth classes, and the nursery she had spent so much time preparing for her first child.

It took Bonney almost eight months to adjust to a change that Steve had adjusted to in minutes. Steve never made his million. The business failed eight days before their baby was born, and they moved again. Steve eventually learned his lesson, and today he doesn't make any major change unless Bonney is in agreement. He tries to give her ample time to adjust to other changes as soon as he can foresee them. However, Steve will never forget the loving sacrifices his wife made so many times. He even realizes that questions like "What about our parents?" or "What about the nursery?" can be more meaningful than money.

Husbands can also make their wives feel stupid, inadequate, or like an unnecessary member of the family when they make most of the decisions alone. Many husbands treat their wives as if they don't know anything at all. When a decision comes up in their area of expertise or with regard to financial dealings, their wives might as well forget about participating as far as they are concerned.

Jerry had to lose money before he would respect his wife's judgment. He considered a number of ways to invest some of his earnings, from apartments, to real estate, to the stock market. After talking to developers and reading literature, he decided to buy a lake-front lot in a planned retirement community. He reasoned that if he bought the land during the early development stages, it would be worth quite a bit of money in five to ten years. When Linda found out about his plans, she hesitated to invest their money.

But Jerry thought, *What would she know anyway?* and signed the contract in spite of her objections.

Sometime later when he wanted to sell the land for quick money to invest in a better project, he found it was difficult to sell. Jerry and Linda will probably still have it when they are ready to retire. If Jerry had consulted Linda, not only would he have saved a great deal of money, but he could have given her self-esteem a boost. After all, what's wrong with becoming "one flesh" with our mates? That's God's design!

We husbands would do well to remember that everyone has a different stress-tolerance level. When you ignore your wife in making decisions, you add stress to every area of her life. As I've said before, stress will definitely take its toll by eroding her physical health.

As with so many areas of my marriage, I had to discover this the hard way. As I mentioned earlier, when my work load demanded that I travel a great deal, I didn't ask Norma if she could handle three small children alone; I just assumed she could. As a result of the extra pressure, she came to me on the verge of a physical collapse. I had to take a less responsible position in my company, but I learned the importance of taking care of my family. They bring me much more joy and fulfillment than any job. Today I can enjoy my work more because my family is always beside me. When a man learns to enjoy his family above all else, his activities and his friends take on an even greater meaning as well.

I look back on the past with grief when I think of incidents like the following: Norma and the three children were to pick me up at work at 5:00 P.M. to go for hamburgers. Just as she drove up, I was called to a last-minute staff meeting. I explained quickly that I would join her in a few minutes. Instead, the meeting lasted two hours. I wasn't apologetic, though. I was angry because she had not waited lovingly and patiently for me in the car while appeasing our three hungry children.

If only I could relive that experience! I would say, "Honey, they just called an unexpected meeting. Would you like to go back home and wait for me and feed the children? Then you and I can eat together later." Or I would explain to my associates that I had a previous commitment to my family. Let's face it, not much is usually accomplished at meetings held that late in the day. (And your colleagues' wives might benefit from it, too.)

Finally, arguments are probably the most common side effects of major decisions made apart from any discussion. As anger sharpens the tongue, turning it into a fierce weapon, husbands and wives can end discussions by attacking each other's character. Words spoken during the heat of an argument are sometimes never forgotten. My wife can still remember ugly things I said when we were dating.

If a woman feels threatened during a discussion, she may become angry and demand her way. If her husband doesn't understand that she is acting that way because he threatened her security, he may feel his ego is being attacked or his leadership questioned. And both will pursue the issue like wild dogs, fighting to be the leader of the pack. Instead, each should enter the other's world to achieve mutual understanding.

Suppose a husband who is having difficulties with his wife comes up with the idea of the two of them taking a short vacation for a few days to better their relationship, while leaving the kids with grandma. His wife may say, "You're pressuring me." He feels he has been verbally slapped in the face. He wasn't trying to pressure her, and furthermore, he sees no logical reason *why* she should feel that way. Tempers flare, and argument #1,241 begins. But who's counting? The point is, if a woman says she feels pressured, take her word for it—SHE FEELS PRESSURED! Try to enter her world to discover why she feels that way—don't argue that you didn't intentionally try to pressure her. If your idea somehow has caused her to say she *feels* pressured, then she *is* pressured.

The chart below gives an example of how to eliminate trivial arguments before they snowball into major flareups.

If she says. . .	Typical response from a husband	Try this instead. . .
"You're putting pressure on me."	"I'm not pressuring you. I just wanted to do	"Honey, I can sure understand that you're pressured. If you feel what I'm saying is pressuring you,

		then I can sure accept that. That's not my intent, but I can understand that you feel that way. Can you share at this time any of the reasons why you feel that way?"
"I hate going to the beach. I don't want to go."*	"You used to like the beach before we were married."	"I know I should know why you don't want to go to the beach, but could you tell me just once more some of the reasons why you don't?"
"No, I don't want to go to the ball game with you. I hate those ball games."	"I try to do things with you. The least you could do is to go with me once in a while and support me in something that I enjoy doing."	"Honey, is one of the reasons that you don't like to go because I ignore you so much when I'm at a ball game?"†

HOW TO MAKE DECISIONS TOGETHER

Once you have found a method that works, stick to it. Whenever my wife and I try to take shortcuts, we get into trouble.

After a quick discussion about moving to the country, we located the home of our dreams. I wrote an ad for the paper to sell our home and bought "For Sale" signs to put in the front yard. A neighbor walked across the street to ask how much I was asking for our house. When I quoted the price, he said it was far too low; it might reduce the market value of other houses in the neighborhood.

A vague uneasiness began to gnaw at me. Since Norma and I had not discussed every detail of this upcoming move, I tried to call her but couldn't reach her. I cancelled the ad and plucked the signs out of the yard. When Norma finally arrived home, we filled out the chart we usually use for major decisions and decided, after weighing

*She may have several reasons for saying this, one being that she is embarrassed about her figure. At that point a husband needs to be tender, understanding, and gentle. Remember, some women do not feel as relaxed in a bathing suit as a man might.

†If she says yes to that question, ask her for other reasons she resists going to a game. (Remember, if you react negatively to her reasons, she'll be less willing to share her true feelings with you in the future.) You may need to give her "room to breathe" and come back to it all another time. If she says no, ask her to explain why, tenderly and with a real desire to understand her and value her opinion.

advantages and disadvantages, that it was not a good idea for us to sell our home at that time.

The simple chart we use helps us reach total agreement on important decisions. We first list all of the reasons, pro and con, for doing something. Second, we list all the reasons, pro and con, for *not* doing it. Third, we evaluate each reason. Will the decision have lasting effects? Is the reason selfish, or will it help others? Finally, we total the pros and cons and see which wins, not *who* wins. Although you may think you have in mind all the reasons you need to make the decision, seeing them ranked in black and white simplifies and streamlines the decision.

The pro-and-con chart forces us as a couple to consider as many facts as possible. For instance, if I am counseling someone, I find I usually cannot help the person until I know plenty of facts about the particular situation. The fewer the facts, the foggier a situation appears. But the more facts I have, the clearer the picture and the easier the solution. If I ask a person to write down all the facts on a piece of paper, often he or she can come up with the solution on his or her own.

Let me give you an example of how the chart works for my family.

A Major Decision—Should I Change Jobs?

This move would mean moving a thousand miles and would involve a cut in pay.

1. List all the reasons, pro and con, for changing jobs and moving my family a thousand miles. (I'll only put down a few of the reasons we used, for purposes of illustration.)

If We Move

What we will gain (pro)

1. We will be able to raise our family in a smaller town.

2. We will gain a greater opportunity to help families in a concentrated way.

3. There are many more camping spots where we're moving, and the weather is warmer year-round.

4. Two of our best friends live in that town.

What we will lose (con)

1. We will be taking a cut in pay. Could we adjust to that?

2. Do we really want to live in a small town and lose all the conveniences of a major city with nice shopping centers?

3. We'll have to move away from our friends whom we love so much.

4. Can we afford to buy our own home?

5. There's not a major airport for convenient travel to my Family Workshops.

2. List all of the reasons, pro and con, for *not* moving my family to a new location and a new job.

If We Stay

What we will gain (pro)	*What we will lose (con)*
1. We will maintain our present salary.	1. We will lose our opportunity to help families on a personal and consistent basis.
2. Our children will be educated at a private school.	2. We will lose the opportunity for our children to live in a warmer climate with a greater opportunity for involvement in sports and activities.
3. We will continue to use all the shops and stores that we know so well.	3. We'll lose our chance to join a church that we as a family really enjoy attending together.
4. We will continue all the contacts we have for buying various items at discount.	4. We will lose our opportunity as husband and wife to work on our life goals together.

It's important to list reasons for *doing* something and *not doing* something. It forces us to think of different aspects of both viewpoints.

3. Evaluate each of the reasons given in #1 and #2. Make your decision based on your evaluations of #1 and #2.

"Vote YES on the Big Move," Kari's sign read. She had plastered signs all over the house to gain votes in favor of our move to another state. Like a campaign manager, she actively tried to get our other two children to cast their votes for her side.

When voting day came, I passed out a ballot to each family member. The suspense mounted as I read each vote aloud until finally the votes were tallied. "Yes" won unanimously.

The doctrine of majority rule doesn't apply here. If one member had voted "No," I believe it would have been important to consider *why* that member had voted differently. An essential ingredient in making a happy family is total agreement. Discussion should stay open until everyone can agree when possible. Creative alternatives can be considered when it looks as though one member is going to "hang the jury."

What to do if husband and wife are deadlocked
on an important decision.

Instead of looking for a referee for the ensuing battle, they should postpone the decision as long as possible in order to gather additional facts. If it comes down to the "wire," they need to decide what is best for the family, and if they still can't agree biblically, he should make his decision with the *family's* best interest in mind. A loving, understanding attitude can melt a wife's heart and give her the security she so desperately wants in times of difficult decisions, even if it takes time to adjust to a decision.

FOR PERSONAL REFLECTION

1. Is a husband instructed to submit to his wife (Eph. 5:21)?
2. What do the verses before and after Ephesians 5:22 mean, where a wife is instructed to submit? Also check Colossians 3:17–19.
3. Since a husband is to love his wife as Christ loves the church, it is essential that we know how Christ loves. What can we learn about Him from Matthew 20:25–28?
4. Write out a simple definition of submission. Consider Romans 12:10.

10

A Successful Marriage ...
It's Easier
Than You Think

*"While
I was with them,
I was keeping them
in Thy name
which Thou hast
given Me;
and
I guarded them."
John 17:12*

WHEN I WAS newly married, I often asked other couples if they could tell me the secrets of a happy marriage. They would usually say, "You and your wife will have problems, but if it's meant to be, you'll stay together. If not, you'll separate." Later, when I worried about staying close to my children, people would answer, "Your teenagers will rebel. It's just normal."

These philosophies seemed so pessimistic that I became discouraged whenever our domestic harmony was threatened during an argument. I couldn't find any articles or books written on how to become a warm, loving family.

However, today I can say without reservation that my wife is my best friend. This has come about because we have practiced a principle learned from several successful families. Practicing this principle also has eliminated any significant disharmony in our family and has drawn us all closer.

I learned this principle by interviewing over a hundred couples across the nation. I chose them initially because they seemed to have close relationships and their children, though many were teenagers, all seemed to be close to their parents and happy about it. They were enthusiastic families—radiantly happy in most instances.

When I spoke to different groups, I would scan the audience, looking for the family that seemed the happiest. Then I would interview them afterward. I often talked to the wife alone, then the husband, and finally the children. I always asked them the same questions: "What do you believe is the main reason you're all so close and happy as a family?" Without exception, each member of each family gave the same answer: "We do a lot of things together." Even more amazing to me was that all the families had *one particular activity in common.*

I can truthfully say I have tested the suggestions of these families enough to prove they are valid. I no longer fear my family will break up. Nor do I fear my children will reject my wife and me as they grow older. That's because my family is practicing the things those other successful families suggested.

Share Experiences Together

Jesus left us an example by sharing His life with the disciples. They traveled, ate, slept, healed, and ministered *together.* He guided, guarded, and kept them; then He prayed for them (John 17). His example of togetherness and oneness constantly inspires me to become "one" with my family by scheduling many times to be together.

Since every family I interviewed specifically mentioned *camping,* I looked into it as a possible recreational activity. Norma's first thought was of bugs, snakes, dirt, and all sorts of creepy-crawleys. She didn't like camping. Though I had been camping only a few times, I couldn't remember having any insurmountable problems. We decided to give it a try. Norma reluctantly agreed, frantically clutching a can of insect repellent and stuffing mosquito coils into her purse.

We borrowed a pop-tent camper and headed for Florida. We found a beautiful campsite in Kentucky, and though I was nervous being all alone in the woods, I didn't say anything. After we parked next to the only bright streetlight within fifty feet of the showers, we built a campfire to roast hot dogs and marshmallows. It was peaceful. No one was around to distract us. We put the children to bed around nine, and then Norma and I stayed up to enjoy a romantic evening. A distant thunderstorm entertained us with a light show as we enjoyed a warm breeze. Though the lightning came closer and closer, we thought it was passing to one side of us and went to bed with light hearts.

The children were asleep as I crawled into a tiny bed with Greg, and Norma joined Kari. We were lying close enough to touch hands while we whispered softly. I thought, *Boy, this is really the life. I can see why everybody likes to camp.* But my feeling of serenity was blasted away as the storm began to lash furiously around us and knocked out the streetlight beside our tent. It was pitch black except for the frequent jagged streaks illuminating the sky. Thunder rumbled, shaking the ground beneath us, and the wind began to howl. Rain beat against our tent until the water forced its way through, soaking our pillows.

"Honey, do you think this camper is going to blow over?" Norma asked faintly.

"No, not a chance," I said. I really thought the camper was going to *blow up*. I knew we were going to die. But within an hour, the storm's wrath cooled enough to let the stars shine through again. We lay there breathlessly on our soaked pillows, each wondering silently whether camping was the life for us. I was also curious as to why camping played such an important part in drawing families together. Of course, any family that faced sure death together and survived would be closer!

Colorado was the destination for our own trip in our own trailer. We could hardly wait to experience the beauty of snow-capped peaks and sniff the aroma of pine trees. I could already hear the sizzle of rainbow trout frying in the pan. As we started up the mountain, our station wagon slowed from 50 miles per hour to 30, then to 25, then to 20, until we finally slowed to the pace of 15 miles per hour. "Hot" read the temperature gauge. I felt like I was wired to the engine because my palms were sweating so. Our children sensed the tension in the air and became hyper and loud.

"I've got to stop at the next pull-off area," I told them. My nerves were frayed as I pulled over. All three kids jumped out immediately. I hadn't even had time to worry about the overheated car when our youngest, Michael, screamed at the top of his lungs.

His older brother, relieving some pent-up energy, had kicked what he thought to be an empty can. Unfortunately, it was half-full of transmission fluid. The can had landed upside down on Michael's head, and he was covered from head to toe, a terribly unhappy little boy. His nose, his ears, even his mouth were dripping with it. Not expecting such a calamity, we had no water in the trailer to clean him up. We worried that he had injured his eyes because he blinked rapidly the rest of the trip.

I've mentioned only the tragic times of our camping experiences, but we've also had tremendous experiences hiking to tops of mountains and exploring the out-of-doors. But the real significance of camping will be understood, I believe, when we get to the third point discussed in this chapter.

Doing things with your family may cost you a little extra money, but it's worth every penny.

For example, Norma called one day to ask if I would like to buy a water-skiing boat and equipment. Though I was unsure at first, the idea seemed to appeal to everyone in the family. We purchased an "extremely experienced" model. When we were bouncing across the lake on our first time out, I noticed my wife holding on to the side as if she feared we would capsize at any moment. I thought I had everything under control, yet panic was clearly written on her face. She gripped the windshield with one hand while the other had a death grip on the bar beside her.

"Norma, what's wrong?" I questioned.

"I hate boats," she said slowly.

"You've got to be kidding. You hate boats? You're the one who called me up and said you wanted to buy the boat, and now you're telling me you hate boats? Would you like to explain that?"

I slowed our speed and let the boat idle so she could relax enough to talk to me.

"All my life I've been afraid of boats," she said. "I've just always had a real problem with boats." I sat there in total bewilderment.

She labored to explain that she hated boats, but she knew she could learn to like them. She enjoys them much more now, further convinced that boating and skiing will knit our lives together. She determined to endure boating long enough to learn to like it for the family's sake.

Not long after our first boating experience, I sat next to an executive from Boeing Aircraft on a flight to Seattle. When I asked him about his family, he told me they were very close.

"What is the most important thing that holds your family together?" I asked.

"Several years ago," he said, "we purchased a yacht and as a family we traveled around the various inlets and islands in the Seattle area. My family enjoys boating so much that it has provided a tremendous way to knit us together."

I wish all fathers felt that way.

One man sadly admitted that when he and his children meet for a rare get-together they hardly have a thing in common.

"It's a sickening experience," he said, "to have your children back home for a visit and have nothing in common. You know, the only thing we ever laugh about as a family is when we remember the one time we took a three-week vacation. We rented a tent and camped. What a vacation! We still laugh at those experiences."

He didn't have any other fond memories of family togetherness. His wife had her women's clubs; he had his men's clubs; the children had their activities. They all grew apart in separate worlds.

"Now that my wife and I are alone, we have very little in

common," he lamented. "We are two lonely people lost in our five-bedroom house."

The simple principle of sharing life together has permeated every area of our family life, from supporting Greg and Michael in soccer to supporting Kari and Greg in piano. As much as possible, we look for ways to spend time together—cooking, fishing, putting the kids to bed, gardening. Everything we do as a family assures me of our unity later in life.

When I think of a trip to Hawaii, I envision snorkeling, scuba diving, spear fishing, or anything related to being in the water. My wife thinks of an orchid lei as she steps off the airplane, dining in romantic restaurants, renting a car and sightseeing during the day. Our desires are completely different. We feel that although a husband and wife both need time to enjoy separate activities, they also need to step into the world of their mates to taste each other's interests.

While my wife is shopping, I might be snorkeling, but at night we would dine together in a very romantic place. At times my wife would want to snorkel with me, and I would enjoy sightseeing with her. I'm not saying that I would rather be touring than snorkeling or that she would rather slip on a wet suit instead of a new dress, but we believe it is important to compromise in order to share experiences. Afterwards, when the trip is only a motel receipt in your wallet, it's experiences you shared during the trip that will draw you together.

I often ask couples if they ever do things together. When I ask about vacations and the husband's face lights up while the wife grimaces, I usually conclude they took their vacation at the husband's chosen site. It was probably a dream to him and sheer torture for her and the children.

Consider the following suggestions before planning a family outing.

First, find out what activities you and your wife and your children would like to do together. Next, consider everyone's schedule to see if the planned outing will force hardship on anyone involved. For example, we agreed as a family that Greg should not be involved in group sports until this season because we felt we should be camping on weekends, instead of sitting on bleachers watching one member play football. From time to time, we adjust our schedule to make sure our family activities are not forcing one member to miss an important event.

At this point, ask your wife to name ten activities she would enjoy doing with you throughout the year.

1. _____

2. _____

3. _____

4. _____

5. _____

6. _____

7. _____

8. _____

9. _____

10. _____

Next, ask her to rate which activity of the ten is the most important to her. Don't be surprised if she prefers doing some things alone—or if she doesn't enjoy being with you at all. If she has no desire to share activities with you, reflect on your attitude toward her in the past. Have you been critical or bored? Did you pout when you had to do something she wanted to do? If so, she will remember those times and tend to avoid involvement with you in the future.

Now, let's go on to the second suggestion for becoming a close-knit family.

Recognize Everyone's Need to Belong

You and I know the good feeling we have when we're able to say, "I belong to this club." "These are my friends." "The club needs my help."

During an interview with a pro-football cheerleader, I learned how much wives need to feel that sense of belonging. She told me she loved the way her husband treated her when she returned from a two-day trip. He was so excited to have her home. He pampered her, telling her how much he had missed her. But his appreciative attitude usually wore off in about two days. Then he would start taking her for granted again.

Why do we sit glued to the television as though our wives didn't exist? It seems we realize our love for them most when they're out of our lives for a few days. But after we've had them with us for a while, the "ho-hums" set in, don't they?

The principle of belonging is powerfully illustrated by an experience I had with my daughter. When Kari was nine years old, I sensed an undefined barrier between us. I couldn't detect anything specific. We just weren't close. I didn't enjoy being with her, and she didn't enjoy me either. No matter how hard I tried, I couldn't break through the barrier. From time to time, Norma would comment that I preferred my sons over my daughter. I said, "One of the reasons is because the boys are more responsive to me."

"You'd better do something to strengthen the relationship now," Norma said, "because when Kari gets older it will be much harder." So, I tested the value of belonging and decided to take Kari with me on my next seven-day business trip. Though we still weren't close, she became excited as we planned what to do and where to stay. During the plane trip we worked on her multiplication problems until it almost drove me crazy—and the man in front of us. We stayed with a farm family in Washington the first night. I noticed the rapport Kari and I felt as we laughed and sang around the dinner table with their numerous children; we were actually enjoying one another's company. At times we didn't even talk. It seemed enough just to be together. Kari seemed to have just as much fun in that farm home as she did helping me with my meetings. I let her distribute some of the material so she really felt she was a special part of my team. And she was.

We decided to take the scenic route from Portland to Seattle. I wanted to show her the small "poke and plum" town near Portland where I was raised. It's so small that by the time you "poke" your head out of the window you're "plum" out of the town. After we had a flat tire near the Columbia River, we changed it together and then walked down to the river to gather driftwood for a memento. We tried to make it up a snow-covered mountain, but had to turn around and go all the way back to Seattle the long way. We will both remember that trip, good times and bad.

I have *never* sensed a barrier between us in the years since that trip. I feel complete harmony and oneness in Kari's company. She still has the piece of driftwood sitting in her bedroom, a silent reminder of our bond and her special relationship with Christ; on it is engraved her salvation date.

Let Hard Times Draw You Together

Foxholes make lasting friendships. Haven't you heard the stories of buddies who shared the same foxhole during wartime?

Whenever they meet, there is an instant camaraderie that no one can ever take away from them, a feeling born from surviving a struggle together. Trials can produce maturity and loving attitudes (James 1:2–4).

Families have foxholes too. Even when a crisis inflicts deep scars, the dilemma can draw the family closer.

Maybe it's the crises in camping that have such a unifying effect on a family. Any family that can survive bugs, poison ivy, storms, burnt sausage, and sand in the eggs has to come out of the ordeal closer. During a crisis, you have only each other to rely on. We all look back on the mishaps that occurred during our camping trips and *laugh*, though it wasn't a bit funny at the time. Like the night Norma awakened me at two in the morning so cold that she asked, "Honey, could you take us home?" Though we were two hours from home, I abandoned my cozy bed to pack and leave. She called me her John Wayne on the way home, but at the time I didn't feel much like The Duke.

Our camping fiascos have been numerous. *Only two more hours and home sweet home*, I thought after our first camping trip. Tension electrified the air as we all longed to be home with hot water and familiar beds once again. Now when we look back on the experience we laugh, and our laughter binds us together as husband and wife and as parents and children.

THE ONE ACTIVITY
THAT WIVES ENJOY THE MOST WITH THEIR HUSBANDS

Many women have told me about the importance of intimate communication with their husbands—special togetherness times— after the children are in bed, during the day on the telephone, at breakfast, at dinner, at a restaurant over a cup of coffee. These special sharing times can be the most enjoyable part of a woman's day.

My wife agrees that an intimate sharing time with me is the one thing she enjoys most about our relationship. We make it a point to have breakfast together as often as possible at a nearby restaurant just to talk about our upcoming schedules. I ask her questions about what she needs for the week and what I can do to help her and vice versa. I enjoy our discussions because I know she enjoys them. But more importantly, I would really miss those times of intimate communication if we ever neglected them.

To really understand each other during our conversations, we use a concept seldom taught in the classroom. It's called the "revolving method" of communication. Though it's very simple, you'll find it a tremendous help in avoiding misunderstandings. It involves four steps:

1) I ask my wife to share her feelings or thoughts with me.
2) I respond by rephrasing what I think she said.
3) She answers either yes or no.
4) If she answers no, I continue to rephrase what I think she said until I get a yes response.

My wife goes through the same four steps when I am explaining my feelings to her.

Our communication is more meaningful since neither of us *assumes;* we automatically know what the other is saying. (In the past, misunderstandings over implied meanings confused and ruined many discussions.) This process has nearly eliminated misinterpretations in our marriage.

FOR PERSONAL REFLECTION

1. How can Paul's example of discipleship in 1 Thessalonians 2:7–11 be applied to a family relationship?
2. Plan out a simple way to become "one flesh" (Eph. 5:31). Use the exercise below to help you.

What activities can we share together in life?

A. The Christian Life
   Church
   Prayer—when, where, how often?
   Bible study—when, where, how often?
   Witnessing
   Helping others

B. Trips or vacations

   What would our dream trip be? What would it include?

C. What are two of my favorite activities?

   Describe in detail at least one activity.

D. What are two of my wife's favorite activities?

   Is there any way to combine our favorites?

E. What is one activity in life I fear or feel inadequate to face?

   How could my mate help me overcome this fear?

11

So You Want
A Perfect Wife

*"For
I will not
presume to speak
of anything
except
what Christ
has accomplished
through me."
Romans 15:18*

"IF YOU WERE more submissive to me, we wouldn't have near as many problems," I used to say to my wife in a holier-than-thou voice. I was sure we would have a harmonious and fulfilling marriage if only I could motivate her to change her attitudes and responses toward me. And I was always thinking of new, creative, foolproof ways to make her change. Of course, my creative ideas usually just made her more resistant, but I didn't let that deter me. After all, most, if not all, our problems were her fault, I thought.

I even said things like, "You're so stubborn and strong-willed you're causing our marriage to decline, to deteriorate."

Or, "If only you wouldn't get so hysterical when we discuss our future plans, I would be more willing to share my life with you. I just can't tolerate your emotionalism."

I believed, at the time, that the husband was the "Captain Bligh" of the ship. When I gave the orders, I expected everyone to "snap to" and follow my leadership without offering resistance or asking questions. My distorted view made me continually critical of my wife's behavior. I can remember threatening her in a rough tone of voice to emphasize the importance of what I was saying. I gave her the silent treatment, clamming up, hoping to gain her attention so she would come crawling to me after seeing the error of her ways. And I can easily recall my persistence in lecturing her over and over again on the same issues.

Lecturing is not nearly as effective as the next three approaches.

BECOME A CONSISTENT EXAMPLE
OF WHAT YOU WANT HER TO BE (ROMANS 15:18)

Studies have shown that children are much more likely to copy their parents' actions rather than their words. I have found the same principle true in adult relationships. A wife is subconsciously much more willing to emulate her husband's attitudes if they have a good relationship and she admires him. Unfortunately, the converse is true also. The more a husband demands that his wife change when he isn't a good example himself, the less desirous she is to improve herself.

I tried to change my wife in a certain area for months. I bribed her, embarrassed her, threatened not to take her on vacations, endeavoring in many "creative" ways to make her change. But the more I talked, the less she seemed to hear. I finally realized how unloving my attitude had been. I told myself I would not say another word to her about her problems until I could control myself enough to change into the tender and loving husband she needed. I was judging her in the same areas I was guilty (Rom. 2:1–2).

HOW CAN A MAN EXPECT HIS WIFE TO GAIN SELF-CONTROL IN AREAS OF HER LIFE WHEN HE DOES NOT HAVE IT IN HIS OWN?

Now *I* was ready to do some changing. "Norma, I've been thinking of trying to change, and I'm ready to start. I'm going to get off your back."

"You know," she said, "I've really been doing some thinking myself, and I really do want to change, especially in that one area that bothers you."

"No, no," I said, "don't do that, because I want to be the first to change. If you change, I won't have as much incentive—you know how competitive I am."

"No, honey, I really want to try harder, and I'm going to change," she replied.

I was so confused because this was the first time she had *ever* been interested in changing. *Then she said something I will never forget.*

"Gary, you know one of the reasons why it's been so hard for me to break some of my habits? It's because your attitude was so terrible. When you criticized me, I lost all desire and energy to try. And you are so hateful about criticizing me that I don't want to improve because it would reinforce your stinky attitudes."

Now that I had taken the pressure off, she told me she could sense the difference in my attitude. "Gary, I really want to change, and you're really helping me now."

The Futility of Lecturing Your Wife

I learned that a husband's tender, sensitive, and understanding attitude creates far more desire within a wife than almost anything else he can do. Unfortunately, I hadn't learned the quality of sensitivity during our early years, and my wife did not always feel free to be completely honest with me for fear of my reactions.

A cold chill runs through me when I remember how much it hurt our marriage for Norma to feel she couldn't tell me her true feelings. One of our most painful experiences in this area began at a family reunion.

We were both tired and irritated after a long day at a family get-together near Lake Tahoe when a disagreement began. I don't know how we found enough energy to have such a fight, but it flared quite easily into an argument. I became more irritated and disturbed when she repeatedly refused to submit to me about my change of schedules. Finally her attitude bugged me so much that I told her I had had it. Here I was, on the staff of an organization that taught others how to have family harmony, and I couldn't even achieve it in my own family. I lived with an uneasy feeling that Norma might blow up at the wrong time and embarrass me. I didn't want that pressure any more, so I decided I had no choice but to quit my job and try a different type of work.

We were both so angry that evening we didn't speak. I awakened at five the next morning with a sick feeling in the pit of my stomach and walked down to the lake to think. I thought through what I would say to my boss and how I would handle the changes about to happen in my life. With a degree of peace, I walked back to the motel to tell Norma of my plans.

She began to cry, begging me not to quit my job. "I was wrong," she sobbed. "I'll change."

Her immediate change in attitude confused me.

"This time you can trust me because I guarantee you this will never happen again as long as we live," she said, still crying. "I really don't want you to quit your job because you will blame me the rest of our lives. Anything you tell me to do, I will do it."

At last, I thought, *she is beginning to see the error of her ways. Now we can get down to the business of developing a more harmonious marriage.*

I couldn't have been further from the truth. Norma had not been completely honest with me. Instead of a change of mind, she was so hurt and offended inside by my critical attitude that her heart had hardened. But since I was threatening her security, to take her away from friends and a home she loved, to move to a different location with no promise we'd even have any money, she hid her true feelings. At that time, I didn't understand how devastating such a threat could be to a woman. Norma fought to save her home the only way she knew—by giving in to me. But it wasn't because she suddenly understood my theory of marriage; it was simply that she had no alternative.

She harbored those resentful feelings for years. Consequently, our relationship could not become what it should have because of her unspoken resentment toward me. She can remember hating me on the inside but smiling on the outside. It makes me shudder to think about it. Since she appeared happy on the surface, I couldn't sense that she was inwardly disgusted with me.

As I look back on the experience today, I realize where I was at fault. I was demanding and insensitive to her needs. I made no effort to understand her physical and emotional limitations and how sudden changes affect a woman. I was also very critical of her attitudes and her fatigue. I threatened her security in a cold, calculating way. Had I been understanding enough to have waited a day or two to discuss what I wanted to do, the outcome might have been different. Only in the last few years have we developed the kind of relationship that allows this type of honesty.

DON'T DEMAND.

SHARE HOW YOU FEEL

The second way to increase your wife's desire to improve your marriage is to *share* how you feel instead of demanding that she improve.

Let me clarify the "sharing" principle by breaking it down into four parts.

Learn to express your feelings through loving attitudes: warmth, empathy, and sincerity. Loving attitudes dramatically increase a woman's desire to hear your comments. Warmth is the friendly acceptance of a person, the feeling that a person is important enough for your time and effort. Empathy is the ability to understand

and identify with your wife's feelings. Can you put yourself in her shoes and see the situation from her vantage point? Sincerity is showing a genuine concern for your wife both in public and at home. A comment such as, "You won't believe my old lady" gives your wife good reason to be an "old lady" when you go home.

Try to avoid using "you" statements when sharing your feelings. When you say to your wife, "You never clean up this house," or "You never have dinner on time," or "You always yell at the children," you will find she is apt to dig her heels in deeper to resist you. According to psychologist Jerry Day, "you" statements make her more determined to have her own way. When a husband says in anger, "Can't you ever think about my feelings for a change," she thinks, *His feelings! What about my feelings!* "You" statements seldom make your wife think about you; they usually infuriate her because she knows you're not concerned with her feelings.

Wait to share your feelings until your anger has subsided. When you are angry, the tone of your voice alone is likely to provoke the wrong reaction in your wife. You might even spit out words you really don't mean. While you are waiting to cool off, either remain silent or change the subject to a neutral one. If your wife asks why you are quiet, answer her honestly. Try to avoid sarcasm and say something like, "I need a little time to think this through so I can better understand my feelings." Psychologist Henry Brandt encourages a husband and wife to be honest enough to say, "I'm angry right now, and to discuss our problem would be disastrous. Could we wait until I've cooled off?" By waiting, you will be able to have a discussion instead of an argument.

Replacing "you" statements with "I feel" messages after you have both cooled down is a better way to share disagreements. Here are a few examples of what I mean:

Areas Your Wife Needs to Improve	Typical "You" Statements to Avoid	Examples of "I Feel" Messages
She doesn't respect you.	"You don't respect me like you should."	"Honey, you probably don't realize this, but I really feel discouraged whenever I hear you say disrespectful things to me." (Plug in the statement she uses that discourages you.)
She doesn't accept you	"You're always trying to make	"Honey, I don't blame you for saying a lot of the things you say to

the way you are.	me into some-body I'm not."	me. Many times we're just not in the same world. *But I honestly don't understand many of the ways I offend you.* And I feel that you're not accepting me for who I am."
She is impatient with you.	"You never give me a chance. Would you get off my back and give me a break, I'm not perfect. I'm not as bad as Sarah's husband.	"Honey, I think you deserve a gold medal for putting up with me, and I wish our relationship was better for your sake. I wish I were more skilled in taking care of you, but it's probably going to take me a long time to learn these new habits. Many times I lose my desire to try when you're critical of me for not improving as fast as you wish I would."
She is critical of you in front of others.	"You make me sick when you criticize me like you did tonight. If you ever say that again I will never take you to another party. You sure made a fool of me tonight."	"Honey, I know how much you enjoy being with your friends. Would there be some time in the near future when we could talk about how I feel when we're at those parties? I hate to bring it up, but there's something you do that dampens my desire to be with our friends together. I really feel embarrassed and low when you criticize me in front of them."

Last, try to abandon "I told you so" statements. No matter how it's said, if it means "I told you so," eliminate it from your vocabulary. Such statements reflect an arrogance and self-centeredness that can be harmful to your marriage. Here are some of the more typical ways of saying "I told you so":

"If you had done what I asked you to do in the first place, this wouldn't have happened!"

"I knew it . . . just like I thought. I only asked you to do one thing . . . I can't believe that you . . . you never listen, do you? . . . See-e-e-e-e?"

"You always have to do it your way, don't you? Well, I hope you're satisfied now."

"I'm not going to say it but . . . maybe someday you'll learn to take my advice."

Can you think of any additional ways that you say to your wife, "I told you so"?

1. _____

2. _____

3. _____

4. _____

5. _____

If you can't think of any at the moment, ask your wife if she can remember some of them. Norma could.

I search out the ways I have hurt Norma's feelings, and she does the same with me. She is secure, knowing *I won't allow* her to mistreat me. She likes to be held accountable for how she makes me feel. I, too, believe it is important for a husband to have the courage to share his feelings with his wife. A lion can roar and growl, but it takes a real man to say it gently. Tell her you need comfort. Let her know you need praise. (I feel I need the same basic treatment Norma does. If she wants me to improve as a husband, it is essential that she knows what encourages or discourages me in the process.) You are the only one who can tell your wife what you need.

CREATE CURIOSITY

The third way to increase your wife's desire to improve comes from the old saying, "You can lead a horse to water but you can't make him drink." But you *can* make him drink if you put salt in his oats. The more salt you put in his oats, the greater his thirst and the more he drinks. The more curious you make your wife, the more she will want to listen. This principle has been aptly named the "salt principle." *Be stingy in sharing your feelings. Don't share them with your wife until you have her full attention.* Once you master the salt principle, you will be able to gain the attention of anyone, even when he or she knows what you are doing. Simply stated, the principle is:

> NEVER COMMUNICATE YOUR FEELINGS OR INFORMATION YOU CONSIDER TO BE IMPORTANT WITHOUT FIRST CREATING A BURNING CURIOSITY WITHIN THE LISTENER.

The salt principle is so powerful that I can gain the attention of my family, even if their eyes are glued to the television. If I want my children to go to bed immediately, I can use the salt principle to get them there without threats, taunts, or screams. Christ left us the example by His method of teaching and motivating people. He used parables to create interest. In fact, He advised us not to teach truth to the uninterested (Matt. 7:6).

The salt principle is so powerful that I have gotten myself into trouble using it. During a speech to a large group, someone asked a question that made me say without thinking, "Do you realize a wife can gain six attitudes that really motivate her husband to want to improve?" The moment those words left my mouth, I realized I was in trouble. A woman's hand went up. "What are those six attitudes?" she asked. I inwardly groaned as I realized I could not discuss those six attitudes and finish the topic I had started. Lowering my head, I apologized to the audience for tantalizing their curiosity. I didn't forget this salt episode because after the meeting I was mobbed by curious ladies. I can't say I felt like Burt Reynolds, but I did have to spend an hour after the meeting explaining the six attitudes. Now if you're wondering what those six attitudes are, you can find them in the Part II of this book.

Let me use four steps to illustrate how to catch your wife's attention when you want to share your feelings.

First, clearly identify the feeling you wish to communicate to your wife. For example, you want her to understand how discouraged you become when she corrects you in public.

Second, identify some of the areas your wife wants you to change. Perhaps your wife would like you to show affection for her by holding her hand or putting your arm around her in public.

Third, use her area of high interest, salted with just a pinch of your feelings, to stimulate her curiosity. Use her high interest for affection in public and say something like, "Honey, when we're out in public or with our friends, I just want to put my arm around you and show everyone how proud I am of you. But there's something that you do occasionally that takes away my desire to hold you."

And fourth, add a little more salt by asking a short question to further arouse her curiosity. Say something like, "Do you know what you do?" Or, "I probably shouldn't say anything at this time, right?" Or, "Would you be interested in hearing what it is that causes me to feel this way?" If she isn't interested by this time, try it again later. Add a larger dose of salt to your statements.

Below are four examples of how a husband can "salt" his wife to listen to his feelings.

Area you wish your wife would change	"Salt" statements that motivate your wife to change
1. She resists your sexual advances	"Honey, do you know what really encourages me to make our marriage better? (No.) It's when I see us working together in building our marriage. (Oh, that's good.) I can think of a major area that makes me feel that you're not pulling with me. (Oh, what's that?) Is now a good time to talk about it? (Yes.) Well, I feel misunderstood and rejected when you don't respond to me at night. Could you tell me what's wrong?" *(Be extra gentle and tender during the ensuing discussion. You may find out that she feels offended or any number of possibilities, but you don't have to solve the problem in one discussion.)*
2. She monopolizes the conversation at parties	"Honey, I know you want to go to their home next week, but there's one thing that keeps happening when we're together that really drives me away from social gatherings in general. (Oh, what is it . . . gulp.) Well, I'm not sure I can really explain it without offending you. (Gulp, gulp.) Do you really want to talk about it? (Yes.) Well, I feel left out at parties by you." *(Ask her how both of you could balance this problem. Maybe you could talk a little more and she a little less. If you discuss a plan before going to the party, you will enhance the possibility of it being more enjoyable for both of you.)*
3. She doesn't want to talk when you're alone with her	"Honey, here we are again, talking about improving our relationship. You still want that, don't you? (Yes.) The best relationship possible that we can build together? (Yes.) There's one thing I don't understand that happens to us during different times of the week, and I think that it is not going to help our relationship, especially after the children are grown and married and we're all alone. (Oh, what's that?) Well, it sort of involves the

quiet times when you and I are all by ourselves and I'm really wanting to talk to you, but you don't seem to have this same desire to talk with me. I'm just wondering if there's something I'm doing that I'm not aware of, because I really want to talk with you but I don't sense that same interest in you. Maybe I'm not being sensitive to your fatigue, or whatever. I'd just like to know, because I really feel left out when you don't talk to me when we're alone."

4. She nags you about household repairs

"Honey, I don't blame you for doing one particular thing to me from time to time, because I'm sure I deserve it. But, when you say one thing to me it really causes me to lose interest in repairing things around the house. (Oh, what's that?) Well, I know it has something to do with me, and I haven't been able to figure it out yet. But in the meantime, it's not helping me to want to fix things around here. (Well, what is it? Tell me.) Maybe you can help me. Would now be a good time for you to help me figure out why you do this particular thing to me? (Yes, dear, whatever it is, let's get it out in the open and talk about it.) Well, you see, honey, I feel so unmotivated when you, sometimes in irritation or in anger, tell me five times to do something and I just can't remember to do it. As much as I want to, my mind just gets occupied with other things and I just can't remember. I really want to help around the house. How can we figure out together what needs to be done to help me get these things done and help you not to nag me about them? I feel really disinterested in doing it when you're nagging me."

In summary, if a man truly wants his wife to improve and their marriage to be strengthened, he should be the example of what he wants to see in her before saying anything to her. He should be courageous enough to share his feelings and avoid accusing her. And finally, he should use the "salt principle" to gain her full attention before sharing his feelings.

FOR PERSONAL REFLECTION

List the changes you desire in your wife and then write out your own projects to become her example. Romans 15:18; 2:1–2.

12

Watch Out!
It Can Happen
To You

"A man's pride
will
bring him low,
but
a humble spirit
will obtain
honor."
Proverbs 29:23

"NORMA, I REALLY think you should take a couple of days away from the kids considering all you've faced during my absence, all the guests you had to entertain, the wedding shower, painting Greg's room. . . . I'll get a babysitter, and you just relax. I don't think you're holding up too well." I was trying to get back to work on this book, and somehow it irritated me that Norma sounded nervous and looked uptight.

She said, "I didn't need that. It makes me feel like you don't think I can handle things on my own."

"But I don't think you're handling yourself well," I said with a scowl and a harsh voice. "Surely writing a book involves more pressure than staying with the kids!"

Then the principles in my book flashed before me and broke through my irritation. I realized I was irritated and nervous and that Norma was bearing the brunt of my insensitivity. I had blown it again!

"You're right. You didn't need that. You *are* doing great. When will I ever learn?"

The next morning she came over to my hideaway motel for breakfast, and we again discussed how I had missed a chance to encourage her. My motives were to help, by my insensitive words came out of a doubt that I *really* was the kind of husband I should be. If I were the right kind of husband, maybe my wife wouldn't have to feel so nervous and rundown. My thoughts had been, *Honey, only a*

169

week and I'll be finished with both books. Please hang on. What will people think of my book if you don't look like I'm making you happy?

Norma said she understood and reminded me that my offensive behavior comes less and less often, that the periods of disharmony get shorter and shorter as we learn how to restore our relationship.

Why are those hard times fading away? Two reasons:

1. I *admit* my offensive ways and quickly accept the fact that I haven't arrived.

2. I *earn* her forgiveness sooner by following the ideas in chapter 5.

(And we are *both reaching* for the best possible relationship. That helps a lot!)

"But," you ask, "when can I relax and enjoy the fruit of my labor?"

Do you remember the story of the young couple who separated for a year until the husband learned how to regain his wife's affection? (See chapter 2.) She couldn't live with his lazy, insensitive, dominant, selfish mannerisms.

He followed many of the principles shared in this book for five years after they reunited, and she was regaining a romantic love and starting to blossom. Then he made the *big mistake! He relaxed and wanted a little return for his years of effort.* He assumed that now he could start enjoying the fruit of his labor. He slowly reverted to his old habits and attitudes: lazy, insensitive, dominant, selfish. Once again she started to lose her feelings of love for him.

Today he is starting all over again. Fortunately, this time they both desire a better marriage and both are seeking help as a couple.

Building a successful marriage is a lifelong endeavor.

Don't relax! And never assume that you've arrived! Pride always comes before a fall (Prov. 29:23)!

Or, you say, "I'm tired of starting all over again."

One man couldn't stick with it. He kept forgetting some of the principles shared in this book. His wife was ready to leave him, and nothing seemed to help, until one day I said to him, "Jim, each time you fail to comfort her and each time you lose your temper, you're back to the starting block in her mind—at that point she still wants to leave you."

"That does it," he said. "No way am I going to keep starting all over again." *And he didn't.* That was the end of his angry outbursts.

You may take great strides forward, but each time you slip, your wife may think you haven't changed a bit. Remember, it took my wife two years to believe me.

FOR PERSONAL REFLECTION

1. How does the secret of prayer relate to becoming a more consistently loving husband?

    Luke 11:5-8—the secret is in verse 8.
    Luke 18:1-7—the secret is in verse 5.

2. How many times should a husband forgive his wife and keep trying to build a loving marriage? Matthew 18:21-22.

Part II

Marriage Building
Principles for the Wife

13

Lasting Relationships
Don't Just Happen

"An excellent wife,
who can find?
For her worth
is
far above jewels."
Proverbs 31:10

JIM STARED SILENTLY at the television set while Carol ached inside, wondering why he was angry at her again. They had only been married a year, and Carol could already see their relationship deteriorating. She couldn't help but wonder if she would soon join the millions of other couples whose marriages have ended in divorce. When she finally broke the silence by asking Jim what was wrong, he refused to answer her. Hurting for a few minutes, she repeated the question. His response wounded her so deeply she began to doubt her adequacy as a wife.

He said, "I'm sick and tired of you taking everything so seriously. You're just too sensitive! If I had known you were this emotional, I probably never would have married you. But since we are married, I think you need to do your part. Cut out the overreacting and stop being so touchy about what I say and do. If we're going to have any kind of marriage, you have to stop being so childish!"

Sound familiar? With these harsh words, Jim unknowingly has set their relationship on a destructive path leading to some very unattractive changes—changes, which will likely lead to the ultimate disintegration of their relationship. Jim's main problem, shared by thousands of other husbands, is that he fails to understand the basic difference between the natures of men and women. Jim has taken two of his wife's greatest natural strengths, her sensitivity and intuitive awareness of life, and labeled them weaknesses. In response to Jim's reproof, Carol, like thousands of other wives, will begin to form a calloused, hardened attitude toward life in general and Jim in particular. If their marriage lasts more than a few years, Jim will find to his dismay that Carol's sensitivity has finally been subdued and that he has lost most or all of his attraction to her. If only he could remember that her sensitivity was one of the first things that attracted him. If only he understood that her alertness was one of her greatest strengths, and if he began treating her with tenderness, gentleness, and kindness, their relationship would grow stronger and more fulfilling.

The emotional and mental differences between men and women (described in detail in chapter 15) *can* become insurmountable obstacles to a lasting, fulfilling relationship when ignored or misunderstood. However, those same differences, when recognized and appreciated, can become stepping-stones to a meaningful, fulfilling relationship.

Women, for example, have a tremendous advantage in two of life's most important areas: loving God and loving others (Matt. 22:36–40). Women have an intuitive ability to develop meaningful relationships and a desire for intimate communication, and this gives them the edge in what Jesus described as the two greatest commandments. Loving God and others is building relationships. God said that it was not good for man to dwell alone, and He created a significant Helper and Completer—woman. Men definitely need help with making and maintaining relationships, but *how* women help so that men listen and receive it is the thrust of this book.

When a woman understands her strengths for what they are, her self-image will be practically indestructible, no matter how her husband belittles her. When both husband and wife understand each other and begin to respond to one another accordingly, their relationship can blossom into the marriage they dreamed of. Carol can begin to make Jim aware of her deeper needs for love, assurance, and security, without feeling selfish for desiring fulfillment of her needs. Unfortunately, at the rate Jim and Carol are going, it probably won't be long before they join the ranks of the one-million-plus couples divorced each year in the United States.

But don't despair! *Your* marriage does *not* have to become part of these awesome statistics. With the right tools, you *can* carve a more fulfilling marriage out of a seemingly hopeless one, and this book will provide you with many of those tools. But the tools by themselves will never get the job done. They have to be picked up and used *properly* and *consistently* if they are to bring the intended results.

If your husband is willing to work beside you, you'll strengthen your marriage that much faster. I believe the greatest benefits will result when you both read this book. When a husband understands his wife's needs and learns how to meet those needs, the relationship will grow more quickly.

In counseling, I have found that *if* I can get the husband to do his part *first*, it's much easier for the wife to carry out her responsibilities in the relationship with greater enthusiasm and commitment. Unfortunately, women are usually more concerned about deepening their marital relationships than men. That's why your book was written first; I felt that *you* would be the one with the greater interest in strengthening your marriage and the one to initiate change in the relationship.

I also believe that you will be the *key* to motivate your husband to read his part of this book. Consequently, a whole chapter in this book (chapter 17) explains how to motivate your husband to read Part I. If he reads carefully, I feel confident that he will *begin* to become aware of the special person you really are and will begin treating you with more tenderness, gentleness, sensitivity, and understanding.

If your relationship with your husband is less than you desire and he shows little concern for your feelings, you may at first find it difficult to take the steps given in this book. However, if you are willing to overlook his lack of response for the moment and put forth some extra effort, the ideas presented in this book *can work*. I am also confident that your husband's desire for a better relationship will increase in response to the *changes* he *sees* in you.

I have spoken to hundreds and hundreds of married women. I found very few who did not want an improvement in their relationships with their husbands. Some women were more content than others, but most of them longed for more loving and romantic husbands. Many said they wanted their husbands to love them more than he loved anyone or anything. You might think, "That's impossible. There's not a man alive who loves like that!" But I have personally seen a growing number of husbands transformed into "impossible" lovers. The changes necessary don't just happen though, men *make* them happen when they know *what* to do!

ONE BIG REASON MARRIAGES FAIL

All too often, people marry before acquiring the knowledge and skills necessary to take care of their mates: to meet their emotional, mental, and physical needs. One of the ironies in our society is that a person has to have four years of training to receive a plumber's license, but absolutely no training is required for a marriage license.

Our educational system doesn't even require communication courses basic to the meaningful development of any relationship. As a result, many men and women enter marriage with virtually no knowledge of how to meet the *basic* emotional and mental needs of their mates. And I must confess, I was certainly among the untrained when I married. It has taken my wife, Norma, and my friends many years to help me become a more loving husband.

It is typical for a man to marry without knowing *how* to talk to his wife. Some men don't even know that their wives *need* intimate communication. Often a man is completely unaware of his wife's sensitive nature. He doesn't know that things he considers trivial can be extremely important to her—things like anniversaries and holidays. Nor does he realize why such things *are* special to her, and so he is unable to meet her needs. Many men don't understand a woman's physical cycles and the hormonal changes she experiences. They don't realize how a woman's home, children, family, and friends become an interwoven part of her identity.

Many women step into marriage equally handicapped. They don't understand that admiration is to a man what romance is to a woman. They don't realize that a man generally relies on reasoning rather than intuitive sensitivity.

It is obvious, then, that if both husband and wife lack the vital knowledge and skills to meet each other's needs, their needs will go unmet. One of the great psychiatrists of our time, Dr. Karl Menninger, said that when our basic needs are not met, we move in one of two directions. We either withdraw in "flight" or turn to "fight." The woman who takes the "flight" approach is certainly not escaping her problems. As she runs, she begins to doubt her self-worth. On the other hand, if she takes the "fight" approach, she may become an unattractive nag to her husband.

I believe the ideal marriage evolves when the wife concentrates on meeting her husband's needs and the husband concentrates on meeting his wife's needs. That combination builds the lasting qualities of a giving relationship.

This book was written to show women how to motivate their husbands to improve their relationship. Changes don't happen overnight, but the principles, in this book have been proven over time in thousands of marriages. I know they work. If a woman is willing to spend the time and energy necessary to apply these principles, I am confident she will see her marriage become more of what she desires.

If you want to become a great painter, you must be dedicated. Learning to master the essential techniques and skills of painting comes first. Then, after you have painted hundreds of canvases, you might display your work as an inspiration for young artists to follow. In the same way, I believe this book will give you many of the essential techniques and skills fundamental to making your marriage, with time and effort, a living example for others to follow.

Since this book was written to meet the needs of thousands of people, some of the principles and ideas contained in it are, naturally, general and far-reaching. It cannot possibly answer all of the specific questions every woman would like to ask, but it does attempt to address the major aspects of love and marriage.

FOR PERSONAL REFLECTION

Why is a wife so important to her husband? (See Genesis 2:18; Matthew 22:36–40.)

14

Eight Ways
Husbands Hurt
Their Wives

"And if he sins
against you
seven times a day,
and returns to you
seven times,
saying,
'I repent,'
forgive him."
Luke 17:4

ON A FLIGHT from Philadelphia to New Orleans, I mentioned to one of the stewardesses that I was writing a book about marriage. I told her one of the chapters discussed ways that a man hurts a woman without even realizing it. Before I knew it, I had been whisked up to first class and three stewardesses were telling me all of the ways their ex-husbands had hurt them. The three seemed amazed that a man could understand how words and actions, which seemed so innocent to their husbands, had inflicted hurts they, as women, could never forget.

For most couples with whom I counsel, a week rarely passes without the husband saying or doing something that unintentionally offends the wife. The following true stories illustrate *eight* ways that husbands hurt their wives ... without even knowing it! However, I have seen men *stop* inflicting these hurts when their wives began applying some of the appropriate principles discussed in detail later.

HE FREQUENTLY CRITICIZES YOU

Jim was great at finding all of Sarah's faults.
Sarah had just slipped into her swimsuit and couldn't wait to get down to the beach. It was the first day of their vacation. Jim walked in, pinched her on the side, and casually remarked, "We better watch how much we eat on this trip." It seemed innocent to Jim, but Sarah thought he was really saying, "You're fat and ugly." The hurt

was so deep that even to this day, five years and a divorce later, Sarah is extremely self-conscious in a swimsuit. (Oddly enough, Sarah is an attractive woman with a good figure.)

Several weeks after Jim made this remark, Sarah decided to try to do something about her figure. She concluded that ice skating would give her the necessary exercise. When she told Jim about her decision, he sarcastically said, "What do you want to do, become an Olympic champ?" To her, he was really saying, "I can't believe how stupid you are to come up with such a ridiculous idea. You're not worth the money it would cost."

Jim not only called attention to her weight problem but also criticized her for wanting to improve. Although he didn't realize it, Jim could find fault with almost anything Sarah said or did. He thought he could motivate her to change through sarcastic comments. Since a woman is not hard and calloused by nature, hurtful criticism rarely provides motivation to change. It usually brings deeper despair, which results in a diminished desire to please her husband. Chapters 22 and 24 will show you *how* to motivate your husband to replace his criticisms with appreciation and gratefulness.

HE DOESN'T PAY ATTENTION
TO YOUR WORDS AND IDEAS

The only way Julia could hope to get Harry's undivided attention would be to magically transform herself into a TV program.

It was 11:00 at night, and Susan, half-asleep, answered the phone. Across the line came the sobs of her mother thousands of miles away.

"What's wrong, Mom?"

Her mother replied, "I have to take $450 out of savings and buy your father a new color TV."

Now fully awake, Susan asked, "What happened?"

"For weeks I have been trying to get your father's attention long enough to explain a sensitive problem your little sister has had. I couldn't drag your father away from the TV set long enough to tell him. Finally I couldn't take it any longer. I marched into the den with a hammer, stepped between him and the TV, and with one blow smashed the screen in!"

"Mom, it could have exploded and you could have been hurt."

"I know, but I really didn't care. I just wanted him to listen. You know what your father did?"

"What?"

"You're not going to believe it. He just got up, walked into the bedroom, locked the door, and turned the little TV on to the program he had been watching in the den. He didn't say a word. He just went right back to ignoring me."

This example may seem extreme, but many wives are understandably offended by their husbands' lack of attentiveness. When a wife begins to talk, it almost seems like a mechanism goes off inside the husband's brain that says, "Now's the time to pick up the newspaper, turn on the TV, or start trying to solve the latest problem at work." He may show his inattentiveness by focusing his eyes on something else (like the spot on the tablecloth) or by simply gazing with a blank expression into his wife's eyes while his mind retreats to other playgrounds.

BUT when it's his turn to talk, he not only demands her attention, but expects her to remember every detail, as if the entire conversation were permanently recorded in her mind.

A woman can be deeply hurt by her husband's inattentiveness because it indirectly tells her that he considers her concerns insignificant and unimportant.

Don't despair. Chapter 20 will teach you how to gain his consistent, undivided attention . . . AND IT WORKS.

HE DOESN'T ASSUME ENOUGH
OF THE HOUSEHOLD RESPONSIBILITIES

Mike thought his only responsibility was to bring home the paycheck.

At 6:45 on Friday morning Mike was just beginning to wake up. As he heard the three children yelling at each other, he noticed that his wife, Betty, had left their bedroom door open. "Just once I wish I could sleep till seven," he muttered. Then he yelled, "As long as you're going to leave my door open, can't you at least keep the kids quiet so I can get some rest?"

He didn't stop to think that Betty had been up for an hour, fixing the children's lunches, getting them ready for school, and cooking breakfast at the same time. And he had the nerve to tell her she wasn't even doing that right because she had left his door open and disturbed his sleep. *Why doesn't he get up and help me? Do I need any less sleep than he does? Are the children my sole responsibility?*

If Mike had had the audacity to take it one step further that morning by asking Betty why she never made a hot breakfast for him, she probably would have told him, "If you want a hot breakfast, set your cornflakes on fire!"

Like a lot of men, Mike thinks his responsibility to his family ends when he leaves the office.

And so does Tom.

Jenny, a stewardess, came home half-dead after a grueling four days in the air. As usual, her "welcome-home" consisted of four days' worth of dirty dishes, four days' worth of unemptied ash trays, and four days' worth of mess scattered all over the house. As she walked into the family room, her husband kept watching the 6:00 news and greeted her by saying, "I'm really glad you're home. This place is beginning to look like a dump."

Don't feel you're the only woman with a husband who doesn't help out much around the house. Probably you don't even talk about it with him because he makes you feel like a nag. Quick to remind you how hard he works and how much pressure he bears, he may even make you feel like a failure because you can't do it adequately by yourself.

Chapter 25 should be just the good news you need to help your husband assume a fair share of the household responsibilities. And you won't have to nag at all.

YOUR NEEDS AND DESIRES
ARE ALWAYS SECONDARY TO HIS ACTIVITIES

Fred was always too busy with something else when his wife needed him; but he always found time to watch TV, read the paper, or go out with the boys.

Fred was a wealthy architect who frequently told his wife he needed several days without her interruption to "think through" a design. However, he had no problem taking a break to watch TV, play a round of golf, or go to lunch with his friends.

In fact, even when he wasn't working on a project, he was usually busy doing things he wanted to do, rather than spending time with his wife. She finally *resigned* herself to the fact that she and her world were not important enough to compete for his attention and companionship.

There are at least six ways you can increase your husband's desire to consider your needs. These are discussed in chapter 19.

HE TRIES TO EXPLAIN YOUR HURTS
INSTEAD OF JUST TRYING TO UNDERSTAND
YOUR FEELINGS AND EMPATHIZE WITH YOU

When Sandy put a dent in Mark's new car, she needed his shoulder . . . not his mouth.

Sandy works hard to make a nice home for her husband and their children. One afternoon while pulling their car into the garage, she hit a post. Knowing he would be upset, she was already in tears by the time he came out of the house. Mark could have become her knight-in-shining-armor by putting his arm around her and simply saying, "That's okay, dear. I know how you feel. Forget the car. I'll take care of it. What can I do to make you feel better now?"

Instead, Mark ran up to the car, looked at the dent, looked up at Sandy, and said, "Where did you get your driver's license . . . Sears & Roebuck? Get out of the car and let me park it." Then he went on to tell her how elementary it is to avoid the posts and drive correctly into the garage.

Men are great lecturers on everything from losing weight to taking care of the house. But how can you get a man to step off the podium and learn how to give you his shoulder to lean on while he quietly and gently comforts you? In chapter 22, I reveal three steps you can take to teach and motivate your husband to comfort you in those tense times when he's tempted to lecture or ignore you.

HE ACTS AS IF HE'S SUPERIOR AND YOU'RE INFERIOR

Larry always acted as if he were smarter and his ideas were better than Joann's.

Larry and Joann both graduated from college with honors. His degree was in engineering, hers in home economics. Month after month, Larry said and did things that made Joann feel as if she added no significant intellectual worth to the marriage. He never took her advice, yet he was always quick to express his opinion, even when it related to her areas of expertise. From cooking to room decor, he could always tell her how to do it better. Also, he was usually making comparisons: his major to her major, the difficulty of his work versus the ease of hers, etc. He consistently demonstrated to her that he neither appreciated her qualities nor respected her talents. Essentially, he made her feel like a doormat.

God never created a woman to be a doormat. She is meant to be a vital, life-giving part of the home. Women have many rich, natural qualities not natural to men. Some of these qualities are detailed in the next chapter. Chapters 23 and 24 explain how your husband can gain a genuine respect and admiration for your uniqueness.

HE SHOWS PREFERENCE TO OTHERS OVER YOU

It seemed only natural for Brad to defend John; after all, John was his best friend.

Karen wasn't married to Brad for long before she learned that she should never express her lack of appreciation for any of Brad's friends or relatives. One day Brad came home from work and saw Karen popping a chicken into the oven. He was delighted because that meant he would have time to toss the football with John for a while. On the way out, he told Karen that he was going over to John's house. She replied, "I hate him. You always spend time with him when you come home instead of with me." Brad stopped dead in his tracks and came back in. He told her she should be ashamed of herself after all John had done for them. John's encouragement had kept them together during their courting days, and John's encouragement had helped them through their first difficult months of marriage. Now she was acting immature and childish, attacking the one who had been more like a brother than a friend.

When she started crying, Brad thought she understood the point he was making; he thought she was feeling ashamed. Not quite! His statement said to her loud and clear that he preferred John over her as a person and as a companion. As time went on, she learned by his words, actions, and attitudes that he preferred many people over her: relatives, business associates, friends, secretaries, even casual acquaintances. Never did he defend her to anyone, and yet he always rose to everyone else's defense anytime she voiced a criticism.

You'll be happy to know that now, years later, Brad consistently prefers Karen above all others. Anytime there is a disagreement between her and anyone else (even his mother), he takes her side and tries to help the other person see the matter from Karen's point of view. In fact, some of his close friends can't understand why he has so much fun spending more recreation time with his wife than with them. In chapter 28 I discuss five practical things you can do that will inspire your husband to prefer you above all others.

HE DOESN'T GO OUT OF HIS WAY
TO ADD ROMANCE TO YOUR RELATIONSHIP

Maryann still can't forget "the day" Frank forgot.

Frank was on a business trip, but Maryann knew she would soon be getting a call or a card or a telegram, or maybe even a bouquet of flowers from him, wishing her a happy birthday. When the mail came around noon, she ran to the box, but there was no card from Frank. She was disappointed at first but finally realized that he had probably decided on something more creative. After all, according to his associates, he was one of the most creative men in his company.

By 6:00 in the evening she ruled out flowers and a telegram because it was after business hours. *He must be planning a call,* she thought. She finally fell asleep around midnight—still nothing. The next day she was depressed but figured he would probably be bringing a surprise when he got home. When he came home, his hands were empty. He had completely forgotten about her birthday. She never said anything, but now, after sixteen years of marriage, she still hasn't forgotten. In fact, she confides that he doesn't do any of the romantic things he did when they were younger. Most of the romance, the unexpected "little things," are gone.

Isn't it amazing how some men who are so romantic before marriage can become so unromantic afterward? It almost seems like a piece of their brain was removed when they said "I do." They literally can't remember how to be romantic. When confronted directly, they are quick to question, "Well, what do you want me to do, buy you flowers or something?" As if there were one thing they could do to make everything right. Ironic isn't it . . . you probably didn't even have to give them a suggestion on romance before marriage, but now they need an entire education.

Other actions and comments can inflict hurt, causing deep depression and despair. Some of the deepest pain you feel comes from being criticized for simply responding to some of his negative qualities. For years I thought a very close friend was married to a "nag." Then I realized her nagging was partly a result of his irresponsibility and laziness in so many areas.

Another friend told me she wished she could explain to her husband that he has trained her to yell. It's the only way she can capture his undivided attention, fleeting as it is! I'm happy to say that she learned how to gain his undivided attention on a consistent basis in a way that has brought encouragement to both of them.

The goal of this book is to equip you with positive steps of action that will build and strengthen your relationship and fill it with genuine love that lasts. Don't think it's too late. I've seen too many marriages that were supposedly "lost causes" rebuilt beyond the wives' wildest expectations. And yours doesn't have to be the exception.

Before we can go any further, however, there are several rarely discussed differences between men and women that must be understood in order to have a full appreciation for the principles we'll discuss later.

FOR PERSONAL REFLECTION

The biblical concept of forgiveness has *two* basic thrusts:

1. to release a person from the just guilt and consequences of his/her actions toward us, and
2. to release a person from the basic cause for his/her offensive behavior.

Have you considered the commitment of truly helping your husband learn how he offends you and also helping him become free from whatever causes him to be offensive?

Forgiveness is a lifelong process (Matt. 18:21, 22). How many times do we forgive others?

15

The Hidden Reasons
Men Act the Way
They Do

*"And
let the wife
see to it
that
she respect
her husband."
Ephesians 5:33*

HOW CAN A man say something to his wife that cuts her to the core
and an hour later expect her to respond romantically to his advances?
Why does a man feel obligated to lecture his wife when he sees that
her feelings are hurt? How can a man lie next to his crying wife, giving
her the silent treatment, when she so desperately needs his
compassion and concern?

These situations are not the exception; they are the norm in
American marriages. When couples come to my office for help, they
are usually surprised that I don't fall out of my chair in total shock as
they tell me their feelings. They can't believe their experiences are
common. Every marriage and every person is unique, yet the
problems people experience are practically universal.

Many of the problems couples experience are based on one
simple fact. Men and women are TOTALLY different. The differences—
emotionally, mentally, and physically—are so extreme that if a
husband and wife don't put forth a *concentrated effort* to gain a
realistic understanding of each other, it is nearly impossible for them
to have a happy marriage. A famous psychiatrist once said, "After
thirty years of studying women, I ask myself, 'What is it that they
really want?'" If this was his conclusion, imagine how little your
husband really knows about you!

The purpose of this chapter is to help you understand some
differences between you and your husband that are responsible for

many of the problems within your relationship. This chapter should be encouraging to you because it will enable you to see *why* he does many of the things that hurt you. Chances are, you have always assumed he didn't care about the fact that he hurts you.

The fact is, he is a man, and many of the hurtful and calloused actions you have witnessed are simply the result of his basic nature as a man. This does not mean you have to resign to living with a calloused or insensitive man—quite the contrary. Once you understand some of the basic differences we will discuss, you will be able to help him balance his natural tendencies.

Before we look at precise physiological and psychological differences, let me first draw your attention to the general differences and how they affect your relationship. The best example I can think of to illustrate these differences is to compare the butterfly with the buffalo. The butterfly has a keen sensitivity. It is sensitive even to the slightest breeze. It flutters above the ground where it can get a panoramic awareness of its surroundings. It notices the beauty of even the tiniest of flowers. Because of its sensitivity, it is constantly aware of all of the changes going on around it and is able to react to the slightest variation in its environment. Thus, the butterfly reacts with swiftness toward anything that might hurt it. (Try to catch one without a net sometime.) If a tiny pebble were taped to its wing, the butterfly would be severely injured and eventually die.

The buffalo is another story. It is rough and calloused. It doesn't react to a breeze. It's not even affected by a thirty-mile-an-hour wind. It just goes right on doing whatever it was doing. It's not aware of the smallest of flowers, nor does it appear to be sensitive to slight changes in its environment. Tape a pebble to the buffalo's back and he probably won't even feel it.

The buffalo isn't "rotten to the core" just because he goes around stepping on pretty flowers. In fact, the buffalo's toughness is a tremendous asset. His strength, when harnessed, can pull a plow that four grown men can't pull.

The analogy should be obvious. Your husband is the buffalo (Don't say amen too loudly!) and you're the butterfly. He may tend to "plow" through circumstances, while you "feel" life and your surroundings with much more sensitivity. The "pebble on the butterfly's wing" may take the form of a sarcastic remark, a sharp criticism, or even an indifferent attitude. Whatever it is, it can hurt and even crush you, while he may not even notice what he's done.

The analogy ends in that the buffalo can never take on any of the butterfly's sensitivities, and the butterfly will never benefit from the buffalo's strength.

Such is not the case with your marriage. Your husband CAN learn how to be gentle, sensitive, and romantic, but he probably won't learn by himself; that's why I've written this book . . . to show you how you can help him. You must realize that your husband doesn't understand how much his cutting words or indifferent attitudes actually affect your feelings. He can learn, but you'll need to help him.

Now, let's take a look at some of the differences between men and women. We will discuss mental, emotional, physical, sexual, and intuitive differences. Each section is by no means exhaustive but will at least give you a better understanding of the differences we tend to overlook.

MENTAL/EMOTIONAL DIFFERENCES

Women tend to be more "personal" than men. Women have a deeper interest in people and feelings, while men tend to be more preoccupied with practicalities that can be understood through logical deduction.

Dr. Cecil Osborne says that women tend to become "an intimate part" of the people they know and the things that surround them; they enter into a kind of "oneness" with their surroundings. A man relates to people and situations, but he usually doesn't allow his identity to become entwined with them. He somehow remains apart. That's why a woman, viewing her house as an extension of herself, can become easily hurt when it is criticized by others. (One woman in her midfifties said she enjoys a card or flowers from her husband because they separate her from her identity with her home and family. The gift singles her out as an individual, with an individual's identity and self-worth.)

Because of a woman's emotional identification with people and places around her, she needs more time to adjust to change than a man does. A man can logically deduce the benefits of a change and get "psyched up" for it in a matter of minutes. Not so with a woman. She focuses on the immediate consequences of the change and the difficulties it may involve for her and her family. She needs time to get over the initial adjustment before she can begin to warm up to the advantages of the change.

Steve and Bonney had been struggling to make just enough money to put food on the table. His small business was requiring eighteen hours a day on his part, and she was putting in at least eight hours a day (and was seven months pregnant). Steve flew East to show his business ideas to a multimillionaire. The man was

193

impressed and made Steve a generous offer. Steve could hardly wait to call Bonney and tell her the great news.

It took Steve less than five minutes to accept the offer. It was the only "reasonable" course of action. He called Bonney and told her the news in "logical" order so she could get as excited as he was. He told her, "First, you won't have to work any more. Second, he's giving me 20 percent of the profits (He says I'll be a millionaire in a year.). Third, you won't believe how beautiful it is back here, and he's going to pay all the moving expenses."

Steve was shocked when Bonney began to weep uncontrollably. At first he thought she was crying for joy (I know it's hard to believe that he actually thought that, but remember, men can be like buffalos.).

As soon as Bonney caught a breath between sobs, she had a chance to ask some questions, which Steve considered totally ridiculous. (In fact, he thought her mind had snapped.) She asked questions like, "What about our parents?" and "What about our apartment—I just finished the room for the baby?" With her third question, Steve, with all of his masculine "sensitivity," abruptly terminated the phone call. She had the nerve to ask if he'd forgotten she was seven months pregnant!

After giving her an hour or two to pull herself together, he called her back. She had gained her composure and agreed to move East and leave her parents, her friends, her doctor and childbirth classes, and the nursery she had spent so much time preparing for her first child.

It took Bonney almost eight months to adjust to a change that Steve had adjusted to in minutes. Steve never made his million. The business failed eight days before their baby was born, and they moved again to another place, still 3,000 miles from home. Steve eventually learned his lesson, and today he doesn't make any major change unless Bonney is in total agreement. He tries to give her ample time to adjust to other changes as soon as he can foresee them. However, Steve will never forget the loving sacrifices his wife made so many times. He even realizes that questions like "What about our parents?" or "What about the nursery?" can be more meaningful than money.

PHYSICAL DIFFERENCES

According to Dr. Paul Popenoe, founder of the American Institute of Family Relations in Los Angeles, a book could be filled with the biological differences between the sexes, excluding those differences related to reproduction. Here are a few of these differences:

Men and women differ in every cell of their bodies. This difference in the chromosome combination is the basic cause of development into male or female as the case may be.

Women have greater constitutional vitality, perhaps because of this chromosome difference. Normally, they outlive men by four to eight years (in the U.S.).

Women's basal metabolism is normally lower than men's.

They differ in skeletal structure. Women have a shorter head, broader face, less protruding chin, shorter legs, and longer trunk.

There are also internal differences. Women have a larger stomach, kidneys, liver, and appendix, but smaller lungs than men.

In bodily functions, women have several important ones totally lacking in men—menstruation, pregnancy, lactation. Women's hormones are different and more numerous than men's. These hormonal differences influence behavior and feelings.

The thyroid gland behaves differently in the two sexes. Women's thyroid is larger and more active. Consequently, it enlarges during pregnancy and during menstruation; it makes her more prone to goiter, provides resistance to cold, is associated with the smooth skin, relatively hairless body, and thin layer of subcutaneous fat.

Women's blood contains more water than men's (20 percent fewer red cells). Since the red cells supply oxygen to the body cells, women tire more easily and are more prone to faint. Their constitutional viability is, therefore, strictly a long-range matter. When the working day in British factories was increased from ten to twelve hours under wartime conditions, accidents increased 150 percent among women, but not at all among men.

In brute strength, men are 50 percent above women.

Women's hearts beat more rapidly (80 beats per minute vs. 72 for men). Their blood pressure (10 points lower than men) varies from minute to minute, but they have much less tendency to have high blood pressure—at least until after menopause.

Women's breathing power is significantly lower than men's.

Women withstand high temperatures better than men because their metabolism slows down less.

SEXUAL DIFFERENCES

Women's sexual drive tends to be related to their menstrual cycles, while men's drive is fairly constant. The hormone testosterone is a major factor in stimulating men's sexual desire.

195

Women are stimulated more by touch and romantic words. They are far more attracted by a man's personality, while men are stimulated by sight. Men are usually less discriminating about those to whom they are physically attracted.

While a man needs little or no preparation for the bedroom, a woman needs to be emotionally and mentally prepared, often hours in advance. Her preparation requires tender consideration, while harshness or abusive treatment can easily remove her desire for days at a time. When a woman's emotions have been trampled by her husband, she can almost be repulsed by his advances. Many women have told me that they feel like prostitutes when they're forced to make love while feeling resentment toward their husbands. However, a man may have NO idea what he is putting his wife through when he does this.

These basic differences are the source of many conflicts in marriage. And they usually surface soon after the wedding ceremony. The woman intuitively has a greater awareness of how to develop a loving relationship. Because of her sensitivity, initially she is usually more considerate of his feelings and is enthusiastic about developing a meaningful, multilevel relationship: that is, a relationship having more facets than just a sexual partnership. She wants to be a lover, a best friend, a fan, a homemaker, and an appreciated partner. The man, on the other hand, does not generally have her intuitive awareness of what the relationship should become. He doesn't have an intuitive awareness of how to encourage and love his wife or how to treat her in a way that meets her deepest needs.

Since he doesn't have an understanding of these vital areas through intuition, he must rely *solely* upon the knowledge and skills he has acquired in these areas prior to marriage. Unfortunately, our educational system does not provide an adequate training program for a young man before marriage. His only education may be the example he observed in his home. For many of us, that example might have been insufficient. Most men enter marriage knowing everything about sex and very little about genuine, unselfish love. Your example and help may be your husband's only hope for acquiring the knowledge and skills necessary to love you and your children in the way that you need to be loved.

I am not saying men are more selfish than women. I'm simply saying that at the outset of a marriage a man is not as equipped to *express* unselfish love as a woman is. (You and I both know that women can be every bit as self-centered as men.)

Norman was planning to invest over $50,000 in a business opportunity that was a "sure thing." He had scrutinized the opportunity from every angle and had logically deduced that it couldn't miss. After signing a contract and handing over a check to the other party, he decided it was about time he told his wife about the investment.

Upon hearing a few of the details, she immediately had an uneasy feeling about the deal. When he sensed her uneasiness, Norman became angry and asked her why she felt that way. She couldn't give a logical reason because she didn't have one. All she knew was that it just didn't "sit right." Norman gave in, went back to the other party, and asked for a refund. He was told that he was crazy but was given his money back. A short time later, ALL of the organizers and investors were indicted by the federal government. His wife's intuition had not only saved him $50,000, but it may have kept Norman from going to jail.

What exactly is this "woman's intuition"? It's not something mystical; rather, it is an unconscious perception of minute details that are sometimes tangible, sometimes abstract in nature. Since it is usually an "unconscious" process, many times a woman isn't able to give specific explanations for the way she feels. She simply perceives or "feels" something about a situation or person, while a man tends to follow logical analysis of circumstances or people.

Knowing now that men and women cannot, without an effort, understand each other's differences, I trust that this chapter has given you a little more hope, patience, and tolerance as you endeavor to strengthen and deepen your relationship with your husband. With this in mind, we're ready to begin to discover how you can help your husband become more sensitive.

FOR PERSONAL REFLECTION

List specific ways you differ from your husband in building relationships:
   with each other
   with your children
   with relatives
   with friends
   with your church

16

Helping
Your Husband
Become More Sensitive

*"A gentle answer
turns away
wrath,
but
a harsh word
stirs up
anger."*
Proverbs 15:1

AFTER TWENTY-FIVE YEARS of being single, Sandy was finally marrying the man of her dreams. Sandy had been dating Larry for four years and thought she knew him inside-out. Their courtship had its ups and downs, but all things considered, she knew their love was so strong that living happily ever after would be as natural as waking up in the morning.

The wedding day finally came, and it was everything she had dreamed about—Larry really was Prince Charming. Then came the honeymoon. Almost immediately she began to see a side of Larry she didn't know existed. On the fourth day of the honeymoon, Larry decided Sandy would enjoy seeing where he used to work in the summers during college. So they began their five-mile hike at the 8,000-foot level of the High Sierras (something every woman dreams of doing on the fourth day of her honeymoon). By the time they arrived at their destination, she was exhausted. Since they had to be back at the lodge by dark, they had time for only a short rest.

By the time they got back to the camp, she had a new concept of physical exhaustion. Prince Charming was tired too, so they immediately went to bed. (Actually, he leaped and she crawled.) To her total amazement, the Prince didn't want to go to sleep—he had more exciting things in mind. From that point on, she began to see marriage as a growing conflict between two self-natures that wanted their own needs met before considering the needs of another.

She had entered marriage thinking Larry would be dedicating himself to meeting her needs. After all, he said in his wedding vows that he would love and cherish her for better or for worse, for rich or for poor, in sickness and in health, until death. In his particular vows, which he had written, he even said he committed himself to provide for all of her needs for the rest of his life. But the vows were quickly becoming mere ceremonial words, and her needs were obviously becoming secondary to his.

She thought she could change him through confrontation by demanding in various ways that he become considerate of her needs. After eight years, things had only become worse. She finally resigned herself to the fact that her relationship with Larry would never improve. Larry, of course, was convinced that the marriage problems were Sandy's fault. He considered her demanding and argumentative. She no longer respected or appreciated him as she had when they were going together.

Today, six years later, Larry is no longer the same self-centered, inconsiderate, demanding husband that he was. Sandy's eyes sparkle when she talks about all the ways he shows his love for her daily, the way he considers her desires even above his own needs. He has become the sensitive husband she always dreamed about. He provides all the strength she'll ever need and yet loves her with gentleness and care. WHAT HAPPENED? Simply stated, Sandy began using five important principles whenever she approached Larry about his insensitivity to her.

No one likes to be criticized, regardless of how much truth lies behind the criticism. Whether we are male or female, six or sixty, when someone corrects us, we automatically become defensive. Yet honest communication is vital to marriage. These two basic truths appear contradictory. How do you honestly tell the one you love about something you find displeasing or aggravating without prompting that familiar, defensive glare or indifferent shrug?

> YOUR HUSBAND CAN BECOME MORE SENSITIVE THROUGH *INDIRECT* METHODS, RATHER THAN THROUGH DIRECT CONFRONTATION!

The following five principles outline that indirect approach. A husband is far more apt to receive your comments about his insensitivity when he hears them expressed through these five principles.

1. *Learn to express your feelings through three loving attitudes: warmth, empathy, and sincerity.* These are common words, but what do they mean? Why are they so necessary?

   a. *Warmth* is the friendly acceptance of a person. It's considering a person to be *important* enough to give your time and resources to—to share his concerns, not because he has earned it, but simply because he's a human being.

   b. *Empathy* is the ability to understand and identify with a person's feelings—simply being able to put yourself in his shoes and see a situation from his viewpoint.

   c. *Sincerity* is showing a genuine concern for a person without changing your attitude toward him when circumstances change.

Your husband may resist your help unless he *sees* these three attitudes within you. These are attitudes that *anyone* can develop. (There is growing evidence in the field of psychology that unless psychiatrists are able to develop these three attitudes within their personalities, their patients will tend to resist their help. In fact, many professionals say that a patient can be helped more by a friend who has these three attitudes than he or she can by a professional who lacks them.)

What happened in Sandy's marriage is now happening in countless marriages, and it *can* happen in yours. The exciting fact is that you *don't have to wait* for your husband to change, even though he may be the primary source of most of the problems. You can start the ball rolling by yourself, and the exciting changes discussed in this book *will* come about!

2. *Learn to share your feelings when angry or irritated WITHOUT using "you" statements.*

Dr. Jerry R. Day, a psychologist from Tucson, Arizona, strongly encourages wives to avoid using "you" statements. For example, "You make me sick" or "You're always late" or "You've always got the answers." "You" statements usually cause a man either to dig in and fight or to promptly leave your presence without resolving the issue. Either way, it makes him more determined to have his own way and causes you to lose ground in the situation.

For example, the statement, "You're never home on time" will tend to cause him to reason, "Who is she to set my schedule; the world doesn't revolve around her—I'll come home anytime I want!"

The statement, "Can't you think about *my* feelings for a change?" makes him think, "Her feelings! What about *my* feelings?"

Or the statement, "Can't you get up earlier and take care of the kids just once?" can cause him to think, "I can't believe how hard I work every day for this family, and now she wants me to do her job."

3. *Learn to WAIT until your anger or feelings of irritability have subsided before you begin to discuss a sensitive issue.*

No matter what you say or how you say it, if you're angry or irritated at the time, it probably will provoke a wrong reaction in him. While you're waiting to cool off, either remain quiet or change the subject to one you can talk about. If your husband wants to know why you're quiet or why you're changing the subject, say to him quietly, "I need a little time to think this through so I can better understand *my* feelings."

(I AM NOT saying that you have to eliminate the feelings of anger from your life. I understand how hard it is to deal with anger. However, when those times arise, avoid discussing a sensitive issue in the heat of anger. That way, neither of you will exchange words you will later regret.)

4. *When you have cooled off, replace "you" statements with "I feel" messages.*

Here are a few examples of what I mean:

Instead of confronting your tardy husband as he walks through the door with, "You never come home on time," greet him with an understanding statement like, "Must have been a hairy day" or "I'll bet you're tired." LATER (maybe even a day or two later, at a time when he's relaxed), begin to share your feelings in the context of your uniqueness as a woman. If you can creatively share your feelings in a positive context, that's even better. For example, "You know, there are some things that you do that really make me feel loved and appreciated, like coming home for dinner on time or letting me know if you'll be late. Those are the ways that you show your love for me. I really need that."

Instead of waking your husband with the words, "Can't you get up early and help me take care of the kids just once?" wait until a time when he's not tired and try something like this: "You work so hard for this family. I wish I had your stamina so I wouldn't need your help in the mornings, but I really need your help or I'm afraid I'm not going to have what it takes to meet your needs. And taking care of you is becoming more important to me than ever before." Or . . . "You work so hard for this family, I hate to ask anything else of you. But I do know something you could do that would make me feel extra-special. Often it's difficult for me to handle the pressure of getting the kids ready for school. It would really make me feel like I'm special if you could help me take care of the kids before school."

By learning to share your feelings calmly, you will gradually wear down his tendency to react sharply in anger. It may take time, but if you persist, you will see changes. The principle that "A gentle answer turns away wrath" (Prov. 15:1) really works as long as your soft answer is not said with a self-righteous or sarcastic attitude.

You should keep sharing your feelings until he understands. You may have to tell him over and over again for weeks that something he does makes you feel worthless. At first he'll defend his actions or tell you why your feelings aren't warranted or logical. Just keep telling him that you're not trying to justify your feelings; you're just trying to explain them honestly to him. Whether he thinks they're logical or not doesn't change the fact that you have those exact feelings. You are unique, and even if you were the only person in the whole world with those feelings, he still needs to understand how you feel.

5. *Abandon "I told you so" statements.*

Such statements can take many forms and should be completely eliminated. They reflect arrogance and self-centeredness, and only set your marriage relationship back. Here are some of the more typical ways of saying "I told you so."

"If you had done what I asked you to do . . ."
"I knew it!"
"Just like I thought."
"I only asked you to do one thing and . . ."
"I can't believe you."
"You never listen, do you?"
"Seeeeeeee?"
"You always have to do it your way, don't you?"
"Well, I hope you're satisfied."
"I'm not going to say it. . . ."
"Maybe some day you'll take *my* advice."

List at least five ways that you have said, "I told you so."

1. _____

2. _____

3. _____

4. _____

5. _____

As you begin to apply some of the principles discussed in this chapter, you may encounter a bit of failure and frustration. Some of your noblest efforts may be criticized or ridiculed, but don't give up.

There is an age-old principle I see proved every day in marriages all over the nation: You reap what you sow. If you persist in developing and expressing the qualities in this chapter, you will ultimately see those same qualities developed in your husband.

Dr. Howard Hendricks says studies reveal that children are more likely to follow their parents' ideals and instructions because of what they see their parents *are* rather than because of what they hear their parents *say*. I believe the same principle applies with the husband-wife relationship. When he sees the qualities in your life that you desire for him, he will be motivated to make those same qualities a part of his life.

FOR PERSONAL REFLECTION

Write out ten gentle phrases you could use during irritating times with your mate, such as those times when he uses your shaver or promises to run an errand. Remember Proverbs 15:1.

17

Motivating
Your Husband
To Listen To You

> *"The Lord's bond-servant*
> *must not*
> *be quarrelsome,*
> *but*
> *be kind to all,*
> *able to* teach ...*"*
> *(emphasis mine).*
> *2 Timothy 2:24*

LOIS HAD A pretty good marriage by today's standards. She considered her husband a good provider and an excellent father. However, the romance had faded from their marriage, and her feelings of affection toward Mark were very inconsistent. She decided she would do all she could to make her marriage what she wanted it to be. She began reading various books on what she could do to be a better wife and was gaining enthusiasm each day.

After several weeks, she stumbled across two books written for men, telling them what they could do to strengthen their marriages. She brought them home for Mark and decided to give them to him after dinner. The moment of truth finally came. She walked over to Mark with a sweet smile and said, "Honey, I've really been working hard lately to learn how to become a better wife so I can be what you deserve to have. I found two books that can help a husband better understand his wife. Would you read them for me?"

Mark gave her a condescending look and said, "We'll see."

Not giving up at that sure sign of defeat, she said, a little more defensively, "I've been reading a lot of books lately and really working hard to make our marriage better. This is the least you can do."

Mark gave excuse number four on man's "Ten Most Widely Used Excuses" list. He simply said, "Sweetie, you know how busy I am these days. I'll really try when my schedule slows down." She knew that could be a while, because in two years of marriage she had never seen his schedule "slow down."

But there was something Lois could have said that would have motivated Mark to read both books within three nights. In fact, he probably would have taken time off work to finish them the next day.

This principle is not given to be used as a manipulative tool. Manipulation usually results in anger, hurt, worry, fear, and other negative emotions, but genuine love causes joy and fulfillment. Manipulation can't wait to get, and love can't wait to give. If your motive for using this principle is based on love, on enriching your husband's life, it can help you enter into a more loving, attentive conversation with him. You'll be able to search out his deepest needs and selflessly dedicate yourself to meeting those needs.

It's called the "salt principle." Salt makes people thirsty, and the goal of this principle is to create a thirst for constructive conversation in which both you and your husband can learn about each other's needs.

Simply stated, the principle is this:

NEVER COMMUNICATE INFORMATION YOU CONSIDER TO BE IMPORTANT WITHOUT FIRST CREATING A BURNING CURIOSITY WITHIN THE LISTENER.

This principle is so easy to learn that even a child can master it. One day my seven-year-old daughter came running into the house crying. I called her over and asked what was wrong. She told me that her little girlfriend never listened to her. Every time Kari would start to tell her girlfriend something, the friend would interrupt and start talking. Kari told me she felt like she didn't have anything important to say because her friend would never listen.

I asked Kari if she would like to learn a way that would make her friend want to listen to her. She was all ears as she hopped up into my lap, and I asked her, "What were some of the things you wanted to say to your friend?"

She replied, "I wanted to tell her what I did with my dollhouse, but she didn't want to hear."

I told Kari that first she had to get her friend's attention with a statement or two that would make her friend want to hear more. She would have to make these statements with *enthusiasm*. We decided she could say something like, "You won't believe *what I did* to my new

208

dollhouse!" Then she would pause and come back with a second statement, "My *parents* couldn't even believe what I did with it."

When I came home from work the following evening, Kari was all smiles. She told me that our plan had worked so well that her girlfriend not only listened to her, but came over and played with the dollhouse.

Obviously, for adults the situations are more complicated, although the principle remains the same. Arouse their curiosity and you've got their attention!

Faye was worried because Jack was too busy to spend time with their son Randy.

Jack's work schedule kept him so busy that he spent very little time with Randy when he was home. Faye realized how much their son needed him, but Jack was usually too preoccupied to listen. Faye decided to give the salt principle a try, and here's how it went:

Faye: (salt)	I heard some very discouraging news from school today about Randy.
Jack:	Oh, no, what was it?
Faye: (more salt)	I don't know what we're going to do about it . . . I'm really worried.
Jack:	Well, what is it?
Faye: (big salt)	Unless you can help out, it will probably end up *costing us* a lot of money.
Jack:	Faye, what are you talking about?
Faye: (The words "special help" begin to resalt for the next thing she's going to say.)	Randy's teacher called and said Randy has a reading problem. Unless he gets *special help*, it could handicap him for the rest of his education.
Jack:	What do you mean "special help"?
Faye:	The teacher explained that if you or I didn't do something about it, we would probably have to pay a lot of money to have it corrected later. She said the longer it goes uncorrected, the worse it will become.
Jack:	What could we do now?

Faye: (salt)	Well, there's not too much I can do, but she did say there was something you could do.
Jack:	What's that?
Faye: (more salt)	In fact, she said if you would do it consistently, it would provide just what he needs to whip the problem. I told her you were very busy and I didn't know if you could find the time. . . .
Jack:	I'll make the time . . . what is it?
Faye:	She said that the basis of the problem involves motor skills. If you could do something like beginning to throw the football with him consistently, his hand/eye coordination would increase and she would be able to help him get his reading up to par.

Today, four years later, Jack still plays football with Randy. Jack not only enjoys their time together, but he also has the satisfaction of knowing that he has done something to help Randy in school that no one else could have done. All of this was a result of Faye's taking the time to creatively communicate a genuine need using the salt principle.

Knowing that you need to arouse his curiosity is one thing, but actually doing it is quite another, right? You're probably wondering, "So now what? How do I apply the salt principle to my circumstances?"

Let's examine the principle a little further to see what it really means.

HOW TO CATCH YOUR HUSBAND'S
INTEREST AND KEEP IT

1. *The first step is to clearly identify the need or concern you wish to communicate to your husband.*

In our first illustration, Lois wanted Mark to learn more about what a woman needs from a man, and, more precisely, she wanted him to read the two books she had just purchased for him on the subject. In the second illustration, Faye wanted Jack to begin spending more time with Randy.

2. *The second step is to identify related areas that are of high interest to your husband.*

This is where Lois failed and Faye succeeded. Lois simply communicated what she was interested in (a happier marriage) but failed to relate her interest to any of her husband's interests. He could not see that he needed any help in becoming a better husband, so becoming a better husband was not of particular interest to him.

Faye, on the other hand, succeeded on this point. She knew her husband's business schedule was of greater interest to him than spending time with Randy. However, she also knew from past discussions that he was extremely interested in their son's education. She identified that interest and remembered Randy's teacher's comments about his reading problem. Since a big part of Randy's problem was his hand/eye coordination, she figured anything Jack could play with Randy to increase his hand/eye coordination would help solve the problem. And then she thought of football. She saw how she could relate Jack's interest (Randy's education) to her interest (wanting to see Jack and Randy have more time together) and also see Randy's reading problem corrected.

Lois didn't have to fail on this point with Mark. Having been married only two years, Mark has told me that his sexual appetite is much greater than Lois's (which is usually the case). I am sure Lois was aware of Mark's high interest in increasing her sexual desires. This is the area of *high interest* she could have used to increase his interest in reading the two books. In the next steps I'll show you how she could have accomplished this.

3. *Using his area of high interest, share enough information to stimulate his curiosity to hear more.*

Since Lois knew of Mark's never-ending physical drive, she could have started with the statement, "I can't believe these two books! I began reading them while you were at work, and I started to get so turned-on I had to put them down. I was really wishing you were home so we could make love."

Knowing Mark, I guarantee that she would have had his undivided attention. Even the Super Bowl would have been turned off at this point.

4. *Add a little more salt. Don't answer his response to your first dose of salt; rather, pause and build his curiosity even more.*

Mark probably would have responded to the first dose with one of the following:

—You're kidding. What did it say?
—Really? Let me see it.
—It's not too late. I'm home now.

Now Lois applies her second dose of salt, *without* giving any relief to Mark's budding curiosity, with a statement like this: "They really are unbelievable. They tell a man just what he needs to do to prepare his wife mentally and emotionally for sex. Those authors really understand what it takes to turn me on."

5. *Use a short question to gain a commitment to his pursuit of your interest or to teach him what you're trying to communicate.*

Lois, at this point, can gain a commitment from Mark to read the first book by asking him one of several short questions: "Have you ever read a book like this that tells you the five things that women can't resist?" or "Have you ever read about the five things you can do that turn me on?"

Lois's goal was not to turn her husband into a manipulator of her sexual desires, but to get him to read two books that would encourage him to do the things that would build up their emotional relationship. She knew the "five things" would motivate her husband to treat her with greater tenderness and respect which, in turn, would help her to be more sexually responsive.

6. *After you have taken these five steps, if he still doesn't show sufficient interest or commitment, keep adding salt.*

Lois could further salt with a statement like, "I'm glad you haven't learned any of these yet; my sexual drive would probably get so strong we'd never get any work done around here."

As I said at the beginning of this chapter, the salt principle is irresistible if used correctly. Every aspect of loving and communicating can be used either beneficially or detrimentally—the salt principle is no different. To use it effectively, there are a few things you definitely want to avoid.

"WHAT NOT-TO-DO" WHEN SALTING!

1. *Do not begin the conversation with a plea or request for his attention or time.*

When you are going to use the salt principle, never start the conversation with statements like the following:

—Can I see you for a minute?
—I really need to talk to you!
—Can we talk about something really important a little later?
—I've been waiting a long time to talk to you. Can we *please* talk tonight?

Introductory statements like these usually generate a negative response because some husbands can't visualize setting aside time "just to talk." Chances are, you'll get hurt from his lack of interest. The dialogue below shows a typical example:

Alice: I would really like to talk to you about a few things after dinner tonight. Okay, dear?

Fred: There's a game on tonight that I've really been counting on seeing. Besides, I've got some work to catch up on.

Alice: Well, how about when you're done? This is really important.

Fred: Look, I'd like to talk, but it's been a tough day and I'm really tired. Maybe tomorrow.

Alice: There's always something else . . . you never want to spend time with me. . . .

And from there the fight is on. Instead of using an introductory statement, start out with a statement that creates curiosity.

2. *Do not start your conversation with your main concern or your solution.*

For example, if Faye had opened her conversation with the statement below, she would have evoked a different response from Jack.

Faye: Dear, Randy needs more of your time, and throwing a football would help his reading problem. Could you start playing football with him?

Jack: I'd love to play with my son, but I just don't have time. You know my schedule.

3. *Don't try to persuade him with your first few statements.*

Often women tend to think the only way they can get their insensitive husbands to do something is to shove them into action with a strong statement or threat. This may work for the short-range, but it can cause him to hear "Wolf! Wolf!"

Faye: Dear, you have to start spending more time with Randy or else there're going to be real problems.

Jack: *Don't* tell me what I have to do. I don't have time to play with him and do my job too. Why don't I quit work, and I'll stay home all day? Then I'll have *lots* of time to play with him.

DON'T GIVE UP! SALTING REALLY WORKS, EVEN WHEN A PERSON KNOWS WHAT YOU ARE DOING

If you don't succeed the first time you use the salt principle, don't give up. You may have to use it several times before you become skilled at it, but given time and practice, it will work! I've never met anyone who couldn't do it as long as he or she just kept trying. Surprisingly, it works even if the other person knows what you are doing.

Use the following exercise to help you tailor this principle to some of your immediate needs and concerns. Also, the principle of "salting" will be more solidified in your own thinking if you take some time to do this.

1. *List four of your current needs or concerns that you would like your husband to understand more fully.*

(For example: a material need, your feeling about someone, an activity you would like to do with him, or a "hurt" that you want him to understand.)

1. _____

2. _____

3. _____

4. _____

EXAMPLE

1. *My feelings about his mother*
2. *My fear of moving again*
3. *My need for understanding instead of lectures*
4. *My need for more companionship with him*

2. List five areas that are of very high interest to your husband.

(For example: hobbies, business projects, career and related interests, religious concerns, friends, sports, TV programs.)

1. _____

2. _____

3. _____

4. _____

5. _____

EXAMPLE

1. *Success in business*
2. *Sexual fulfillment*
3. *Concern for the total welfare of the children*
4. *Acceptance among the men at his office*
5. *Relationship with God*

3. *Write down at least two statements or questions that would create curiosity about one of your four concerns or needs.*

Try to relate it to one of his five areas of high interest.

1. _____

2. _____

EXAMPLE

1. *Do you know what psychologists say is the greatest determining factor in the emotional stability of a child?*
2. *If you and I would decide to work on this together, not only would our children gain emotional stability, but I would probably develop a stronger sexual desire just by being around you.*

She is talking about her need for companionship *and* she is relating it to two important areas of his life—his concern for their children's welfare and his desire for greater sexual fulfillment. In this example, the wife had remembered that she had read that children become better balanced when they see consistent affection and warmth between their parents. She tied all of this together and created two "salty" statements.

The more you use the salting principle, the more effective you will become in applying it. You'll find that it not only works with your husband, but with anyone whom you want to listen to you with undivided attention.

FOR PERSONAL REFLECTION

What example did Jesus give us of the salt principle? He never wasted His time sharing important truths with people who were not interested. He even taught against teaching truth to the disinterested (Matt. 7:6). Jesus used parables and questions to arouse curiosity.

18

Motivating Your Husband To Change

"If any of them
(husbands)
are disobedient
to the word,
they may be won
without a word
by the behavior
of their wives"
(emphasis mine).
1 Peter 3:1

HOW MANY TIMES have you tried to tell your husband that you need to be loved emotionally during the day-to-day routine if he wants you to enter wholeheartedly into intimacy with him? You need gentleness, affection, thoughtfulness, and romance *before* you go to the bedroom if you are to give of yourself unreservedly *in* the bed. In the same manner, he must see certain qualities in your life that make him *aware* of your needs and receptive to your feelings before he can respond to those needs and feelings.

Because a man may enter marriage with such a low level of knowledge and skill to meet a woman's needs, it is essential that his wife teach him what her needs and feelings are and, ultimately, show him how he can meet those needs. He becomes far more receptive to learning about your needs and how he can fulfill them when *six qualities* are present in your life.

All six are probably present in your character to one degree or another and, if they are nourished, they will grow stronger and have a greater influence on your personality. As this growth takes place, your husband will have a much greater desire to learn how to love you in the way you need to be loved.

When you were in school, you may have noticed that some courses were much more enjoyable than others simply because they were taught by an instructor you liked. It was easier and more enjoyable to learn from teachers who possessed certain character qualities.

When the qualities of courage, persistence, gratefulness, calmness, gentleness, and unselfish love are present in a person's character, it is easier to receive his or her words and to follow his or her instruction or example. This is no less true for your marriage. These qualities must be present in some degree before your husband will really want to learn from you.

COURAGE

Courage is the inner commitment to pursue a worthwhile goal without giving up hope.

Many women have ALREADY given up hope that their marriages will ever be any better. When a woman's hope for a better marriage has faded, her attractiveness to her husband diminishes and the "life" of the relationship gradually declines.

Regardless of how discouraged you may be, however, it is *never* too late to rekindle your hope and bring renewed life into your relationship with your husband.

Joyce and Greg had been married for three years. Joyce was pregnant with their first child when she discovered Greg was seeing another woman. Her affections had already begun to fade before she found out about the other woman, and when his affair came to light, her affections died completely. Their relationship went from love, to hate, to indifference.

One day at lunch she broke the usual silence and asked Greg what he was thinking about. With two words he shattered what little hope she had left. "About her," he responded. After he went back to work, she told God that she had no hope left. But she didn't stop there. She went on to pray that if He could give her hope or give her a new love for Greg, she would receive it.

To her surprise, she found herself doing kind little things for Greg, even though she didn't like him. Within three weeks, Greg began to notice such a change in Joyce that he found himself more attracted to her than to the other woman. He even felt ashamed for the way he had been treating her. He broke off his relationship with the other woman and joined Joyce in her growing commitment to build a more fulfilling relationship with each other and with Christ. For Joyce, courage began when she told God that she was *willing* to receive a new hope and love for Greg.

Both Joyce and Greg tell me that their relationship now is so much deeper they can't even imagine how empty it used to be.

The *first step* toward increasing your courage is to commit yourself to *pursue actively* a more fulfilling relationship with your husband and to build a better marriage. One major roadblock to a happy marriage is maintaining unrealistic views of what a good marriage is. These unrealistic views begin in childhood and culminate with the wedding ceremony. That's why psychologists say that when you and your husband said "I do," SIX people were united in marriage.

On the bride's side stood
1. The person you thought you were
2. The person he thought you were
3. The person you ACTUALLY were

On the groom's side stood
1. The person he thought he was
2. The person you thought he was
3. The person he ACTUALLY was

The growth and joy in marriage come from combining these six different expectations into a unified, realistic relationship. And, yes, it *is* possible, and it *can* be done. That's what learning to love is all about, and that's exactly what you are learning as you read this book. Couples who've been married for years have as much to gain in their relationships as do newlyweds.

One newlywed recently told me that when she married her husband she thought she was marrying one of the last sensitive men alive. Within a year, she learned he was not at all as sensitive or "naturally romantic" as she had thought. She thought he had sneaked out and had brain surgery that altered the part of the brain that affected behavior. Before marriage, it seemed as if his considerate ways of caring for her flowed naturally from his inner being. Now she is disappointed and even irritated that such actions are not a natural part of his manner. In fact, he has to stop and think about how to carry out even the smallest acts of kindness. When she voices her discontent, he gives her a puzzled look and asks, "What am I supposed to do?" Like most women, she is further irritated because she feels, "If I have to tell him what to do, it takes all of the meaning out of it!"

I've heard her story repeated hundreds of times. That's why it is important to have a clear mental picture of what constitutes a good marriage. Rather than having me tell you what I think a good marriage is, let me do something a little different. Which of the following would make your marriage what *you* would like it to be? Check as many as you like.

My marriage would be much better if my husband . . .

☐ would make me feel respected and more important than his work, his relatives, his friends, and his pastimes.

☐ would really try to understand my feelings and needs and learn how to respond lovingly to them.

☐ would genuinely desire and seek forgiveness when he hurts my feelings or the children's feelings.

☐ would consistently feel and express sincere appreciation for who I am and what I do.

☐ would recognize my sensitivity as a strength and welcome my encouragement for him to become more sensitive.

☐ would understand my unique physical limitations and enthusiastically take an active part in dealing with the children and household responsibilities.

☐ would allow me to lean on him emotionally for comfort when discouraged or distressed, without criticism or lectures.

☐ would respect me enough to *welcome* my opinions and advice when making decisions that affect our family.

☐ would want to be my best friend and would want me to be his.

☐ would not try to impose values and ideals upon me that he is not applying himself, eliminating any double standard.

Each one of these descriptions is a worthwhile *attainable* goal. In the chapters that follow, each is discussed in detail. You will be given precise steps of action that you can begin to take immediately to make these goals a reality in your marriage.

While the first step toward increasing your courage is to commit yourself to an active pursuit of a better marriage, the *second step* is to commit yourself to *endure the pressure* that may come from your husband as you begin to pursue a better marriage, keeping in mind that his desire to enrich your marriage is probably far less at this point than yours.

Shortly after their wedding, Denise was shocked at the difference between Jerry's behavior as a husband and as a boyfriend. She became discouraged, but after joining a group of couples with whom I meet, she made a commitment to pursue a better marriage. For the first few months, she encountered increased pressure and resistance from Jerry. One day when she was sick, she tried to share her feelings of weakness with him, telling him how much she needed his comfort and help around the house. His offhand reply was, "Oh, come on, gut it up . . . you can do it." He went on to imply that his mother never acted that way when *she* was sick.

Jerry didn't change overnight. On another occasion, Denise (a schoolteacher) asked him to visit her school to see how she and her students had decorated the classroom. It had taken a lot of work and creativity on her part, and she was really proud of the results. Once again, Prince Charming rose to the occasion by sarcastically saying, "I don't ask you to come see my office. Why make me come see your classroom? Besides, if you've seen one classroom, you've seen them all."

But the story didn't end with Jerry's sarcasm. Because Denise had made the second commitment, "to endure the pressure that comes from pursuing a better marriage," Jerry has changed. He has entered into the same commitment to build a better marriage. He is becoming more and more sensitive to Denise and now takes an active part in assuming many of the household responsibilities. That alone has helped draw them much closer. He's beginning to respect Denise, her unique qualities, and her unique sensitivities.

You may or may not encounter pressure or resistance as you begin a more active pursuit of a better marriage, but it's important that you commit yourself to endure any pressure that may come. If you wait for him to initiate a better relationship, it may be a long, long wait.

PERSISTENCE

Persistence means continuing to pursue a goal until it is achieved.

For years, Ken's way of dealing with Carla's hurt feelings was to give her a lecture on or a rational explanation for why she was hurting and how she could stop. These ranged in length from the brief "you're too sensitive" all the way to the twenty-minute complex analysis of her entire situation. Carla always assumed it was just his way of trying to tell her he was superior by making her feel at fault. If someone didn't talk to her at the party and she deduced they didn't like her anymore, Ken would simply tell her, "Oh, they were just too busy . . . you're just taking it too seriously." If she had an argument with his mother, his mother got his understanding while Carla got comments like, "You overreacted," or "I can't believe how you hurt mom's feelings."

After Carla realized that men have to learn how to respond to women's feelings, she began to tell Ken each time she needed comfort, "Don't lecture me . . . just hold me and understand." This didn't do a bit of good the first six or seven times she tried it. She still got his lectures (although they kept getting shorter). Finally Ken (genius that he is), realized that Carla was simply asking him not to preach at her but to comfort her with silent gentleness. He tried it once and noticed a completely different response in Carla. She recovered from her hurt feelings much faster than when he tried to explain away her feelings.

Ken told me that although it was hard not to lecture the first few times, his quiet response was so much more effective that it has now become natural. If Carla had tried to help him change by sharing her feelings only once, nothing would have happened. But she persisted, and now both she and Ken are enjoying the benefits of her persistence.

Several years ago I met a man who had been very successful in his work with teenagers. He had influenced thousands of young people in a positive way. When I asked him the secret of his success, I was surprised by his answer. He said, "It's simple. For every 200 ideas I try, one works!" One of the teenagers from his youth group, Jill, followed his example after she married.

Since the first week of their marriage, Jill had noticed how Dave always showed preference for his family over hers. When they moved across the country for Dave to attend graduate school, she thought she would be free of rating second to his family. Unfortunately, 2,000 miles wasn't far enough. Phone calls, letters, or visits with the family continued to add fuel to the fire. Whenever Jill found fault with any of Dave's family, Dave would always rise to their defense. Time after time she would try to tell Dave how deeply it bothered her that he preferred his family over her, but Dave always defended himself.

A few years after graduate school, Dave finally had the chance to relocate near their hometown. He thought Jill would be thrilled because it meant living near her family too. He couldn't understand why she cried when he told her about the opportunity. Once again she explained that she was afraid to live near his family because of his preference for them. As usual, he defended himself and couldn't see it from her viewpoint.

On vacation they visited their hometown. As they were leaving his family, he asked her, "Tell me one more time why you don't want to move back?" She explained once more, and it finally got through. Since then, he has had many opportunities to demonstrate his preference for Jill. She now feels so secure that she is looking forward to the possibility of returning home. Once again, the wife's gentle persistence brought lasting benefit to her and her husband.

GRATEFULNESS

Gratefulness is a sincere appreciation for the benefits you have gained from others.

A survey was recently taken among several thousand workers, asking what their employers could do to motivate them to work harder. The employers were amazed that the number-one response had nothing to do with income or benefits. The majority of workers stated that *the one thing* their employers did to make them want to work harder was to *express appreciation* for their individual efforts.

If gratefulness motivates a person to try harder on the job, why won't it motivate your husband to try harder in the home? The answer is, IT WILL! Gratefulness expressed through praise is one of the highest motivations for men. If you want your relationship with your husband to become more fulfilling, it is essential that you develop a grateful attitude.

Praise expressed from a grateful heart is essential to our walk with God. We actually enter into His presence through praise (Ps. 100:4); and our faith in Him is proven through our willingness to thank Him in all circumstances, no matter how destructive we may think they could be (1 Thess. 5:18; Rom. 8:28). We haven't learned to walk with Christ until we learn to say "thank You, Lord, for 'that.' I don't understand it, but I trust that You can work it for my good because I love You."

Kathy and John had been married for eighteen years. When Kathy came to my office, she was distressed because John was an alcoholic. In spite of the problems that resulted from his alcoholism, she was still committed to pursuing a better marriage. I told her that gratefulness expressed through praise could provide a powerful motivation for John to overcome his problem. We also talked about the other qualities discussed in this chapter, and how she could develop them in her life. When she left my office, she had an enthusiastic desire to begin practicing some of the steps immediately.

Several weeks later there was a knock at my door, and when I opened it I had to catch my breath. To my surprise John had come up to my office to talk with me. He told me that since his wife had come to see me there had been so many changes in her life that she was like a new person. He went on to say, "She's become so loving and appreciative, I just can't go on hurting her anymore. Would you help me?"

This couple's story graphically illustrates the power of these inner qualities and, more specifically, the power of gratefulness to motivate a man to want a better relationship. You may be wondering what qualities Kathy found to be praiseworthy in her alcoholic husband. She used her greatest strength to detect these qualities.

It should be evident by now that a woman's greatest strength is her sensitivity. Sensitivity can become your best friend in your effort to detect admirable qualities in your husband. When I first mentioned to Kathy that she needed to express gratefulness to John, she gave me a bewildered look and said, "What's there to be grateful for? Do you know what it's like to live with an alcoholic?" I explained to her that there are many positive qualities that can have negative expressions. We talked about a few of her husband's negative traits in order to detect some positive qualities she could begin to praise.

The most obvious problem she could think of was his self-pity. Self-pity can be a negative expression of compassion, so I asked Kathy if she had ever sensed that John was concerned for the welfare of others. Her eyes lit up immediately. She said she had always noticed how quick he was to show concern for those who had misfortunes.

I asked her if she had ever noticed whether he was sneaky about hiding a bottle or getting away for a drink. Once again she smiled. Craftiness is often a negative expression of creativity. (One of the most creative men I ever read about had been a thief for more than twenty years.) When I explained that craftiness and creativity are often different expressions of the same characteristic, she told me that John's job required a great deal of creativity. In a matter of minutes we had picked out two qualities for which she could begin to praise him. In order for her praise to be sincere, she would need to use her sensitivity to detect the proper times and opportunities to express praise. (NOTE: The following list may help you use some of your husband's negative traits to discern his admirable qualities.)

Negative Behavior	Positive Characteristics
Slow	Cautious, attentive to details
Careless	Easy-going, lenient
Fussy	Careful, likes to do things right or "first class"
Can't say "No"	Peace-loving, gentle with people, compassionate, helpful
Talks too much	Thorough, expressive
Too strict	Disciplined, self-controlled, thorough
Pushy	Determined, aggressive, persuasive

DEVELOPING A GRATEFUL ATTITUDE

The *first step* in developing a genuine attitude of gratefulness is becoming aware that the benefits in your life have come from two main sources: other people and God. When confronted with this idea, one man said that it simply was not true. He started in business with nothing and had become extremely wealthy. He said, "No one ever gave me anything." He was asked how far he could have gone in business if he hadn't learned to read or write. His obvious reply was, "Not far." Then he lowered his eyes and acknowledged that someone else had offered him an invaluable asset that he had used most of his life. Before he knew it, he could think of dozens of people from whom he had received countless benefits.

If you stop to think about it, there are very few benefits in your life for which you can take sole credit. Before going any further, take time to complete the following exercise.

Developing Gratefulness
Exercise #1

In column A list ten of the most treasured benefits in your life. (For example: your children, education, talents, material possessions, abilities.) In column B list the name of at least one person who contributed to the corresponding benefit listed in column A.

COLUMN A	COLUMN B
Ex. My children	Ex. Husband, Dr. Shaughnessy, Nurse
1. _____	1. _____
2. _____	2. _____
3. _____	3. _____
4. _____	4. _____
5. _____	5. _____
6. _____	6. _____
7. _____	7. _____
8. _____	8. _____
9. _____	9. _____
10. _____	10. _____

The *second step* in developing a grateful attitude is learning to minimize your expectations of your spouse. Expectations can be one of the most destructive forces in your marriage. They can bring unnecessary disappointment and discouragement to you and your husband.

Imagine that you have no money in savings and are suddenly hit with a hospital bill of $2,000. Banks and finance companies turn you down, but a friend agrees to give you a loan. You promise to pay it back in six months. Six months later when you have just saved enough to pay your friend back, you are hit with another bill. So, you spend what you've saved and have nothing left to pay back the debt. Ten days later your friend calls and asks, "Where's the money?" You explain what happened, and she says, "You promised to pay me back in six months, so get me the money," and she hangs up. Chances are, you'd look for the nearest bottle of Pepto-Bismol.

The next day your friend calls back to ask if you have the money yet, saying she needs it desperately. When you tell her that you still don't have it, she cries and says she's going to call every day until you send the money. By this time, not even Pepto-Bismol will help.

And yet, this is the position in which you place your husband with your expectations. You are constantly holding a debt over his head that he cannot pay because he does not have the resources.

For eight years Ben had been living under the weight of Sue's expectations. Each time he bought her something, either it wasn't enough or it was too late. When he would finally fulfill her expectation, she would express the attitude, "It's about time." He felt like no matter what he did he could never please her. Then Sue stopped expressing her expectations and began expressing appreciation for *any* attempt Ben made to please her. Ben didn't realize what was happening at first, but after a couple of months it dawned on him that he couldn't remember the last time Sue had asked for anything, especially furniture for their home. He was so encouraged by her change in attitude that he bought a whole houseful of furniture, exceeding any of her former expectations.

Ben wasn't the only one who found a new joy as a result of Sue's diminished expectations. Sue discovered that fewer expectations increased her happiness because she allowed her husband the freedom to surprise her.

The best way I know of decreasing your expectations is to change your focus from your husband to God. Psalm 62:1–2 gives us the freedom to expect life from God alone; and Philippians 4:19 assures us that our God will supply all our *needs* through His riches in glory in Christ Jesus. (Those two verses have allowed Norma to take her focus off me meeting her needs and put it onto God meeting her needs.) As we rest in Him, we become free to help those around us because we're not expecting anything from human sources, but only from the Lord.

By diminishing your expectations, you can free your husband of a burden that you force him to bear, and you can free yourself from unnecessary disappointment. Diminishing your expectations does not mean getting rid of your needs or wants. That is humanly impossible. It simply means eliminating your time limit and preconceived ideas about when and how those expectations will be fulfilled. The following exercise may help you keep tabs on your expectations.

Developing Gratefulness
Exercise #2

Make a list of your expectations under each category.

Your Material Needs

Ex. New Sofa

_____

_____

_____

_____

His Attitudes

Ex. Impatient with children

_____

_____

_____

_____

Your Emotional Needs

Ex. Praise for a good meal

_____

_____

_____

_____

His Habits

Ex. Throws dirty clothes on floor

_____

_____

_____

_____

The expectations you listed above are like bombs set to destroy your relationship. The only way to deactivate them is to *get rid of the timer.*

CALMNESS

Calmness is an inner peace that allows you to respond quietly to a stressful situation without fear.

Let's go back to the analogy of the butterfly and the buffalo. The butterfly is delicate and sensitive even to the slightest breeze. The buffalo, on the other hand, isn't even bothered by a thirty-mile-an-hour wind. Although your sensitivity is one of your greatest strengths (because it allows you to "feel" things so much more intensely), it can also be a source of discouragement and despair if you do not balance it with calmness.

I'm not even beginning to imply that you should do anything to reduce your sensitivity. In fact, if your husband has succeeded in making you more calloused, it is important that you regain the sensitivity you have lost. The more sensitive you are, the more beauty, gentleness, tenderness, and "feeling" you can bring to your family and your environment.

At the same time, however, because you are aware of what's going on around you, you may easily react to the slightest changes. When we over-react to a situation, we sometimes can cause greater problems than the ones to which we are reacting.

With a car full of noisy Girl Scouts, Jenny was driving on a rain-slick highway, taking them to their meeting. A cat started to run out in front of the car; Jenny over-reacted and swerved radically to avoid it. The car started fishtailing back and forth across the highway until it slammed into a ditch. Several children were injured, but she had missed the cat. A minor adjustment with the wheel would have enabled her to miss the cat and still maintain control of the car, but she over-reacted to the situation.

The same thing can happen on your "emotional" highway. Your sensitivity enables you to "see" many potential problems that your husband may overlook. You may sense your daughter's hurt feelings when your husband uses harsh words to correct her, while he may be totally unaware that he has even wounded her. Correctly used, your sensitivity can enable you to be aware of your daugther's reaction and, in the right way at the right time, to provide her with the needed comfort. Eventually, it will even enable you to teach your husband how to detect such hurts and, by example, teach him how to bring healing.

The wrong way to use your sensitivity in this situation would be to quickly over-react by criticizing your husband in front of your daughter or by defending her action which provoked his correction in the first place. The first step in developing a calm attitude is to *control* your tendency to over-react.

After thirteen years of marriage, Frank and Evelyn were finally going to have their dream trip to a South Sea island. They were especially excited because part of their expenses were being paid.

Three weeks before the trip, Frank learned that the expenses would be far greater than he had anticipated. The meals would be especially costly, but he didn't worry about it because he figured, "How much can we eat anyway?"

When Frank called Evelyn and casually mentioned this, Evelyn did not take it quite as calmly. She knew from past experience that when it came to vacations, Frank was so tight with his wallet that he squeaked. She immediately envisioned all the other couples going to fancy restaurants and Polynesian luaus, while she and Frank would sit in their room feasting on peanut butter sandwiches and a carton of milk. *Without any explanation of how she was feeling,* her reply to Frank was, "I really don't think I want to go."

In the past, Frank would have responded to such a statement with, "If that's the way you feel, we'll cancel the trip." An argument would have followed, and her *over-reaction* probably would have cost them the trip of their dreams. However, this did not happen. Frank was learning to be sensitive to his wife, so he responded to her statement with the question, "Why do you feel that way?" Evelyn was able to *calmly express* her concerns, and Frank assured her that if she would like, she could carry the money designated for meals and they would dine wherever she liked.

Over-reacting not only decreases your husband's desire to meet your needs, but it also forces you to go through many problems that could otherwise be avoided.

The second step in balancing your sensitivity with calmness is to realize that the relationship principles discussed in this book *will* bring about a change. These principles have worked for thousands of couples, including many whose situations appeared very hopeless. At this point, you and many other readers may be saying, "There is no situation more hopeless than mine." You may be right, but see if yours is worse than Mike's and Gail's.

The only way to describe Mike and Gail's marriage was "who hates who the most?" They only stayed together because they didn't have enough money to live apart. They had no feelings of love toward their two children. They viewed them as two mistakes who came along and messed up their lifestyle. Each day after work Mike would stop at a bar, meet another woman, go out and get drunk, and come home late at night. Each night he and Gail would have violent fights with Gail coming out on the losing end since Mike was 6'2'' and 190 pounds. Gail's greatest hope in life was to have enough money someday to leave Mike and the kids.

One day someone told Gail how she could gain a genuine, lasting love for Mike. She was also told how she could begin to develop inner qualities and express those qualities in a way that would motivate Mike to go through similar changes. She began to apply a simple but life-changing principle. Nothing changed the first week, but by the end of the second week Mike had noticed such a radical change in Gail that he entered into the same commitment she had made. They fell in love with each other and in love with their children. In the thirteen years that have followed, they have helped hundreds of couples to build more fulfilling and lasting relationships. What was the principle Gail used? She began applying what the Bible calls *a quiet spirit* (1 Peter 3:4).

In 1 Peter 3:1–6, the apostle Peter describes four qualities God makes available to any woman. These qualities not only please God, but are highly motivating in changing a husband. One of these, the "quiet spirit" mentioned in verse 4, is the heart of inner beauty in a Christian woman.

Here's what Gail did. Like the holy women of old, she hoped in God and preferred her husband's needs to her own. She submitted herself to God, trusting Him to meet all her genuine needs (Phil. 4:19). She became anxious for nothing, but in *everything*, by praying and thanking God before she received from Him, she let God know her requests, and this *peace* began to *guard* her heart and mind in Christ Jesus (Phil. 4:6–7). She knew her needs would be well taken care of, so she was then free inside and able to focus on Mike's needs; that is, she had a quiet spirit—inner calmness. This calmness crowds out the fear so common in a wife's responses to her husband (1 Peter 3:6).

GENTLENESS

Gentleness is showing tender consideration for the feelings of another.

While I was visiting with a friend, we began talking about one of the most unusual couples either of us had ever known. What made them unique was that in their eighteen years of marriage they had never yelled at each other. I know this sounds hard to believe, and you might assume that the husband, Herb, is a Caspar Milquetoast kind of guy. Nothing could be further from the truth. Herb is an excellent athlete with engineering degrees and a very successful business. The fact that he has never yelled at Helen doesn't mean he hasn't yelled at anyone else.

The question is: How can a man who is as aggressive and self-motivated as Herb go eighteen years without yelling at his wife? As my friend and I thought about this, we looked at each other, smiled, and blurted out the answer in unison, "How could *anyone* ever yell at Helen?" Helen is a living picture of gentleness.

Have you ever noticed the difference between the way a father handles a newborn baby and the way he plays with a three-year-old? The first time I held my newborn son I was extremely careful and was so concerned I might hurt him that I handed him back to my wife rather quickly. By the time he was three, we were roughhousing almost nightly. Why was I less gentle with a three-year-old than I was with a newborn? When he was newborn, I was convinced that he was very fragile and that I needed to exercise the utmost care just to keep from hurting him.

The key motivation for gentleness is maintaining an awareness of the extreme fragility of other people's feelings. It was only natural for me to become less gentle physically with my son as he grew stronger. Unfortunately as time went on, I also became more calloused to my son's feelings because my busy schedule distracted my attention. Basically, I did what most of us do—I began to take Mike for granted. The more we take others for granted, the less gentle we tend to be in our relationship with them. We lose sight of their precious value and fragile inner person.

In other words, "The more we value something, the more gentle we will be in handling it." If I handed you a three-thousand-year-old, paper-thin Oriental vase worth $50,000 and asked you to take it to the bank, would you handle it any differently than if I gave you a 59¢ plastic vase and asked you to take it down the street?

Something happened to Mike that completely renewed my awareness of his priceless value and the fragility of his life. We were staying at a large motel, and I was swimming with my three children. While I was roughhousing with Kari and Greg, Mike was floating around in his Donald Duck inner tube. I turned around and saw the inner tube floating by itself in the deep end of the pool. Down in the water I saw Mike lying on the bottom of the pool—motionless, except for his soft, blond hair moving back and forth with the motion of the water. My heart was gripped with grief and fear as I dived down and brought him to the surface. After he recovered, I knew it would be a long time before I would take him for granted again. That was two years ago, and our closeness has continued to grow ever since.

There may be times when it is difficult for you to fully appreciate the priceless value of your husband, but the fact remains that he is a very special creation of God with needs, disappointments, hurts, and feelings just like anyone else. In the chapters that follow, we will be discussing specific ways you can express gentleness in your relationship with your husband and children.

Unselfish love is an action directed toward fulfilling another person's needs.

Nearly all of us enter marriage believing our love for our mate will never fade. Yet in the U.S. today, for every two marriages, there is one divorce. For too long we have accepted Hollywood's portrayal of love as the type of love for which to strive. It doesn't take long to discover that mere passion which revolves around sexual gratification is not sufficient in itself to establish a lasting relationship. Unfortunately, too many couples begin their marriages thinking this type of love is all they need.

There are at least three kinds of love, each totally unique. Of the three types of love—affection, passion, and genuine love—only the latter provides an adequate foundation for the other two types. If this type of love is missing, the relationship will most likely not be long-lasting. One of the most exciting virtues of genuine love is that God can build it within your character without the help of affectionate feelings (Gal. 5:22; Rom. 5:5). Before we look at genuine love, let's first consider the other two types of love.

Affection

The first type of love is recognizable when someone says, "I have fallen in love," or "I no longer love my husband." It's possible for people to "fall in love" and "fall out of love" because affection is based upon someone meeting *our* needs or living up to *our* expectations. As long as they meet our emotional, mental, and physical needs and live up to our expectations, we remain "in love" with them. When they cease to meet those expectations or fail to meet our needs, we can easily lose the affectionate feelings we have for them.

Passion

The second type of love is aptly described by the word "passion." This type of love is mainly centered around our need for sexual fulfillment. Like the first type of love, it is based upon our partner's ability to meet our needs—more specifically, our desire for romance and sex. This is the basis for most immature marriages—two young people longing for each other and getting married to guarantee that their mate will always be near to meet their needs. Passion is the weakest foundation for a marriage, as is evidenced by the high divorce rate among teenage marriages. A marriage must have passion to be fulfilling, but if passion is the thread that weaves the marriage together, the marriage has a much greater chance of unraveling.

Genuine Love

Genuine love is totally different from the first two types. Affection and passion make us aware of our own needs and cause us to look to others to meet those needs. Genuine love, as evidenced by Christ, searches for the needs of others and seeks opportunities to meet those needs (John 15:11–13). Simply stated, genuine love says, "I see your need; please allow me to meet it." Or as the apostle Paul defined it, "I submit myself to meeting your needs—your needs are my master" (Gal. 5:13–14). The focus of genuine love isn't receiving; it's giving. When a person receives genuine love from someone else, it can be one of the most powerfully motivating forces in his or her life.

I received a "D" in geometry the first time I took the course in high school. This qualified me for the "privilege" of taking the course a second time. I hated mathematics, and the second time around I was getting another "D." Midway through the course our teacher became ill and was replaced with a substitute. When the substitute walked into the classroom for the first time, we all gasped silently. His face was so disfigured that for the first week we looked out the window when we raised our hands to ask a question. By the end of the second week, his face was no longer a distraction because we felt the love he had for each one of us personally. He had begun to seek out what each one of us needed to improve our understanding of geometry. It was obvious to us that his highest concern was meeting our individual needs for learning the subject. He demonstrated his genuine love for me by staying after class on many occasions, doing everything he could to broaden my understanding of the subject. His eyes sparkled and his smile made him a very attractive person. His hidden beauty was what we all began to see. I was so motivated by his expression of love that my grade went from a "D" to an "A" in only six weeks. I went on to minor in mathematics in college as a result of this experience.

Genuine love doesn't necessarily spring from feelings. Its basis is primarily *a concern* for the welfare of another. Although the feelings of affection will follow, genuine love is initially an *action* directed toward fulfilling another person's needs.

The *first step* in developing genuine love for your husband is to begin valuing him as God does (John 3:16). It's committing yourself to care because he's worthwhile and because God cares a great deal about him. As you obey God's word in John 15:11–13, you receive the joy and peace Christ speaks of as a reward. God's plan is so terrific: you gain the life He promised, and you meet the deepest needs of your loved one at the same time.

In chapter 9 we will discuss the five basic needs of a man and how to meet them. But to genuinely love your husband, you have to go beyond those five basic needs and discover needs that are uniquely his. This *second step* involves using your creativity to meet his needs. This step is also discussed at length in chapter 21.

FOR PERSONAL REFLECTION

Developing these six inner-beauty qualities is a lifetime commitment. As these qualities become more and more a part of your character, your husband will find it much easier to learn *from you* what it takes to have a more fulfilling relationship. The remaining chapters will give you precise steps to help you begin motivating your husband to pursue a fulfilling and caring relationship. Many of these steps will produce visible results almost immediately. Others may take more time.

19

How To Increase Your Husband's Desire To Spend Quality Time With You

*"And
let the wife
see to it
that she respect
(admire)
her husband."
Ephesians 5:33*

BEFORE I MARRIED, there were certain types of girls that attracted me. They not only attracted me, but lots of other men as well. Finally, I decided to pinpoint the qualities they had that we all liked. By discussion and observation, I discovered at least six qualities they had in common. I believe that by taking these actions you can increase your husband's desire to set aside special moments with you: 1) Admire him; 2) Express a positive attitude on a consistent basis; 3) Focus more energy and concern on your inner beauty than on your outer appearance; 4) Compete with all his interests; 5) Use your unique feminine quality of gentleness; 6) Seek his opinion in your areas of interest.

ADMIRE HIM

Just as there are physical laws, such as the law of gravity, that govern our daily activities, so there are equally forceful and consistent relationship laws. One is the law of admiration. It reads: *People are attracted to those who admire them and repelled by those who belittle or look down on them.* Admiration is one of man's deepest and most important needs. That's probably why the Scriptures teach wives to admire their husbands (Eph. 5:33). The apostle Peter states that admiration can even motivate a husband spiritually (1 Peter 3:1–2).

237

The word *admire* (or *respect, honor*) in the Scriptures basically means "to attach high value to another." When the Word speaks of "fearing God," it simply means that God is to be most important to us—number one in our lives—and that is the beginning of wisdom (Prov. 9:10). Admire, respect, fear, and honor are similar in meaning, and all tell us to consider one another very worthwhile (Rom. 12:10).

The law of admiration is an extremely important part of this book, for it is the basis of all lasting, growing relationships. The vital part is that you don't have to like a person to admire him or her. Admiring someone is a choice, a decision, a commitment, an act of our will. It's telling ourselves, "God loves and values that person, and so can I."

Your husband might irritate you, belittle you, offend you, ignore you, or basically nauseate you, but admiration looks beyond what he does to who he is. It's unconditional.

Men tend to gravitate toward those who admire them.

The following quiz may pinpoint reasons why your husband does not want to spend as many hours with you as he does watching TV or pursuing other interests.

Quiz

1. *Have you ever shown more appreciation or admiration for other men than for your husband—perhaps for a pastor, a teacher, or another woman's husband?* Even without his conscious realization, your husband can be hurt by your esteem for other men. The questions, "Did you see Sarah and Jim at the party? Could you believe the ring he bought her?" may be telling your husband that Jim is more successful and generous than he is, that Jim treats Sarah better than your husband treats you. Or the statements, "I love being with Joan and Tom. Have you noticed how considerate he is?" may cause your husband to immediately assume that you believe he is not as considerate as Tom. Any statement of comparison, whether direct or implied, can tell your husband that you admire someone else more than him. Some men even avoid church because they feel they could never measure up to the minister their wives brag about on a weekly basis. Areas that are especially sensitive to a man include his job, his friends, his family heritage, and his intelligence. Be careful not to praise other men in his presence unless you are able to show even greater appreciation for your husband at the same time, or unless he is already secure in your admiration of him and your relationship is solid.

2. *Have you belittled or criticized your husband, his abilities, his character, or his activities?* This is especially destructive if done in

front of his friends or children. Even the military—not generally known for its sensitivity to feelings—recognizes as the first basic principle of leadership, following basic training, that it is totally unacceptable to belittle a man's character or ability in front of others. I can think of nothing that demoralizes a man faster than criticism in front of his peers or his children.

3. *Have you ever had a tendency to exert pressure on him to do something until it gets done?* Nagging is another word for pressure from a wife that makes her husband feel incompetent and irresponsible. Rather than motivating him to fulfill his responsibility, it makes him want to ignore it. As you keep nagging, he will seek other people who don't constantly remind him of his inadequacies. It's facial expressions and tone of voice that belittle and devalue a person.

4. *Do you find your trivial discussions turning into arguments?* He may view such discussions as an insult to his ability and intelligence, while you may be more realistically aware of the long-range problems caused by ignoring small things. But instead of challenging his unwillingness by arguing, look for indirect ways to expand his awareness of your world and get him to consider the full implications of what he is saying. (We'll go into more detail on this later in chapter 9.)

5. *Do you ever find yourself questioning his explanations of his behavior?* For example: If he calls you from the office to say he has to work late, do you ask him something like, "Do you really have to work late tonight?" With that one question, you imply you really don't trust his judgment. All he hears is your challenge of his judgment. No one likes to spend time with a "suspicious judge."

6. *Can you think of at least three things that you have complained about in the last week* (his schedule, his time with the kids, his lack of help around the house)? Complaining has the same effect as nagging. It repulses him.

7. *Have you ever compared your level of awareness to his?* This lies at the heart of distinguishing maleness and femaleness. The apostle Peter calls a woman "the weaker vessel." The Greek word for *weaker* means "more sensitive" or more "fragile" (1 Peter 3:7; Rom. 14:1). Since women tend to be more aware of relationships and the nurturing aspects of life, it is reasonable to assume that your husband is not as aware as you are that something is missing between the two of you. If you expect him to desire the same level of intimacy as you, and if it offends you when he doesn't notice what seems obvious to you, your facial expressions and tone of voice may communicate a judgmental and belittling attitude. Many women think their husbands lie awake at night thinking of offensive things to

do to them. Well, it's just not true. Those things come natural for most men! If she doesn't understand that a man's basic drive is to conquer and find his identity in his vocation or activities, a woman can become hurt because she takes his attitude of indifference personally. She thinks he doesn't like her or the children. He interprets this anger or hurt as a put-down of him, especially if she says, "You should have known . . . or realized . . . or paid attention. . . ." The best way to begin helping a man indirectly is to accept him as a man and value him for what he is today and for what he will be through your loving and patient help. (Incidentally, we men need what a woman can give us for our own sake and well-being. We need to be more aware of feelings and what builds lasting relationships.)

PRACTICAL WAYS TO BEGIN EXPRESSING ADMIRATION FOR YOUR HUSBAND

In my discussions with various men, I have found that there are a variety of ways that their peers, secretaries, employers, and friends make them feel important. I have taken the ten most frequently suggested and have written a brief description on how you can apply them in your relationship.

1. *Begin to seek your husband's advice and opinions on decisions.* Consult him for reactions to furniture selection and arrangement, style and color of clothing, dinner options, etc. In doing this, try not to ask him open-ended questions like, "What do you want for dinner tonight?" Even though you have good intentions, you force him to think through something he may consider your responsibility. However, if you ask, "What would you like for dinner—steak or spaghetti?" he appreciates your consideration. Don't overdo it though, for it might indicate to your husband that you are becoming too dependent and uncreative. Rather, maintain a balance by looking for special opportunities to seek his opinions and advice. As you carefully evaluate his ideas, he sees you consider him valuable.

2. *Make an effort to remember your husband's past requests and desires and begin to fulfill them when possible.* A close friend of mine told me his wife had done something that made him feel very special. Several weeks before he had remarked to her, "I wish I could watch just one football game from start to finish without getting interrupted." One day as he started to turn on a game, his wife came into the den, took both kids by the hand, and said, "Let's go up for a nap." After putting them to bed, she came in and said, "I'm going to go shopping now, and I hope you're able to enjoy this game without any interruptions. I've taken the phone off the hook so you won't be

disturbed by any calls." What amazed him was that his wife remembered his comment made several weeks before and evidently had looked for the opportunity to do something about it. In appreciation, he began to work on some long overdue household projects.

Some facts about human relationships are as predictable as the laws of nature. As the example above proves: *no one can continually ignore considerate, loving actions.* If you make your husband feel special, you increase his desire to do the same for you. (However, if he takes advantage of you, use the idea of sharing your feelings in chapter 23.)

In the spaces below, list five requests your husband has made or implied. It could be a special event he wants to see or an activity he's been wanting to do; maybe a special meal you haven't made for a long time or one of his favorite desserts. As you begin to fulfill some of his past wishes, you may not receive any immediate encouragement from him. He may even say, "It's about time!" Rely on sheer willpower in difficult moments to see this project through, because the more you do it, the more fulfilling it will become for you.

1. _____

2. _____

3. _____

4. _____

5. _____

3. *Look for occasional opportunities to draw attention to your husband's positive qualities when you're with other people.* For example: Praise him to your children, calling attention to his positive character qualities. If you are with friends and he says something worthwhile, tell him you think it makes a lot of sense and ask him to explain it further. Or, relate to friends or relatives a specific incident in the past week that highlights one of his positive qualities. For example: "John is so considerate of my feelings. The other day I hadn't said a word about how I felt, but he could tell I was down. He came over and put his arms around me. Then he told me he knew I was troubled and asked how he could help."

I can't begin to express how good I feel inside when people occasionally tell me something positive my wife has said about me. It makes me feel appreciated—I want to go home and put my arms around her as soon as I can!

4. *Make an effort to gain an appreciation for your husband's occupation, trying to understand how important he feels his job activ-*

ities are. Many men are frustrated with their jobs, feeling that no one really appreciates their worth or value, their talents and abilities. When you appreciate what your husband does, you may become his *only* hope for achieving genuine self-worth. Until he really believes that he is worth something, he will have difficulty focusing his attention on the worth of others—including you.

Don't ever belittle his job or the importance of his activities on the job. Nothing destroys a man's self-esteem more than to hear his wife cutting down his efforts to support her. Though you may not criticize his efforts, you may belittle them by being ignorant of them. If you cannot accurately explain to someone else your husband's job responsibilities during his normal working day, you don't know enough about his job. Don't try to gain this knowledge from him at one sitting, but over a period of time begin to investigate by asking a few questions to gain a clearer understanding of how he spends his day, the types of projects he works on, and how his duties affect or support his fellow workers. (Be careful not to imply by the manner of your questioning that you think he loafs on the job.) Also, he may put down his job by little comments. When a man feels unimportant because of his job, it tears away at the very heart of his being. Help him discover the value of what he does.

5. *Carefully consider what your husband says without hasty negative reactions.* I am not promoting blind obedience, but rather open-minded listening. Often we demand *our* way on issues that could have been worked out in another way without creating major problems. If you have a tendency to react immediately when you hear his ideas, discipline yourself to withhold your reaction until his entire thought "sinks in" and you've had a chance to consider his idea fully. You will avoid unnecessary tension in your relationship, and he will enjoy being with you more. This is a good time to introduce the concept of submission. Submission is a beautiful biblical teaching that best illustrates genuine love. Unfortunately, it has been misused until today the word is filled with distasteful connotations. Probably the most abuse has fallen from the hands of misguided husbands and "leaders" who have the mistaken idea that authority means "boss," decision-makers without regard for those under their authority.

Jesus said both in words and by example that anyone who wishes to be leader or ruler must first learn to be servant of all (Matt. 20:26–27). *Leaders are lovers.* They serve—submit to—and listen to those whom they would lead.

When a husband is loving his wife with understanding, gentleness, warmth, and communication, it is relatively easy for her to submit to him as a person. But even if your husband is not a loving person, you should still be practicing submission—love in action. It communicates to your husband that he is valuable and that his needs are more important than yours at the moment. (Equally important, husbands are to submit to their wives—more about this in his book—Ephesians 5:2).

A summary of this special biblical secret—*submission*

- I submit to God. I'll ask Him, and wait for Him, to meet all my needs (Ps. 62:1; Phil. 4:6–7, 19).

- I realize how valuable I am to Christ because He gave His life for me (John 3:16).

- While waiting for my needs to be met through Christ, I'll attend to the needs of those around me. I'll forget about my needs because God's taking care of them (Eph. 3:19–20), and I'll focus on what I can do for others (John 15:11–12).

---

6. *Don't let two days pass without expressing appreciation for at least one thing your husband has said or done during those forty-eight hours.* Just a reminder. Don't forget how much nicer it is to be with people who make you feel special than with those who don't.

7. *Use your sensitivity to detect your husband's personal goals, and lend him your support as he pursues those goals.* His personal goals may involve advancement in his company, higher income, or special pastimes. A very successful businessman in Texas told me that his wife has always been supportive of his personal goals. Once she knew how important it was to him to be well-respected by others in his field, she helped him in a variety of ways to achieve this goal—through improving his taste in clothing, encouraging good personal grooming habits, etc. (He welcomed her help in this area because she didn't force her opinions upon him.) She encouraged him during times when he felt like quitting and praised him each time he attained any of his goals.

8. *Begin to admire your husband in nonverbal ways.* Studies of communication between husbands and wives have proven that words alone are responsible for only 7 percent of the total communication. Thirty-eight percent of marital communication is expressed through voice tone, and 55 percent through facial expressions and body movement. In other words, when you say something to your husband, the words themselves account for only 7 percent of the meaning. Take the phrase, "I love you." It can be said in a way that

communicates, "Of course I love you; I pay the rent, don't I?" or it could be expressed in a way that says, "I adore you and couldn't live my life without you." Or, "I desperately need you to fulfill my needs right now." That's why I have heard so many wives responding to their husbands' "I love you" with, "You sure have funny ways of showing it." Here are a few *nonverbal* ways to show your husband how important he is:

1. Be attentive to his concerns when he comes home.
2. Look as attractive as possible when he comes home.
3. Prepare appetizing meals.
4. Show interest and ask questions about his job, activities, problems, achievements.
5. Listen attentively by focusing your eyes on him.
6. Don't make him compete with the TV, the dishes, or even the children when he's trying to talk to you.

9. *Genuinely desire and seek your husband's forgiveness whenever you offend him.* Both men and women tend to avoid those who offend them. (One of the most common complaints children make about their parents is that parents never admit they are wrong.) The key to "wiping the slate clean" with your husband is not saying, "I'm sorry." That's a phrase even children exploit to avoid a spanking. When we have been offended by someone, we usually don't want to hear a glib "I'm sorry." We want to know that the person realizes he or she was wrong and that he or she hurt us. I believe there are a lot of "wrong ways" to ask forgiveness. They are wrong because they do not bring us into harmony with the person whom we have offended and they may not communicate the person's value to us. For example, avoid saying:

1. I'm sorry *if* I was wrong; I *hope* I didn't hurt you.
2. I'm sorry I did that; I really didn't mean it to hurt you.
3. I'm sorry I said what I said, but you were wrong too.
4. I'm sorry. Next time I'll try to be more careful.

With apologies like these, your husband will feel you are not accepting full responsibility for your action. You are either minimizing the degree to which you hurt him or you are minimizing your role in inflicting the hurt. As a result, he may sense that your apology is insincere. Though he may say, "I forgive you," he will be saying to himself, "She really isn't sorry at all. She's just trying to get rid of her guilt."

One of the best ways I have found to ask forgiveness is, unfortunately, the hardest and the least creative. All it requires is that you go to your husband, look into his eyes, and say, "I was wrong in what I said or did. Can you forgive me?" Two things will happen when you ask for forgiveness in this way. First, your husband will desire to restore the relationship and will be more prepared to forgive you; and second, it is likely to exert pressure on him to ask for forgiveness in the future for the ways he has offended you. As a side benefit, it makes him feel important—you are telling him indirectly that you care for him enough not to leave him with hurt feelings.

EXPRESS A POSITIVE ATTITUDE ON A CONSISTENT BASIS

While in college I dated a lot of different girls. Eventually I met a girl who had a particular *quality* that attracted me like a magnet. Even though I was still dating others, I called her almost every day, spending an hour or two on the phone with her.

The magnetic quality that kept me racing for the telephone was this girl's positive attitude. She was always so much fun to talk to, never doing or even saying negative things. Instead, she was always encouraging and positive. Four years later we married, and today, after fourteen years of marriage, her positive outlook on life continues to be a tremendous source of joy and strength. She uses her alertness and awareness to look beyond surface issues, and she often sees positive benefits in situations that appear dark and hopeless to me.

If you want your husband to yearn for quality time with you, then it is essential that you develop and express a positive attitude. You might say, "But if you knew my husband . . . if you knew what I'm going through . . . it's just impossible for me to develop a positive attitude." Just ask yourself these questions:

- How do I act around our dinner guests when I have a headache?
- How do I act when I'm in a hurry at the grocery store and run into a friend with problems?

We usually find it easy, or at least necessary, to have a positive attitude around our friends and associates. Don't you agree that our mates deserve the same consideration?

When your husband comes home from work, the worst thing you can do is greet him with a negative comment about something he forgot to do or some disaster you encountered during the day.

I am not saying that you shouldn't talk about negative things. But I am stressing that there is a right way and a right time to talk about them. Wait until he's had a chance to rest or until the house is quiet after the kids have gone to bed. If a negative situation is so important that you have to confront him with it as soon as he comes home—then use the salt principle (chapter 17). Negative greetings should be the exception, not the rule. Your husband's homecoming should be as peaceful as possible (unless your son has just been arrested or the IRS wants to audit your tax return immediately).

Have you ever wondered why people gravitate toward the negative rather than the positive? The answer is simple. Our very natures tend to be negative. It seems no matter how good a situation is, we are able to find something negative in it. For example, which of the following sets of numbers attract your attention most quickly?

$$2 + 2 = 4 \quad 5 + 6 = 11 \quad 7 + 8 = 17 \quad 8 + 8 = 16 \quad 9 + 11 = 20$$

Which of the five words below attracts your attention most quickly?

read   love   crisp   develp   smart

Notice that your eyes automatically dwell on the incorrect problem ($7 + 8 = 17$) and the misspelled word (develp).

We all tend to notice the negative. So most of the information in our newspapers and on television broadcasts revolves around negative issues. And that's why we all enjoy a "juicy tidbit" of gossip.

Negative thinking, especially about ourselves, is a major cause for an overall negative outlook on life. What we say to ourselves about a problem actually has stronger effect on our feelings than the problem itself. We all tend to bombard ourselves with short sentences like: "I'm no good." "I'm a failure." "I can't do anything right." "He doesn't like me." "This guy is driving me crazy." "I'm coming unglued." "You're blowing my mind." "I'm sick and tired of this." All these short, negative statements focusing on the bad side of things produce a negative attitude. The ultimate result of a lifetime of negative thinking is frustration, despair, and depression. In fact, a psychiatrist recently told me he believes two words alone can keep a person in a mental institution: "If only. . . ."

It's very important to understand that much of depression and discouragement is directly related to negative thoughts. If at 9:00 A.M. we start thinking, "I'm no good," or "I'm a failure," or "He doesn't like me," we'll be depressed by 11:00 A.M.

Our feelings *follow* our thinking and/or actions. If our thinking and actions are positive, then our feelings *will be* positive in a matter of hours (The Scriptures teach that as a person "thinks within himself, so is he" [Prov. 23:7]).

GAINING A POSITIVE ATTITUDE

I once counseled a young wife who had been sexually attacked when she was a young girl. I could see by the expression on her face that she was still discouraged and distressed about the incident and embarrassed to talk about it. Feeling she had been cheated in life, she was somewhat resentful that God had allowed such a horrible thing to happen. Still unable to eliminate her deep feeling of shame over the situation, she began to discuss how she felt about it now as an adult.

I began by telling her she would never be free from the resentment, shame, and negative attitude resulting from her experience unless she could first see the benefits which resulted from the attack. She looked at me like I was crazy when she asked, "What benefits?"

"I'm going to ask you a very difficult question based on two Scriptures—1 Thessalonians 5:18 and Romans 8:28. Do you think that right now you could thank God that this *happened* to you?"

"You've got to be kidding," she said. "I could never thank God. The only thing I could ever be thankful for is that I didn't become mentally ill because of the attack. I'm thankful for that."

"I'm not asking you to be 'thankful' that it was a terrible experience. I'm just asking you to be willing to say, 'Thank You, God, for that attack because I know You can turn it into good. I just can't see the good now'" (Isa. 61:3; Rom. 8:28).

She didn't think she could do that, which was understandable. However, I told her she could work through her feelings, and then I asked her if she would like my help. She responded, "By all means."

"First, let's look at your dating life before you got married. Did you ever let anyone take advantage of you sexually when you were dating?"

She replied, "Absolutely not! When that man did that to me, I said no other man would *ever* take advantage of me again."

"So in other words, because that happened to you as a child, you never got involved in any immorality in high school or college. Consequently, you have been spared the hurts that can come from an illicit relationship. It may have even saved you from the consequences of pregnancy before marriage. In essence, that man gave you a vaccination that may have saved you from worse problems," I said.

"Yeah, I never thought of it like that, but that's exactly what happened," she replied.

"Now I'm going to show you the most important thing of all. You received a gift at the very time the attack took place. Do you know what I'm referring to?"

"No, what is it?"

"You received a priceless quality that will enable you to better love others in a genuine way. That is, *greater sensitivity*. How alert are you to your children's needs and your husband's needs?"

"Very alert!"

"I can believe that. It's only natural that when something terrible happens to us, we become even more aware of and sensitive to the sufferings of those around us. Awareness and sensitivity then become the basis for genuine love—being able to detect another person's need and having the motivation to meet that need in the most effective way."

I continued by asking what kind of man she had married. Was he calloused or gentle? She said her husband was a very loving, tender, gentle man. She considered him a wonderful husband. It became increasingly obvious to both of us that because she had been abused by a man, she had become more aware of her need for a gentle and compassionate husband. She realized how the experience had "sensitized" her to the type of husband she really needed.

By the time she left my office, she had all the reasons she needed to thank God for her past. After being in bondage to negative feelings for years, she was set free simply by thinking through the positive factors involved.

The first step in gaining a positive attitude is to discover the benefits of the negative situation. (Incidentally, I haven't heard of a situation yet that lacked positive benefits.) It often seems the more tragic the situation, the greater the positive consequences. I am not saying that the beneficial outcome of a negative situation justifies the situation. Absolutely not. I am saying that as we recognize the *positive side* of a negative situation, we can be liberated from the chains that tie us to guilt, resentment, despair, and any other negative feeling which has held us captive.

With this principle, I must include two cautions: First, I am not providing an excuse to do something wrong, with the rationalization that something good will come of it. I believe that such reasoning is shallow and perverted in that the wrongdoer is always the loser (Luke 17:1–2). Second, people who are suffering from tragedy don't need flippant statements such as, "I know you can find some good in this if you really try." So first be sensitive to their emotions and their immediate needs for *comfort*. When the time is right, after empathic comfort has been extended graciously and gently, then you can begin to help them see the benefits of their problems.

The more you discover the inherent benefits of *your own* problems, the more positive your attitude will become. As a result, your husband will desire to spend more time with you.

FOCUS MORE ENERGY AND CONCERN ON YOUR INNER BEAUTY THAN ON YOUR OUTER APPEARANCE

It's obvious that women and men alike usually spend more time and energy trying to groom their exteriors than strengthen their interiors. A woman should do everything she can to make herself physically attractive to her husband.

However, outer beauty will only attract a man's *eye*, but inner beauty will keep his *heart* (1 Peter 3:1–6).

We discussed at length in chapter 18 several inner beauty qualities that can melt almost any man's heart: courage, persistence, gratefulness, calmness, gentleness, and genuine love. For your convenience, I will review in capsule form the working definitions of each of these qualities:

1. Courage: The inner *commitment* to pursue a worthwhile goal without giving up hope.

2. Persistence: *Continuing* to pursue a goal until it is achieved.

3. Gratefulness: A sincere *appreciation* for the benefits received from others.

4. Calmness: An inner *peace* that allows you to respond quietly to a stressful situation without fear.

5. Gentleness: Showing *tender consideration* for the feelings of another.

6. Genuine Love: Meeting the *needs* of another, prior to your own personal needs being met.

As you develop these qualities, your husband will want to spend more and more time with you.

COMPETE WITH ALL HIS INTERESTS

Every wife needs to ask herself these searching questions:
"Why would my husband want to spend more time with me?"
"Would *I* even want to spend more time with me?"
"What can I do to make myself more attractive?"
"What can I do to become more attractive to my husband?"
"How can I become more attractive than his other interests?"

The first step in competing for your husband's attention is to make yourself more interesting and attractive. For example, one woman deeply resented being second to other people or her husband's job.

After harboring this resentment for several years, she finally began to understand WHY he preferred the company of others. During one particularly miserable trip, she had been moody and grouchy most of the time because her husband had been busy with other people. After giving it a great deal of thought, *she realized* that her husband didn't want to spend time with her because the things she enjoyed simply were not interesting to him (visiting dress shops, jewelry stores, etc.). After that wretched vacation, she determined to make herself more appealing and fascinating.

So while her husband took an extended trip, she decided to make some drastic personal changes. She lost weight, changed her hairstyle, and purchased a few fashionable outfits. But *most importantly*, she began to change some of her attitudes. She made a special effort to work on qualities of inner beauty. When her husband sighted her waiting at the airport after his trip, he said he honestly wondered, *Who's the beautiful blonde in the sunglasses?* He couldn't believe the difference. He not only began to spend more time with his "new" wife, but he became more alert in areas where he had never shown any sensitivity whatsoever.

When your husband comes home from work each night, how do you look? Is your hair fixed up? How about your clothes? When he goes into the kitchen or dining room to eat dinner, is the table setting attractive and neat? Do you fix some of the food he really likes the way he likes it? In every area of your life, discover how you can be so attractive that he would rather be with you than anyone or anything else. (Remember, this effort is not just for your benefit; it is for his, too, in all his relationships, especially with your children.)

Giving admiration or respect is the second step in competing for your husband. He hungers for sincere admiration and respect, and he will gravitate toward those who admire him, his personality, or his talents. This need for admiration motivates men to spend time on committees, run for political offices, and enter various competitive sports. In fact, many men compete in strenuous events just to receive a trophy—the tangible symbol of accomplishment.

The third step in competing for his attention requires that you show more interest in his life than anyone else does—more than his friends, his colleagues at the office, or any of his associates. Imagine the impact on your relationship if you gave your husband a daily dose of genuine interest. He would probably leave friends or work early to get home to you. Don't laugh! It's possible.

I remember a young woman who came to my office emotionally broken and distraught after her husband had told her he had been seeing another woman. He was planning to leave, although he would stay until their baby was born. When he told her, she became hysterical. She said, "As I thought about losing him, I was so upset that my very reaction repulsed him. I'm sure that even my facial expression communicated an intolerable ugliness to him."

The remaining weeks would be a precious commodity. I told her to use every available moment to compete with the other woman. She did just that. She recalled some of his favorite meals and fixed them. She jotted down his interests and began centering her conversations around them. Giving attention to her appearance, she tried to look her best each evening when he came home from work. And above all, she never demanded that he remain at home, although she knew he was probably going out to be with the other woman. She became more fluent in her admiration of him and began to do little things she thought would mean a lot to him. At first he resisted her efforts, telling her she was wasting her time. *But she persisted.*

Within three months, her husband had quit seeing the other woman because of the changes he saw in his wife. He said he saw a beauty in her he had never seen before, the inner beauty she had worked so hard to develop. Her strong interest in her husband, plus sensitivity to his needs, had overcome anything the other woman could offer.

USE YOUR UNIQUE FEMININE QUALITY OF GENTLENESS

Have you ever been driven to the point of losing control? Screaming, swearing, breaking things in outbursts of anger *can* result from the need for a deeper relationship with your husband. As he fails to meet this need, you become so frustrated that you explode from time to time. These explosions may rearrange the furniture, but they do nothing to change his behavior.

I'm sure you're keenly aware of your husband's deficiencies; however, it is of upmost importance that you refrain from confronting him with them in anger. As we've said before, a man has a tendency to fight his conscience; and if you become his conscience, he'll either fight you or flee you. Whichever route he takes, you've lost your goal of spending more time with him.

You need to tell your husband how important it is to spend time together. But tell him in a gentle, loving way at the right time. Explain to your husband some of the important occasions you'd like to spend with him—anniversaries, birthdays, holidays, and other times that are special to you. *Then find out what times he would like to share with you.*

It's also important to discuss the types of activities you would like to do together. That is, times you'd like to be alone with him or out with friends, with your children or without your children. (Ever tried an overnight campout with him alone? Just remember—when the sun goes down, a couple of hours remain when some great uninterrupted communication can take place.) Let him know that when he spends time with you, he's really doing himself a favor. Explain that the closer your relationship becomes, the more responsive you'll be in meeting his physical needs. Explain, too, that as your relationship grows you'll gain a stronger desire to do things especially for him—fixing special meals, dressing the way he prefers, attending sporting events with him. I believe one of the best ways you can recognize and meet your husband's unique needs is to develop and maintain open communication through a growing relationship with him.

I often wondered what provoked some women to eat their way to obesity. Would you believe, one reason is a lack of communication? It's true. I found that their compulsive eating is often directly related to apathetic husbands. Just the feeling of an incomplete relationship can cause some women to turn to the refrigerator for comfort. As a woman gains weight, her husband's rejection, combined with her feelings of guilt, puts even more pressure on her. Frustrated and nervous, she becomes more compulsive in her eating. The only way she can get off this vicious treadmill is to communicate to her husband—*in a gentle way*—that she needs his understanding and acceptance.

By explaining your feelings and needs gently, lovingly and calmly, it becomes obvious that you're not being selfish in asking him to spend quality time with you. A lack of time with him affects you and your relationship with him.

SEEK HIS OPINION IN YOUR AREAS OF INTEREST

One of Bonney's majors in college was home economics, including training in interior design. She is an extremely creative woman and needs no help from her husband in decorating a room. Whether choosing wallpaper or carpeting, picking lamps or arranging furniture, she has the ability to create just the feeling she wants in a room through tasteful choice of decor. Steve is aware of his wife's talent; he realizes Bonney needs no help when it comes to furnishing their home. But on many occasions she has made him feel needed and appreciated by seeking his opinion on carpet samples, fabrics, etc. She never belittles his taste, and as a result, he tells me he always looks forward to doing things with her.

Many men appreciate it when their wives ask for help. My wife can always get me to join her simply by starting a repair project. If she asks me to do it, usually I'm not interested. But as soon as I see her struggling with some repair, I jump in and we fix it *together*. I really enjoy it when she gently asks for my help without expectation and then expresses gratefulness for my time. You may think, *Why should a woman even have to do all that to get her husband to spend time with her? It just doesn't seem fair!* I agree with you. But the fact of the matter is that men are buffalos and women are butterflies. Your buffalo may never gain butterfly sensitivity unless you provide the motivation.

However, you should beware of several pitfalls at this point. First, when you recruit his help, don't criticize him for doing the job worse than you would have done it yourself. Criticizing his work is the fastest way to discourage him from working side-by-side with you again. If he does something which fails to meet your standards, bite your tongue.

Second, if he gives an answer you don't like when you've asked his advice, don't start an argument. You can easily avoid arguments by offering him choices you know you can live with when you ask for his advice. For example: If you want his opinion of wallpaper, don't give him a wallpaper book with five hundred samples. Narrow the field to several different patterns with which you are satisfied. Then ask him to decide which of those patterns he prefers. If he doesn't like any of them, go back and study the books and then bring him several more choices.

My last caution is: Be selective about asking for his help, and never embarrass him.

Immediately after graduate school, our income was much too low for us to buy ready-made draperies for our living room. So Norma made them at home, with my assistance. After a crash course on how to use a sewing machine, I worked with Norma almost from start to finish on those curtains. They weren't the best-looking in the world, but we enjoyed our joint accomplishment. And I gained a greater appreciation for all the little things that go into sewing and making drapes.

Sounds good, right? Wrong!

I'll never forget the day that I was driving down the road with the chairman of the education board, on which I served, and he said, "I was talking with your wife, and she told me that you helped her make some curtains." He gave me a funny look and asked, "Do you really enjoy sewing?" I was so embarrassed that I vowed never again to help my wife in any area which could be misconstrued by others. If she had said something like, "I really appreciated my husband's help in designing our curtains," it wouldn't have been as embarrassing. But I felt ridiculous when people knew I actually sat at her sewing machine and made curtains. It was even worse to be asked if I really enjoyed sewing. Now that I'm more "mature," I wouldn't mind admitting something like this. But at my young age my ego just couldn't take it.

The six motivating factors discussed in this chapter really work. It would be impossible for anyone to develop and apply all of these overnight, but in time, you will have countless opportunities to use each one. When you do, you will find your husband gravitating toward your admiration and respect; your positive attitude will be a source of encouragement and strength that he'll begin to depend on more and more; and everyone will gain by your commitment to him.

FOR PERSONAL REFLECTION

1. Why would a husband believe the Word without a word being spoken by his wife? 1 Peter 3:2.
2. How does Romans 12:10 apply to the word *submission*. Carefully define this word for your own relationship.

20

How To Gain
Your Husband's
Undivided Attention
On A
Consistent Basis

"An excellent wife,
who can find?
For her worth
is far above
jewels."
Proverbs 31:10

ON A RECENT flight to Los Angeles the pilot announced that a world-famous cheerleading squad was aboard and would be strolling the aisles singing "Happy Birthday" to anyone who had a birthday that month. When they finished singing, I asked if I could interview the married members of the group for a book I was writing. They graciously consented, and I had the opportunity to spend more than an hour with two of them. One had been married for a year; the other had been married for three years. Both were articulate, intelligent, and physically attractive.

I started our interview by asking them what was the greatest single disappointment in their marriages. Their answers? Each said it was nearly impossible to get her husband's undivided attention unless he had ulterior motives.

I wasn't surprised that they gave the same answer. I have heard it from hundreds of women, young and old, attractive and unattractive. The "inattentive husband" seems to be a universal complaint among women. Both of the cheerleaders said they had given up any hope of seeing a change in their marriages. They had slumped into what society says is "only natural."

It *isn't* "only natural," and it *can* be changed! No matter what your situation is, there are at least four ways to gain your husband's consistent, undivided attention. Both of the NFL cheerleaders were excited to learn how to make their husbands eager to listen, and you, too, can be encouraged by the changes possible through use of the following principles.

LIGHT UP

Something about my father attracted me like a magnet. When school was out, many times I would rush to his hardware store instead of going out with my friends. What drew me to my father? Why did I prefer a visit with him over some of my favorite activities? As soon as I set foot in his store, it seemed as if his whole personality lit up. His eyes sparkled, his smile gleamed, and his facial expressions immediately conveyed how glad he was to see me. I almost expected him to announce, "Look, everybody, my son is here." I loved it. Although I didn't realize it at the time, those tremendously powerful nonverbal expressions were the magnets that drew me to him.

Ninety-three percent of our communication is nonverbal. Your husband can be attracted or repelled most often, then, by your nonverbal behavior. If he comes home from work to a worn facial expression that says, "Oh, brother, look who's home—Mr. Gripe," or "It's only you," then of course he will be repulsed. Whenever you see him, you've got to "light up" with enthusiasm, especially in your facial expressions and tone of voice. That light comes from the inner knowledge that he's valuable. Norma shows that sparkle whenever I walk in the door, and consequently, I want to spend time talking to her and listening to her. If she "lights up" when a particular subject is mentioned, she increases my desire to talk about that subject; as a result, I enjoy listening to her, her opinions, and her needs.

As a husband "sees" your sincere expressions of his worth, he will be drawn to you (1 Peter 3:1–2).

The students in a psychology class picked up on the powerful effect of "lighting up" when someone is talking. They met after class without the professor and decided to try an experiment. Every time the professor walked close to the room heater (a radiator) they agreed to appear more attentive—sit up straight, liven their facial expressions, take notes more diligently—to look as interested as possible without being too obvious. Each time their professor walked away from the radiator, their interest in his lectures would dwindle noticeably—they would look at each other with bored expressions, slouch in their chairs. Their experiment proved the "lighting up" principle. Within a few weeks the professor was giving his entire lecture while seated on the radiator.

While I was in college, I decided to try a similar experiment of my own. I asked my ten-year-old niece, Debby, to make up one hundred sentences using any one of the following pronouns: he, she, we, they, it, or I. I had predetermined that every time she used the pronoun "he," I would make encouraging movements with my body or positive expressions with my face and tone of voice. Each time she used other pronouns, I would sit back in my chair, look bored, and mumble in an indifferent tone of voice.

By the time we reached the fiftieth sentence, Debby was using the pronoun "he" in every sentence and continued to do so until we finished. Unaware of what I had been doing, Debby said she thought I had been checking on her sentence structure. She was unaware of her frequent usage of "he." Since then I have used the "light up" technique to demonstrate that I am genuinely interested in what others are saying. I've also found that my positive nonverbal communication increases others' interest in what I say.

I encourage you to use this technique to show your husband how *important* he is. It's an invaluable way to build a more loving relationship.

LEARN MORE ABOUT HIS INTERESTS AND VOCATION

Many men allow their hobbies to be a consuming passion. They live, breathe, eat, and sleep their hobby or vocation. One woman told me she wanted to build a deeper relationship with her outdoorsman husband, but she knew nothing about hunting and fishing. She decided the only way to become knowledgeable about her husband's interest was to take up hunting and fishing herself. She actually had no desire to hunt and fish, but she *did* desire a deeper relationship with her husband.

First, she asked him to teach her how to shoot a gun. They spent hours at the firing range as she endured the necessary practice. Next on the agenda—a fishing trip, which proved frustrating due to her lack of skill. So, she practiced casting in their backyard and found that her enjoyment increased as her skill improved. In the early weeks of "training" she became discouraged and thought the whole idea a waste of time. But she persisted. Now an excellent marksman, she enjoys hunting and fishing with her husband. Not only have their shared experiences drawn them closer, but more importantly, they have developed a common interest which they both enjoy discussing. It's easy for her to gain his undivided attention simply by beginning a conversation about hunting or fishing and then moving to other subjects.

If you feel your husband lacks the patience necessary to teach you one of his hobbies, don't let it stop you from learning. Simply seek another source of instruction. Professional instruction is readily available in almost every sport or interest. Try the lessons to see if you've got what it takes to "stick it out," and then surprise him after you've gained some proficiency. If you tell him about your intentions before you start, he might not believe that you will follow through. He might even discourage you from trying.

Nearly every man is interested in some type of sport—either as a spectator or a participant. Whatever sport your husband enjoys watching on TV, try to develop an appreciation for it. At first it may bore you to tears, but as you learn the rules, techniques, etc., you will enjoy the sport more. Pay as much attention to what's going on as your husband does, otherwise you will be distracting. If he is watching a football game and you decide to do a little knitting on the side, chances are you'll drive him up the wall. As far as he's concerned, interest without attentiveness is really no interest at all. (Incidentally, the more you find out about the personal lives and families of professional athletes, the more your interest will increase.)

As we mentioned in chapter 19, every man needs to feel admired. Because he spends the largest part of his day at work, his identity becomes linked to his job just as your identity is linked to your home and family or your own vocation. If you aren't excited about his work, it's nearly impossible for him to believe that you admire him for anything. Consequently, it is extremely important that you learn enough about his responsibilities to express a genuine interest in them. You can't learn everything about his work overnight. Take your time about it.

One woman told me she was repulsed by her husband's occupation as a trucker. She categorized all truckers as morally loose, rough, crude, and dirty. Although she never *said* anything negative to him, her nonverbal behavior got the message across. And slowly but surely, her husband lost interest in spending time with her.

I encouraged her to take a closer look at the trucking industry and the tremendous services it provides for our society. I reminded her that nearly everything she owned was delivered via truck . . . virtually every other industry is dependent on the trucking industry . . . a truckers' strike practically paralyzes our society. I told her about the numerous times my family has been assisted by truckers willing to stop and help when our cars were broken down on the highway.

I suggested that she begin to ask her husband about the different types of goods he delivers, the towns he goes through, the people he meets, and the discouraging problems he faces. Within a month she had a new appreciation for the value as well as the difficulty of his job.

USE THE SALT PRINCIPLE
TO GAIN YOUR HUSBAND'S ATTENTION

In chapter 17 we discussed the salt principle and how it works. If you are still somewhat unsure about this principle, it might be good to review that chapter before you read further.

The salt principle is undoubtedly the most effective way to gain your husband's undivided attention. Although learning to use this technique does take some practice, once you've mastered it, you will invariably gain his full attention—even if he knows what you're doing. Remember to use this technique with a loving, gentle, kind attitude. If your attitude or tone of voice reflects pride or cockiness, your husband will only resent your attempt to arouse his curiosity. He will consider it a weapon, especially if you use it to create curiosity and then refuse to fulfill it with something like, "Well, I'll just tell you later when you have a better attitude!" I can't think of a better way to immunize your hsuband against the effectiveness of the salt principle.

With the right attitude, the salt principle is so powerful that it works even when the listener is in a hurry or under pressure. You don't have to wait until your husband is free from tension and deadlines to stimulate his curiosity. Just give it all you've got with salty questions, pleasant facial expressions, and a gentle tone of voice.

TEACH YOUR HUSBAND TO LISTEN TO YOU

By now I hope I've made one point clear: *most* men do not understand women. Since you know your needs better than anyone else, you can be your husband's most effective teacher. He needs to learn from you *why* it's important to listen to you and *how* to listen.

First, explain why it's important to you that he spend time listening with his undivided attention. (The woman called "virtuous" [also, "excellent"] in Proverbs 31:10 was so called because she had convictions and influence. Convictions bring influence. When you're sold on something, like the importance of a better relationship, it will show through your facial expressions.) Let him know that when he doesn't listen to you attentively, it makes you feel unimportant and unappreciated. Explain that this, in turn, decreases your desire to meet his needs. Make it clear, however, that the opposite is also true. When he consistently listens to you with attentiveness, you feel more important and have a much stronger desire to meet his needs with greater creativity. You may have to tell him these things repeatedly before they sink in. But each time the opportunity arises, you have another chance to stimulate his curiosity.

In addition to explaining *why* you need his undivided attention, you must show him *how* to give it. Discuss the nonverbal means of communication with him. As he learns to understand your feelings by looking at your eyes and facial expressions, your communication and your relationship will deepen. Gently remind him that his partial listening doesn't do any good, that you don't want to compete with work, sports, and TV.

Be careful not to let your times of communication deteriorate into arguments. Use your sensitivity to learn how to side-step issues, words, or mannerisms that ignite an argument. Some women concede that the only way they get their husband's undivided attention is to start an argument. Unfortunately, that's not the type of undivided attention which builds a healthy relationship. Let your communication be as encouraging and delightful as possible.

Learning to gain your husband's undivided attention on a consistent basis will be a major undertaking. However, gaining his attention is not an end in itself. It is a means to develop several beautiful facets to your relationship. One of those facets, helping your husband become aware of your emotional and romantic needs, will be discussed in detail in chapter 21.

FOR PERSONAL REFLECTION

Why was the Proverbs 31 woman so honored by her husband?
Proverbs 31:10–31. List ten inner qualities of this woman.

21

How To Increase Your Husband's Sensitivity To Your Emotional Needs And Desires

"An excellent wife
is the crown
of her husband,
but
she who shames him
is as rottenness
in his bones."
Proverbs 12:4

MOST WOMEN HAVE a short, simple definition for romance and emotional tenderness—"the little things." Ever tried to explain to your husband what those "little things" are? One woman told me, "My husband thinks he's doing me a big favor by buying me a new toaster. But for some reason, that just doesn't mean as much as it would for him to greet me early in the morning by taking my hand or kissing me on the cheek to tell me that he thinks I'm really special."

A woman can become so much a part of her children, her home, and her daily routine that she often loses her identity as an individual. Consequently, she feels a deep need to be singled out, loved individually. No woman wants to be viewed merely as the wife, the other laborer, the cook, the cleaning lady, the mother, the ironing service, the laundress, or the family chauffeur. It's not enough that her family show deep appreciation for the role she fulfills. She has a need for her husband to draw her out of that demanding role and love her for *who she is* rather than for *what she does.* Once he gains a sensitivity to her emotional needs and desires, he can begin to fulfill them with creative actions that women call, "the little things." (For your husband's benefit, I discuss this in greater detail in the book *If Only He Knew.*)

You can provide your husband with the motivation and the

knowledge necessary to meet your needs by cultivating three new skills: 1) sow seeds of love; 2) explain your unique needs and desires; 3) express your gratefulness without expectation.

SOW SEEDS OF LOVE

We reap what we sow (Gal. 6:7). You've heard it a hundred times, but it's just as true now as it was thousands of years ago. If you're rude and contentious, people will respond to you in the same way. Conversely, if you're thoughtful and gentle, it's difficult for others to respond with anything less. As you detect your husband's needs and make special efforts to fulfill them, eventually he will notice your efforts and appreciate you. Out of his appreciation will grow a desire to enrich your relationship. If you start by sowing seeds of love and care for your husband, soon you'll be reaping his love and appreciation.

Discover your husband's distinctive needs.

Some women presume to know all of their husband's needs without even asking them. But I have never met a man who could say his mate knew *all* about *all* of him.

It's always fun to meet the wife who thinks she has her mate completely figured out. In total confidence she says, "I know exactly why he does that," or "I know him inside out." But all I have to do is ask a few questions to reveal that the "know-it-all" partner knows a lot less about her spouse than she thought. Many couples, thinking they know each other intimately, have actually lived on a superficial level for years. Unfortunately, marriages of this type are the norm rather than the exception.

Get past the superficial by discovering the individuality of your mate. Although your husband is similar to other men, he is totally unique . . . one of a kind. He is different in temperament, personality, childhood, adolescence, family relationships, heritage, talents, goals, aspirations, successes, failures, frustrations, and disappointments. You must abandon the idea that he's just like all other men, another common, everday, average guy. Finding out *who he is* and *what he feels* can be one of the most stimulating and rewarding investments of your life. Sometime you might ask him, "What really fulfills you as a man?" Listen carefully as he shares some of his deepest feelings. Make a list of the things he shares, and demonstrate your interest in them by talking about them from time to time. Try to discover the things that hurt and disappoint him. In other words, begin to really know your man.

Next, consider some general needs common to men. As you

think about them, keep in mind that you may have to tailor each one to fit your own husband.

NEEDS COMMON TO MEN

Men need to be loved.

Obviously, if your husband preferred living alone, you wouldn't be married to him right now. Every man needs to know that someone, somewhere in the world cares about him. He needs to feel warm, friendly acceptance from another person. He needs to know he has a committed, intimate friend who will like him no matter what he does. Just like you, he needs the security of genuine love. That's why the older women are to teach the younger women to love their husbands (Titus 2:4).

Genuine love is far more than a feeling; it's the kind of love that lasts a lifetime. It means a commitment to care for the loved one unconditionally. It says, "I'm committed to you no matter how you treat me or what happens." Genuine love does not depend upon emotions or circumstances. It takes full advantage of the present to bring meaning and joy to the lives of others. If your marriage is to become all that you long for, you must *begin today*, right now, to develop the unconditional love which forms the foundation of a fulfilling marriage.

As you begin to develop genuine love, it's quite possible that you will lack romantic feelings. Don't be discouraged. I guarantee that if you persist in expressing genuine love in actions and words because he's worthwhile, eventually the feelings will follow. And the romantic love you once shared with your husband will return. The notion that genuine love is something you feel at all times is a drastic misconception. Feelings are changeable—they can come and go. But love is an unchanging commitment. Your husband needs to sense your unconditional acceptance of him as a person—that you value his opinions no matter how he phrases them; that you are concerned for him no matter how unnerving his habits. He needs to know that you carefully, thoughtfully listen to what he says and that you consider his words and actions worthwhile.

Men need to be admired.

Men will do almost anything to gain the admiration of others. They will literally search for someone to love and respect them—and you can be that someone to your husband by letting him know you're interested in him, that you desire to know what's behind his decisions and the direction he's going.

Take advantage of the variety of ways to express genuine admiration. When he's down, don't react with disgust. Maintain respect for him as you comfort him quietly and gently. When you've hurt his feelings, admit you were wrong and ask for his forgiveness. When he shares an idea with you that doesn't sit right, don't come unglued. He needs the confidence and security of knowing that you won't react negatively to his ideas. Give him the same confidence that you have in the chair you're sitting in—a confidence that allows him to rest and relax with you. (If you need more ideas on how to admire your husband, refer to chapter 19.)

Men need to be understood and accepted.

You can't hide it. Your husband can sense it a mile away. I'm talking about that subtle thought you've probably had since you married: "I'll make him over someday." Sorry, but with that attitude, you probably won't.

Show him acceptance and understanding as he is. I'm not saying you have to accept his offensive ways without any hope of change. Just accept the fact that your husband needs to be taught—in creative ways—how to meet your needs. Remember, you are *in the process* of teaching him, and he is *in the process* of learning. If you're on the same train, don't expect him to get there before you do.

Men need to know their advice is valuable.

If you can stay on the "right side" in the following ways, I believe you will demonstrate to your husband that his advice is valuable.

You shun his advice by . . .	*You welcome his advice by . . .*
picking up the newspaper or sewing while he's talking.	putting aside all other interests while he is talking.
rolling your eyes.	giving him your full attention, eyes focused on him.
yawning.	pointing out positive or helpful aspects of his advice.
criticizing before you've heard him out.	letting him have the floor until he has fully expressed his opinion.
trying to get in the last word.	thanking him for the time he spent sharing his advice.

Men need to feel appreciated.

Your husband probably feels that his biggest contribution to you and your family is the financial support he provides. Obviously, then, one of the best ways to show your appreciation for him is to thank him regularly for his diligence and faithfulness on the job. Even if you are providing part of the income, it is crucial that you show him how grateful you are for his provision.

Aside from financial support, your husband also demonstrates his care for you in "little ways." Maybe he keeps your car maintained, or perhaps he empties the trash twice a week. Try to keep a mental list of little things he does that save you time and effort. Then thank him for them as often as possible. When he feels he is meeting the "big and little" needs of his family, his self-respect increases. As a result, he will begin to feel a deeper love for his appreciative wife.

EXPLAIN YOUR UNIQUE NEEDS AND DESIRES

Make a list of the needs and desires you would like to see your husband fulfill. Divide your list into four categories: emotional needs, physical needs, spiritual needs, and mental needs. In some areas you may have an overflow of needs, and in others you may have to struggle to think of one need. But delve into your feelings until you believe your list is complete. Condense the list into the smallest number of vital needs so it doesn't appear overwhelming.

As you explain the list to your husband, remember to discuss one need at a time until you've covered each subject. Your husband may have trouble accepting the importance of some of your needs, so you may have to discuss the differences between men and women where sensitivity is concerned. But be sure to maintain the right attitude while explaining. When you appeal to him for understanding, avoid self-pity, jealousy, or whining. These approaches are repulsive to anyone, especially your husband.

Finally, as you begin to discuss your needs, be sure to use the salt principle when appropriate. Look for creative ways and times to share these needs. For example, you might want to write your husband a letter explaining a few of your deepest longings. Be careful not to accuse or imply failures on his part; just explain how you feel. Let him read it alone if he chooses. Be sure he can read it during a calm, tension-free time of the day.

The Worst Approach

One woman told me she was extremely discouraged about her husband's lack of interest in her. He had a tremendous drive and interest in his work, his friends, his pastimes, but almost no interest in her or their children. She talked on and on about how much she had tried to get him to change. Nothing seemed to work. When I discussed it with her husband, I found she had continually confronted him with his failures as a husband. He said she always seemed to choose the wrong time to talk about their problems— "Just when I was trying to unwind." To top it all off, she came across as a combination of prosecutor, judge, and jury. Just before he went to bed, just as he got home from work, almost anytime he "let down" around her, she started condemning and reasoning.

I began to see that she had what I call a "contentious spirit," *one that always contends for its own way.* She was constantly pushing him into a corner, trying to make him see her point of view. Even the Bible describes the effects of a contentious woman. She dries out a man like the searing desert sun; she drives a man to the corner of a rooftop; she drips on a man like a steady rain (Prov. 25:24; 21:19; 27:15).

What perfect analogies. Around the house, this woman's habits were as annoying as a constant dripping—like a leaky faucet. Her contention was like the sun beating down on a wayfarer in the desert. No matter where her husband turned, he couldn't get away from it. He found no oasis of relief because she continually reminded him of his failures. Finally, her actions had forced him to the corner of a rooftop with nowhere else to go.

Want to know what brought him down off the roof in a hurry? His wife got rid of her contentious spirit. Consequently, she inspired a tremendous change in her husband. Today she describes him as a much more loving husband who meets her needs in ways she never even dreamed possible.

Explaining your feelings and needs is not the same as voicing complaints. One couple, who constantly bickered, determined to go through a whole week without voicing any criticism. Rather than argue, each time either of them became irritated, they wrote it down. Each time either was annoyed by the other's failure, he or she wrote it down. They placed each "complaint" slip in one of two boxes, a "his" and a "her" box. At the end of the week, they planned to open the boxes. He would read her complaints and she would read his.

Saturday night finally arrived, and he decided to go first. He opened the box and began to read the dozens of little notes, one at a time. His eyes reflected the hurt and disappointment in himself as he read her complaints. "You've been promising to fix the screen door for six months, and it's still not fixed." "You never put your socks in the dirty clothes." "I'm getting sick and tired of having to pick up after you everywhere you go." He was sincerely grieved by all the ways he had offended his wife.

Then it was her turn. She opened the box and pulled out the first slip of paper. She read it with a lump in her throat. The next note brought tears to her eyes. Picking up three more notes, she read them quickly and began to weep. Every note in the box read, "I love you." "I love you." "I love you."

Like many wives, you may have been fooled into thinking that one day your complaints would finally remold your husband into the perfect mate. But I hope the example above clearly illustrates that unconditional love and tenderness, not complaints, can transform a cranky opponent into a humble, loving partner.

However, it is important to verbalize your feelings. One wife touched her husband's heart with a note she wrote him. He actually changed his weekly schedule to include more time with her. The note read: "Many days I feel like a shining little red apple—one of the top ones in a barrel. Everyday you come by and choose one, but never me. Your hand comes close, sometimes you even lift me up, but always you choose another. I've got a little worm growing inside me, and each day I become less attractive. I long for the day that you choose me!"

EXPRESS YOUR GRATEFULNESS WITHOUT EXPECTATIONS

Recently I received a card in the mail from my wife. In it, she said that she loved me, that every year of our marriage was more fulfilling, and that she appreciated some of my recent attitudes and actions. There were no hints of hidden expectations in the card. She didn't ask for a thing, but she sure made me want to do more for her.

Through the years, Norma's "no beg" attitude has inspired me to search for creative ways to express my love to her. And it all started with some tattered furniture in the early years of our marriage.

Norma was sick and tired of the pitiful "late garage" style furniture we owned. For months she begged me to replace it. "Gary, it's just awful. I'm so embarrassed when our friends come over. Plee-e-e-ase, can't we get some new furniture?"

I felt like a slave to her expectations. *No matter what I do, she'll never be satisfied,* I thought. *I'm not about to buy her any new furniture with that attitude.* (What a domineering attitude I had then!)

One day it dawned on me. *She hasn't said a word about that furniture for over a year. She hasn't even dropped hints about it.* Sure enough, Norma had completely given up her expectations to the Lord (Ps. 62:1–2). She started focusing more attention on her inner qualities. At that moment I was willing to do anything for her. I was so grateful for her "new" attitude that I asked her how much money *she* would like to withdraw from our savings account for new furniture. Then we marched down to the local furniture store and bought a couch, lamps, tables, chairs. . . .

Norma's complaints accomplished nothing, but her non-demanding patience accomplished everything. Around our house we've noticed several factors make it easier for any family member to change: expressing the change you desire to see without attaching a time limit; showing appreciation for the slightest move toward change; showing acceptance and love regardless of change.

FOR PERSONAL REFLECTION

Using 1 Peter 3:1–6,

1. Write out your own definitions of admiration, and
2. design one practical application for showing gratefulness this next week. See also 1 Thessalonians 5:18.

22

How To Gain
Your Husband's
Comfort and Understanding
Instead of
Lectures and Criticism

*"To sum up,
let all be harmonious,
sympathetic, brotherly,
kindhearted, and humble
in spirit;
not returning
evil for evil,
or insult for insult,
but giving a blessing."*
1 Peter 3:8–9

IT WAS THE dead of winter, and Lois felt like she had been cooped up in the house for weeks. She had been invited to a women's luncheon so she jumped at the chance to get out of the house. She got in her car, turned the key, and to her dismay the battery was dead. Realizing her plans were ruined, she rummaged through her purse for the house keys. Suddenly she remembered she had left the keys inside the house. It was definitely "one of those days" ... she couldn't go to the luncheon, she couldn't get into the house, her neighbors weren't home, and there wasn't a phone nearby. Her only choice was to trudge to a phone in the bitter weather. On the way, a high school student recognized her and offered her a ride. She decided to go to her husband's office instead. Discouraged and depressed, she needed her husband's comfort.

Enter husband—irritated and angry. He just couldn't believe she had locked herself out of the house. And to top it all off, she had the gall to embarrass him by coming to his office during work hours. Just so it wouldn't happen again, he let the harsh words fly. Of course, his words produced nothing but more frustration and hurt feelings in Lois.

Why do men find it so much easier to lecture their wives than to comfort them? If you could climb into a man's mind, you would see that when he is confused or hurt he seeks a *logical explanation* for his feelings. Once he has made a clear analysis of the problem, he usually feels relieved. It is only "logical," then, that he respond to your problems in the same way. In essence, he thinks he can "talk you out of it."

But if your relationship with your husband is to be strengthened, it's vitally important that he learn when and how to comfort you. You shouldn't feel guilty about your need for someone to "lean on." That need is not a sign of weakness, as some would have you believe. It's simply a part of our human nature. We all need to lean at times.

I believe there are least three steps you can take to increase his awareness of your need for tender comfort.

GET EXCITED OVER HIS ATTEMPTS TO COMFORT YOU

The first step in motivating your husband to comfort you is to respond in a big way each time he does the slightest thing to comfort you. This is called *positive reinforcement*. It demonstrates how much you appreciate his understanding. I'm not telling you to try out for cheerleader each time he comforts you. Just remember to do something special for him—maybe a day, even a week later. Perhaps a special meal, a romantic night in the bedroom, or an unexpected love note in his lunch box or wallet. If there was anything you particularly liked about the way he comforted you, call attention to it. Regardless of what you do to show your appreciation, be sure he sees the link between your gratefulness and his act of comfort. Incidentally, he needs to learn how to comfort you as much as you need to receive it. He needs it for his own personal well-being and joy (John 15:11; Col. 3:12–15).

It's extremely important that you never ridicule or belittle any of your husband's attempts to comfort you. Even when his attempts are inadequate, rather than calling attention to his failure, praise him for anything positive in his actions. (Even the attempt itself is a move in the right direction!) Never try to gain his comfort by criticizing him for not comforting you.

Imagine for a moment that your son has just been taken to the hospital. You need someone to lean on emotionally. The anxiety is almost more than you can bear, but your husband just stands there. You're thinking inside, *Why don't you just hold me and reassure me?* So you blurt it out, "Don't just stand there. Come here and hold me." Now you've called attention to his inadequacy, compounding the anxiety and concern he feels for your son. Unfortunately, his natural response is to resist all the more.

People always respond more favorably to positive reinforcement than to negatives such as criticism or ridicule. In building your relationship, it's of utmost importance that you praise him for his attempts to be a comfort to you. But that's just the first step in motivating him to offer his emotional support.

TEACH YOUR HUSBAND
HOW TO COMFORT BY BEING HIS EXAMPLE

The second step goes back to a principle we discussed in the previous chapter—you reap what you sow. One of the most effective ways to teach your husband how to comfort you is to discover how he likes to be treated when he's down. Teach by example. When you sense that he is fearful or uncertain, ask him to tell you how he feels. Tell him you understand. If he reacts to you, saying something like, "Don't treat me like a little kid," then try another approach. Perhaps he feels unmanly or childish in your comforting arms. In that case, you can comfort him with your words and facial expressions. He won't resist when you learn to comfort him the way he needs to be comforted.

To some men, emotional support means taking their side in a conflict. For example, when John was in college, his fiancée broke their engagement and decided to marry one of his best friends. John's only consolation came when his roommate, Ted, responded with deep empathy: "John, I don't know what's wrong, but I know you're hurting. If you want to talk about it, or if there's anything I can do, just say so. If you don't want to talk about it and you want to be left alone, I'll just wait in the living room until you feel a little better."

John, touched by his roommate's concern, revealed that his ex-fiancée was marrying a friend. "I just need some time to be alone," he said.

When Ted walked into the other room, John overheard him say to his girl friend, "Your best friend Sue just went and got engaged to another guy. How do you like that?"

That was just the type of comfort John needed. His roommate really understood how he was feeling!

Try to detect the most meaningful ways to comfort your husband in each situation.

TELL HIM GENTLY HOW YOU DESIRE TO BE COMFORTED

The third step is to teach him how you, as a woman, need to be comforted. It's important to remember that his natural inclination may be to solve your problems "logically" so that they don't arise again. Much of this is covered in the book *If Only He Knew*, but chances are you'll still have to be his main teacher. After all, you're the one he is learning to comfort.

You may remember the story I told earlier about the wife who received a lecture virtually every time she needed comfort. She had to remind her husband four or five times, "Don't try to tell me why it happened. Just hold me." He finally got the message. Had she not persisted, he never would have learned how to comfort her. (One encouraging point: they had been married nine years before she tried to teach him how to comfort her, but it only took a few weeks for him to catch on.)

One woman who had left her husband said, "I just can't stand the thought of going back into that situation. He offends me in so many ways, and then he never comforts me when I need it. I just can't go back." I asked her if she would be willing to teach her husband how to comfort her. She gave me a funny look and asked, "What do you mean, teach him?"

"When you're in a stressful situation, or when you're discouraged, how do you want him to treat you?"

"I'd like him to put both arms around me and gently hold me. Then I'd want him to tell me that he understood or at least that he was trying to understand."

"Well, why don't you teach him that?"

"You're kidding! He'd think I was crazy. And besides, why should I have to teach him? He should do it on his own. I'd feel stupid having to tell him things like that."

I changed my approach a little. "Has he ever said things to you like, 'Honey, I don't know what you want me to do when you're discouraged. Should I cry, or kiss you, or . . . ?'"

Her eyes lit up and she said, "Yeah, it's amazing the number of times he's said that he didn't know what to do, or how to act, or what to say. I even remember him saying, 'You just tell me what you want me to do.' But I always thought he was being sarcastic, and I was offended because he couldn't figure it out by himself. I thought if I had to tell him it really wouldn't mean anything anyway. Do you mean some men really need to be taught the little things, like how to hold a woman tenderly?"

My answer was an obvious "yes." A lot of men avoid soft words and tender comfort because they have never been taught how to use them. Also, they simply don't understand the positive effects they will have on their wives and the sense of well-being they themselves will receive. I have found that once a man has learned why and how to comfort, he gains a real appreciation for the role it plays in his marital relationship.

During most of our marriage, my wife could never expect to receive comfort from me whenever she made an embarrassing mistake. I usually ridiculed her or got upset. But eventually, she began to share with me her need for sympathy, compassion, and understanding. Just when I was starting to get the hang of it, my newly acquired knowledge was put to the royal test. I came home one Saturday to find my camper parked at an angle in the driveway—not unusual in itself. Unfortunately, a large section of the garage roof was lying next to it in the driveway. Like most men, the first thought that came to mind was money. How much would it cost to fix it all? I felt like going into the house and screaming at my wife for her carelessness.

As these thoughts raced through my mind, I recalled the many times she had told me how she needed to be treated in upsetting situations. I walked up to her, put my arm around her with a smile, and choked out the words, "I'll bet you really feel bad. Let's go into the house and talk about it. I don't want you to feel bad for my sake."

Inside, I held her for a minute without saying anything. She told me she had dreaded my reaction as much as the accident. "That's okay, honey," I said. "We'll fix it. Don't worry about it." The longer I held her and the more I comforted *her*, the better *we* felt.

When we walked out to survey the damage, I realized it wasn't as bad as it looked. The roof hadn't splintered; the part that fell had sheared off neatly like a puzzle piece. All that was needed were some nails and a little paint. Within a few minutes, a friend had heard about the accident and had driven into my driveway with a pickup and tools; in an hour we had it completely fixed.

When we were finished, I thought to myself, *A couple of hours ago I could have crushed my wife's spirit, strained our relationship, and made her feel like an idiot ... all over an hour's work.*

Even though I thought Norma would be the only one to gain from my understanding attitude, in the long run I actually benefited the most. The increased admiration and respect I received from her provided an even greater incentive for comforting her. If you let your husband know that you deeply admire him for his comfort, he, too, will have an increased desire to comfort you.

FOR PERSONAL REFLECTION

Think of at least three future stressful situations that would cause you to desire comfort. Discuss these with your husband and explain exactly what you would need if any of the three situations occurred.

23

How To Motivate
Your Husband
To Receive Your Correction
Without Defensiveness

"The heart
of her husband
trusts in her,
and
he will have
no lack of gain."
Proverbs 31:11

"**YOU PAY MORE** attention to that stupid dog than you do to me," Sheila yelled at her husband. "How can a grown man love a dog more than his wife?" Resentment had been gnawing at her for years since Bill took up the habit of playing with Peppy before bothering to say hello to her. Finally the anger and hurt burst through her self-control. Bill reacted with more anger. Another argument had begun.

In this chapter you will learn how Sheila could have handled her complaint to get the result she desired. Read and study the following seven ideas to learn how to motivate your husband to *accept correction* without a nasty argument or a defensive response. Then give them a try. We think you'll be in for a nice surprise.

USE THE "SANDWICH" APPROACH

Always layer your slice of correction between two pieces of praise. For example, if your husband complains that you overspend on the children's clothing, use the sandwich approach: First, the bread . . . "Honey, I really appreciate how hard you work to provide so many nice things for us. You really do love us." Next the meat (your correction) . . . "Sometimes I feel like you think I'm spending money frivolously, buying more clothes than the children need. I just want you to know that I really try to watch how much I spend, and I

buy only what I think they need." And now the other slice of bread . . .
"But most of all, I just want you to know how much we appreciate
your hard work to make all this possible. The kids and I were talking
about what a fantastic father and husband you are. . . ."

Usually, the apostle Paul began his letters with praise before
he sandwiched in his reproofs. Look how he started the Book of
Philippians: "I thank my God in all my remembrance of you" (1:3).
Even defensive people are more receptive to correction when it's
cushioned with kind words.

One policeman used to dread stopping speeders, even though
it was part of his job , because of the hostility he encountered. He was
miserable on the job until an older patrolman shared his secret.
"Every time I pull someone over, I do something very important. It's
the one thing that keeps me from getting negative reactions."

First, he approached the traffic violator with a smile. *Second,*
he greeted him or her with a friendly "good morning" or "good
afternoon." *Third,* he asked, "How's your day going?" with genuine
concern. Usually the motorist would explain he had been having a
miserable day. But by the time he told his problems to the interested
patrolman, he was relaxed and congenial. Only then did the patrolman ask to see his license. After writing the ticket he would say, "I
hope your day improves for you."

The younger policeman tried this approach and found it
rarely failed. It can work for you and your husband too. Approach
your husband with a smile and friendly words. Then find out what is
troubling him. Once you've discovered the "burr under the saddle,"
you'll be much more understanding of his irritating behavior and
better equipped to offer constructive criticism. Remember, a soft
word turns away anger (Prov. 15:1). The more gentle and careful we
are, the more others can receive our criticisms.

One caution about the sandwich approach. You should praise
your husband from time to time without any corrective comments.
Otherwise, he might become wary of "sandwiches."

TRY THE "PUZZLE" APPROACH

You can't put a jigsaw puzzle together without all the pieces,
and you can't solve a problem without all the facts. (In Spanish the
word for puzzle is *rompecabezas,* which literally means "break your
head." And that's just what your husband feels like doing when you
don't give him all the pieces.)

The more facts I have about a disagreement between Norma
and me, the easier it is to find a clear solution to our problem. The
first fact I obtain about her feelings or beliefs represents only one

piece of the overall picture. When I lay it down on the table, it doesn't give me much of an idea about the finished picture. So, I add more pieces by asking questions, and the picture begins to take shape. Occasionally I try to force the wrong pieces together, but she lets me know when I do. Sometimes I try to guess what the completed picture will look like, but only when the pieces are fitted together do I know for sure. Often the finished picture (solution) is so simple that we wonder why we didn't see it right away.

Your husband can't put a solution together when you throw him one tidbit of information and stop at that. Nor can he wade through all the facts when you give him five hundred at once. Make it a point to give him one piece at a time until he has all the facts. (Simply give him the facts and let him draw his own conclusions.) When you don't focus on the consequences of his actions in a judgmental way, you'll be amazed how much easier he accepts correction. He may need a week, a month, six months, or more. The length of time depends on the individual problem, your attitude when you give him the pieces, and the strength of your relationship.

Incidentally, the puzzle approach is also useful when making personal decisions or helping your children learn to make sound decisions. Any fuzzy problem comes into focus when you take time to gather all the factors.

REPLACE "YOU" STATEMENTS WITH "I FEEL" STATEMENTS

Rather than expressing your feelings, "you" statements imply judgment and criticism; they place the blame on your husband. Try to replace "you" with "I feel."

Think back to the beginning of the chapter when Sheila accused Bill with, "You pay more attention to that stupid dog. . . ." Her "you" statement made her husband so angry and defensive they couldn't even discuss the problem. If she had used an "I feel" statement, the results would have been much different.

"Honey, I know that it's not intentional, but I feel like Peppy means more to you than I do. I know how ridiculous this must sound, but I just wanted you to know how I felt."

"Why do you feel that way?" he asked.

"Well, because when you come home from work, I feel you spend more time with Peppy than with me. This may sound insignificant, but if our relationship is going to grow and become all we want it to be, then it is important that I share my feelings."

Had the conversation continued, she could have gently shared a possible solution, but only at his request. "Why can't my husband come up with his own solutions?" you may ask. Unfortunately, some husbands probably wouldn't notice the problem if they tripped over it. In most cases, your husband will need a gentle nudge to notice and correct a problem.

MASTER THE "SALT PRINCIPLE"

Imagine that your husband is totally engrossed in a televised football game between two of the best teams in the nation. Then you make one statement that's enough to tear his attention away from the game and put it all on you. Impossible you say? Read on.

The "salt principle" stimulates your husband's interest in subjects he would otherwise find dull. The secret is in the manner of presentation. If you master the salt principle, he will practically beg to hear what you have to say, be it praise or correction. But you have to withhold your correction until you've created so much curiosity that he can't wait to hear it. The chart below illustrates the skillful use of the salt principle in correction.

Areas You Wish He Would Change	How to Tell Him By Asking Questions
He's too critical.	"Honey, what bugs you the most about the bosses you've had?" If he mentions criticism, grouchiness, etc., ask him how it made him feel. He'll probably respond with, "It really took the life out of my job." Now the door is open for you to explain your feelings. "Honey, that's sort of how I feel when you're critical of me. It takes the life out of sex and makes it hard to respond to you physically."
He's too harsh.	"Honey, do you think it's possible for our relationship to improve every year?" "Yeah, sure I do." "Well, you know, if we could correct one *big* thing this year, I feel sure our relationship would be much more fulfilling. Would you be interested in hearing about it!" If he says yes, then you can respond with, "Honey, when you're harsh with me about something I've done wrong, I really feel like pulling back from you,

especially when I'm already aware of my mistakes. I'd just love it if you would comfort me first, just hold me tenderly, and ask me how I'm feeling." If he says he is not interested in hearing about that "one big thing," wait until later and add more salt to create greater curiosity and interest.

He ignores you.

"Honey, could we talk about how I can overcome some difficult feelings I have when we're at parties?" If he says yes, you might say, "Sometimes I feel all alone, just standing by myself while you're off with other people. I know you need those times with your friends, but I feel left out. What do you think we should do?" You might suggest a creative alternative. Perhaps at some social gatherings you could plan to stay with your husband while at others you could go off with friends. Or, you might decide on a balance of time together at each social event. Another solution might be to agree on a signal you could use at parties to show your husband you'd like to be with him more. The signal might be a move toward the group with whom he's talking or a casual glance at him across the room. As long as your husband agrees to this solution, you won't have to fear being called a "tag-along." And having talked it out before the party, you will feel more at ease, more secure, more involved while you're there.

SET AN EXAMPLE
BY ENTHUSIASTICALLY RECEIVING HIS CORRECTION

An attitude of understanding and receiving his criticism not only is a wise decision, but will increase your love for him. That's what it says in Proverbs 9:8. When your husband finds fault with you, don't dig in your heels by offering a countercharge. Show him by example how to receive criticism without defensiveness. Admit that there is some degree of truth in his criticism, however small. When you're alone, reexamine his criticism and try to accept its valid points. Then get to work on the necessary changes. Talk about a heart melter! Nothing gets to the "perfect" husband faster than a pliable wife.

If you really want him to receive correction willingly, then actively *seek* constructive criticism from him. If you sense he is perturbed about something, ask him to tell you all about it. Draw him out about things you might have done to irritate him. When you see him building barriers between you, don't wait for him to explain. *Seek* his correction willingly. Only the wise seek reproof and they inherit honor (Prov. 3:35). We reap what we sow.

MAINTAIN OPEN COMMUNICATION WITH YOUR HUSBAND

Take down the barriers your offenses may have built by earnestly seeking your husband's forgiveness. Don't give him any excuse to avoid communication by leaving the lines crossed. It is crucial that you clear up each and every offense you cause if you want your husband to receive your correction in the future. Use your sensitivity to detect subsurface problems when your husband seems to shut you out, making sure there are no hidden barriers to your correction.

EXPLAIN WHY YOU NEED TO CORRECT HIM

I am often amazed at my wife's foresight, insight, perception, sensitivity ... she foresees the consequences of my decisions long before I carry them out. Like most women, she perceives the subtle effects my decisions have on our home and children. I consider it her *responsibility* to share her observations with me. They are invaluable. By sharing your unique womanly insights, you afford your husband a special steering mechanism that can keep your whole family moving in the right direction. You may not have all the answers and you may not be right all the time, but your insight is a priceless resource to your husband. Explain to him in a tactful way that you would like to help him make the best decisions possible. Share with him that you sometimes notice different angles on a problem that he might be interested in. If you explain your insights in this way, he won't be threatened by a know-it-all attitude.

FOR PERSONAL REFLECTION

Read several chapters of Proverbs and notice the number of times Scripture encourages us to seek correction from others and why we should seek it. For example, try chapters 1, 12, and 13.

24

How To Gain
Your Husband's
Appreciation and Praise

"Her children
rise up
and
bless her;
her husband also,
and
he praises her."
Proverbs 31:28

"HI, HONEY. JUST a little note to tell you that I love you and miss you. Hurry back to me!"

John smiled to himself as he folded the note and put it back in his wallet. During his ten-year marriage he has had to travel a lot. He usually arrives at his hotel discouraged and lonely. But through the years his wife has made those times of separation a lot more pleasant by hiding cards, letters, even cookies in his suitcase.

"I get a warm feeling whenever I find a surprise," he says, "because I'm reminded of her love for me. It really makes me feel better, though I still miss her."

John kept one of her notes in his billfold during his last business trip. Whenever he was down, he took it out and reread it. The note was a constant reminder of her love and appreciation for him.

John's wife gained his praise and appreciation by freely showing appreciation for him. I have found that everyone has a deep hunger for praise and appreciation. Never in all my years of counseling have I heard a woman complain of too much praise from her husband.

But I have heard the opposite. "My husband is always so critical. If he would only appreciate the things I do." Though many wives may feel there is no hope, I know a husband can learn to praise his wife. I have found two ways a woman can increase her husband's appreciation for her and at the same time stimulate his outward expression of appreciation.

SHOWING APPROVAL FOR YOUR HUSBAND

As you read earlier, men hunger for appreciation from others. They will gladly receive recognition from secretaries, employers, employees, friends, or anyone else willing to give it. A man's need for approval is as strong as your need for security in financial matters and family relationships. When a man knows his wife approves of him, he enjoys her companionship. He will find himself spontaneously complimenting her in response to the approval she gives.

Instead of demanding appreciation from your husband or shedding tears when he doesn't give it, try the approaches suggested below.

The Direct Approach

One way to show approval is the "direct" approach— expressing esteem for your husband verbally or through letters, love notes, and cards. I'm looking at two cards my wife sent me last month. In the past, I would have opened them and thought, "Isn't that nice?" before tossing them into the nearest trash can. But the more cards and letters I receive from Norma, the more anxious I am to reciprocate her "written praise." Now when I receive a note from her, I usually keep it for several readings. When she sends cards that cite specific qualities she appreciates in me, I feel inspired to think about her praiseworthy qualities and reciprocate with a card.

Though it's true that all men need appreciation, not all men like the same *form* of appreciation. Be careful to avoid forms your husband might find gushy or overly sentimental. You can discern what will encourage your husband and what will embarrass him by trying several ways until a few really hit home.

My heart goes out to one Baylor University coed who hired a fraternity group to sing a Valentine love song to her fiancé. She expected him to react dramatically to the surprise she planned, but he never mentioned it to her.

"Jim, how did you like your Valentine song?" she finally asked.

"Oh, yeah," he said. "I heard it, but I didn't really understand why you did it. It was kind of confusing to me."

His response left her hurt and confused. She honestly wondered if he cared for her at all. This pointed example illustrates something I hope each woman will remember long after this book has been read: men think differently than women.

The exercise below will help you learn how to show approval for your husband. In the left column, list ten admirable areas of his life. In the right column, record how you intend to praise him in that area. You may want to tell him personally or with a special note hidden where he'll be sure to find it. However you choose to do it, let it be your way of saying, "Honey, I really approve of what you've done and who you are." Remember, we can value someone even if they irritate us.

Things You Approve of About Your Husband	Direct and Creative Ways to Show Your Approval
1. _____	_____
2. _____	_____
3. _____	_____
4. _____	_____
5. _____	_____
6. _____	_____
7. _____	_____
8. _____	_____
9. _____	_____
10. _____	_____

The Indirect Approach

The "indirect" approach is another way to show approval for your husband. Husbands and wives were using this approach long before the flood of marriage books hit the market.

Norma's mother had this approach down pat years ago. Through good grooming and an encouraging 5:00 P.M. greeting, she showed "indirect" approval for her husband. Every day she prepared for his homecoming by bathing and putting on fresh clothing. Norma says she can't remember a single time when her mother greeted her father with problems or complaints. Instead, she let him relax and made him feel important by the extra time and effort she spent to make one part of his day happy.

Norma's mom was a good teacher. I have never come home to the wife portrayed in cartoons—dressed in a sagging, torn housecoat and curlers as permanent as light fixtures. Norma always looks good and smells good.

I could list thousands of indirect ways to show approval for your husband. Norma knows plenty of them. Just to name a few: she welcomes my suggestions about her wardrobe; she introduces me to new friends with a tone of voice that reflects admiration for me; and she constantly tells our children how much she appreciates me.

I remember the time when I came home from work dead on my feet, too tired to protest when my daughter climbed into my lap with sticky fingers. "Daddy, mommy says you work real hard to take good care of us." A warm sensation spread over me, and suddenly I didn't feel so tired. (Chances are, your children will let your husband know what's being said "behind his back." I hope for his sake that it's good.)

Praise your husband to his male friends and their wives. Just think what good gossip you'll spread when you say positive things about your spouse. Quite a switch from the usual complaints!

At this point, make a long list of the indirect ways you can show approval for your husband. Pick two or three of the best ones and be sure to apply them during the next week.

Three Ways to Alienate Your Husband

Wives often alienate their husbands by *unknowingly expressing disapproval of them.* Here's how one woman's disapproval drove a wedge between herself and her husband.

Joan always greeted Frank at the door with pushy advice about this problem or that decision. He began to dread his homecoming each day because he envisioned Joan as a stalking lion, ready to pounce on him.

One evening, before he could even put down his briefcase, Joan pounced. "I heard what you said to the Jacksons at the company party. I thought about it all day." Frank's stomach knotted in a hot wad as he blocked out her words. But her shrill voice pierced his defense. "Frank! Frank! You never listen to me. I want you to call the Jacksons right now and invite them to dinner next week. We have to be friends with them if you ever want to get anywhere in the company."

I can't believe she thinks I'm so dumb, Frank thought. *Why does she keep pushing me?*

A man often interprets his wife's bossiness as a lack of approval. *She must not think I'm too capable, judging from all the advice she gives me.*

In defense of many wives, I recognize that the passive nature of the typical husband forces a wife to "take over." I hear how very frustrating it is for you. My encouragement is that a natural response doesn't always gain the result you desire. Another paraphrase of Ephesians 5:22 is, "Let your husband take care of your needs just as you allow the Lord to love you."

Another way wives show disapproval for their husbands is by *discrediting their feelings or desires.* As a highly skilled art critic, one wife decides to quietly dispose of his pitiful Rembrandt reproduction. As an expert seamstress, another wife criticizes that "custom-made" suit he got on sale. Or, on a more realistic plane, the veteran gardener ignores her husband's desire to plant a pine tree on the front lawn and opts for a maple instead.

If you will listen closely, you can hear your husband expressing his desires every hour. Right now he may be mumbling behind his newspaper about chicken spaghetti with sour sauce and cherries on top like his mother used to make. Pick up on his subtle statement and make it for him. If you don't, he'll wonder whether he's worth anything to you. Resentment may spring up alongside his doubt, and soon he'll make unconscious efforts to eliminate things that please you. "I know what you want, but I don't want to do it" becomes the sad response of many husbands.

You may have to run on sheer willpower to respond to your husband's desires at first. But remember, good feelings usually follow loving actions. Who knows? You may even learn to like his mother's chicken spaghetti concoction.

As proof of your good intentions, write down at least ten things you know are important to your husband. Schedule one or two a week for him. The best way to obtain a completely accurate list is to ask him. "Honey, I'd like to sit down and find out what things in life are really important to you." His response may provide a list that will outlast your retirement years.

The third and most common way wives show disapproval of their husbands is by *contradicting them.* Have you ever sympathized with a husband who could hardly get a word out of his mouth before his wife jumped in with both feet to correct him. "No, that's not the way it was. It was like this...."

Contradiction is hardly an invitation to most husbands. No one wants to live with a know-it-all.

When Frank and Mary came to my office for marital counseling, she was by far the more "motivated" of the two. She not only answered the questions addressed to her but also those addressed to her husband.

"Now, Frank," I asked, "how do you see the situation?"

Before Frank could utter a sound, Mary would interrupt and say, "He'll say something about me, but it won't be true. He exaggerates."

I rarely become irritated in counseling sessions, but this time I began to boil within.

I asked, "Frank, what do you think the problem is?" and Mary said, "I think it's that he never spends any time with me."

Time after time, Mary answered Frank's questions. Even when he did speak up for himself, Mary had a countercharge that put him to shame. Several perplexing questions came to mind. Was the woman deaf? Had I misunderstood them when they introduced themselves—was her name Frank and his Mary?"

This kind of problem usually indicates a very passive, non-communicative husband. She's had to answer for him if any type of communication was to occur between them. However, after awhile he interprets this method as a put-down.

I suggest that with this type of person you: 1) direct questions to him in a loving, accepting manner to draw him out; 2) wait for him to express himself; 3) praise him for each genuine idea he expresses.

List the ways you have contradicted your husband lately and make a silent promise to forsake them in the future. Each time you are tempted to contradict him in front of someone, step into his shoes and imagine the embarrassment he will feel.

GENTLY TEACH YOUR HUSBAND
ABOUT YOUR NEED FOR HIS APPROVAL

Judy loved teaching because her principal commended her regularly for her skills and methods. Rarely did a day pass without a gentle, encouraging word from him. It seemed the more he praised her work, the better she became.

Imagine the effect constant praise would have on your attitude as a wife. You would work harder each day to BE the mate your husband talked about. You would also be absolutely free to praise him once you knew your work was appreciated. Don't be embarrassed to request his praise. There's nothing wrong with the boost you receive from sincere praise.

Norma once overheard a grocery store clerk explain how much she loved her job because the friendliness of the customers made her feel accepted and needed. "And my boss and the other clerks tell me I do a good job, too," she said. "I'd rather be here where somebody appreciates me than at home with that husband of mine. Even if I fix a ten-course meal, he doesn't notice. But just let me be late with dinner once! Then I hear about it."

This woman needed to admit her need for his approval. If a woman can't admit her need for praise, then her marriage will become stale and superficial. Her feelings of love and responsiveness will dry up, and she will start building walls to keep her husband at a distance. A woman will never completely feel like her husband's helper and completer until she *hears* how she is helping and completing (Gen. 2:18).

Be specific with your husband about *when* you need his praise. Try something like, "I know you want a happy marriage. Dear, would you like to know what you can do to make me a very happy wife? It won't cost you a thing. No energy—just a little creativity."

"What?"

"You can show your approval of me by praising me for who I am and what I do. For instance, I especially need your praise when I fix a special meal for you or go out of my way to do something extra. I just need to know how you liked it. I need it, and it's okay to need it."

Perhaps you can best explain your need for appreciation by relating it to one of your husband's personal experiences. When one husband asked his wife why she wouldn't take a vacation with him, she responded, "Would you want to take a vacation with your old boss?" (He had just quit his job due to harsh criticism from his boss.)

His wife gently explained, "When you criticize me, I feel like you do when your boss criticizes you. I feel defeated when you ignore the good things about my meals and point out what I forgot, like—"The salt isn't on the table," or "You didn't buy the right kind of butter. Even though we both have jobs, I feel you expect me to fix dinner while you watch television. I feel less than a person."

Dale broke down and cried. Within six months, he was a completely different person. Having conquered the temptation to complain, he is now free to meet his wife's need for approval and praise.

LIGHT UP WHEN HE PRAISES YOU

The last way to teach your husband about your need for approval is to "light up" whenever he praises you. Reward him with enthusiasm and excitement, making him subconsciously desirous of praising you more often.

As human beings, we all need and respond to praise. There is nothing shameful about longing for an occasional "pat on the back." So, demonstrate your legitimate need by responding to your husband's praise with a cheerful face and bright expressions. He will be sure to remember it next time you need approval.

FOR PERSONAL REFLECTION

Memorize Ephesians 4:29. List the words you can use to build up (edify) your husband. Then list the words that tear him down so you can avoid these. What comes out of our mouths should encourage and lift another (Ephesians 4:29).

25

How To Help
Your Husband
Share Responsibility
For Your Children
And the Household Needs

*"The ones
who are married,
they are concerned
about
how they may please
one another"
(paraphrased).
1 Corinthians 7:33–34*

WHEN YOUR HUSBAND bolts through the door at 5:00 P.M., where is he headed? What does he look forward to after work each day? A snooze underneath the newspaper in his easy chair? Maybe a good hour with the sawdust and skill saws in his workshop?

Is it so unrealistic to wish that he looked forward to being with *you* in the evenings, helping with the children and household responsibilities? No, it's not. I believe this chapter will help you to motivate your husband to strengthen his relationship with you by *sharing* responsibilities for the house and children. In other words, it will help your husband think in terms of doing things *with* you rather than leaving the whole "job" to you.

Dr. James Dobson, a leading psychologist, says his real work in life begins when he gets home at night—helping his wife with the children and developing relationships with them through meaningful activities. I would like all men everywhere, including your husband, to be a part of one of life's greatest challenges and obligations—family life. Here are four ways to increase his desire to "join the family."

CREATIVELY EXPLAIN YOUR NEED FOR HIS HELP

In general, a man doesn't understand a woman's need for help with the children and household responsibilities. Also, he may not understand how his neglectful ways affect your feelings of "going it alone."

The only way your husband *may* ever understand you is for you to explain it to him. Many women, fearing ridicule, are ashamed to tell their husbands when they are physically exhausted. Once while lecturing on this subject I described the tremendous fatigue many women endure raising preschool children. A woman in the audience later told me that as I spoke she literally relived the pain of raising three children without her husband's help. Not only had she suffered physical exhaustion, but emotional anguish as well when her husband belittled her duties in comparison to his in the "hard business world."

Due to the widespread misinformation about homemaking, many women shudder to admit their occupations as housewives. They feel like martyrs or second-class citizens. If a husband detects these attitudes in his wife, he too will begin to look on her with disdain. Soon his sarcastic verbal and nonverbal communication will cut into her inner-being, damaging her self-image severely.

You must paint a picture of yourself for your husband's benefit. Let it portray your physical limitations and your unique needs. Without it your husband may expect more than you're able to give. Paint another picture for him that shows exactly what you do around the house and with the children. Explain how many times a day you change your son's diapers, chase the children out of the street, and pick up after them. Help him picture the fatigue and pressure you face, knowing you'll never catch up with the housework. Open his eyes to the boredom you feel as you fold and refold, straighten and re-straighten, tie and retie. Then tell him about the mental drain of answering hundreds of, "Mommy, can I . . ?" questions.

While my coauthor put into words the daily tasks many women face, he said he felt an overwhelming grief about how blind he has been to his wife's hard work the last nine years. "Gary, I can't let her do all of this by herself," he said. "She's told me about these things for years, but I never realized till now what she's really been going through. As I think back, I've heard or seen her do every single thing you mentioned."

I learned the greatest lesson of my life not in college or graduate school but right in my own home. In one single lesson, I gained a deep understanding of what my wife goes through every day of her life. If every husband in America could undergo my experience, the wives in America would be enthroned as queens. What was the lesson? My wife had major surgery and spent two weeks in the hospital. During that time I took care of all three of our children. I cooked the meals—all forty-two of them, not counting the eighty-four snacks in between. And I attempted to fulfill the thousands of household responsibilities in my "spare time." I soon realized it would take all I had just to keep up with the kids and do "surface" cleaning. I couldn't do half the work my wife normally did. One day she asked, "Have you been able to clean out the closet?" Clean the closet? Good grief, I had been stuffing things in the closet just to get them out of the way! Once I even lost one of the kids and found him lodged between the basketball and the dirty clothes! "Honey, I haven't had time to clean out the closet. I'm exhausted!" I responded. All those additional tasks she crammed into her schedule made me realize how frustrating and exhausting housework can be without help.

I'm sure you realize that the average husband gets up Sunday morning, dresses himself, expects breakfast and glares because his wife isn't ready on time for church—while she's supervised dressing the children and everything else that goes into the preparation. Many of us men haven't even noticed it.

Perhaps you are one of the few completely organized women who can keep her household in perfect order with no assistance. I don't see how any woman can do that unless she neglects everything else in life to become the family maid. It would be far less backbreaking to gain your family's support in housekeeping. Try the following simple suggestion: Make it a game for each family member to pick up one misplaced item each time he or she leaves a room. That way, no one has to pick up everything, but everyone picks up something. And you don't have to face the frustration of straightening the house each time your family "blows through."

Another suggestion: Once you've explained your need for his help, appeal to your husband for help on the basis of his physical *strength* and *stamina*. Let him know when you need his strength to move a dresser or lift a heavy box. Tell him how much more lively you would be in the evening if he joined with you in your many projects. And remember, share your needs in a gentle, non-threatening way.

One newlywed husband snubbed his wife's request to help with the dishes. Frankly, he considered it beneath him. His mother had never expected that kind of help from his father. Besides, the dishes were her job. He worked all day and figured he had a right to come home and relax. He had his job and she had hers. *She probably sees an easy way out of her job now that I'm around,* he thought. But his attitude changed immediately when his wife finally explained that she just wanted to be with him, to talk to him and enjoy his company.

It's likely your father-in-law didn't help his wife around the house. If that's the case, your husband probably feels housework is unmanly. He may fear getting caught in the disgraceful act by friends or relatives and being tagged "henpecked" for the rest of his life. Or, he may simply doubt your need for help as he remembers his mother's "Lone Ranger" abilities.

Let me give you an example of how to empathize with your husband in this area: "Honey, I want you to know how much I appreciate your hard work. I realize you probably don't feel like helping me around the house after a hard day's work, but it sure would help me to meet your needs as a wife if you could do some things *with* me. Besides your physical help around the house, I'd also enjoy your company. You're just fun to be with."

After such a gentle suggestion, if your husband implies you've concocted a clever plan to get him to do your work, then try again another time. This is the perfect opportunity to express two of the inner qualities we talked about earlier—courage and persistance. Keep explaining in a gentle, creative way how much you need his at-home involvement, especially if you're working outside the home.

Looking back, I now see the damage I caused in my own marriage by expecting my wife to do what she was never made to do. I "forced" her to labor beyond her physical capacity, expecting her to help me maintain the yard, carry furniture, lift heavy boxes; I often even added errands to her overloaded schedule, thinking she had plenty of free time. And to make sure she wasn't loafing, I played Inspector General. "Norma, tell me what you got done today." If I had only known then what I know now!

A close friend shared my sentiments recently as he recalled the birth of his second child. Calloused and ignorant of women's needs, he let his wife resume her normal chores too soon after a very difficult childbirth. For the next three years she endured severe pain until she finally had to have major surgery. He said he now realizes that the pain and mental anguish she suffered could have been easily prevented by his tender understanding and help.

Remember, you're doing him a big favor by helping him *understand* you. "Husbands ... live with your wives in an understanding way ... and grant her honor ... so that your prayers may not be hindered (1 Peter 3:7).

EXPLAIN HOW HIS HELP
WILL BRING LASTING BENEFITS TO YOUR CHILDREN

Many child psychiatrists say children desperately need to see a genuine loving relationship between their parents. They have found that children who see a deep affection between their parents have fewer mental and emotional problems in life. Children whose parents are in conflict can lose their self-worth and can slip downhill into psychological problems.

The answer is not to focus all your affection on your children. Dr. Alfred A. Nesser of Emory University School of Medicine warns against centering the family primarily around love for the children. He believes even a longstanding marriage can disintegrate if the husband or wife gives more love to the children than to his or her mate. In the book *Seven Things Children Need,* John M. Drescher said, "The wife who loves her children more than her husband is endangering *both* her children and her marriage."

For your children's sake, it is crucial that you and your husband do everything possible to strengthen your love relationship. One of the best ways to demonstrate your love for each other is to do things together around the house. While you enjoy your husband's company, your children will be developing self-worth and security in the knowledge of their parents' healthy relationship.

MOTIVATING HIM TO HELP
BY SHOWING ENTHUSIASM FOR HIS HELP

Throughout this book we've stressed the importance of expressing approval through praise or other indirect methods. Perhaps the most forceful method is "lighting up"—showing enthusiastic appreciation with an appropriate facial expression. When you "light up" in response to your husband's help, you not only increase his feelings of self-worth, but you provide an incentive for him to help you in the future.

I've heard many wives say, "Whenever my husband helps around the house, he makes such a big deal out of it that I'd just as soon do it myself." Those women are forgetting that it *is* a big deal to him. He really believes any work he does after 5:00 is "overtime." Whenever he does a chore at home, large or small, he probably feels he's the greatest husband in the world. Don't pop his balloon by belittling his help. Instead, praise him and show genuine appreciation. Tell him you think he's extra-special since many husbands won't help their wives at all. Your praise will deepen his love for you and increase his desire to help you.

My mother had a knack for making me feel special. A widow for many years, she often needed my help around the house so she could work to support our family. Whenever I came home from school, the kitchen cupboard was usually stacked with breakfast and lunch dishes. Occasionally I cleaned up the mess, doing the best "little boy" job I could. When my mother came home from work and found it clean, she lit up with vivacious facial expressions. Then she felt my forehead, acting as though she thought I was sick. She never criticized my job, though I spilled plenty of water and broke a few dishes. She made such a big deal out of my little chore that I really felt great. The appreciation she showed made it all worthwhile.

When your husband does a "big thing" around the house, you can take one of two approaches. You can either drive him out with what he did wrong or draw him in with what he did right. Don't give your husband any excuse to avoid helping you in the future—no wrinkled brow, no disgusted grunt. Those of you who lean toward perfectionism will have to go extra-heavy on the patience until your husband learns how you want it done. Just accept his help, whatever its form, and correct it later.

And remember: It's never too late to change. One husband refused to help his wife with any household duties during nineteen years of marriage. But a personal crisis motivated him to change within three months. Now he clears the table after each meal and looks forward to washing the dishes with his wife. He also helps her with the laundry from start to finish. (His wife could have lost ground in their relationship by insisting on her special towel-folding method. Instead, she had fun showing him how to do it until he finally learned her way.)

GAINING HIS HELP BY INTRODUCING HIM
TO A REAL "MAN'S MAN"

One summer several years ago our family took a short vacation at a lakeside resort. We felt we needed a rest from all the pressures at home, a nice "family only" time together. But it didn't turn out to be just family. At the resort I met another husband whose relationship with his wife made such an impression on me that from then on I enjoyed helping my wife at home and with the children.

Strong and athletic, this man was a professional coach whom I had admired at a distance for some time. I enjoyed everything about him except the way he treated his wife. You'd think she was a queen the way he helped her. For one shocking week I watched him help prepare meals, set the table, and clean the table. He frequently offered to help without being asked and always took the major role in correcting the children rather than expecting her to assume total responsibility. Once he even encouraged his wife to read a book while he did the chores. Did he ever show me up! Next to him, I felt like such a failure as a husband and father that I almost wished I could pack up and go home.

You might suspect that his wife acted like she ran the show. Not so. She obviously loved him deeply and showed sincere respect for him at all times. She treated her husband like I wanted my wife to treat me. But I didn't dare compare her to Norma. After all, how could I expect that kind of treatment when I wasn't willing to give the same?

Maybe this "man's man" wasn't so dumb to put on an apron and bury his arms in dishwater. As I watched him with his wife and saw the love they shared, I began to realize I was the real dummy. If I wanted my wife to treat me like his wife treated him, then I would have to earn it. Many times I have been grateful for that man's tremendous example.

You may not know anyone like him, but keep your eyes open for a man whom your husband respects. If that man treats his wife the way you want to be treated, then try to spend more time with the couple so your husband can benefit from his example. However, *never* push your husband to change by comparing him to the other man. Believe me, your husband is much more likely to change as *he notices* his friend's living example.

GAINING HIS HELP WITH A SUGGESTED "HONEY-DO" LIST

Some husbands won't like my next suggestion at all. However, many will find it helpful in learning how to get involved in their wives' household responsibilities.

My wife frequently gives me a list of four or five jobs she needs help with on Saturdays or after work hours. She's always careful not to overwhelm me with too many tasks per list. And she always explains any details about the list that would otherwise be unclear. Like, "Honey, the doorknob I wanted you to install wasn't available at the hardware store so I need you to order it from the catalog." I happen to enjoy fixing mechanical things, but your husband might not. If that is the case, don't put jobs on his list that are frustrating and/or impossible for him. Give him enough jobs to get him involved and lighten your load but not so many that he dreads your next list. And above all, try to include jobs he can do *with* you.

Once you've made your list, stimulate your husband's curiosity about it. Explain how his help will directly improve your relationship, make it easier to meet his needs, etc. If he still reacts negatively, either drop the idea for a while or decrease the number of tasks until he begins to see the benefits of helping you.

FOR PERSONAL REFLECTION

As you pray that your husband will fully understand you and your motives to *share* your life with him, including the household responsibilities, learn the deep meaning found in Luke 18:1-6. With a calm spirit of expectancy from the Lord, patiently approach the Lord with your requests. And with this same spirit, approach your husband.

26

How To Motivate Your Husband To Meet Your Material Needs

"Be anxious
for nothing,
but in everything
by prayer and supplication
with thanksgiving
let your requests
be made known
to God."
Philippians 4:6

PERHAPS THE FIRST thing newlyweds learn is that two can live as cheaply as one—for half as long. Getting lifestyle in line with income is a tough requirement during those first years of marriage. It often sparks a war that can end in divorce court.

What one partner finds an absolute necessity, the other views as an unnecessary luxury. She may have kept a weekly hairdo appointment since the time she could walk. And her fashion-conscious husband may have been adding a shirt and tie to his wardrobe each month for the past fifteen years. So we're off to war over twenty-five dollars left in the till at the end of the month. He just has to have a new shirt and tie, and she knows she'll become the laughingstock of the community if she doesn't get her hair done. Husbands whose wives don't work outside the home often feel it's "my money" and rationalize with statements like, "If I'm going to be respected on my job, I have to look and feel successful." Statements like that can send a wife down Guilt Boulevard. She begins to feel guilty about wanting anything for herself. That, of course, is a primary motivation for women to seek outside employment—"So I can earn my own money." But even those wives who stick to the necessities may feel they have to justify or explain where each penny went. Their husbands may gladly fork over four or five hundred for a new toy and then grill their wives over a ten-dollar extra on the grocery bill.

Since their environment becomes an integral part of their lives, women often suffer depression when their homes are not an expression of themselves but an expression of what they can afford. "That picture is not my taste. It's just my budget." Obviously the solution is not an extravagant shopping spree to make your home the perfect illustration of you. However, you can gain the freedom to make your home an expression of yourself one step at a time. I am not suggesting that you neglect your family's basic needs in favor of home improvement. But it is possible that a portion of your husband's paycheck can be channeled toward your needs. This chapter will give you the essential tools to motivate your husband to cheerfully meet your needs as a wife, a mother, an individual, and a homemaker. After all, providing for his family is a basic biblical responsibility (1 Tim. 5:8).

Through the years I have pinpointed five ways husbands have been successfully motivated to meet their wives' needs. These five will not necessarily have the same effect on all men, so you will need to determine which approach has the best potential for your husband. For many of you, trial and error may be the only way to discover the best approach.

EXPRESS YOUR MATERIAL NEEDS
WITH CONVICTION AND ENTHUSIASM

For twenty years, Carol had "beat around the bush" when expressing material needs to her husband, Ken. Like many women, she feared the "third degree." Her husband had established a dependable routine of questions for those times when she expressed needs. As a result, Carol had developed a dependable justification which she used to prepare Ken for every need. Hardly a positive approach, hers was like a whimpering puppy's. She was always painfully mindful of her last "offensive" request and even more afraid of making another. Her husband usually responded with little or no interest. When he did give in and give her some money, his begrudging attitude made her feel even worse. But she finally grew tired of her approach and his response, realizing she was a worthwhile individual with opinions and ideas as valid as his. So, she decided to begin expressing her needs in a direct, positive way. Without apology or explanation, she said with a smile, "Dear, I need to buy a new coat for Tommy. It's getting cold, and the other one is worn out. I need thirty dollars because I'm going to buy it today."

She was shocked by her husband's response. "Hey, that's

great. Thanks for taking care of it." He gave her the money, no questions asked. (Keep in mind that money was no problem for Ken. He had plenty of it, but kept it in a tight fist.) All it took was a logical presentation with confidence and conviction on Carol's part. Once Ken sensed the urgency of the need, he was willing to loosen up and meet it.

Many women meet less resistance, criticism, and questioning when they express their needs directly to their husbands. Though the direct approach may fail with some husbands, I do know it works on me. I really appreciate my wife's straightforward, enthusiastic, and logical way of expressing the needs of our family. "Conviction and influence" is the Hebrew meaning of the "virtuous" woman described in Proverbs 31:10–31.

Even outside my home I am influenced daily by this principle. When people approach me with a long preamble of excuses, invariably I lose interest in helping them. Their excuses attach a "low priority" tag to their needs as far as my time is concerned. When I hear, "Mr. Smalley, I really would like to talk to you but I hate to take up your time," I think to myself, *I'm really too busy to help him.* On the other hand, when people ask for my time with conviction and enthusiasm, I am usually eager to meet with them. "Gary, I've come up against a tough problem, and I need some answers right away. I wanted to get moving on it, and I know you're the person to help me. Could you take some time? It's very important." Of course I will. I get enthused about helping people like that because I know they are ready for a solution. They are coming to talk because they want answers right away.

Here again we can focus on the value of women. Since women appear to be more observant about relationships, it would be reasonable to assume that you more readily notice the special physical needs of your family and your children. And since men tend to be more preoccupied with their vocation, they need reminders. Recognize your strength and let your husband *see* your convictions and enthusiasm.

Let me also remind you that timing and attitude are crucial to the effectiveness of this approach. Be particularly sensitive to your husband's state of mind before you approach the subject of needs. He may need time to relax, take a shower, or jog before you begin the discussion. Once he's ready, share your needs and your feelings honestly but not critically. Take care not to accuse your husband of being unconcerned. Above all, avoid anger. It can provoke your husband to dig in his heels and rationalize his attitudes more than ever.

An enthusiastic attitude can evoke just the opposite response.

When a husband picks up his wife's contagious enthusiasm, he too will consider her needs top priority. Get the enthusiasm flowing by recognizing that your needs are valid and worth expressing with confidence. Your husband will notice the difference and begin to acknowledge your special awareness of needs.

APPEAL TO HIS SENSE OF LOGIC

Most men require an orderly presentation of facts before they can make a decision. That's why it's important that you learn how to express needs in a way he can "process" them. Any time you want to present a need to your husband, ask yourself the following four questions:

1. Why do I need it?
2. What is the best product on the market?
3. Where can I buy it for the lowest price?
4. What will be the consequences if I don't buy it now?

Why do I need it?

This question will help your husband see the benefits of the purchase you want to make. Even a new dress or a beauty shop appointment for you can have positive effects on your husband and family. What may appear a selfish request on your part is often a potential benefit for your family. How so? Don't you feel 100 percent better with a new hairdo? Doesn't it affect the way you treat your children and your husband at the dinner table? If so, all you have to do is record *why* you want to make a particular purchase and the positive effects it will have on your husband and family. Then simply present the facts in a calm, orderly manner.

What is the best product on the market?

Even though you've finally decided you really need that sofa, you're not quite ready to approach your husband. Now you must discover the most effective way to meet the need over the long run at the lowest cost. You should decide on the style and brand that will give you the longest life at the lowest expenditure. The cheapest sometimes ends up being the most expensive. For example, one sofa may seem a bargain at $400. But if it is constructed so cheaply that it lasts for only two years, the pro-rated cost of that "bargain sofa" is $200 a year. On the other hand, a higher quality sofa may cost you $600 and last six years. Although it cost $200 more initially, in the long run it costs only $100 a year. I'm not suggesting that the highest quality merchandise is always best for you. Many of your purchases will be limited by your income. However, if you can postpone your purchase and save for the best long-term buy, you will demonstrate wisdom and business ability to your husband. And the fact that you've researched the available products will impress him with the seriousness of the need. Telephone several stores and ask a salesperson to give you the brand names of the best merchandise. After several calls, one brand may be mentioned as the best by four or five salespeople.

Where can I buy it for the lowest price?

I doubt that you need help in this area. Most women are excellent shoppers. The one thing I do want to point out, though, is that your husband needs to know you have checked the prices in *several* stores. I'm always impressed when Norma can show me the high price tags in three or four stores and then the low price tag where she intends to make a purchase. It makes me feel more secure, knowing she's not getting taken by a salesperson. Comparative shopping, since it takes time and effort, proves that my wife isn't on an impulse-buying spree.

What will be the consequences if I don't buy it now?

As you consider the answers to this question, the weak supports for your need will fall away, hopefully leaving the genuine urgency for it. Thoughtful consideration may reveal you really don't need to make the purchase in the time frame you originally established. If that is the case, the time pressure will be lifted like a burden from your shoulders. On the other hand, you may discover serious consequences that would result by not making the purchase immediately. That kind of evidence would communicate the urgency of the need to any husband.

After you have the answers to each of these four questions, you should be ready to make a logical presentation to your husband. If after plenty of research you still don't know which item to buy or where to buy it, then get your husband in on the act. Anything you can do together will strengthen your relationship.

EXPRESS GRATEFULNESS
FOR THE NEEDS HE HAS ALREADY MET

There are plenty of creative ways to express gratefulness for the material needs your husband has met. One wife expressed gratefulness by getting rid of a piece of furniture her husband hated. When he noticed it was gone, she told him she had disposed of it to express appreciation for the way he had met a family need.

LEARN TO BE SATISFIED WITH YOUR HUSBAND ALONE

For years I was burdened with my wife's material expectations and had little motivation to meet her needs the way she desired. But suddenly she changed course. Nearly every day she expressed genuine appreciation for me. Material possessions took a back seat. After a full year of her direct and indirect appreciation, I finally realized that she did love me just for being me, not for what I did for her. Soon I was looking for every opportunity to meet her needs and our family's needs. I didn't think of denying her that furniture she wanted for years. Now that I knew her expectations weren't on the furniture, I felt free to buy it for her. We made a major project of it and spent several thousand dollars furnishing our home the way that she had always wanted.

I have met wives so content in their personal relationships with God, their husbands, and their families that they are able to live happily in circumstances as they are, with the philosophy, "What you've got is not nearly as important as who you've got."

KEEP A "HONEY-DO" LIST OF MATERIAL NEEDS

This last approach may turn many men off, but for some, like myself, it provides a handy reminder of genuine needs. A "Honey-Do" list is a record of material needs you would like your husband to meet within a given period of time. The items on the list should be reasonable and attainable for your husband with your budget. It serves as a "preview" of family needs, releasing your husband from the pressure of unexpected expenses. Use your sensitivity to determine whether your husband would genuinely appreciate a list like this. If you sense he is interested, begin to work on the list *together* and put the items in order according to their importance. If you notice your husband feeling burdened with the list, by all means revise it or tear it up. Its purpose is to ease, not increase his load.

I'm for all husbands meeting their wives' material needs in a loving way. I'm confident that you can motivate your husband to do this by living the five approaches I described in this chapter. But I hope you will keep your affection and desire centered upon the Lord and your husband instead of material possessions. Only *relationships* afford lifelong satisfaction.

FOR PERSONAL REFLECTION

Application of Philippians 4:6–7:
1. Make a list of your important household needs.
2. Calmly and expectantly let the Lord know about your list of needs.

3. In a spirit of thanksgiving let your husband know about your earnest prayer list. Let him know that if God directs him to help, you'll be thrilled.
4. Accept the Lord's *peace* as you *wait* for Him to answer your prayer, possibly and hopefully through your husband.

27

How To Increase And Deepen Your Husband's Affection for You

*"He
who sows sparingly
shall also
reap sparingly;
and he
who sows bountifully
shall also
reap bountifully."
2 Corinthians 9:6*

TIM GLANCED ACROSS the breakfast table at Ruth. As he looked at her, he came to a sickening realization—"I don't feel any love for her anymore . . . why am I even married to this woman?"

Obviously, Tim's ailment couldn't be cured with two aspirin and plenty of fluids. He was suffering from the age-old problem of unrealistic expectations, thinking his mate would always be the twenty-year-old he married. But she had changed in the past eight years.

Typically, most of us expect our mates to retain their original physical and emotional attractiveness. But a funny thing happens on the way to retirement . . . we change. And if we change the things our mates once found attractive, we have to replace them with something better.

Even in the courtship phase of your relationship, his affection for you didn't "just happen." It grew in response to something he liked about you. Perhaps his feelings were stirred by your appearance, your personality, or the way you made him feel. If you have disposed of those positive qualities, his love for you may have dwindled to apathy.

During the courtship days, you probably had limited exposure to your fiancé. It was easy for each of you to put the other's needs or best interests first since you didn't have to do it twenty-four-hours a day. Obviously, if your fiancé was putting your best interests first and fulfilling your needs to the neglect of his own, your heart was melting daily in response to him, and vice versa.

After marriage, things quickly changed. The exposure was no longer limited to times when you were both "at your best." His own interests began to take precedence over yours and vice versa. Under these circumstances it didn't take long for swelling affections to subside.

That's why "the other woman" is at such an advantage. She can offer the new attractions your husband assumes you have lost. She can quickly stir the deep, romantic feelings your husband longs to feel toward you. In the context of their brief encounters, both of them can temporarily subdue their self-centered natures and put the best foot forward.

What specifically can you do to increase your inward beauty which is naturally reflected through your eyes and facial expressions and definitely increases your attractiveness?

KEEP A SPARK BURNING

There are several ways you can "keep a small spark burning" in your husband's heart for you. I know that you would love to see your husband initiate romance, but you may have to light the fire yourself for a while. Even though you begin to practice some of the following ideas, your husband may not fall head-over-heels in love with you overnight. However, his affections will change gradually. So don't be surprised if someday you wake up and he's the one kissing *you* on the cheek. Be prepared, in the meantime, for his shock, laughter, or even negative response to your romantic attempts. Just let him know that you love him and that you are trying to express your love in special ways. The ideas I suggest are by no means all-encompassing. There are probably thousands of ways to bring romance into your relationship. Hopefully mine will serve as a springboard for your own creative ways.

Plan activities that will make him feel special.

Here you can let your imagination run wild. Although the possibilities are endless, you know what type of activities would make your husband feel special. Perhaps his favorite meal by candlelight or a weekend getaway to his favorite resort. Whatever the activity, you can always enhance it by wearing his favorite perfume or a dress he really likes.

By planning special activities from time to time and adding a little variety, you will be showing him how special you think he is. He may not offer praise right away. Don't expect it. If you persist, eventually he will respond with praise and increased affection.

Occasionally be the initiator in the sexual area of your relationship.

Men usually initiate sexual advances in marriage, and do not really need preparation to be sexually aroused. A woman, on the other hand, needs to be prepared with gentle loving romance. Her responsiveness to sexual advances may even be affected by her husband's behavior over the past days and weeks. Although you understand this, your husband may not. Even though it may seem unnatural, it is important that you occasionally initiate intimacy if you wish to increase his affection for you.

If you have been belittled, crushed, criticized, or beaten down through the years, it may be extremely difficult for you to initiate sex. Many women have said that making love with their husbands without being emotionally prepared makes them feel like prostitutes. For a woman to engage freely in love-making, she has to give her whole self to her lover. When she is unable to do this because of his bad treatment or inadequate preparation, she feels as if he is simply using her body. If you have felt similarly toward your husband, it may sound nauseating to initiate sex with him on sheer willpower. However, as your relationship grows and deepens, you will find it more natural to give yourself to him and even initiate sexual intimacy.

When you do initiate it from time to time, use imagination to make the bedroom and your appearance as inviting as possible. Perfume, candlelight, gentle words, and a soft touch are just a few of the ways you can add creativity to the occasion.

Another way to make the occasion more fulfilling for you and your husband is for each of you to concentrate on meeting each other's sexual needs. I have found that a selfless, giving attitude contributes most to sexual enjoyment. A man's greatest fulfillment comes when he puts his whole heart into stimulating his wife and bringing her to a climactic experience. At the same time, a woman is most fulfilled when she concentrates on meeting her husband's needs. Selfish sex does nothing but remove the potential for maximum pleasure.

Needless to say there are dozens, if not hundreds, of books written by authorities on how to make the bedroom experience more fulfilling. But I firmly believe that sex at its best happens when a husband begins to meet his wife's emotional needs on a daily basis. All the techniques and atmosphere in the world can't warm up a neglected wife.

Remain flexible.

Most women would like to have their days scheduled from beginning to end, with no surprises. Schedules can be beneficial when they provide a guide for the day, but they can also become inflexible taskmasters. The day is ruined for some women when one item on their schedule has to be changed. All they can think about when their husbands come home is, "I'm behind on my schedule, and tomorrow will be worse if I don't catch up before bedtime."

If you want your marital relationship to deepen, it is very important that you learn to be flexible. I believe there is nothing as important to you or your family as a good, loving relationship with your husband. Your flexibility can make your husband feel really special and can keep that "spark" in your relationship. When he comes home and sees that you are willing to set aside your schedule for an unrushed conversation, he feels valued and loved.

Occasionally I come home late at night after meeting with a couple or a group. It really means a lot to me when my wife wakes up and spends a few minutes listening to me unwind as I tell her about my evening. Sure she's making a sacrifice, but it makes me feel important and deepens my affection for her.

Your schedule is important, I realize. However, you need to maintain a balance by being able to set aside your priorities from time to time to pay special attention to your husband and his needs. That's genuine love.

Keep yourself in good physical condition.

Health's most bitter enemies are lack of sleep and an improper diet. When they team up with constant stress, they can leave a woman irritable—not exactly an invitation to her husband's affection.

Believe it or not, one major answer to the problem of fatigue, listlessness, and irritability is regular vigorous exercise. One psychologist told me that exercise not only improves one's physical condition but also provides an excellent remedy for discouragement and depression.

Establish a routine of regular, vigorous exercise, whether it be jogging, bicycling, an exercise class, or working out at a health spa. (Be sure to consult your physician if you have any health problems that might be restrictive to certain types of exercise.)

INCREASE YOUR RESPONSIVENESS TO YOUR HUSBAND

A man loves a responsive woman. In fact, a man's self-confidence is directly related to the way others respond to him. A man will tie his affection to those who respond to him and remove it from those who don't. There are at least two ways you can increase your responsiveness to your husband.

Maintain an openness and willingness to yield to him.

I am not talking about the doormat concept of blind submission. God gave you a mind and feelings that He never intended your husband to trample underfoot. But I am talking about the willingness *to be open* to whatever your husband has to say. A willingness to hear him out and yield, if you can do so without violating your own conscience. This type of submission is not a sign of weakness, but a sign of genuine maturity (Eph. 5:22).

You know your child is growing up when he or she begins to notice and defer to the needs of others. Likewise, adults demonstrate maturity when they are willing to submit for the sake of one another. A man needs to have a submissive attitude toward his wife by considering her feelings and unique personality when making decisions. He needs to be willing, at times, to yield to her preferences. The more mature we are, the more willing we are to yield to one another.

In marriage, submission is not always simultaneous. Someone has to begin. If it doesn't start with your husband, then why not let it start with you. Perhaps he'll take advantage of your submission at first, but eventually he may take up your mature approach himself.

Carefully consider what your husband says without reacting to him.

Give attentive consideration to what your husband says *without* reacting negatively. Don't just accept the surface meaning of his statements. Ask questions and probe gently until you have a thorough understanding of what he's really trying to say.

Don't play mind reader. Too many wives assume they know their husbands well enough to predict what they are going to say. Some wives even claim to know their husbands' hidden motives. If you're going to assume anything, I hope that you will assume pure motives on your husband's part. If you do, you will be much less resistant and much more responsive to his statements. Don't react to his statements while he's speaking, but consider them and retain anything of value in them.

"You're just being weak," one husband said when his wife asked for an occasional "I love you." Needing reassurance of his love, verbally she had been slapped in the face. Obviously her affectionate feelings were dampened by his comment. Had she only stepped out of the circle of offense and taken time to consider his response, she could have learned a lot—that she needed to share why his expressions of love were important, that he approached the subject from a different reference point, and that he had *not* intended to hurt her.

As you become more responsive to your husband by learning to yield and not react, you will increase his self-confidence and self-worth. As a result, he'll gain a deeper affection for you.

KEEP THE IMAGINATION IN YOUR RELATIONSHIP ALIVE

Most of us are not fond of our daily ruts. We flock to the unusual, the novel, the unexpected in life. It's no wonder that routine marriages break up. There are too many interesting carnivals all around. When a wife can predict her husband's every mood and a husband can predict his wife's, their marriage is in for trouble. As they say, "Variety is the spice of life." So let's put some spice into your marriage.

I jog two to five miles every day, but I never take the same route two days in a row. I don't want my jogging to become monotonous. Variety keeps it interesting. The same holds true for your marriage relationship. Monotony can't set in when you add variety to your dinners, your conversations, your outings, your dates, your sex life, and your appearance.

One of the best ways to keep the imagination alive in your realtionship is to be well-informed. Ask your friends how they add creativity to their marraiges. Read books and magazines about subjects that would stimulate interesting conversation. My wife contributes so much to the variety of our marriage because she is constantly learning. She not only keeps her mind alert by reading, but she also takes courses on nutrition, gourmet cooking, and other special subjects. It seems she always has something new and interesting to talk about.

CLEAR UP YOUR PAST OFFENSES TOWARD HIM

In chapter 19 we discussed the importance of clearing up offenses against your husband. It would probably be beneficial to review that chapter now.

Each time you offend your husband without clearing it up, you drive a wedge in your relationship. Nothing will remove that wedge except your humble request for his forgiveness. Write down at least three or four things you have done recently to offend your husband. Then go to him with a humble attitude and ask his forgiveness as we discussed in chapter 19. You might even take it a step further and ask him what other areas of your life offend him.

Sally was afraid to try this because her close friend had been blasted when she asked her husband how she could improve as a wife and mother. "But I'm still planning on doing it," Sally said, "because I saw how much it improved my friend's marriage." Sally's friend had finally let her husband's correction sink in and take effect. "She stopped dominating and let him lead out in public," Sally told me, "and it really improved their relationship."

Perhaps the greatest step toward maturity is learning how to admit when we are wrong. When we can humbly seek another's forgiveness, we not only clear the offense but we also gain the respect of the offended one. What takes more courage—ignoring your offense or admitting it? The only time I ever sensed a negative reaction when I asked for forgiveness was when I asked with an accusing attitude. When others sensed a lack of genuine sorrow, they often reacted with bitterness or anger. But when they sensed a sincere grief on my part, their respect for me seemed to increase. Not only is God drawn to the humble—so are others (James 4:6).

REMAIN A CHALLENGE TO YOUR HUSBAND

I've discovered a deep truth in Proverbs: "If a man is hungry, almost anything is sweet; if he is full, even honey is distasteful" (Prov. 27:7, my paraphrase). What a powerful statement of human nature —we all tend to desire what we cannot have and become bored with what we have conquered.

Before you married, you probably were your husband's number one challenge. He got more of a charge out of winning you than anything else in life.

A man is often willing to set aside everything—relationships, projects, vocation—in order to pursue the woman he wants to marry. Unfortunately, soon after the wedding his sense of challenge departs, and he "buries himself" in projects, vocation, and other relationships. "Ah, but if I play hard to get, that'll get my husband's attention," you say. No, that may only frustrate him. But if you maintain a confident independence, showing him that he is not your sole purpose for living, he will feel challenged once again.

Before we were married, I dated my wife sporadically over a period of four years. It seemed Norma was always available. I could call her on a moment's notice and she was always ready to go out with me. She was easy to talk to, and I loved being with her. But I took Norma for granted—perhaps because she was always available when I called her.

Then one day I heard she was dating another guy. For some strange reason my affection for her increased immediately. I thought I was going to lose her. I pursued her vigorously—all the way to the altar. But once we were married, the challenge was over. Boredom began to set in for both of us. Through many of the principles in this book, we overcame the boredom, and to this day Norma remains a challenge to me. I know she is not totally dependent upon me for her happiness. She has a deep relationship with God and looks to Him for her ultimate fulfillment (Ps. 62:1–2; Eph. 3:19–20).

USE YOUR NATURAL ATTRACTIVE QUALITIES

Several years ago a friend of mine was attending a retreat for college students. He had been married for about four years and was actively involved in counseling college-age young people. On the retreat, a very attractive young blonde came to him for counseling. In a moment of emotion, she put her arms around him seeking his comfort. He tells me that to this day, six years later, he can still remember her soft and gentle embrace. He said that in the course of his marriage his wife, who had been so gentle and affectionate when they were dating, had never touched him so softly. But one moment with that young girl had melted him. He said he hasn't seen her since, but he's never forgotten her soft voice and gentle touch.

What has happened to all the lovable characteristics that first attracted your husband to you? Perhaps it was your quiet, gentle voice . . . your gentle spirit . . . your ability to listen . . . your vivacious personality . . . your keen mind . . . your sense of humor . . . whatever qualities made the total person to whom he was initially attracted. Have some of them gotten lost through the years? Do you scream for his attention now? Are you too busy to listen to him? Have you lost your sense of humor?

I realize that your husband's inattentiveness through the years may have drained you of some of these qualities, may have driven you to scream or throw things, may have caused you to ignore him. But if you are to recapture his attention, you must somehow recapture and exhibit those qualities unique to you that first drew him to you. (These same qualities are very likely what might now attract him into the arms of another woman who exhibits them.)

GENTLY TEACH HIM BY SHARING YOUR FEELINGS

Your husband may think he is one of the most affectionate men ever to walk the face of the earth. If he's not, are you willing to teach him how to be? Maybe he assumes going to bed with you is all the affection you need. But you and I both know nothing could be further from the truth. When you do share your feelings, wait for the right time and the right circumstances. Present your feelings as clearly and logically as you can. If he reacts negatively to them, wait for another time. But be persistent. Try not to pressure him, but patiently and gently explain to him how you feel.

Sharing your feelings takes persistence, but it also takes a method that really helps a man to better understand your true feelings. The most effective method I'm aware of is called "feeling word pictures."

These are feeling words related to a man's interests or past experiences.

Here are some examples:

- I feel like I'm a sixty-minute cassette tape and you play me romantically at night like I'm a ten-minute tape.
- I feel like a towel after a full day of washing dirty trucks.
- I feel like a two-hour-old McDonald's hamburger.
- I feel like a worm after catching a big fish.
- I feel like a golf ball after 18 holes for one important tournament, discarded or ignored.

FOR PERSONAL REFLECTION

List at least five ways you are enriching your husband's life and your marriage. Remember 2 Corinthians 9:6.

28

How To Become Your Husband's Best Friend

"It is
not good
for the man
to be alone;
I
will make him
a helper
suitable for him."
Genesis 2:18

ONE OF THE most important objectives of this book is to help you become your husband's best friend. If you achieve this goal, many of the other objectives we talked about will automatically fall into place. A best friend is someone with whom you share intimately, someone with whom you love to spend time. Maybe that doesn't describe your husband's feelings for you at present—or your feelings for him. But don't give up hope. In this chapter we will discuss some additional ways you *can* become his closest companion.

SHARE COMMON EXPERIENCES TOGETHER

Within a period of three years, I interviewed more than thirty families who were very satisfied with their inner-family relationships. Theirs was not a superficial satisfaction, but a deep love and fulfillment. The families came from diverse geographical and social settings, and their economic bases ranged from very modest to very wealthy. But all of the families had two things in common, one of which was a concern for togetherness. In each case, the husband and wife tried not to schedule independent activities that would take them away from each other or from their children on a consistent basis. They also avoided activities that would not contribute to the well-being of the total family.

Careful planning was an essential key in these homes. Though a certain degree of flexibility was present for the pursuit of individual interests, each family member worked to create a mutually supportive unit. The family, it seemed, became a "person" in itself, nourishing itself and protecting its best interests. Typically, the husband and wife spent some time in joint acitivites, but more time in activities including their children. When one of the family members participated in an individual activity, the others made an effort to support him or her. (For example, the whole family would turn out for a Little League ball game.)

The other striking factor common to all these happy families was their love for *camping*. My wife and I had never been inclined toward campfires and army cots, but when I discovered that all thirty "ideal" families were campers, we decided to give it a try.

I borrowed a "pop-up camper" and we made plans to camp our way from Chicago to Florida. The first night on the road we arrived in Kentucky. It was a beautiful night, and I thought, *I can really see why this draws families together.* We talked around the campfire, sang songs, and roasted hot dogs. By nine o'clock we were pleasantly tired and tucked in bed. A romantic bit of lightning flashed in the distance followed by a gentle roll of thunder. Then it happened! That gentle thunder became a deafening boom that seemed to hover over our camper. Terror seized my little troop. Rain beat against our camper so hard that it forced its way in and soaked our pillows.

Norma and I were both frozen in terror when she squeaked, "Do you think the camper will blow over?"

"Not a chance," I said. *But it might blow up*, I thought to myself.

Who would consider camping after a horror story like that? We did. In fact, we've endured far worse at times. It seems some of our worst tragedies and arguments happen on camping trips. And that's precisely why we've become avid campers. So many things can go wrong that a family is *forced* to unite just to make it through the tough parts of the trip. The good side of camping enables a couple and their children to share the beautiful sights and sounds of God's creation. For years afterward, they can reflect on the tragic and happy experiences they struggled through together. The feeling of oneness lingers *long* after the camping trip is over.

Your first attempt at scheduling family activities may be difficult due to over-commitment. If your husband or family is already worn out with too many activities, they won't be exuberant over your new ideas. You may even be too tired to consider them yourself. But you can *make* time for them by learning to use the simple word "no." When you are asked to commit yourself to an activity that you know would not benefit your family in the long run, simply say no. Or tell them you need to discuss it with your husband. If necessary, let him step in and act as a shield by saying no.

Not all individual activities are non-productive or harmful to family life. Your love for antiques and your son's love for caterpillars makes for a healthy balance. There is no reason to cut out or infringe upon all individual interests. Flexibility will allow togetherness and individuality.

However, one family member should not expect another to participate in distasteful or offensive activities. And no family member should attempt to be another's conscience. I don't believe you should force yourself to violate your own conscience just to be together as a family. (Not participating in distasteful activities is an important part of Romans 14.) Neither should you condemn those in your family for any of their activities. If a certain family function is distasteful, simply share in a gentle, noncondemning way that you would rather not participate. I have found that when a wife stands firm on her personal convictions in a nonjudgmental manner, it only adds to her family's respect for her.

ATTACK AND CONQUER TRAGEDIES AS A COUPLE, NOT AS INDIVIDUALS

Lasting friendships are built in foxholes. Nothing binds two people together faster than a common struggle against the enemy. Virtually any crisis can draw you and your husband closer, whether it be a stopped-up sink or your unwed daughter's pregnancy. No one hunts for tragedy, but if it strikes at your door, you can strengthen your marriage by dealing with it as a team.

One of America's great preachers tells how a tremendous sorrow united his family. He and his wife faced the "typical" marriage problems and their teenagers were going through the "typical" years of rebellion. Their family life was pleasant but not intimate. One day, to everyone's amazement, his wife came home and announced she was pregnant. No one was unusually excited; the last thing they felt they needed was another mouth to feed and keep quiet.

Soon after the baby was born, things changed. He became the apple of everyone's eye. His sweet, gentle spirit was apparent from the day he came home from the hospital. The children were so in love with him they argued over who would get to babysit with him. When the baby was only a year old, he became very ill and had to be rushed to the hospital. The whole family waited anxiously for the doctor's report. That sweet little boy had leukemia. For three days and nights the family waited together in a single room, watching over their baby, praying and hoping he would live. On the third day he died. Overwhelmed with grief, they went home to start a new life without him. Never again would they take one another for granted. Their mutual love and commitment would remain strong. Without a doubt, the death of their baby was the greatest tragedy any of them had ever experienced, but out of it came a tremendous love, intimacy, and appreciation for each family member.

MAKE IMPORTANT DECISIONS TOGETHER

It was the Fourth of July, and Norma and I were getting ready for a picnic when we burst into a heated argument. After a few minutes, things had only gotten worse. We could see we were going to be late for the picnic, so we postponed the argument till later.

I was fed up with our history of arguments. It seemed we couldn't stay out of a fight for a day. I asked Norma, "Would you be willing to try a new approach for a few weeks?" She agreed.

What we agreed upon that day has had a powerful impact on our marriage. It has forced us to communicate on deeper levels than I ever thought existed, helping us to gain an understanding of our individual viewpoints. It has forced us to look beneath surface opinions and discover the very root of our own thinking. When we disagree about a sitaution, our commitment to this principle helps us verbalize our feelings until we understand each other. Six years have passed since we made that commitment, and it continues to work far beyond our expectations. (It's been keeping us out of arguments ever since!)

On that Fourth of July *we agreed never to make final decisions on matters that affected both of us unless we both agreed.* If we don't arrive at unity before the bus gets here, we don't get on it. We've relied on this principle in all sorts of situations. Both of us assume responsibility for sharing our feelings honestly because we know we can't go anywhere until we're in agreement.

One man told me he would have saved more than thirty thousand dollars in the stock market if he had put this principle into action six months earlier. I'm always glad to find men who are willing to admit the value of their wives' counsel. After all, no one knows a man better than his "best friend."

DEVELOP A SENSE OF HUMOR

Class reunions always bring out the funny memories of former days. Here in this corner Jack is breaking up the group clustered around him with his old sophomore jokes. Over there by the punch bowl Janet is laughing uncontrollably as she's reminded of that practical joke on her first double-date. It seems we all did more laughing in our premarital days.

You probably weren't somber and sad when your husband married you. So, if you want to be his best friend now, you may need to add a little humor to your relationship. No need to buy a clown suit. Just look for ways to tickle his funny bone. Clip those comics or cartoons that strike you as funny and save them for his enjoyment during lighthearted times. Be willing to losen up and laugh heartily when he tells a good joke. There are countless ways to add humor to your marriage. Be willing to set aside the serious quest for romance at times to enjoy just having fun together as friends.

UNDERSTAND YOUR OWN PERSONALITY TRAITS
AND YOUR HUSBAND'S

We didn't develop all of our personality traits. Many of them were inborn. There are four basic temperaments that affect our personalities and all of us *tend* toward one of those temperaments. According to Tim La Haye, these four personality types can be labeled the talker, the leader, the legalist, and the unmotivated. If you don't understand your personality type and the way it interacts with your husband's, you are likely to suffer unnecessary pain and misunderstanding. Each personality type has its strengths and weaknesses. When you better understand the strengths and weaknesses of your husband's personality, you can work in harmony with him to compensate for his weakness. If you don't understand his personality type, you may react to his weaknesses whenever they clash with yours.

There is so much material on the subject of personality types that to go into detail would require another complete book. However, I have attempted to give a brief description of each personality type, some of its strengths, and some of its weaknesses.

Take this simple test to determine your own personality type and your husband's type. (You each might be a combination of two types.) Check the appropriate boxes with an X for your husband and an O for you. The point of the test is to show that each of us has a unique personality type and that we *tend* to marry opposites (those who complement us).

Becoming best friends is not an automatic process just because you live together. You have to learn to compensate when you are confronted daily with the faults and weaknesses of your mate.

The Outgoing Types
(Extrovert)

The Shy Types
(Introvert)

I *The Talker*	II *The Leader*	III *The Legalist*	IV *The Unmotivated*
☐ forward looking	☐ cold—unsympathetic	☐ gifted	☐ calm & quiet
☐ inventive	☐ determined & strong-willed	☐ moody	☐ casual
☐ undisciplined	☐ insensitive & inconsiderate	☐ analytical	☐ easygoing
☐ charming	☐ independent	☐ negative	☐ idle
☐ weak-willed	☐ hostile—angry	☐ perfectionist	☐ likeable
☐ restless	☐ productive	☐ critical	☐ spectator
☐ warm	☐ cruel—sarcastic	☐ conscientious	☐ diplomatic
☐ friendly	☐ decisive	☐ rigid & legalist	☐ selfish
☐ disorganized	☐ unforgiving	☐ loyal	☐ stingy
☐ responsive	☐ self-sufficient	☐ self-centered	☐ dependable
☐ unproductive	☐ visionary	☐ aesthetic	☐ stubborn
☐ talkative	☐ domineering	☐ touchy	☐ conservative
☐ undependable	☐ optimistic	☐ idealistic	☐ self-protective
☐ enthusiastic	☐ opinionated & prejudiced	☐ revengeful	☐ practical
☐ obnoxious—loud	☐ courageous	☐ sensitive	☐ indecisive
☐ carefree	☐ proud	☐ persecution-prone	☐ reluctant leader
☐ egocentric	☐ self-confident	☐ self-sacrificing	☐ fearful
☐ compassionate	☐ crafty	☐ unsociable	☐ dry humor
☐ exaggerates	☐ leader	☐ self-disciplined	
☐ generous		☐ theoretical & impractical	
☐ fearful & insecure			

Your "best friend" relationship with him will require perseverance, patience, understanding, genuine love, and the other qualities we discussed throughout this book. As you put into practice the five suggestions we discussed in this chapter, I am confident your friendship will deepen.

FOR PERSONAL REFLECTION

List the specific ways you have been a helper or completer to your husband (Gen. 2:18).

List additional ways you could help or complete his life.

Please Don't Forget

First, don't expect miracles overnight. Nearly everything of genuine worth takes time to perfect. These principles *do* work when applied over a period of time with persistence and a loving attitude.

Second, seek after the Lord with your whole heart, and you will find Him real and fulfilling (Luke 11:9; James 4:8).

Third, don't panic or give up when you fail. As you begin to apply these principles, you may "blow it" frequently. For example, you may find yourself using "you" statements instead of "I feel" statements without even thinking about it. Don't worry. It takes time to change habits. When you find yourself failing to apply a principle, make a mental note of the situation and vow to respond correctly the next time a similar situation arises. As time passes, you'll find yourself succeeding more frequently and failing less often. Don't fall into the trap of thinking that you're a failure just because you have failings. You're only a failure when you've given up all hope and effort to succeed.

May God bless you as you dedicate yourself to a more fulfilling and loving relationship. Remember, He wants it for you as much as you do (John 15:11-13).

Resources

Brandt, Henry, with Landrum, Phil. *I Want My Marriage To Be Better*. Grand Rapids, Michigan: Zondervan Publishing House, 1976.

Collins, Gary. *How To Be a People Helper*. Santa Ana, California: Vision House Publishers, 1976.

Day, Jerry. Clinical Psychologist, Tucson, Arizona: Ideas on stress management.

Dobson, James. *What Wives Wish Their Husbands Knew About Women*. Wheaton, Illinois: Tyndale House Publishers, Inc., 1975.

Drescher, John M. *Seven Things Children Need*. Scottdale, Pennsylvania: Herald Press, 1976.

Gothard, Bill. Director and lecturer, from the Institute in Basic Youth Conflicts. Oakbrook, Illinois.

Hardisty, Margaret. *Forever My Love*. Irvine, California: Harvest House Publishers, 1975.

Hendricks, Howard. *What You Need to Know About Premarital Counseling*. Waco, Texas: Family Life Cassettes, Word, Inc.

Hockman, Gloria. "A New Way for Families to Solve Problems Together." *Family Weekly*, July 16, 1978, p. 6.

Jones, Charles. *Life Is Tremendous*. Wheaton, Illinois: Tyndale House Publishers, 1968.

LaHaye, Tim and Beverly. *The Act of Marriage*. Grand Rapids, Michigan: Zondervan Publishing House, 1970.

LaHaye, Tim. *Understanding the Male Temperament*. Old Tappan, New Jersey: Fleming H. Revell Company, 1977.

Nair, Ken. *Discovering the Mind of a Woman*. Laredo, Texas: Fiesta Publishing Co., 1982.

Osborne, Cecil G. *The Art of Understanding Your Mate*. Grand Rapids, Michigan: Zondervan Publishing House, 1970.

Wheat, Ed. Family Physician, Springdale, Arkansas: Tapes on sex in marriage: "Sex Technique and Sex Problems in Marriage," and "Love-Life for Every Married Couple."

Joy
That Lasts

To four outstanding, supportive couples,
who know the secret of having JOY THAT LASTS:
Jim and Jan Stewart, Ben and Ann Kitchings,
Charles and Dorothy Shellenberger,
and Rick and Joan Malouf

Contents

1

Reaching Bottom Is
the First Step Up

EVERY CRISIS, NO matter the magnitude, is a step toward an enriched life, but try to explain that concept to a hurting couple.

Gerald, a tanned, athletic-looking man dressed in a golf shirt and custom slacks, wept in my office. Next to him, with a dazed look on her face, sat his wife, Martha. Although flooded by the sunlight that brightens Phoenix more than three hundred days a year, this couple could not escape their gloom as they told me about their teenage son, Don, who had rejected all of their standards.

This couple had done their best to raise Don in a Christian environment, but now that he was an adolescent he spent most of his time at parties, often strung out on drugs, with no apparent ambition for school or a career. This personal tragedy had robbed Gerald of his enthusiasm for his job as president of his own company. The possessions he'd worked so long and so hard to acquire—two homes, expensive cars, a forty-foot yacht—no longer satisfied him.

Martha's hurt ran even deeper. For years women at the club and at social events had spoken of her family as a model. Now she overheard snatches of conversation from those same women using her family tragedy as the latest bit of gossip. Each new painful episode that unfolded with her son added to her shame and left her emotionally exhausted. Martha felt she had little reason to continue living.

Stories like this permeate society, and they are not limited to the wealthy. No matter what our circumstances, whether we own much or little, we cannot live for long without feeling cheated by life. We eventually will experience despair and discouragement.

All of us will one day lose loved ones through death or separation. Illness will hamper some of our lives. Some of us will lose precious possessions, be victimized by violent climes, jilted by friends, financially ruined by bad investments, heartbroken by rebellious children, or unjustly fired from well-paying jobs. And some of us will waste our time worrying that these things will happen. Every day people face rejection, loneliness, and hurt feelings. And they envy the success and apparent happiness of others.

Many believe God is pulling a cruel prank when He allows us or loved ones to suffer unjustly. Others repeat (or whisper under their breath) words similar to those spoken by the people in Isaiah's time: "My way is hidden from the Lord, and the justice due me escapes the notice of my God" (Isaiah 40:27). Those of us who have felt betrayed by God understand Gerald and Martha's discouragement.

Gerald and Martha did not know, however, that *their troubles actually brought them a step closer to the richest life possible*. They were on the brink of a life filled with joy and peace without realizing how close they were.

How could I help them? They would not accept simplistic formulas. They hurt, and they needed to know that someone understood their pain. They didn't need theoretical answers; they needed hope. A road map and a few words of encouragement from me wouldn't be enough to help them find their own way out of their circumstances. They needed a personal guide.

"He jests at scars, that never felt a wound," Romeo said in Shakespeare's *Romeo and Juliet*. The only way for me to help Gerald and Martha was to "feel their wound." Although I had never experienced the pain of having a rebellious child, I too had known rejection. Nine years earlier I had been deeply wounded by my closest friend. Although the crisis didn't involve my family, I felt the pain of rejection as intensely as any parent of a wayward child. Yet that difficult experience opened for me the door to the most enriching discovery of my life.

To help Gerald and Martha I told them my personal story of rejection and discovery. I had helped my best friend build a small company into a leader in the industry, only to lose my position and friendship. Then for two years I wallowed in a marsh of despair, wondering if I could ever again experience the level of fulfillment I'd found in my work and unique relationship. In the midst of my mental and emotional anguish, however, I had discovered the doorway that leads to fulfillment. Quietly I told Gerald and Martha my story.

As a young man fresh out of graduate school, I had met Dale at the church where I was assistant pastor. He owned a small company that sold health food products. Through seminars and written materials, he taught people how to live healthy and fulfilling lives.

Dale's charisma captivated me. Like a modern-day John the Baptist, he called people to a combination of well-rounded physical health and moral purity. And he lived what he preached. He was totally committed to his work and spoke boldly about selling people a great product while bringing America back to Christian values. Accepting his invitation to work for him was the easiest decision I'd ever made.

My wife, Norma, didn't share my enthusiasm. In spite of my excitement, she told me several times that she felt I would regret working for him. But I "knew" better. I believed Dale was a modern-day prophet who had a vision to change America, and I was going to help him.

That was in 1968. Six of us manned the company headquarters in a suburb of Denver. We doubled the size of the business in the first year and doubled it again the next. We could hardly contain our enthusiasm when we realized that everyone in the United States would be using our products within fifteen years if we continued the same rate of expansion.

I began to arrange for major hotel ballrooms to hold Dale's meetings. We packed out conferences in Seattle, Long Beach, Chicago, Dallas, and Kansas City. To see entire hotels and convention centers filled as Dale motivated people to live healthy lives staggered me. And then to see people fill our coffers by buying our line of natural food products, books, and other materials was more than I could believe.

I opened regional offices in ten cities, hired managers to supervise warehouses filled with our products, and trained a growing number of distributors to promote Dale's philosophy. On the road every month, I interviewed prospective employees, approved office leases, negotiated agreements with hotels and convention centers, and conducted motivational seminars of my own for our employees.

My most significant memories, however, were not of packed conferences, exciting business transactions, or constant travel and first-class accommodations. What meant the most were the times Dale and I slipped away to a remote cabin in the Colorado Rockies. There we would spend a couple of days praying, developing new conference and promotional materials, dreaming of new products for our research department, and plotting strategy to take our message and products beyond the U.S. border to the entire world.

Every few hours we would take a break and toss rocks into a trash can, competing like two kids to see who could make the most shots. Sometimes in the evening Dale would tire, and I'd keep him awake, motivated by the thought of sending new material to our distributors or conducting our seminar in a new city. People's lives were being transformed by Dale's work, and I passionately believed it had to spread as quickly as possible.

Dale was everything I could want in a friend; in fact, in many ways he was like a brother. We shared much more than the vision to help people. Since we were nearly the same size, we often borrowed each other's clothes. Many times I walked into my office and found a new shirt or tie on my desk—a present from my best of friends.

Sometimes Dale would call me late at night, embarrassed that he couldn't remember who had borrowed his car. I would drive the four blocks to our headquarters to pick him up and often we'd go out for a late dinner. Inevitably I would have to pay because money meant little to Dale. Frequently he didn't even have his wallet. But he was a generous man. When Norma's car was in the shop, I'd simply go into Dale's office and he'd give me the keys to his car. His door was always open, and I was involved in most of his meetings.

Dale was married, but spent little time with his wife. The many exciting things happening at work demanded most of his time and energy, and our friendship took a great deal of his time as well. In many ways, I too made my relationship with Dale a higher priority than my own wife and family. I believed I was in an ideal situation that would last until I retired. Dale and I shared our possessions, our personal dreams, and our vision for the company.

In the ninth year of our intimate friendship I began to detect a subtle change. By then our headquarters complex teemed with more than one hundred employees. We were no longer a small, intimate family. New managers with MBA degrees had strong ideas about how to run the company. Personality clashes and distrust replaced the warmth of our office. Upper management jockied for Dale's time.

One afternoon I walked into Dale's office and asked for his car keys. Without looking up from his paperwork, he informed me that we had a new policy. "The staff will no longer borrow each other's cars," he said, and with that I was dismissed. In the days that followed I was also informed that I had to knock before entering Dale's office and that I was no longer needed in some important meetings I would have attended a few months earlier.

Like a jealous suitor, I was hurt and confused by this sudden change in our working and personal relationship. I kept wondering what I had said or done to cause Dale's response.

In the week that followed I learned, "through the grapevine," that some of the new management team did not approve of my qualifications and were threatened by the amount of access and influence I had with Dale. So almost overnight they had gotten me moved from the fireplace off into a cold, damp corner.

During this same time of tension and change, our accountant, a longtime friend, came to me with devastating news. He felt sure that three of the company officers who were very close to Dale were engaging in unethical business practices with company funds.

Dale had established such high standards with his product, conferences, and company that we enjoyed an unblemished reputation with our customers and suppliers. The behavior of these men would eat away at our credibility and threaten the existence of our company.

I made an appointment for the accountant and me to see Dale. On a Friday afternoon we laid before him all the facts about our staff problem. Then I made what I believed was a very logical recommendation: that we fire the three managers and deal openly with the people that were affected, before any serious damage was done to the company.

Dale rejected my idea. Looking me straight in the eye he said that he appreciated my information but he didn't believe the offenses merited any disciplinary action.

This was not the Dale I knew. I felt as if I were a stranger in the presence of a man I once knew intimately. As I sensed how far apart we had moved I felt the lifeblood of our relationship draining away.

Throughout the next week I was so emotionally devastated that I could barely muster enough strength to return to work. For nine years all my energy had been devoted to Dale and his cause. But suddenly the cause was hollow, and so was I. Rejected by my best friend and completely drained of my enthusiasm, I didn't know where to turn.

Years later, Dale admitted that keeping those managers was a mistake. Company growth leveled off and even declined as a result of that decision. For me, however, the effect was immediately devastating. For several days severe depression sapped all my energy, and I lost all enthusiasm for the cause that had captivated my life for so many years.

Gerald and Martha listened attentively as I related my story. When I stopped for a moment, Martha asked, "How did you ever overcome that?"

I told her that for a long time there was no one I could talk to. Dale had been my spiritual confidant. He was respected in the Christian community, so I didn't feel I could seek counsel from anyone who knew about our work without sounding like a disgruntled employee. It was even difficult to express my fears to Norma. She had warned me about working with Dale, and I wouldn't humble myself to admit her intuition had been right.

It took nearly two years and a career change before I understood the answer. In the process, I began to realize a tremendous truth:

> Trials can be our greatest experience, for they can lead to the source of lasting joy.

Through this devastating experience I discovered the secret to a life so fulfilling that today it is almost impossible for circumstances to rob me of my joy for any length of time.

I drew a picture of a cup and explained that it represented my life. Then I showed Gerald and Martha how I had filled my cup from the wrong sources. Dale and my job had satisfied me for almost nine years, but when things started going wrong they became like acid, eating holes in the walls of my life until everything fulfilling and meaningful had drained out. Through that experience I learned the secret to keeping my cup filled. There was one source that would not only fill it, but cause it to overflow!

I shared with Gerald and Martha the same principles that are the basis for this book, and when they left my office, they looked hopeful. A few weeks later Gerald called to tell me that he and his wife had gained a new purpose in life. Even their son recognized the change. Gerald kept in touch over the next two years and told me how he and Martha were experiencing fulfillment and peace on a daily basis, regardless of their circumstances. Gradually their son began to change his lifestyle and eventually he entered a local community college to prepare for a career in business.

Many of us are facing difficult circumstances. Some of us hurt because we've been rejected by someone we love. Some of us have climbed over fences to find greener pasture but found only desert instead. Some of us have followed a rainbow only to find the pot of gold an illusion. And some of us are worried that the good life we enjoy may evaporate.

As incredible as it may seem, those who recognize themselves in any of the above circumstances are on the brink of discovering an exciting life. In fact, problems are the tools that help us fill our lives with lasting joy, peace, and love. But most of us do not even recognize the tools, much less know how to use them.

I never understood this myself until I lost almost everything of value. During my search for meaning and purpose after my devastating experience with Dale I discovered several biblical tools that turned my tragedy into triumph. In the following pages I'd like to help you identify and learn to use them in your own life. These tools help us build up our self-worth, regulate our negative emotions such as anger, worry, fear, and envy for our benefit, and equip us to go on a treasure hunt to find the "gold" that is buried in every trial.

The message that God intends us to live in a perpetual oasis may encourage us for a season, but before long we will run into trials, and with them a dry, barren desert. Crossing a desert unprepared can be deadly. My prayer is that this book will help you prepare for inevitable desert experiences and show you how to find the true source of refreshment. This discovery will lead you to the source that is always running over, never running dry. I missed out on this refreshment for years because I kept trying to find something tangible that would finally satisfy me. I learned instead that even having it all wasn't enough.

2
Having It All Isn't Enough

STEVE AND BRENDA were excited about their future. They were young, talented professionals who deeply loved each other. Steve had just completed medical school and looked forward to a surgical career. Brenda was a nurse at the county hospital. They had dated since high school, and now that Steve had finished his training they finally felt free to marry. Their wedding was the talk of their small town. They had so much going for them—a promising financial future, important positions in the community, and a deep love and commitment to each other. They never could have imagined the tragedy that would shatter their expectations and destroy their lives.

Four weeks after their wedding, Brenda contracted a rare form of hepatitis from an emergency room patient she had treated. Doctors immediately hospitalized her but their treatment was ineffective. She weakened daily and within a week had died.

Steve's dreams died with her. He had never considered the possibility that the one he loved could be taken from him so abruptly. After the funeral, overwhelmed by his devastating loss, he walked aimlessly around town for hours. In the following days he couldn't bear to go to his office. Often he would sit in his darkened apartment, tears streaming down his face.

Two weeks after the funeral, in an act of desperation, Steve tried to take his own life with an overdose of pills. If his parents had not become concerned when he didn't answer their phone calls, Steve's attempt would have succeeded. Now, several years later, Steve still struggles with chronic depression and has never reached his potential as a surgeon. His life is frozen in a tragic experience from his past.

Most of us will never face such a tragedy, but sooner or later all of us must come to grips with life's insecurity. We may move through life unaffected for weeks, months, even years, but eventually each of us will suffer some form of loss or disillusionment. The feeling of loss will be more traumatic for some than for others, but all of us will have to deal with its effects.

I never considered suicide after my experience with Dale, but like Steve, I experienced a deep sense of loss. For several months after leaving the company, I frequently woke up at three or four o'clock in the morning with my stomach churning like a stormy sea. I desperately wanted to understand why I was experiencing such misery. If the Christian life that I believed and spoke about was true, why was I so unhappy? Why couldn't I rise above this disappointment and move on with my life?

One morning I awoke at four o'clock with the familiar pangs of anxiety engulfing me. To keep from disturbing Norma, I quietly slipped out of bed and tiptoed down the hall. My eight-year-old son heard me. "What are you doing, Dad?" Greg whispered.

"I'm going downstairs to study," I told him.

"Can I go with you?"

After pouring Greg a cup of juice I sat down with him at the kitchen table and admitted to him that I was going through a struggle and couldn't seem to find the answer. He listened and tried to understand. "Greg, there has to be a reason why I keep getting my feelings so hurt. Do you remember the time we went fishing and you lost that big trout? You cried and I had to hold you for a long time?" Greg nodded. "That's a little like how I've felt for the past few weeks. I feel like I had a trophy fish right at the edge of the boat—but it got away. I feel such a deep sense of loss that I can't feel joy anymore."

Greg didn't understand, but talking to him helped me crystallize my thoughts. Perhaps if I could explain what I felt to an eight-year-old boy, I could understand it myself. "Greg, I think I've been making the same mistake over and over. Maybe that's why I'm so miserable." I looked at his nearly empty cup of juice and suddenly had an idea. "It's like my life is a cup, and until recently it was filled with joy and peace and love. But lately a big hole has been drilled in it and all the life has drained out. Instead of joy filling my cup, anger and fear and hurt feelings have taken its place."

"But what made that hole?" Greg asked.

As I talked, I realized I had been expecting relationships to keep my cup filled. I grabbed a note pad and drew a picture. "I think it's becoming clearer to me! Greg, tell me if this makes sense."

I drew as I talked. "As I think about it, Greg, I'm not looking for life just in relationships; actually I'm looking for life in at least four different places. And fulfillment from these four places floods into my life through a network of hoses and faucets. The problem is, someone has turned off the spigot!" I showed Greg the picture and he said he understood.

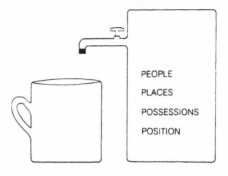

PEOPLE

PLACES

POSSESSIONS

POSITION

> For the first time I began to realize my major mistake: I was expecting to find fulfillment in people, places, possessions, and position.

Not only did I no longer receive fulfillment from these sources, it was as if the satisfaction they once had given me was now destroying me.

That late-night conversation with Greg changed my life. For the first time I began to understand why my emotional and spiritual life had been like a small sailboat on a large lake. On nice days with gentle breezes I would skim across life's surface, refreshed by the wind and invigorated by the spray. But when the storm clouds came (and they always do), I had no safe harbor to sail to and no anchor strong enough to help me ride out the storm. The lake that once provided pleasure and fulfillment suddenly became life-threatening.

In my own personal life, and with people I am trying to help, like Gerald and Martha, I always take time to look closely at the four areas that cause so many of us to miss out on a satisfying life: people, places, possessions, position.

PEOPLE—WE CAN'T CONTROL THEM

For the first thirty-five years of my life I thought people were supposed to make me happy. My wife, children, friends, relatives, boss, fellow employees—all were part of a group I felt should fill my cup. This belief caused my problem with Dale. I enjoyed our friendship so much that I began to expect it to continue unchanged forever. In a subtle way, I shifted from following Dale's leadership to expecting him to cooperate with my goal of enjoying our unique friendship. I became more interested in our meetings than in the goals of the corporation. Preparing material and planning new strategies, at first a means to help more people, became ends in themselves—ways to spend time with Dale.

I had similar expectations of my family. I wanted them to appreciate the great movement I was in and to serve me by submitting their desires to the goals of this great work. I remember one winter day in particular when Dale called a special meeting at 5:00 in the afternoon. Through my office window I could see Norma waiting in the car for me. Snow had started to fall, and the children were pleading to play outside but weren't dressed appropriately. Rather than excuse myself from the meeting, even to tell her how much longer I'd be, I expected her to understand and wait patiently in the cold with the kids for forty-five minutes. After all, I was helping to bring a spiritual and physical revival to our country. What could possibly be more important?

It was years before I realized, with grief and embarrassment, that I'd selfishly expected my wife and kids to serve my ambition. No wonder Norma and I weren't receiving much joy in our lopsided relationship.

I see this attitude frequently in dating and marriage relationships. Take, for example, a woman who dreams for years about finding "Mr. Wonderful." She believes this man will fulfill her deepest longing for intimacy. She pictures him sitting next to her on an overstuffed love seat in front of a warm fire, his arm around her, talking for hours. She sees them discussing their plans for the future, their next vacation, and how they'll redecorate the living room. She knows he will diligently fix things around the house, keep her car running smoothly, and be there to support and encourage her when she is discouraged. She often thinks of her husband-to-be as a waterfall cascading into her life, a never-ending source of fulfillment that will make her life overflow with meaning.

This woman doesn't know she is setting herself up for the very heartache she is trying to escape. A few weeks into marriage she will realize that her husband, in many ways, can't or won't cooperate with her expectations. The relationship she expected to bring security may actually make her more *insecure*. Her husband may be the type who notices every attractive girl who walks by. He may be so wrapped up in his work that he shows little interest in her work or activities. He may be too tired to fix her car or make necessary household repairs. Even his interest in touching her may seem to have only sexual connotations.

Before long this woman, who once had so many dreams, begins to feel used and taken for granted, almost as if he had hired her as a maid. Not only is he not filling her cup, but his insensitivity has started to wear small holes in it and her emotional energy is draining out. Eventually she may even lose the level of love, happiness, and peace she had when she entered the marriage.

When her husband fails to meet her needs, she may think of an alternative: "If my husband isn't going to meet my needs," she reasons, "I'll have a family. Children running around the house are what I need to be fulfilled!" Too late she will discover that children, rather than filling her cup, have an amazing capacity to drill very large holes in it.

A man may also enter marriage with many expectations. He pictures how his wife will respond to him. Each day she will comment on how gifted he is as a lover, husband, and father. Without question, she will prepare delicious meals every night and always respond warmly to his sexual desires.

But soon he too discovers that not only is she unable to fill his cup, but she chips off the enamel until leaky cracks develop. Like her, his insecurity increases, and he may begin to think he married the wrong person. He may even begin to look around for another woman who he thinks will better meet his needs and become his ultimate "cup filler."

Husbands and wives are not unique. Many others are frustrated because they look to people to fulfill their expectations. Children may long for greater love and better communication with their parents. Parents may feel "taken advantage of" by their children. Employees often feel that employers do not care about them as people. Employers may feel that employees have no sense of loyalty or gratitude. And many Christians feel betrayed when certain "super Christians" succumb to temptation and turn out to be just as human and just as prone to failure as anyone else.

In Proverbs we read, "Hope deferred makes the heart sick" (13:12). Many husbands, wives, children, employees, employers, and friends put their hope for fulfillment in other people, which eventually leaves them empty and frustrated inside. Researchers like Albert Bandura and other sociologists believe this is a major cause of many social problems. Their research on anger and acts of violence related to anger shows that a key contributing factor is "frustrated expectations," the same thing that leads to divorce, runaway youth, suicide, battered mates, kidnapping, drug and alcohol abuse.

I am grateful I finally began to see this principle, because my unrealistic expectations of others kept me from gaining the fulfillment I sought. People, no matter how perfect, could never fill my life.

But if that is true, where can we turn?

John and his wife, Joan, went through emotions similar to mine. Each expected fulfillment from the other. When they didn't find it they thought a new home might help. They built a beautiful house on several acres in a suburb of San Francisco, but they still had trouble getting along. John felt they needed a change of location, so he built a beautiful mountain cabin. That didn't solve the problem either, however, because they fought just as well in their cabin as in their spacious San Francisco home.

Relying on a location or special place to bring us lasting joy is like taking a snapshot of a beautiful setting. When we get the picture developed it never quite recaptures the beauty we beheld.

Joan wasn't impressed by the places John provided for her, so she decided to test her wings, to get free from the man who was robbing her of joy. When she left she took their child with her.

After several months of being on her own away from home, Joan discovered the secret of having her cup filled with lasting joy. John noticed such a change in her that he asked what she had found. Her explanation led to the restoration of their relationship as he too realized that permanent happiness didn't dwell in a spectacular home or mountain cabin.

People today look to all types of places to fill their cups. In the United States, the first place most couples expect to find fulfillment is in their own home. Indeed, few of us can be content without a proper home. We're concerned about the neighborhood, the number of bathrooms, the view, and appropriate furnishings and coordinated interior decoration. Whether we rent or own or live in an apartment or a sprawling split-level, we expect pleasure and satisfaction from our home. We even feel cheated if we're not living in the right location. But getting our dream home can cause more anxiety than not getting it. Often we end up worried about making mortgage payments, how or where to add another room, and what security system to install to protect our investment.

When Norma and I finally bought our first house five years after we were married, everything about it—the smells, the fresh paint, the new neighbors—excited us. But after the initial thrill wore off, we noticed how loud the neighbor's dog barked and the continual loud music from their patio. They did nothing to control their dandelions, so their weeds quickly spread to our grass.

As we settled into the routine of living, our house became ordinary. Our friends' new home was more spacious and had more conveniences. We began to think we too needed those things. But the more things we bought, the more things needed fixing. The bigger the house, the bigger and more expensive the problems and the more time and effort they consumed.

I admit that I have enjoyed fleeting moments of satisfaction from our home in Arizona, but it frustrates me more than it satisfies me. My garage door breaks an average of twice a year. The hinges on the back gate have fallen off. Swarms of aphids have set up housekeeping on our roses. Dust from the expansion of our family room kept circulating through the house after construction. My lawn is always dying, either because I gave it too much water or fertilizer or not enough. My sprinkling system breaks whenever a car pulls too close to the edge of the lawn. And I've lost the war against weeds. Sometimes I'm tempted to dynamite the front yard and start over, but that would damage Dad's orange tree.

In my travels across the country and overseas I've visited in many homes and found happy people and miserable people in both small apartments and spacious dwellings, which suggests to me that where we live has little to do with our level of happiness.

Failing to find lasting joy in a house, many people begin to look outside the home to a place where they can "find it all" while they "get away from it all." They plan a dream trip to Hawaii to enjoy the sun and surf or to Colorado to enjoy the snow and skiing. But all too often it's simply that—a dream.

Vacations can be enjoyable, but the possibilities for disaster are endless—bad weather, lost travelers checks, car breakdown, canceled flights, stuffy motel rooms. Our first trip to Hawaii was an illustration of this.

I was to speak in a gorgeous hotel on the north side of Kauai. We looked forward to a week of sunbathing and sightseeing on the island paradise. But it rained every day. The travel brochure conveniently withheld information about the island's average rainfall, which, where we were staying, was 425 inches a year!

Things we least expect can ruin a vacation we've anticipated for months, or even years. Like the time we planned a special ski trip with our relatives. First we lost the key to our shared apartment and nearly froze while we tried to find the manager. Then my niece got a severe nosebleed as we prepared to make our first run down the mountain. And on my second trip down the slope, stomach flu attacked me unexpectedly. As I tried to hide in the woods to relieve my stomach cramps, I slipped and slid forty feet through the trees. My son, Greg, laughed uncontrollably while I spent thirty minutes trying to dig myself out of the snow and clean myself up.

Because I travel so much, people often tell me they envy me; they think traveling is exciting. They do not realize that traveling drills big holes in my cup. The headache of arranging tickets, rushing to make connections, delayed flights and lost luggage, added to fatigue from jet lag, uncomfortable beds, and flat pillows, drains away any joy that traveling might provide. If you enjoy your family, every day on the road is a day away from those you love most. Most people who look to travel for fulfillment are disappointed.

Places, whether homes or vacation spots, are like a mirage. To a person thirsting for fulfillment, they look like a quenching pool of water. Yet once we reach them we find only sand—and the 10,000 other tourists who beat us to the spot.

POSSESSIONS—WE NEVER GET ENOUGH

If people and places can't satisfy us, perhaps we would be happy if we had more things.

I took a large cut in pay when I parted company with Dale, so I was thrilled when I had a business opportunity that promised to yield at least $200,000 in the first year, and perhaps twice that the following year. Norma and I quickly thought of things we "needed"—a microwave, a new phone system, a sophisticated stereo system, a new washer and dryer. Our house suddenly seemed far too small and outdated. We drove around town and found a beautiful two-story home overlooking a lake. The price was only half of the "minimum" amount we thought I would earn. We began to figure ways to borrow the money for this house in anticipation of our windfall income.

Fortunately the bank never considered our loan request. The amount of money we actually received paid only for those few appliances we bought in anticipation of moving into the new house. Every day those items were a grim reminder that we could not move out of the home we no longer liked.

Money does not provide lasting fulfillment, nor is it the key to the door marked "the overflowing life." I've met as many poor, happy people as I have rich, happy people, and vice versa. Yet many of us live as though cars, campers, and boats bring lasting enjoyment to life.

We see this attitude displayed especially at Christmastime. Millions believe the holiday ad campaigns that tell us which things will bring happiness. But after all the gifts are opened, many of us slide straight into discouragement, even depression. Year after year the pattern repeats itself; new possessions cannot satisfy us for long.

Possessions, like people and places, lose their ability to fulfill us. Trying to quench our thirst from this source is like drinking salty sea water. It shimmers and glistens with promise, but it only leaves us more thirsty and cramped.

If lasting fulfillment is not found in people, places, or possessions, what's left? Disillusioned by these three, many people look to recognition, expecting power or the world's praise to satisfy them.

By the time I started to understand this principle, I had worked in both menial jobs and in what I considered the ultimate in a challenging leadership position for a large corporation. I couldn't imagine going any higher, short of replacing Dale, which I had no desire to do. Yet even at "the top," I finally realized that this position could not provide the continual joy and peace I desired.

Those within the Christian community are not immune. They too fall victim to the myth that they can find fulfillment by achieving position. Some Christians would love to share the limelight with a television personality or be able to sing like their favorite Christian recording artist. "Believers in secular jobs may simply long to be able to work for a ministry-related organization or a church. They presume that if they were working in a Christian environment they would not be bothered by the problems and pettiness they find in the secular workplace. Working in that type of environment, they think, would be like having a perpetual "quiet time."

Unfortunately, even in a ministry setting, certain things about work still leave us lacking lasting fulfillment. One reason jobs do not satisfy is that they all have at least one thing in common: *Work!*

Work is not always fun, especially when we have to do the same thing over and over again. Besides, jobs rarely live up to our expectations. When we reach a position for which we've striven, there is usually so much pressure connected with it that it loses much of its glamour. Like owning a big home, the responsibility can consume all our energy.

Most of us focus on what we expect to gain from our job: money, security, promotions, benefits, or fulfillment. We may find these things for a time, but no job is secure. We must continue to perform well or we will lose it. If the company is sold, new management may decide they no longer need us. The economy may slump. The marketplace may change. And all the while we grow older. Nearly all of these factors are beyond our control, but they undermine our position nevertheless.

Les worked thirty-three years as a lineman for the phone company. He thought he had the ultimate in job security. Because of his seniority, he would be one of the last to be laid off; and that was inconceivable because he worked for the largest telephone company in the world—AT&T. Who could have anticipated that Ma Bell would be forced to break up? Only three years away from retirement, Les learned his job would be phased out.

I discovered something interesting while working with professional athletes. Most of us think they enjoy security with their large, multi-year contracts and the glamour of their positions. Instead, however, I often found them disgruntled when they did not perform well, were not playing as often as they felt they deserved to play, were suffering from a nagging injury, or could not get along with their coach. If a contract with a professional sports team is a guarantee of happiness, why do so many professional athletes demand to be traded or to have their contracts renegotiated? And why do they have so many problems with drugs, alcohol, and divorce? No one is immune from the truth that *position* does not provide lasting security and satisfaction.

How many men and women have sacrificed their family life for a higher position only to discover that the position they sought didn't fulfill their expectations? And in the process they lost their relationship with their children. Instead of the fulfillment they were looking for, what did they find? Hurt feelings, anxiety, fear, stress—the very things they were hoping to avoid.

Other areas breed insecurity as well. Many people think they would be fulfilled if they could lead a great cause, work full-time helping people, become a media celebrity, cut a record album, win a political election, or write a book. Consumed by the excitement of these activities, some ignore the potential cost in time or finances, loss of privacy, and demands from supporters.

We need to refocus our expectations on a totally different source. It's not enough to stop expecting fulfillment from people, places, possessions, or position. After my talk with Greg that morning, I realized where *life did not originate*. But I still did not know how to plug into the genuine source of life. I couldn't imagine how or why I had failed to learn such an important truth during my years of seminary, church involvement, or in my association with Dale and his seminars. If I didn't know the answer, who did?

My search for answers began with God Himself. My prayer for help was nothing more than a whimpering cry: "God, teach me what I'm missing. What am I failing to understand?" More than eleven years ago I first prayed that prayer, and I can honestly say that the years since have been the most fulfilling, adventurous, and overflowing I've ever experienced.

Here are three reasons why my cup is full today:
1. Negative emotions such as hurt feelings, envy, jealousy, anger, depression, lust, fear, and worry have virtually faded from my life.
2. Positive, life-giving emotions have replaced negative emotions. I regularly experience love for and from others, and my inner joy and happiness does not depend on God's creation. I have an inner calm and contentment—a peace of mind—that I never used to experience.

3. I've learned how to use the painful, emotionally difficult experiences of life to benefit me and those around me.

A fulfilling life has nothing to do with people, places, possessions, or position. When the true source of fulfillment floods us, a deepening sense of security accompanies it, assuring us that the source of life cannot be yanked away.

Once our cup is filled by this source, we are truly free, for the first time, to enjoy God's creation—because we can appreciate it without depending on it for fulfillment. We live overflowing lives because the *source* of life, instead of the *gifts* of life, brings us contentment. How? By finding the well that never runs dry.

3

Finding the Well
that Never Runs Dry

WHERE WOULD I find lasting fulfillment? Learning that I had looked for contentment in all the wrong places for so many years left me empty. Even after I prayed and asked God to show me what was missing, I felt a hollow darkness inside. Then suddenly, as if someone switched on emergency flood lights, I began to realize why I was so discouraged.

It happened in my office on a Monday morning. I had no motivation to begin work and was too disgusted with Dale to attend the weekly staff meeting. I had just received a letter and a check for sixty dollars from a minister I had met a few days earlier at one of our seminars. I reread the letter and felt a wave of embarrassment. The pastor asked me to use the money for a new suit. He had noticed that I wore the same suit for three consecutive years and said his motivation for sending me the check was 1 John 3:17: "Whoever has the world's goods, and beholds his brother in need and closes his heart against him, how does the love of God abide in him?" How could I explain that I didn't need a new suit? Besides, I probably earned three times his salary. I should have sent him money.

Intrigued by his comments, I reached for my Bible and read the five short chapters of 1 John. Bible reading had become no more than a daily ritual for me during this stress-filled time. For weeks I'd read it without gaining any spiritual insights. But this time my mind was unusually alert as I tried to sense even a hint of truth that might help me. The words in chapter two stunned me: "The one who says he is in the light and *yet* hates his brother is in the darkness until now. The one who loves his brother abides in the light and there is no cause for stumbling in him. But the one who hates his brother is in the darkness and walks in the darkness, and does not know where he is going because the darkness has blinded his eyes" (1 John 2:9–11).

Over and over I read those verses. The word *darkness* precisely described my discouragement and lack of enthusiasm. I knew that walking in God's light meant walking in His love; however, I had never equated my lack of love for Dale with hatred. Maybe others could see it, but I had missed it. Not only did I not love Dale, I had actually developed a deep anger toward him. Left to fester, my anger could have turned into hate.

Could this be true? I felt I was too spiritual and mature to stoop to hating someone. I'd never yelled at Dale or tried to hurt him in any visible way. Yet according to God's Word I was walking in darkness, not in light, because I did not love my brother.

Though perhaps not evident on the outside, my angry thoughts and bitterness proved that inside I hated Dale. And though not affecting him, my hate was destroying me. I could not function in more than the routine activities of my job and life. No wonder I didn't sense God's love or have a desire for spiritual things. I was slipping into darkness and wasn't consciously aware of it.

Rarely has Scripture so overwhelmed me. I slid out of my swivel chair and onto my knees. "God, it's hard for me to admit it, but what You've written in this verse is true of me," I prayed. "Now I understand why I don't sense Your presence and why I'm walking in such confusing darkness."

I left the office knowing my conflict was not with Dale. By allowing anger to remain within me unresolved I was fighting a law of God. Blaming Dale had kept me from seeing my own immaturity and lack of love. In my anger, I had set myself up as his judge. I had examined the evidence and mentally pronounced a guilty verdict. Yet I could not possibly know all the reasons Dale had not followed my recommendations. And even if I had known, by judging him and hating him I was superseding God, the only true judge. I recalled James 4:12: "There is only one … judge, the One who is able to save and to destroy; but who are you who judge your neighbor?"

It was time to resolve this. I went home and suggested to Norma that I go away for two or three days to be alone with God. She encouraged me to go, for I'd been impossible to live with. If it would bring me out of my depression, she was eager to give me the time. So I grabbed my Bible, a jug of water, and a pen and paper and headed over to our company's vacant rental house a half mile from our home.

During the next two days, I began to learn the secret of having my cup filled to the brim.

Away from phone, radio, television, and all other interruptions, I spent two days drinking only water, praying, and reading the Gospel of Luke. "Lord," I prayed, "I'm willing to read through this Gospel and as many other books in the Bible as it takes for You to teach me the secret of finding the abundant life You promised."

I spent the entire two days in the Gospel of Luke, though I did refer to other passages of Scripture to confirm what I was learning. Luke 11 was the first chapter to jump out at me. When I read about the disciples asking Jesus to teach them how to pray I thought, *Aha! Maybe this will help me find the answer.* So I prayed, "Lord, teach me how to pray." If I asked God, through prayer, to help me discover the secret to fulfillment, and if He indeed answers prayer, then He would show me the secret I so desperately needed.

The exciting thing about the secret I was about to learn was that it had nothing to do with the people or things around me, or with my position. Furthermore, it had nothing to do with my earthly accomplishments, my level of education, or my financial condition. It had everything to do with understanding Christ's words: "I came that they might have life, and might have it abundantly" (John 10:10).

What I learned from Luke 11 and 18 taught me the greatest secret to life.

DISCOVERING GOD'S BEST

The first clue came in Christ's parable in Luke 11. Can you see in this passage what helped me understand fulfillment?

> And He said to them, "Suppose one of you shall have a friend, and shall go to him at midnight, and say to him, 'Friend, lend me three loaves; for a friend of mine has come to me from a journey, and I have nothing to set before him'; and from inside he shall answer and say, 'Do not bother me; the door has already been shut and my children and I are in bed; I cannot get up and give you anything.' I tell you, even though he will not get up and give him anything because he is his friend, yet because of his *persistence* he will get up and give him as much as he needs. And I say to you, ask, and it shall be given to you; seek, and you shall find; knock, and it shall be opened to you. For everyone who asks, receives; and he who seeks, finds; and to him who knocks, it shall be opened" (Luke 11:5-10).

I acted out this parable in my mind to try to understand it. I pictured myself as the person who went next door to borrow three loaves of bread for my unexpected visitor. I began to knock on my neighbor's door at midnight. "Don't bother us," I heard him shout "We're all in bed. I can't get up and give you anything." But I knew that if he did not help me I would only have to pass the word around the community the next day and he would be ostracized. My neighbor was a good friend. We'd fished together and shared many meals. Our children played together, and I couldn't say how often we had borrowed things from each other. However, those were not the reasons he eventually helped me at such a late hour. He got up and gave me as much as I needed because of *my persistence and in order to protect his reputation.*

Jesus went on to make the application for us. Why are we to continually ask and seek and knock? *Because God's reputation is at stake.* I could pray, "Lord, what's the secret to the abundant life you promised in John 10:10?" I intended to keep asking this question until I got an answer, and I knew God *would* answer because He will not be shamed. I was asking, and God promised I would receive. I was seeking, and He promised I would find. I was knocking, and He promised to open the door to understanding.

From this parable I learned two crucial principles: First, God will not be shamed. He guards His Word and His reputation as did the neighbor portrayed in the parable I'd read. Second, He is faithful to answer the persistent prayers of His children.

RECOGNIZING GOD'S FAITHFULNESS

As I read the next parable, another truth about prayer emerged.

Now suppose one of you fathers is asked by his son for a fish; he will not give him a snake instead of a fish, will he? Or if he is asked for an egg, he will not give him a scorpion, will he? If you then, being evil, know how to give good gifts to your children, how much more shall *your* heavenly Father give the Holy Spirit to those who ask Him? (Luke 11:11–13).

If we humans know how to give good gifts to our children, just think about the almighty God of the universe, our heavenly Father. He promises to give His very Spirit to those who ask. I suddenly realized this was what I was seeking. This was the life He had promised! Life was contained in His Spirit living within me. If I had His Holy Spirit, I would have love, joy, peace, patience, and all the other fruit of the Spirit (Galatians 5:22–23). Ephesians 3:19 states that to *know the* love of God is to be "filled up to all the fulness of God." I know it is God's Spirit *alone* that fills my Cup.

This wasn't new to me—I'd heard it hundreds of times. What was new was *how* to gain God's Spirit and keep that relationship alive.

370

During those two days, I went to God as a child goes to his father. As a hungry son seeking bread, I stated my requests:

- I asked to experience Him within me and that I might no longer expect anything other than Him to fill my life.
- I asked for healthy family relationships and that Norma and I and our three children would love each other and be an example to other families.
- I asked for knowledge and wisdom to be the best possible husband and father.
- I asked God for a friend who could guide me further in this truth. I needed someone who would help me resolve my inner turmoil regarding Dale and help me live an obedient Christian life.
- Finally, I asked God to let me guide others, particularly by preparing me to do more personal counseling so I could share my insights from Him.

Even though God promised to be faithful, I couldn't keep myself from making one stipulation. I asked, of all the people who might be that "special friend" to help me grow, that it not be Jim, a most obnoxious older man in Dale's organization. He had a know-it-all attitude so offensive to me that I found it hard to be around him

The answers to my prayers began almost immediately. First, Dale called me into his office a few days later to discuss how we might resolve the struggle we were having in our relationship. As I stood before him, I wavered as to whether or not I should tell him about all I had been learning and feeling. Just when I was about to open up and express to him what was on my heart, Dale said, "Gary, I think you need to talk to someone besides me about what's been going on. In fact, I've arranged for you to spend a good deal of time with Jim over the next several weeks to talk things out."

Jim! The very person I had prayed I wouldn't have to talk to. I could have resigned on the spot. I was confused and upset with God. I felt as if I had asked for a fish and been given a snake. I couldn't understand why the one person I specifically wanted to avoid was to become a major part of my week.

Though I sensed God's Spirit changing me, I had to struggle to keep from walking out of the room. Yet those two days of prayer and fasting had been so meaningful to me that I prayed instead. "Lord, even though I'm confused and upset, I am not going to try to figure this out. I'm willing to let You prove Your faithfulness in my life"

That afternoon I started meeting with Jim, and almost overnight God used him to pull me further out of my discouragement. Instead of the pride-filled, know-it-all I expected to find, Jim was caring and compassionate. More than I ever thought possible, he understood Dale as well as my conflict with Dale. Instead of lecturing me, he listened and prayed with me. In the time I spent with Jim over the next few weeks my attitude changed from resentment at having to meet with him to feeling rewarded because we were meeting.

This was a major turning point. I began to realize that God was not giving me a scorpion or a snake. He was faithful in answering my prayer. Yet like a loving Father, He knew what I truly needed. I could relax and trust Him even when I didn't understand what He was doing. My confidence in God grew by leaps and bounds as I continued to knock on His door for my other requests.

God had answered my prayer about finding a close friend to help me work through the situation with Dale, and soon I began receiving answers to my other requests as well. I had played to be a godly husband and father and to learn to keep my family in harmony. Without me lifting a finger, God answered that prayer by opening up a door to a ministry I never expected to have any part in.

A good friend and pastor I had met through our business called and asked if I would consider doing three things in his church: First, he wanted me to become a better husband and father so I could teach others out of my own life experiences. Second, he wanted me to develop a ministry to families. And third, he asked me to begin a counseling program at his church.

While Norma and I prayed about this exciting opportunity, an almost identical offer came from another pastor in California. Now I had not only one chance to learn about my family and family ministry, but two!

This dilemma fascinated me, and I've seen it happen many times since. God is so faithful that He often gives several answers to a single request. Those two offers showed me how far I had slipped into discouragement. Before getting into the Gospel of Luke, I had questioned whether I would ever see any answers to prayer or to life and whether I would ever be of any service to God. These opportunities showed me that our ways are never hidden from the Lord and that regardless of our circumstances, He has a task for us to accomplish for Him.

Seeing the things I had prayed for come together reassured me of God's faithfulness. I hadn't sent out dozens of résumés looking for a job, nor had I asked Jim to become my friend. Yet in both cases God, in His own way and timing, had honored my requests, just as He said He would in Luke 11.

Norma and I decided to accept the first offer—to serve as a family pastor at a growing church—and we prepared to move our family to another state. As I began to plan my departure from Dale's company, I felt a renewed love for the people I was leaving. Even though my conflict with Dale had been devastating in many ways, I found I still loved him and knew, finally, that God had used our problems to bring me closer to Him. In fact, I began to understand that if I had never gone through that experience I might never have discovered the depth of God's faithfulness nor become so meaningfully related to Him.

But God had taught me another truth concerning prayer that has become my primary tool for finding answered prayer.

PERSISTENCE—A SECRET TO ANSWERED PRAYER

During the two days I camped out in the Book of Luke, I listened intently each time Jesus spoke about prayer. In Luke 18 Jesus introduced two parables by telling His disciples that "they ought to pray and not lose heart" (v. 1). The first story He used is now one of my favorites; in it lies a fantastic secret to effective prayer. Here's the scene:

Imagine an unrighteous, wicked judge assigned to a small city in Israel. He has no respect for God or man. He is disgruntled because He would rather be in Rome enjoying pageantry, games, and parties. Instead he's stuck with a bunch of farmers, shepherds, and religious fanatics. Every day people line up to present their grievances to him and he passes judgments according to his mood.

In the line of people stands a widow with no one to look out for her best interests or to protect her. Her situation appears hopeless Others take advantage of her, but she has no legal rights. Although many look at her as helpless, she knows the secret to gaining justice. The first time she presents her petition to the judge, he brusquely dismisses her. But she does not give up. After coming before him repeatedly, she finally gains legal protection, "lest by continually coming she wear me out" the judge decides (Luke 18:5).

Jesus said to listen carefully to the story of this unrighteous judge. He pictures an important truth people need to understand. It was the woman's persistence that brought results. Jesus goes on to say, "Shall not God bring about justice for His elect, who cry to Him day and night, and *will He delay long over them?"* (Luke 18:7).

Following my two-day retreat, I imagined myself coming every day as the widow did and lining up before God. From chapter 11, I learned God was loving and that He would be faithful to His children. From chapter 18, I learned to get in God's prayer line every day, a practice I have continued since 1975.

When I line up to pray, my petitions fall into three categories: First, I ask for what God promises to give His children—love, joy, and peace through His Holy Spirit—that's fulfillment. Second, I pray about the needs of my family. And third, I pray for the needs of people around me.

After we moved away from Dale and his business, one of my major needs was to be free of resentment toward him. I knew it was wrong for me to feel betrayed and to desire revenge, but I could not shake myself loose from these emotions. Every day for two years I applied the principle from the parable in Luke 18 and prayed as I jogged: "Lord, I'm in line again, along with many of Your children. I must admit how upset I still am with Dale. I don't know how You're going to do it, but I know You're going to free me. Maybe this is the day! And if not today, perhaps tomorrow!"

After two years of getting in line every day and requesting that freedom, it finally came. A man from my church approached me with an article from a counseling magazine. "This article describes a problem I'm having," he said. "Would you read it and then could we talk about how to solve my problem?"

Even though this man was looking for help for his own problem, the article perfectly described *my* conflict with Dale. It also provided the final pieces of information I needed to resolve it completely.

The article explained that much of Dale's strong drive to achieve came from several conflicts he had never resolved, especially his father's overpowering emphasis on success as measured by how much he produced. Acceptance from his parents came only when he overachieved. In addition, Dale felt compelled to use people to reach his overachieving goals. When they didn't help him achieve, he discarded them, which explained why I was only one in a trail of broken relationships Dale had suffered. Finally I saw why he couldn't repair his own broken relationships.

I also learned that real forgiveness required my prayers and actions to release Dale from the grip of overachieving inner conflict. Dale was crippled by always having to gain approval. Why should I be angry with him? He needed understanding. I needed to love and help him instead of draining away all my emotional energy by being bitter toward him. Once I stopped long enough to *understand* Dale, I was finally able to forgive him. That day I stepped out of that prayer line and never again needed to get back in it. My resentment toward Dale never returned.

Shortly after reading that article, and after God released me from my anger, I drove to one of Dale's health seminars and had a great visit with him. Some of the things that once made me angry reappeared, but this time, rather than bristling and wanting to separate myself from him, I listened and felt genuine love for Dale and respect for his work. I actually wanted to pray for a special blessing of God on his life. That's when I knew I was really free! In fact, we continue to see each other and talk on the phone. I realize now that my problem with Dale was not Dale's problem. It was my attitude.

God not only is faithful to answer our persistent prayers for spiritual needs but for physical needs as well. An example of God's faithfulness in taking care of everyday practical concerns involved my daughter Kari. Every night for approximately two years the two of us stood in line asking God to provide a car. I was earning significantly less than I had with Dale, and our family station wagon was on its last legs and full of rattles. The engine was unreliable, and I had rewired the broken springs in the front seat on the driver's side with coat hangers. I did not have the money to replace the car and did not want to go into debt again, but I never mentioned the need to anyone else.

One afternoon while working with a businessman, we took a break for a hamburger and he decided to drive my car. When he sank down in the seat and leaned toward the door he asked if this was my only car. I said it was. "This is pathetic," he said. I laughed and agreed with him, but was caught totally by surprise by what he said next. "Tomorrow I want you to go down to any car lot in town and pick any car you want. I'll pay for it."

That kind of experience has been repeated again and again in all areas of need. I never presume on God's timing, and I never expect satisfaction from any material thing He gives. Yet time after time His provisions for my physical needs remind me that God is indeed my source of life. Even with things like misplacing my wallet or keys, it's fun to get in line and watch Him resolve the "little" things.

What's exciting about all this is that any child of God can experience the joy of trusting Him. I've learned that I can't take pride in what He does for me because it is His faithfulness, not my spirituality, that makes the difference.

DEPENDING ON GOD FOR LASTING LIFE

Humbled, alert, and convicted, I became childlike, completely dependent on Christ for both life and direction, the exact position He wanted me in. But many of us have a hard time believing God cares so deeply for us.

I once met a woman in counseling who didn't think she could depend on God in the same way she used to depend on her doting father. Sherie was single, 36 years old, and with tears she challenged God and me. "You say God loves me and can meet all of my needs and fill my cup," she said. "But who's going to take care of me? Who's going to talk to me? Who's He providing for me?" Then she added, "I have a car stereo that won't fit my car. It was a gift so I can't return it, and I don't even know the first thing to do about it. Now tell me how God can meet a need like that?"

I did not know how God would meet her needs, but I knew He could, even with her stereo. "Are you willing to ask God to become the source of your life and to depend on Him for every need?" I asked her. At first she couldn't do it because she still felt God had cheated her. We got on our knees and with tears she prayed, "God, I want to depend on you, but I can't." After two more tries, she finally blurted out, "Okay, God, I will completely trust my life in Your hands and let You, in Your timing, fill my life and take care of my everyday needs."

That encounter left her emotionally exhausted, and I honestly did not expect much to happen for a while. But the next morning she could hardly wait to call me. She had called a retailer to see if she could exchange her stereo. The store manager said he didn't carry that model but suggested that she call the factory office. She did. It was after working hours, so a regional manager answered the phone. After some discussion, he recognized her name. Her father had been one of his closest friends in high school. "If you're his daughter," he said, "I'll take complete care of whatever you need."

Stunned, Sherie recognized this as a demonstration of God's faithfulness. In subsequent years, she has filled several notebooks detailing how God has met her specific needs.

Some people may object, saying that everyone experiences similar "coincidences" and that they aren't necessarily from God. Maybe it's not an important question for the small things in life, but when people ask God for fulfillment, peace, joy, and love, and they come in lasting amounts, that's worth shouting about. And aren't those our deepest needs? God is faithful to provide what we need when we get in His line. In the same way a child asks a parent for candy or a new toy, we can petition God for the "small things." If He doesn't give them, perhaps they aren't really needs. But He will fulfill His specific promises, such as those for abundant life (John 10:10) and inner peace (John 14:27).

A FINAL LESSON ON PRAYER

In Luke 18:18-30 Jesus spoke the words that became the basis for the famous quote of Jim Elliott, the missionary to the Auca Indians who was martyred in Ecuador: "A man is no fool who gives up what he cannot keep to gain what he will never lose."

Christ promised His disciples in Luke 18:29-30 that anyone who seeks God's kingdom above home, mate, brothers, sisters, parents, and children will receive many times more *at this time* as well as eternal life in the age to come. But how does putting God first help us in our everyday problems?

Like many of us, Donna needed to learn to put God first in everyday living. She progressed from anger to hatred to apathy toward her husband, Dave, because of an affair he'd had. She was so disgusted that she did not speak to him for days. Donna was surprised when her pastor showed her that her hatred and judgmental attitude were wrong in God's eyes. Until she saw the log in her own eye, she could not possibly help her husband. Donna humbled herself by admitting her own sin. She also learned to pray for her husband and to wait on God to change him.

Over the next several days, a new love for her husband and a previously unknown sense of calm seeped into Donna's soul. She even started doing special things for him. As the weeks went by, Dave noticed the change in her behavior. Captivated by the beauty of her peacefulness, he finally broke down and asked what had happened. When Donna confessed her judgmental spirit and explained her new dependency on God, Dave expressed his desire for the same peace and joy. Together they went back to the pastor, who helped Dave discover what Donna had found. They became one of the most radiant couples in our church, all because Donna escaped from the darkness of her anger and began walking in the light of her new dependency on God. She saw the truth, grabbed hold of it, and found lasting fulfillment in knowing God personally.

In addition to having my life completely filled, I still enjoy the pleasures of knowing and serving people, of traveling to new places, of having some possessions, and of gaining some position. But these things are no longer what I look to for fulfillment; they are simply the overflow.

> If I lost them all I would still be full because I have the source of life itself—a personal relationship with Jesus Christ (1 John 5:11–12).

I once heard a story about a man who died and was given a guided tour of heaven by St. Peter. When they came to an immense warehouse filled with all shapes and sizes of wrapped packages, the man asked Peter what they were. Peter replied sadly, "This is where God keeps all the gifts He intended for His children. These were never claimed." Unfortunately, many today never claim God's promised packages. We leave His gifts in the warehouse of heaven, either because we never ask or because we get out of line too soon.

I do not want anyone to miss out on God's gifts the way I did for so many years, especially the gift of life itself. This new life overflows with meaning so satisfying that the thrill of other pursuits is as fleeting as the momentary excitement of an amusement park ride.

4

Grabbing Hold of Fulfillment

NEVER UNDERESTIMATE THE power of a woman who has yielded her life to God. She not only has strength, but a special, radiating beauty. Norma had that glow during our courtship and when we were first married. After several years of marriage, however, her power and beauty started to fade, and she blamed me for her lack of fulfillment.

Norma was frustrated with me for good reason. Before my crisis with Dale, I traveled nearly fifty percent of the time and was so consumed with my work that I had little energy left for her and the kids. When Michael, our third child, was born, he was sick much of the time and so Norma could not maintain the house and care for the children without my help.

She tried conventional methods to get me to change. She talked to me, she pleaded, she cried. Nothing worked. I didn't change, and neither did she.

But then Norma tried something *unconventional*. Her action motivated me to go to Dale and ask for a different position in the company so I could spend more time at home.

What was this powerful action she took?

> Norma quit fighting. She realized she wasn't fighting me; she was fighting God's plan for fulfillment.

Norma had read about God's love for her. He had demonstrated His love by sending Jesus Christ, His only Son, to give her abundant life. By demanding that I change, she was in essence saying that she could not experience a full life unless God somehow used me to meet her needs. But God was ready and willing to meet her needs, apart from me, if she would only let Him.

With no coaching from me, Norma changed her thinking, admitted she hadn't been seeking God alone, and began her own journey to find God's fulfilling love. Rather than complain to me, she prayed, "Lord, thank You that all I need is You. You know I want a good relationship with Gary and that I want him to spend more time at home. You also know that I'm not very strong physically. I'm so tired that I don't feel I can last much longer under this strain. I'm coming to You with these requests because I know that if I *need* Gary at home, *You* can either make it happen or take away my desire. I'm going to stop fighting Gary and instead ask You either to change him or to meet my needs in some other way."

To find God's fulfillment, Norma took steps similar to those I later discovered. She stopped expecting life from me and started looking to God. She realized I not only would not, but could not, fill her life, so she went to the source of life and asked Him to fill her.

The results were startling. I noticed the change almost immediately. When I came home from work, I sensed a calm spirit in our house. Norma's face was peaceful, no longer tense. Instead of the usual harsh words, her conversation was quiet and she was more interested in asking me how my day had gone than in relating her activities with the children.

After a few days, I couldn't keep from asking what had happened. "Gary, I got tired of fighting you," she explained calmly. "I realized that I wasn't trusting God concerning our marriage and family, and so I decided to stop complaining and start praying. I've told God that I would like you to spend more time at home, and if I really need that, I know He will make the necessary changes." She also grabbed my attention by stating, in a calm and undemanding way, "I think I'm headed for a physical collapse. Michael has been sick so much, and with all the other responsibilities, I don't think I can last much longer."

Imagine what that did to me. I was instantly convicted that my priorities were wrong. And that wasn't all. Because Norma had changed, I *wanted* to spend more time at home. That same week I asked Dale to change my job so I could spend more time meeting my family's needs.

What Norma did summarizes the first three chapters. She stopped looking to people, places, possessions, and position and turned to a trustworthy God Who answers the persistent prayers of His children. He promises life, and He delivers!

Some may think Norma just disguised her selfishness by asking God to change me instead of nagging me to change. I disagree. I encourage wives to ask God for a good relationship with their husbands and children. That request is not selfish. A good relationship benefits not only the wife, but the entire family, the Christian community, and ultimately our nation and the entire world. It also glorifies God, because a godly marriage is a picture of our relationship with Christ (Ephesians 5:22–23).

Once we're into the habit of seeking fulfillment from the world, we won't learn overnight to look to God as the source of life. It took Norma and me several years before looking to the Lord was our natural, first response, and at times we still catch ourselves focusing on someone or something other than Him.

The procedure we follow is not magic. Neither does it need to be kept legalistically like a scientific formula. These are simply guidelines we have followed that we hope you can learn from and adapt to your unique situation. God creates us as individuals, not as carbon copies, so put your own fingerprints on the steps that follow.

STEP OUT OF FANTASYLAND

Many Christians, frustrated by the lack of fulfillment they've found in people, places, possessions, and position, have fallen for the deception that God's Word is not entirely true. They live as though the Bible were a book of myths rather than a living and active guide to fulfillment. For them, the hope of gaining lasting love, joy, and peace is like believing Disneyland is real. And attending church is like the temporary thrill of one of Disney's rides. Behind the splashing water, flashing lights, dark tunnels, and dancing figures are only computers and wires and sophisticated sound systems. Christianity is a make-believe world, a ride they take Sunday after Sunday. It doesn't satisfy, but they keep riding because deep down they want to believe it is real.

Others, looking for a greater thrill, switch to different rides, like a new church, a different speaker, or some new teaching. The new ride is more exciting at first, but no more satisfying in the long run.

Some have quit taking the rides altogether. They are convinced that those who say they find fulfillment in the Lord lack depth and settle for the simplistic solutions found in a make-believe world.

How do we escape the amusement park syndrome where rides go nowhere except up and down, round and round? We begin by admitting that we have sought fulfillment from people, places, possessions, or positions. These four P's describe our personal Disneyland. The entrance to this amusement park is wide, and many go through it. But Christ said the gate that leads to life is narrow and only a few find it.

The call to hand over tickets we've paid a high price for is difficult to obey, but that's the requirement. It's called confession. We must admit we've been standing in the wrong line and step willingly into God's line.

STEP INTO TRUTH

Admitting we've been in the wrong line is only the first step toward reality. We also need to move into the right line. That is what the Bible means by repentance. It's stepping out of one line and into another. It's turning away from one way of thinking and embracing God's way. It's changing directions, rejecting our former source of expectations and accepting a new source, one that will never fail.

How does this concept actually work? Here's an example in an area where many of us struggle—society's emphasis on sexual "freedom." From toothpaste to cars to flowers to resort hotels, we can hardly buy anything that a sparsely dressed woman has not advertised. Because our society is obsessed with sex, lust is a major temptation.

Even though I had a very rewarding relationship with Norma, I was not immune from this temptation. I met a woman at work whom I found very attractive. Through months of periodic contact, I gradually developed a strong emotional attachment to her. As I gained her confidence she began to tell me some personal struggles she was having. I empathized with her and wanted to take her in my arms and comfort her. When I was honest, I knew I really wanted more than that. But holding her would be enough, I told myself.

During those weeks of temptation I was also learning that people cannot give ultimate meaning to my life. At times I desired to be with this woman, but whenever my thoughts strayed I would confess that she was not the source of my life and admit that I was standing in the wrong line. Then I would ask God to make me realize that what appeared to be as harmless and fun as an amusement park ride was actually a real-life thrill ride that would crash at the end.

Once I had confessed my desire to have someone other than Christ fill my life, I would get back into the line that leads to knowing Him personally. Although I didn't know it at the time, the Lord was teaching me an important principle about "staying in His line" during times of temptation.

RETURN TO THE SOURCE OF JOY

Once we have switched lines, how do we continue to experience this gift of life? The apostle Paul writes in 1 Thessalonians 5:16, "Rejoice always." In Philippians 4:4 he commands, "Rejoice in the Lord always; again I will say, rejoice!" Paul is so emphatic about this because the word "rejoice" literally means "return to the source of our joy."

In the case of this other woman, I obeyed Paul's instruction to rejoice by praying, "Lord, You know, and I'm just discovering, that this girl will never fill my cup. If anything, she could drill huge holes in it. Not only would I probably wind up in disharmony with her (that's usually the case with couples who've had affairs), it would undoubtedly do tremendous damage to my family and to Your reputation. But the most foolish result of all would be that I would cut myself off from You, the very source of life. So right this moment, Lord, I'm asking You to fill my cup. Thank You for letting me see this before it's too late. However long it takes, I will stay in Your line until I'm free from her and filled with You."

Over the years a similar prayer of rejoicing has kept me, in many situations, from giving in to such temptations as envy, jealousy, fear, and anger. Rejoicing, even in times of testing, is acknowledging that God is the source of life. And rejoicing brings us to the place where our lives can be filled by the source of life—God Himself.

Ephesians 3:14-21 is the best explanation of rejoicing I have found.

> For this reason, I bow my knees before the Father, from whom every family in heaven and on earth derives its name, that He would grant you, according to the riches of His glory, to be strengthened with power through His Spirit in the inner man; so that Christ may dwell in your hearts through faith; and that you, being rooted and grounded in love, may be able to comprehend with all the saints what is the breadth and length and height and depth, and to know the love of Christ which surpasses knowledge, *that you may be filled up to all the fulness of God.* Now to Him who is able to do exceeding abundantly beyond all that we ask or think, according to the power that works within us, to Him be the glory in the church and in Christ Jesus to all generations forever and ever. Amen.

Note the italicized words: *That you may be filled up to all the fullness of God.* That is God's desire and gift to us. And in the next verse, Paul talks about Him who is able to do *exceeding abundantly beyond all that we ask or think. That's the overflow—the exciting, fulfilling life we all desire. It's waiting for us. We can experience it by rejoicing.*

Rejoicing begins when we acknowledge that God is the source of all life. In fact, He *is* life, which is why we can adore Him and sing praise to Him. Rejoicing reveals faith, because it demonstrates our expectation that God will reveal to us the depths and heights of His love. All of this is so that we may be *filled up to* all *the fulness of God.* The ultimate in ful-fillment.

MAKE GOD YOUR BEST FRIEND

During my time of temptation, I learned that the principle of rejoicing was reliable. Simply going to the source of joy and getting to know Him personally as my very best friend filled my life. Christ wants to he our friend. He said we are His friends *if* we obey His command to love Him and each other. Obeying Him does not mean I am like a slave. He says in John 15:15, "No longer do I call you slaves; for the slave does not know what his master is doing; but I have called you *friends,* for all things that I have heard from My Father I have made known to you."

Most of us have enjoyed a close friendship. When we're with that friend, we're relaxed and free to be ourselves. We enjoy each other's company. I believe rejoicing—returning to each other often—is the key to fruitful friendship. That's why making God our very best friend is the way to lasting joy. To experience God's joy on a daily basis we must become His friend.

I picture myself like the widow standing in God's line, waiting patiently for Him to meet my inner spiritual needs and my family's material needs. I do this while I run every morning. During the half hour to an hour that I'm pounding the road, I enjoy a special, uninterrupted time of building a meaningful friendship with Christ.

Each person must find the time that is right for him or her. It might be while eating or dressing. During quiet moments of Bible reading and prayer. While driving to and from work. While ironing, cooking, or washing dishes. During a break at work. The important thing is that we not let the cares and pressures of everyday living squeeze out our daily personal time with the source of life.

In addition to spending time alone with God, we must also spend time in His Word. Reading God's Word is essential for getting to know His thoughts. In fact, spending time in His Word plugs us into the source of life. In John 6:63 Jesus says, "The words that I have spoken to you are spirit and are life." And in John 17:17 Jesus prays to the Father on behalf of His disciples saying, "Sanctify them in the truth; Thy word is truth."

There is a very important balance between *knowing* Christ and knowing *about* Him. Neither worshiping the Bible nor ignoring it can bring steady spiritual growth. Reading God's Word and not developing a personal relationship with Him is like reading a biography of President Reagan but never getting to know him.

But Christ and the Word are one (John 1:1), so it is impossible to know Him without knowing His Word. And the only way to have an intimate friendship with Him is to communicate with Him, to let His words sink into our souls.

I can understand this better when I think in terms of my relationship with Norma, who is my very best friend. One of the reasons we are so close is because we have security in our relationship through consistent communication, a sharing of our deepest emotions, a communion of our spirits, and regular, meaningful touching. My friendship with Norma helps me know God better as a friend.

Friendship with God is also security. The apostle Paul mentions that security in Romans 8:38–39: "For I am convinced that neither death, nor life, nor angels, nor principalities, nor things present, nor things to come, nor powers, nor height, nor depth, nor any other created thing, shall be able to separate us from the love of God, which is in Christ Jesus our Lord." Just as I'm committed to Norma, I'm committed to God for life, and I know He's committed to me.

Friendship with God is prayer. Just as we cannot know a friend without communicating, we cannot know God without regular conversation with Him through prayer. Prayer is a two-way street. I express my love, devotion, and feelings, and I listen to Him as well. The closer the friendship, the more intimate our sharing. One of the reasons King David knew God so well was because he poured out his emotions in verse after verse in Psalms and contrasted his feelings with the awesome greatness of God. "How precious also are Thy thoughts to me, O God! How vast is the sum of them! If I should count them, they would outnumber the sand. When I awake, I am still with Thee" (Psalm 139:17–18).

Friendship with God is identification. True friendship requires a willingness to be seen together. A person is not truly a friend unless we are willing to be identified with that person. This is one reason communion and baptism are so important, and why physical signs such as kneeling, singing, and other forms of worship reflect our relationship with God.

Friendship with God is dependency. One of the benefits of knowing God as our friend is being able to express our physical and material needs to Him. When we seek to know God, we are promised that our material needs will be met (Matthew 6:33), but we need to remind ourselves constantly that having our physical needs met will not give us life. Life comes only through knowing God, not from the material goods He gives us.

Friendship with God is gratefulness. An important element of a good friendship is mutual admiration, which is another way of saying we should not take each other for granted. We need to be grateful for the friendship, and sometimes we need to express our gratefulness in tangible ways.

By realizing how faithful God has been and wants to be to those who draw close to Him, we can develop a grateful, thankful heart even before we receive answers to our prayers. Paul tells us in Philippians 4:6 to "Be anxious for nothing, but in everything by prayer and supplication *with thanksgiving* let your requests be made known to God." The next verse confirms how God fills our cup. The *peace* of God, which surpasses all of our comprehension, protects our hearts and our minds in Christ Jesus.

During my time of praying about my lust, I was able to thank God for freeing me even *before* He did because I knew He would be faithful and that I would not get out of His line until He helped me. It was His will that I be faithful to His commands and to the wife He gave me, so I was confident that He would answer my prayer for mental and physical purity.

One of the benefits of expressing gratefulness is contentment in knowing that God will fill my cup and provide for my needs. The same spirit that Paul describes in Philippians 4:11 has become mine, for I too have learned the secret of being content in whatever circumstances I am in.

Also, like the great King David, my inner calm and peace continues as I follow his example in Psalm 62. My soul no longer expects anything from God's creation but waits in silence for God only. I command my soul to do the same thing David did: "Wait in silence for God only, for my hope is from Him. He only is my rock and my salvation, my stronghold; I shall not be shaken. On God my salvation and my glory rest; the rock of my strength, my refuge is in God" (vv. 5–7). I have determined to trust Him at all times and to wait for His faithfulness.

DECIDE TO BE FILLED

The feelings associated with gratefulness and contentment may take time to develop. Contentment results from *deciding* to rest in the faithfulness of God. Calmness results from *seeing* His faithfulness time after time. I meet many discouraged Christians who experience little of God's faithfulness because they get out of His line too soon. They don't allow God to answer in His perfect timing. Because they are discouraged, they don't feel like getting back into line. It's a defeating cycle, but we can choose to break it.

Our decision to rest in God's faithfulness can be based on the promises clearly given in Scripture. God promises to be our rock, shield, rear guard, shepherd, king, rescuer, hiding place, living water, bread of life, light, physician, our life-supplying vine, our power to overcome sin, our advocate before the Father, our free gift of eternal life, as well as our source of wisdom, joy, peace, love, and self-control. The list goes on and on.

These promises are facts, given to God's people who stand in His line like the widow in Luke 18. Gratefulness, praise, wonder, and excitement can become real as we witness His work in our lives. The faithful, trustworthy fact, according to His Word, is that He provides these emotions to all who love Him.

The process of discovering and knowing Jesus Christ as the source of life can continue every day for the rest of our lives. Getting to know Christ gives life richness, for we can never fully know the depth of His love. Every day is an opportunity to see a new dimension. Unfortunately that doesn't mean we never get sidetracked or discouraged. The false promises of the world in which we live continually draw us away from the source of life.

Negative emotions also draw us away from God. Anger, loneliness, and hurt feelings can make us feel as if God has deserted us or let us down. Actually, the opposite is true. God allows these feelings to help us see where our expectations are focused, whether on God or on His creation. In the next chapter we will find out how to use negative emotions as an early warning system, alerting us that we need to return to the source of life, which is Christ Jesus Himself.

5

Discovering the Main Cause of Unhappiness

JIM HAD BEEN comfortably married for almost ten years, and he and his wife had a healthy, though somewhat unexciting, relationship. Jim had never been the type to send cards or flowers, but this year he wanted to do something special for his wife on their anniversary. He asked his secretary what he could do to show his wife he really loved her.

"Flowers," she said. "Send flowers. And buy her a big box of candy as well. In fact, you might even find a romantic poem, memorize it, and recite it to her when you give her the gifts."

Inspired by his secretary's suggestions, Jim canceled his afternoon appointments, drove to the florist and to the candy store, and even stopped at the library and found a book of poems. Nearly bursting with excitement, Jim drove to his house, carried his pile of presents to the front door, and rang the doorbell. When his wife answered the door, Jim started to recite the poem he had selected and handed her the candy and flowers.

His wife stared at him for a moment and then began to cry.

"What's the matter?" Jim asked.

"What's the matter?" his wife sobbed. "The garage door opener broke this morning; the baby has been sick and is running from both ends; the dog ate the remote control for the television; and now you come home drunk!"

In this make-believe story, the response Jim received from his wife was the opposite of what he expected. The same thing happens in real life. At one time or another all of us will be in situations in which our expectations are unfulfilled, and unfulfilled expectations are a primary cause of negative emotions and unhappiness. Many people who struggle with negative emotions actually use them as weapons against themselves. Every day, people make statements like, "How could I have gotten so angry at my wife?" or "I can't believe she got that raise. I know I shouldn't feel this way, but . . ." or "For six years I've been dating him. I can't believe it's over."

Many of us deny and try to push away these painful feelings. But consider this:

> Anger, hurt feelings, fear, and lust can actually help us develop a closer, more vital relationship with Christ.

That statement may sound incredible because negative emotions are usually associated with a lack of spiritual maturity and unhappiness. And it's true, allowed to fester and develop, they can draw us away from God. We have all seen numerous examples of how the "deeds of the flesh" (Galatians 5:19) can hurt and damage relationships. But as Christians, we need not become victims of our emotions. Even negative emotions can be the impetus that moves us back to the source of joy.

We can never completely avoid negative emotions; we will all experience anger and fear and loneliness on occasion. The issue is how often we have them and how we use them. There are many ways to respond to negative emotions; some ways are healthy, others are not.

An unhealthy response to negative emotions is to try and stuff them deep inside or pretend they don't exist. The damage of denying our emotions is well illustrated by the story of a Spartan boy in ancient Greece. At the age of seven the boy left home to begin a life-long career of harsh military service. He was taught every aspect of military combat. He learned survival skills and was taught to hide every trace of emotion.

One day the boy captured a fox and was playing with the animal when he saw his instructor approach him. Quickly he stuffed the wild fox underneath his cloak. In keeping with their custom, the teacher questioned the boy at length. The boy calmly responded to the teacher's endless questions, his face never betraying a hint of pain or fear even though the fox was gnawing and tearing at his unprotected body. Finally, suffering from mortal wounds, the boy fell dead at his teacher's feet. He became the model of Spartan discipline, and this story was later used as an example of genuine manhood. Yet those "manly" qualities killed him.

Some Christians view such control of their emotions as a measure of spirituality. No matter how much they are struggling or hurting, they believe they must always present a facade of happiness.

The model Christ gave us, however, was not that of a spartan. Jesus wept at the grave of a friend. He became angry at the money changers in the temple. He was even accused of being a "wine-bibber" and a "glutton" because he attended a wedding and other parties. Denying negative emotions may leave us looking good on the outside, but it can be destroying us on the inside.

A second option is to allow our emotions to run their natural course with the attitude that there's nothing we can do about them. The problem with unchecked emotions, however, is that they can harm others as well as ourselves. Ken and Cindy are an example.

Ken came from a home where everything was always clean and neat; Cindy's family wasn't as concerned about neatness. This difference created a great deal of conflict in their marriage. When Cindy was tired after a hard day's work, she let the housework wait until another day. This frustrated Ken, who constantly fired verbal darts at his wife: "What are these clothes doing in the corner?" "This room looks like the dust bowl." "You expect the ants to clean these dishes?"

One morning Cindy awoke to hear Ken vacuuming the living room at six o'clock. She staggered out of the bedroom and asked what he was doing. "I'm sick and tired of living in this pigpen!" he yelled. Ken's outburst of anger and his degrading comments left Cindy defeated and destroyed her motivation to change. But Ken seemed unaware of the damage his anger caused his wife. Venting his negative emotions made Ken feel better for the moment, but it caused lasting scars in his relationships.

Releasing pent-up emotions may be considered good therapy in some circles, but it comes at a high price. A friend who worked at a psychiatric hospital relayed the tragic story of Brian. Brian had a great deal of anger at what he considered unfair actions his parents had taken. As part of Brian's therapy he was put into a room with an inflated BoBo doll, which was to be used as a punching bag. "Just pretend this doll is your parents," Brian was told, "and use it to release all your hostilities."

After destroying two BoBo dolls Brian fell to the floor in exhaustion. His therapy was termed a success, but when he was released from the hospital a month later he returned home and crippled his father in a fit of rage. Neither denying nor venting our emotions is the answer.

For Christians, another option is available.

> Those who know Christ can use negative emotions as warning signals.

Ken looked at Cindy as the cause of his anger without recognizing that his anger revealed his problem as well.

If Ken had been willing, he could have harnessed the power of his anger to draw him closer to God—even to make him more loving. How is this possible? If we recognize that negative emotions are like warning lights on the dashboard of a car, we can use them to warn us that we are headed for trouble.

Imagine that you are driving me to the airport after I have spoken in your city. We're enjoying a fascinating discussion when suddenly I notice a red light flashing on your dash, warning you that the car is overheating. When I draw your attention to the light, you tell me to ignore it. "It always flashes on and off," you say.

After several miles of traveling with the red light on, I once again mention my concern "OK, OK," you say, "open up the glove compartment and give me a hammer, will you?" I do as you ask, and then, with a smile, you smash the light. "There," you say, "that should make you feel better. Now will you quit pestering me?"

Three miles later the car comes to a halt in a blanket of smoke, and I miss my plane. Because you failed to admit the reality of the problem and acknowledge the warning light, you must now deal with my frustration and your own embarrassment.

Although this story is exaggerated, I regularly see people doing this very thing in counseling. They come to me with warning lights flashing in their lives, but instead of using the valuable information the lights could provide, they ignore or smash them.

Probably the most important thing that negative emotions reveal—and certainly the most destructive—is our own self-centeredness. Just how self-centered are we? I asked a beautiful model that question several years ago.

Mary came to my office and asked for help in her struggles with her husband. As I listened to her complain about his harsh, demanding, and insensitive ways, I noticed that her face reflected a hard, deep-seated resentment. She spent a great deal of time describing his lack of love. He demanded that she dress in a certain way so he would always look good with her. Once when she scratched the car fender he treated her like a child by taking her "toy" away until she "learned how to drive."

She left herself wide open when she paused to say, "I'm really hurting over my husband's treatment. Is there anything I can do to relieve the pain?" This was early in my ministry and today I would probably not use such a bold approach. I forced Mary to face something she didn't want to face when I asked her, "How self-centered do you think you are?"

First amazement, then irritation at my brash question spread across her face. "I'm not very self-centered at all," she responded. "Most of my time is spent taking care of the children or my husband. I have almost no time for myself."

Not sure where this would lead, I asked Mary if I could give her some homework. Her assignment was to write down every time she was angry or had hurt feelings and to ask herself *what she was personally losing* that might cause hurt or anger. She agreed to return in a week and share the results.

During our next appointment Mary confessed that for the first time she realized how many things she unconsciously expected of her husband, her children, and her environment. She had filled three pages with incidents and discovered that every time she was angry or hurt, someone was denying her something she wanted. When I asked her again how self-centered she thought she was she lowered her head as she answered, "*Very* self-centered." I immediately confessed that I too was self-centered and that it was a toss-up as to who was more selfish. But I probably had her beat.

Admitting we are selfish is not easy. I like to be thought of as a caring, compassionate, giving person who always looks out for the best interests of others. But in reality, my best attempts to be righteous are as filthy rags, according to the prophet Isaiah (Isaiah 64:6).

> We all need to admit our level of self-centeredness because out of such an admission comes the freedom to refocus our expectations away from God's creation and onto God.

Let's examine seven common emotions and see how they reveal our self-centeredness, and then explore how each emotion can be used to draw us into a closer walk with God. In the process, we will see how our negative emotions can lead us to the source of our fulfillment.

ENVY—DESIRE FOR GAIN

Envy is the desire to gain what appears to make others happy—a bigger home, a better car, a higher paying job. We think that having these things will finally make us content.

Perhaps we keep our eyes upon Christ most of the day, knowing that He alone fulfills us, but in quiet moments early in the morning, during coffee break, on the drive to and from work, the green cloud of envy settles over us and we wish we had more of what the Joneses have. They appear to be so happy. But if we lived with them for a few weeks, we might discover they are just good actors. Behind their closed door, Mr. and Mrs. Jones may be wishing they had what we have.

I rarely experience envy any more. But for many years it often engulfed me, especially when I traveled with members of Dale's management team. The subject of money inevitably surfaced and we would compare salaries. I could tell that each of us was trying to understand why one person made more or less than another.

I never revealed my salary but I learned that one of my subordinates was making significantly more than I, even though he had far less experience in the business. For several days and nights I felt envy and anger because of that inequity. I formulated several plans to reveal the injustice without sounding like I was complaining. But Dale discovered the mistake about the same time I did and doubled my salary before I even had a chance to talk to him. It had been an innocent oversight. Dale had been so immersed in his cause that he rarely thought about the financial rewards to himself or others in the business. But doubling my salary did not eliminate my envy because there was always someone else in the company who made more money and had more things. I came to realize that money and possessions would never fill my cup. *The only good my envy served was as a reminder that God alone is my source of life.*

The reason I seldom feel envy any more is because I know that nothing others have can permanently satisfy. When I do feel envy, I pray, "Lord, thank You for this emotion. Help me see that what I want can never fill me up as much as You can. In fact, looking for happiness in Your creation is like idol worship in your eyes. I'm glad You honor those who turn from idols to worship You" (based on 1 Thessalonians 1:9).

The next emotion is closely related to envy.

JEALOUSY—FEAR OF LOSS

Whereas envy is wanting something we don't have, jealousy is the fear of losing what we already possess.

Jealousy is what we feel when someone flirts with our mate, when a special friend moves away, or when our position at work is threatened.

In high school, I dated Susan fairly steadily for nearly three years. During our senior year she went to California for a vacation and when she returned she informed me that she had met another guy. Those next few days I was miserably jealous. I lost ten pounds in two days. I couldn't concentrate on my after-school job, and my boss finally told me either to quit or to make up with my girlfriend.

After the boss's ultimatum, I left work early and went over to Susan's house. When I told her how miserable I was, she broke down and cried. What a thrill it was to have her back. But the excitement didn't last very long. Within a month, we were having major problems. I was constantly questioning the relationship. I was never sure she wouldn't leave me again. Instead of being able to relax and enjoy her company, my fear of losing her a second time drove away all my positive feelings and made me suspicious of any other guy who talked to her.

Although I didn't realize it at the time, I can see now that my jealousy actually revealed my own pride. I wanted control of the relationship and of her. If we were going to break up again, I wanted to be the one to do it, not her.

Negative emotions reveal to us that we are viewing the world as if its only purpose is to satisfy our needs. When we expect individuals and things to cooperate with our specially designed program to bring us satisfaction, it's not surprising that we get envious and jealous when those goals are frustrated, delayed, or postponed.

As with envy, to counteract jealousy I approach the Lord in prayer: "Lord, I'm afraid of losing something that I already have. However, I want my treasure to be in heaven, not here. I realize that whatever I have that I enjoy can never permanently fill my cup. Even if I lose something I need, I can come to You, the giver of life, and ask for another . And if You don't want me to have it, I can ask You to take away the desire. Thank You that You, not my possessions, are the source of life."

Some men fear losing their wife because it would end their best friendship as well as their sexual outlet. They fail to remember that God can handle every need. Andre Thornton, a major league baseball player whose wife was killed in a tragic car accident, understands this truth. Andre honestly faced his emotions through prayer:

> I asked God to quench my sex drive, even though since the accident I hadn't felt any sexual feelings whatsoever. But I knew myself well enough to know that someday those desires would return. I knew the temptations that came to professional athletes. I knew the women that hung around baseball teams. There would be opportunities on road trips to get into compromising situations, and I didn't want to do anything to disgrace the name of Christ. So I asked God to kill any sexual desires until He brought along someone to take Gert's place in my life. God was faithful in answering this prayer, too.*

Some people have a hard time admitting that the warning light of jealousy is flashing in their life. But letting it flash too long can cause major problems. Spouses, children, and possessions are simply on loan to us from the Lord. We do not own them. Continually fearing the loss of a person or a possession can end in emotional and spiritual defeat.

*Thornton, Andre, as told to Al Janssen, *Triumph Born of Tragedy* (Eugene, Ore.: Harvest House, 1983), 105.

The next emotion is probably one of the most destructive desires drawing men and women away from God. At almost every men's retreat I teach I am asked to address this subject. At conferences for pro athletes when we have a question-and-answer-time for men only, this topic always comes up first.

LUST—A FANTASYLAND DREAM

Lust makes us think that having some person we don't have would make us happier. Often that person is a figment of our imagination. Even if the person is real, we often attach character traits to him or her that are not real. Usually our lust focuses on sexual involvement. We imagine someone terribly fond of us who prefers our presence and intimacy over anyone else's. We imagine that if we had such a person to hold in our arms, it would be exciting and wonderfully fulfilling. This is a terrible deception, for we forget or ignore the devastating consequences of carrying out our imaginations.

Sensual imaginations reveal our selfish desire for stimulation. Unchecked, sensual stimulation actually increases the desire. We see this exhibited in several ways. For example, one of the primary reasons people smoke or consume alcohol or drugs is to stimulate their physical senses.

As a person continues in this selfish frame of mind, the desire grows until he needs regular and increasing doses of stimulation. That's one reason for the child pornography craze today. Men who stimulate their minds through sensual photographs need increasingly kinkier or more violent pictures to remain stimulated. The same is true with sexual involvement in marriage. If our primary motivation for sex is self-centered—to have our mate stimulate us—we tend to need more and more varied forms of sex to remain stimulated.

Even if we feel we've conquered lust, the emotion can strike when we least expect it. One friend discovered this when he spoke at a Christian conference. Dick's wife was in the final months of pregnancy, so they were not as sexually active as usual. While several hundred miles away from home, Dick suddenly found himself infatuated with a woman attending the conference. She was attractive and seemed to enjoy his company. But while admitting his normal sexual drive was heating up, he also knew that yielding to that desire would bring at best only a very temporary satisfaction. He came face to face with his own selfish desire to be stimulated and realized that the devastating long-term consequences to his ministry, to his wife and kids, and to his relationship with God would far outweigh any momentary pleasure. That knowledge helped him control his physical drive, which took about forty-eight hours to subside.

The motivation behind extramarital affairs seems to be very different for men and women. Men tend to lust for physical release or conquest, viewing women as challenges for satisfying their sexual drives. Women, on the other hand, tend to involve themselves in affairs because of their deep need for communication and a meaningful relationship that is not being met.

How can we use this emotion to strengthen our relationship with God? First, by recognizing the basic motive behind lust. Lust is not serving a person in love; it is viewing a person as an object to be used. This happens even in marriage. With Norma, I had to realize that I was violating God's law by trying to use her for my own happiness rather than loving her by serving her needs.

Second, lust can reconfirm our awareness that God—not another's body, not even our mate's—is the source of our fulfillment. As pleasurable as sex can be, it can never substitute for the lasting joy and satisfaction of knowing God.

Third, in the midst of lustful thoughts, as an act of our will, we can pray something like this: "Lord I know there are times when I wish my mate acted sexier. And there are even times I have thoughts about being in the arms of another person. All the advertisements on TV have tried to convince me it would be exciting. But right here and now I continue to trust You to fill my life with what I need. I am willing to rest and wait in Your faithfulness. I don't even know all I'm trying to gain from these lustful thoughts, but You know, and I know You'll meet my needs as You always have."

Since God knows our thoughts, we can share them with Him and admit we don't understand.

That's what Paul instructs us to do in Romans: "[God's] Spirit also helps our weakness; for we do not know how to pray as we should ... and He who searches the hearts knows what the mind of the Spirit is, because He intercedes for the saints according to the will of God" (Romans 8:26-27).

What practical help call we offer those stuck in the quicksand of lustful desire? Some try to struggle out of the grip it has on their lives through visualization, masturbation, or regular participation in sexual activity. But the more we struggle, the deeper we sink. If no one is available to pull us out, the one way to escape from quicksand is to relax, lie back in the sand, take a deep breath, fill your lungs with air, and allow your limbs to float to the top. We can take similar action with lust by not fighting our thoughts and desires and instead ask Jesus to perform what He promises to do—release us from bondage. He can supernaturally pull us out as we rest in Him.

Another way to escape from quicksand is to slowly move your arms above your head, sink them slightly into the sand, and swim slowly to the edge, as if doing a slow-motion backstroke. Experts say it may take several hours to swim just a few feet. But freedom is as close as the bank. We can do the same thing by persistently looking to Christ for strength and patience.

I have known men stuck in the mire of lust who didn't make it to freedom for several months. It may take a year for some to "swim" to freedom. Day after day we must reconfirm truths given to us by Christ. God promises He is faithful to answer the requests of His children. "Therefore I tell you, whatever you ask for in prayer, believe you have received it, and it will be yours" (Mark 11:24 NIV). And, "If you remain in me and my words remain in you, ask whatever you wish, and it will be given you" (John 15:7 NIV). Real freedom comes from abiding in a close relationship with God and from allowing God's Word to become alive in us. He says in His Word to live a life of love: "But among you there must not be even a *hint* of sexual immorality" (Ephesians 5:3 NIV). And "It is for freedom that Christ has set us free. Stand firm, then, and do not let yourselves be burdened again by a yoke of slavery" (Galatians 5:1 NIV). It is God's will that we experience freedom from lust, so we can stand in His line daily, knowing it is just a matter of time before He will bring us freedom from sexual slavery.

Once we're free from the quicksand, we're usually weak from the effort. Here are four ways to regain strength and remain strong to keep from falling back into the mire.

First, rehearse the negative consequences of sexual involvement, even in the midst of lustful thoughts. Remember what it feels like to be trapped. The consequences are far more than we can mention here, but they include enslavement to passion (Galatians 5:1), reinforcement of our self-centered tendency that diminishes genuine love, callousness of our soul (Ephesians 4:19), and, of course, the possibility of catching a sexual disease. In other words, the truth and life of God is darkened within us when we engage in unrighteousness (see Romans 1:18-32).

Second, memorize sections of Scripture that deal specifically with sexual freedom. After memorizing them, persistently ask God to make your life consistent with those verses. Start with Galatians 5:1-14, Ephesians 5:1-6, and 1 Thessalonians 4:3-7.

Third, for men especially, beware of the anger/lust cycle that often develops. Many men experience their most severe times of lust after a struggle or problem at home or at work. If we fail to make things right after a disagreement or confrontation, we may be setting ourselves up for temptation because such encounters leave us feeling depressed and inadequate. Since none of us likes to feel badly about ourselves, we look for something to perk us up, to make us feel powerful and important again.

Sexual stimulation can have a temporary euphoric effect. Like alcohol or drugs, it can bring about a heightened sense of self-worth—until the shame and reality of our actions bring us crashing down. Some men who never take a drink or try drugs, submit to a life of erotic escapades that is every bit as addictive, and every bit as deadly.

Proverbs has sobering words for those who use any form of lust—actual sexual encounters, fantasy, or pornographic pictures—to make up for feelings of anger or low self-worth. "The lips of an adulteress drip honey, and her speech is smoother than oil; but in the end she is bitter as gall, sharp as a double-edged sword" (5:3-4 NIV).

Giving in to lust does not break the anger/lust cycle; it only intensifies it. Now we are not only angry and depressed about our problem at work or at home, but we are also angry about our lack of self-control. And on top of our shame, those of us who are Christians also have the Holy Spirit convicting us of sin.

Genuine repentance is a biblical solution, but getting furious with ourselves and vowing it will never happen again does little good. In fact, when we browbeat ourselves (a way of punishing ourselves so that God won't, or so that He will "let us off the hook") we actually dig a deeper rut for ourselves and set ourselves up for our next "lust fix."

Unless we truthfully deal with the anger/lust cycle and admit that it is signaling that a relationship needs repair or that we need the help of a Christian friend or counselor, we may continue in the downward spiral for years. This vicious circle of sin can cause even Christians to spin so fast that right seems wrong and wrong seems right.

Finally, realize that for most people gaining freedom from lust is a long-term process, especially for those who have developed a habit of immoral thoughts and actions. You might consider starting or joining a support group for those who struggle in this area. This can be a group of men or women (not in the same group) who testify as to how God has produced freedom and who encourage and support one another in memorizing and meditating on Scripture. They also hold each other accountable, pray with each other, and talk honestly about their entrapment. Much healing can come just by confessing our weakness and praying for each other: "Therefore, confess your sins to one another, and pray for one another, so that you may be healed. The effective prayer of a righteous man can accomplish much" (James 5:16).

Al meets regularly with several other men in a discipleship group. Once he returned from a business trip and reported that his hotel room had a cable movie station. He watched a PG-rated movie, then started to watch a sexually explicit film but caught himself and turned it off. However, he expressed concern about handling temptation on an upcoming ten-day trip. One of the members asked Al to develop a plan to use his time, which he did.

On his return Al had to give a report. He told how near the end of the trip he found himself seated next to a single woman at an athletic event. The thought entered his mind, "You could take her out for dinner and no one would ever know." Rather than allow time to entertain the thought any further, he left the game early. *Knowing he was accountable to men back home helped him resist temptation* because he knew they would ask him how he did.

I have focused on the sexual aspects of lust because it is so out of control in our society. But other forms—such as craving sweets, overeating, and stimulating the senses through drugs and alcohol—can be just as damaging. The thoughts I've shared can apply in any area of sensual temptation that robs us of life.

What warning lights flash most frequently in your life? Jealousy, envy, or lust? Take the time necessary to deal with those emotions.

6

Overcoming
a Major Destroyer
of Joy

HAVE YOU EVER walked confidently out on a long limb only to look back and see someone sawing it from the tree? That's how I felt at a church council meeting years ago. But the hurt I experienced that night led to one of the most important discoveries of my life. A discovery that not only drew me closer to Christ, but closer to the very people who hurt me as well.

Ordinarily church council meetings were uneventful. Routine reports, budget reviews, and voting usually sent everyone home yawning. Confident that I had performed an above-average job for my second year out of seminary, I delivered my report enthusiastically, hoping to add some excitement to the typically boring meeting. The excitement I generated, however, was not the kind I expected. My recommendations concerned what I considered obvious needs, particularly the purchase of a church bus for the youth. I assumed I had the support of the pastor and the Sunday school committee before this meeting. But instead of endorsing my recommendations and expressing what a wonderful job I had done as assistant pastor, each council member started criticizing me. Why didn't I run the youth group as it had been run in previous years? I should slow down in making so many changes. Did I think my ways were superior? They'd been doing things the same way for fifteen years. Why were they suddenly wrong when I came? They were especially critical of the bus because of the complications and negative elements it would bring to the youth group. Plus the cost would be prohibitive.

The sudden and intense criticism stunned me, and I was offended that no one on my committee supported me, not even the pastor. I thought to myself, "They don't pay me enough to take this kind of abuse. Why am I subjecting myself to this? Somewhere there must be a church where people would appreciate my talents. It's obvious this congregation doesn't want me."

I slithered home that night and woke Norma to pour out my woes. I complained about how I'd been mistreated and suggested that I ought to quit. She tried to encourage me.

Unable to sleep, I sat in the kitchen and pondered my situation. I reached for my Bible but didn't feel like reading it. On the scratch pad by the phone I wrote, "Why do people in the church continue to hurt my feelings? Why do they make me so angry?" "Lord," I pleaded, "show me what I can do for these poor people. How can I penetrate the hardness of their hearts? What would it take to break through their stubborn resistance and help them see Your love?" If necessary, I was willing to stay up all night and read every chapter of the Bible to find help. I was tired of having my emotions manipulated by members of the church.

For several hours, I could not figure out what to do to help those people. It never occurred to me that my conflict with the church might be my fault, that I might need to change or adjust some attitudes and actions. I could only think that if they were more supportive, more committed to Christ, more dedicated, then I'd be happy. If they'd only step out of the past and start implementing my fresh ideas, I wouldn't have these problems.

Sound familiar? No wonder Jesus said in Matthew 7:3: "And why do you look at the speck that is in your brother's eye, but do not notice the log that is in your own eye?"

Sometime early the next morning, light began to dawn in my mind and I caught a glimpse of the log in my own eye: I wasn't *serving* these people; I had unconsciously tried to *use* them for my own self-centered goals. I had learned many creative ways to run a church education program in seminary. Implementing those ideas became my goal for this church. Though I never verbalized it, I expected the pastor, the Sunday school committee, and the church membership to follow me without question. Couldn't they recognize the genius of my fresh, creative ideas? I interpreted their negative response to my many new ideas as a personal rejection of me.

When church members did not cooperate with my personal goals I got hurt feelings. But how could they possibly cooperate if they didn't know my goals? I had never shared them—that would have exposed my self-centeredness. I had forgotten what a genuine minister is—one who *serves* the needs of those around him. No wonder the church reacted against me. I had never bothered to find out *their* goals. I hurt their feelings becuase I changed their programs, and they hurt my feelings because they did not cooperate with my unstated goals.

Understanding and Using Hurt Feelings

Hurt feelings are closely connected with anger but are slightly different. Unchecked, they can lead to anger, then bitterness, and even depression. Hurt feelings are those frustrating emotions that emerge from the unexpected. They let us know we are trying to use someone for our own benefit who is not cooperating with us.

Usually, when our feelings are hurt it's because we had hoped that the offending individual would make us happy in some way. We may have expected the person to say or do something that we planned to use for our own fulfillment. When the person didn't cooperate, we may have responded with tears, pouting, an angry reaction, or quiet disappointment, hoping that our reaction might provoke the person to change and treat us in the way we first expected. If the person refused to change, we may have tried the silent treatment for two or three days. We may have been tempted to get even or to run to someone else for sympathy.

Escaping the Pain of Hurt Feelings

That night after my disastrous church council meeting, the first thing I had to do was *admit* my problem. With deep conviction I confessed: "Lord, I never realized until now the fuller meaning of what a real servant is." Somehow I had forgotten that the second most important commandment He gave us is to love one another. I had misrepresented myself as a minister, especially as an assistant pastor. To my shame, I hadn't even taken the time to ask the one I was assisting what direction he wanted to go. Where did the pastor want to take the church? What did he feel was important? What would he like me to do? My primary objective had been to design my own program and to find ways to get everyone, including the pastor, to follow it. Did I only want a successful program that would reflect my talent and lead me to bigger and better positions?

I never did get to sleep that night, and I could hardly wait to get to church in the morning. When I arrived I immediately called the pastor to ask if I could see him. When he invited me into his office, I confessed, "Pastor, that board meeting was rough last night. But it showed me something very important. Early this morning I realized that I have been violating a major biblical principle. For two years I have tried to get everyone in this church to follow my program, my goals, my vision. It's honestly never occurred to me, as your assistant, to ask you where God is leading you to take this church."

"After the meeting last night, I thought the reason you wanted to see me was to resign," he said with a smile.

I asked him to forgive me for my poor example as a minister and as his assistant. Then I asked him to share with me his goals and how I might assist him in reaching them. I wanted to learn how to use all my resources and training to help him, the church council, the youth sponsors, and the members of the church to reach their own spiritual goals.

That was the turning point in our relationship. He not only forgave me, but he immediately started treating me like a son. He still got frustrated with me occasionally, but instead of allowing my feelings to be hurt I would ask what I could do to help remove any roadblocks from his ministry or how I could be an encouragement or comfort to him.

That incident was not the only time I have seen the depth of my self-centeredness. There have been other humbling moments when my feelings have been hurt, even by my loving wife, Norma.

Last summer Norma and I attended a dinner party. During a discussion about the quality of life in Phoenix, I proudly announced that it's like paradise. In the winter you can have a fire in your fireplace almost every night and still swim in an outdoor pool during the day.

When someone asked how cold it actually gets in the winter, I quipped, "It can drop into the low 20s."

Norma laughed and said, "That shows how observant he is," and went right on talking.

I didn't hear anything else she said. My feelings were hurt. I couldn't understand why she would make such a belittling statement and embarrass me in front of all those people. Besides, I was sure I knew how cold it gets in Phoenix. I was tempted to ask the hosts if they had an encyclopedia. I wanted to prove I wasn't stupid.

It bothered me so much that I didn't speak to Norma on the way home. When she asked if anything was wrong, I snapped, "No!" I had a cauldron full of emotions churning within. I was ashamed for feeling so hurt, yet angry that she would be so insensitive. When I finally mentioned the problem, she apologized and said she hadn't meant the statement to come out that way. Yet I remembered her words and still felt irritated.

Before I fell asleep, I prayed, "Lord, as hard as it is to express these words, thank You that my feelings were hurt tonight. This 'red light' helps me see again my own self-centered tendencies. What those people think of me does not matter because their opinions have nothing to do with my self-worth. Only Your opinion matters. Norma didn't mean to hurt my feelings, and my reaction to her comments reveals that I have filled my cup with something that doesn't belong in it—other people's opinions. I expected Norma to say things to make me look intelligent. I guess that shows how quickly we can drift from You. Before I fall asleep, I want to thank You that I can look to You for my fulfillment rather than to Norma or anyone else." My hurt lasted only a few more minutes and was gone by the time I drifted off to sleep.

Even when someone deliberately tries to hurt our feelings we can still apply this principle. We don't have to allow hurt feelings to defeat us.

ANGER—SOMEONE OR SOMETHING IS BLOCKING MY GOAL

Anger is a very close relative of hurt feelings. As another important warning light, it usually indicates that our focus has shifted so that we are expecting fulfillment from God's creation rather than from God Himself.

Anger can erupt at any moment, and it's not always directed at a person. Sometimes we get angry at circumstances, such as a construction detour. The anger we express is evidence that we expect our environment to cooperate and meet our needs. As mentioned in an earlier chapter, we expect the "four P's" to add something to our fullness. We're frustrated because we believe we're about to lose something we thought was secure. Or we realize we may not gain something we expected.

Before a woman marries, she often has clear expectations concerning her future husband. He will communicate all his goals, expectations, and feelings; he will comfort and hold her when she needs him; he will make her feel special.

After three or four years of marriage, however, some of these women conclude that it would have been less painful to remain single. Their blocked expectations are often reflected in anger and expressed in explosive outbursts or nagging irritation. Other women may hold their anger inside so that only their pastors or psychiatrists know for sure. They are the ones who will see the damage caused by repressed anger.

The same thing is true for men—wives and children may frustrate their personal expectations and eat holes in their emotional cup.

One father we know has been furious with his son for three years because he married a girl from a different social class. What the father won't admit is that his anger is actually a reflection of his own self-centered expectations.

When people and things frustrate our personal goals, anger results. My anger level has dropped significantly over the last several years as I've realized that no person or thing can take away what God has given me. If I lose something of material worth, I know God can replace it if I really need it. So I can relax without feeling compelled to manipulate my circumstances.

I'm not completely free from anger, however. I still tend to use people for my own advantage by setting secret goals for them. When they don't cooperate, I become frustrated and angry. This happened when my family agreed we should write a parenting book. Our goal for the book was that it would help parents stay in harmony with their children, build their children's self-worth, motivate them to be courteous, and to help them attain their God-given potential.

What happened on those days when my children were disrespectful or unmotivated or out of harmony—in other words, when they were normal children and we were normal parents? I became angry because they blocked my goal of helping thousands of families through our book. I was afraid that my goal would go down the drain if anyone got wind that things weren't perfect in the Smalley home. So I lectured my children—until I stopped and thought about what I was doing. Then I realized I was standing in the wrong line again, expecting fulfillment from the people reading this book rather than from God.

We have a saying in our house, "Am I making you angry or am I revealing your self-centeredness?" With three honest children and a very honest wife, I must often admit that my own self-centeredness is at the bottom of a problem or disagreement.

> People do not really make us angry.

We may think people make us angry, but most of the time they simply reveal our own selfishness. What usually makes us angry is our lack of control over people and circumstances.

If I get angry at someone who insults me and deliberately tries to make me angry, I am making a personal decision. He cannot *make* me angry. Unless I have been secretly trying to convince him how wonderful I am, there is no reason for me to be upset at his accusation. So once again, anger reveals self-centeredness. I am angry because someone does not think of me the way I want him to think.

Under similar circumstances, parents often become angry at their children. If a child does something to embarrass a parent in front of the parent's adult friends, the parent often becomes angry, because adults (just

412

like teens) want their friends to think well of them. The fear of losing social status or approval has spurred many angry reactions.

One of the most difficult lessons for many of us to learn is to stop trying to gain the approval of others. Expecting to find our true self-image reflected in the opinion of others is like going into a house of mirrors to find out what we really look like. Each person, like each mirror, will tell us something different. One person may admire us for being "open-minded," but someone else may criticize us for "having no convictions." One person may tell us our new outfit is "divine," but someone else might comment, "I had no idea they made outfits like that in your size."

To deal with anger we must come to grips with the fact that we are not all-powerful. Until we can see people and circumstances through the eyes of a sovereign God, we will never be free from trying to control what others do to us and think about us.

Yet all anger is not directed toward others. Many times anger is disgust at our own ineptitude. After speaking to a group of more than four hundred men recently, I berated myself on the drive home. "Smalley, how could you give such a lousy talk? Why in the world did you use that stupid illustration? No one laughed, and it didn't even fit in your outline. They must think you're a real jerk. There goes your reputation!"

In the middle of my mental tirade, I recognized what I was doing and shifted into a prayer: "Lord, thank You that I'm angry and disgusted with myself. Being accepted by those men has nothing to do with my fulfillment. I thank You for loving me and filling me and being so faithful to me for so many years. I want to improve my speaking skills, Lord, and I plan to do that. But I know those skills have nothing to do with You and me."

Then I put some Christian music in my tape deck and sang praise songs the rest of the way home. It took about ten minutes for the anger to subside and for me to feel free, ready to continue with life. I could have spent days feeling like a failure, but instead I used the opportunity to learn more about myself and God.

As we examine the remaining emotions, we may discover we are all more self-centered than we thought. Although recognizing our self-centeredness is never pleasant, unless we honestly admit our selfish motives, we cannot begin to use our negative emotions for positive gain.

Righteous Anger—Is There Such a Thing?

"Loving anger" is a legitimate form of this usually negative emotion, but I rarely see it in myself or others. Righteous anger is spawned by injustice to another and motivates us to help, not harm, both the victim and the offender. For instance, if someone you know is robbed and beaten, righteous anger would grieve with the victim and gently guide that person to emotional health. It would also grieve over the sickness of the attacker and, if possible, firmly and directly love that person to wholeness.

Although there are times to be righteously indignant, those who are honest must admit that most of our anger is the result of self-centeredness. If we are willing, however, we can learn to use this anger to strengthen our relationship with God.

Using Anger in a Postive Way

First, we need to thank God for the flashing light that shows us the connection between our anger and our selfishness. Thanksgiving is an expression of trust and obedience. It's a way of saying we want to follow His way rather than our own.

Second, we need to determine why we're angry. Blocked goals are the most common cause of anger, and anger over blocked goals reveals our selfish nature.

Third, we need to admit our self-centeredness. The promise of 1 John 1:9-10 is that if we *confess* our sin (of selfishness), God is faithful to forgive us and to cleanse us. If we think we're not sinners—if we rationalize our anger and insist that we're not being selfish—we lie and the truth is not in us.

We may feel that admitting our selfish ways degrades us, but being aware of natural tendencies has nothing to do with personal worth. Some people think confessing means they must constantly chant the refrain "Such a worm as I." That is not God's message! However, if we desire a close, dependent relationship with Christ, we must admit daily, and sometimes hourly, that we are tempted to use an aspect of God's creation to fill our cup. Sometimes we may even surrender to that temptation and become angry when the created thing doesn't fulfill our expectations.

Anger imprisons some people. Those who are violent or verbally abusive in their anger, or who are overly critical of themselves and others, probably will need more help than I can offer in a few pages. Never hesitate to ask for help from qualified Christian counselors and pastors, however. Your willingness to face the problem and deal with it is a sign of strength. Also, a number of excellent books can help you further understand why people continue in their anger and how you can break the vicious cycle. I've listed some of them at the end of this book.

Fourth, we need to pray a simple but meaningful prayer express-ing to God that we realize He is the source of life. Here are some examples:

- "Lord, whether or not I make it to my appointment on time has nothing to do with my fulfillment."
- "Lord, the fact that Norma bought white bread rather than whole wheat does not mean I cannot have a fulfilling life."
- "Lord, having to take the time to remove Mike's bike from the driveway cannot rob me of Your joy."
- "Lord, buying the wrong part for this repair job means I'll lose a few minutes, but that won't drain my cup. So what if I have to drive back to the store? It won't mean a thing in a year."

For many people, it is the little inconveniences like those listed above that bring on an angry response. But anger can also be a response to much more serious issues.

Over the past several years we have seen many people with deep emotional struggles resulting from tragic circumstances: a woman whose husband had abandoned her and their four school-age children; a man who had given all his savings (including his retirement fund money) to a "Christian" builder who left town with the money and left behind thou-sands of dollars of debts; a young woman who waited with a chapel full of guests for a groom who never showed up; and a corporate manager who worked for years to reach the top, only to have his company bought out in a hostile takeover, leaving him jobless at age 61.

Possessions, position, places, and people. The loss of these caused severe hurt and anger for each of these people. But when they discov-ered the source of lasting life and recognized their anger as a flashing light warning them that they were operating without the power of a sover-eign God who could more than compensate for their loss, they were able to deal with their loss instead of letting it devastate them.

We helped each one through weeks of necessary grief. Then, when they were ready, we walked with them into a personal, healing relation-ship with Christ.

Martin Luther once said about temptation, "You cannot keep birds from flying over your head, but you can keep them from building a nest in your hair." The same is true with anger. We cannot control the cir-cumstances that make us angry, but we can control how we respond to them. We can resist the temptation to let our circumstances make us angry.

Let's switch gears now and discuss an area that's brought to us by the producers of upset stomachs. This section combines the two emotions that keep many of us up late at night and can hinder all our relationships, especially our relationship with God. We can look at them together.

FEAR AND WORRY—WHAT IF I CAN'T ACHIEVE MY GOALS

How many of us pass through a day without experiencing one or both of these emotions? Fretting about the implications of some action or dreading what may happen in the future is common, but not healthy. All of us are familiar with that gnawing, sickening feeling that eats at our insides when the promotion we expected and needed to meet financial obligations is in jeopardy; when something we treasure is in danger of being lost; when we are given an ultimatum—accept a transfer to a strange city or look for another job; or when a person we respect has lost confidence in us.

Fear reveals our attitude toward personal loss. The greater the loss, the greater the fear. Worry, a form of fear, is preoccupation with the possibility that we may lose something valuable.

One weekend my lawyer told me I needed to call him first thing Monday morning because he had received correspondence from the Internal Revenue Service. For hours over the next two days I worried, imagining all kinds of horrible scenarios—getting audited, owing thousands of dollars, learning I wasn't doing what I should be doing, getting a lien slapped on my house. On and on the thoughts persisted.

To make matters worse, I couldn't reach him on Monday! When I finally talked to him Tuesday afternoon, I learned that he couldn't make a corporate decision about my company without knowing if I intended to change the name of the company. It was a minor question, certainly not worth spending any time worrying about. That same day I received a letter from him saying he had thoroughly checked out our finances with my accountant and everything was in order. How typical. We often waste valuable energy worrying about something that turns out to be insignificant.

Reasons for Fear and Worry

Whenever I begin to feel fear or worry I thank the Lord for the feeling, then test the following six reasons until I understand the source. Simply identifying the reason for my worry often calms my anxiety. I remember these six areas by trying to pronounce a word spelled FRMPTH (sounds like *from the*).

Future—Am I worried about something in my future? For a young single person, it might be college or a future mate or a possible job. Some might worry about earning enough money to provide for a family. Someone who's sick might be anxious about achieving long-term goals. Whatever it is, recognize that it cannot give permanent fulfillment.

Reputation—Am I worried that my reputation will be smeared? Sometimes I fear being on television because I'm afraid I will say something to embarrass myself or my family or God. If that's the basis for my worry, I take the simple steps we'll discuss in the next chapter and the anxiety disappears almost immediately.

Money—Am I worried about losing money or not gaining enough money? I remind myself that money does not provide fulfillment. Like Paul, God can bring me to the place where I am content whether I have much or little (Philippians 4:10-18).

Possessions—Am I worried about losing or not gaining possessions? I identify the items and then remember Jim Elliot's statement: "He is no fool who gives up what he cannot keep to gain what he cannot lose."

Time—Am I worried about not having enough time? I ask myself the following questions: Is someone misusing my time? (If we don't set our own schedules, someone else is likely to do it for us.) Am I procrastinating? Am I up against an impossible writing deadline? I remind myself that God controls time and that He has given me enough to accomplish all He wants me to do. So I resolve to use it wisely and to respond to each interruption as if it came from God. Even if worry about unmet deadlines awakens me in the middle of the night I need not worry about not getting enough sleep. Instead I can use the time for fellowship with God, which in itself is gain. With the Lord, tomorrow's loss or gain cannot affect my fulfillment. So I can relax and even enjoy my insomnia. Usually that helps me fall asleep.

Health—Am I worried about losing my health or getting old? Do I get discouraged when I find more wrinkles and gray hairs? Do I worry about my weight? On these occasions I remind myself that my health is in God's hands and that even poor health cannot keep me from having a fulfilling life. When I was in seminary I worried about my reputation, which caused my stomach to churn, which made me worry about getting an ulcer, which made me worry that people would discover I was not at peace with God, which would ruin my reputation! Of all people, how could a minister not be at peace with God? Now, however, I know that having people think well of me offers only temporary satisfaction at best, but I still need to remind myself often of the futility of trying to convince others of my spiritual value.

One way to counteract fear and worry associated with any of the above causes is to recall memorized Scripture. For example, meditating on portions of Psalm 37, 62, or 103 helps put problems in perspective. Think on the meaning of phrases such as "Do not fret because of evildoers," "Delight yourself in the Lord," "Better is the little of the righteous than the abundance of many wicked," "The steps of a man are established by the Lord . . . when he falls, he shall not be hurled headlong; because

417

the Lord is the One who holds his hand," "[The Lord] is my rock and my salvation, my stronghold; I shall not be greatly shaken," and "God is a refuge for us."

A friend of mine who is a prolific writer used to spend weeks worrying when he sent a proposal to a publisher, wondering how it would be received. Rejection notices devastated him. He worried about what he was doing wrong and what it would take to be published. Rather than motivating him to resubmit his work or to improve his craft, rejection immobilized him, making him unable to write at all for days.

My friend no longer suffers from fear and worry, however. Recently he told me about submitting an article idea to a national magazine in which he really wants to be published. The rejection letter disappointed him, but instead of giving in to depression, he took a short walk and prayed, "Lord, thank You for this rejection. I know that being published in this magazine would be a real achievement, but I also know that it won't give me lasting fulfillment. Lord, I only want to be published where You want me to be. Allow me to be free from anxiety and to continue to do the work You've called me to do. Whether I'm ever published in this magazine or not, I thank You that we're always together. You, Lord, are what brings me life." Within thirty minutes he was back at his desk, working hard on another book, with no feelings of worry to inhibit him.

What makes negative emotions like worry and fear exciting is that we can deal with them as warning lights and move on with productive lives. They don't have to defeat us when we understand Who they point us to.

LONELINESS—NO ONE SHARES MY GOAL

From the moment of birth we need other people. In fact, newborn babies are more helpless than almost any other creature. Yet our need for relationships is a double-edged sword. The fulfillment we find in relationships is sharply contrasted by feelings of emptiness when we are alone.

God Himself is a God of relationships. In the beginning, God said, "Let *us* make man in *our* image (Genesis 1). The Father, Son, and Spirit mirror our need to be in relationship to others and explain the emptiness and frustration we feel when we are alone.

Perhaps one reason the Lord provided us with a "family of believers" is so we would always have spiritual mothers, fathers, sisters, and brothers to love us (see 1 Timothy 5). A loving church can be a haven for lonely people.

Yet for some people, the loneliness they feel is not based on a lack of people in their lives, but on their own selfish actions or desires. Jim's wife, Betty, had just delivered their second child in less than two years. With all the demands on Betty's time, Jim began to feel left out and unwanted. He turned to a secretary at work to boost his self-worth, and in almost no time they were having an affair.

Jim set out to end his feelings of loneliness in a sinful way, and he only compounded his pain. Today, four years later, his wife and children live in another state and the other woman is living with another man. For Jim, the pain keeps driving his loneliness deeper and deeper—and may for years to come.

Although Jim's example is extreme, loneliness can be a symptom of a selfish desire to control another's time or affection—even if it is not best for them or others.

When the birth of Michael, our third child, required me to stop traveling as much, I often shuttled the travel team back and forth from the office to the airport. After dropping them off I'd feel lonely whenever I recalled their parting statements: "We'll miss you in Minneapolis"; "We'll say 'hi' to all your friends in Seattle"; or "We'll bring you some bread from San Francisco." I'd drive back to an empty office, sometimes feeling resentment toward Michael for what he had denied me. I had to learn that only Christ, not those trips nor even the camaraderie, could give me lasting fulfillment. The loneliness I felt was selfish, not genuine. Once I learned that truth, I was free to stay home, where I found out how much more rewarding it was to have extra time with my wife and kids. Since then, I've thanked Michael time and time again for helping me learn this truth.

Like all the other negative emotions we discussed, loneliness can draw us closer to God. How? First, we need to know why we are lonely. Most often we are wishing we had someone near us to share our life experiences. We want someone to return to us the same level of affection we wish to give. Although the desire for companionship is natural and good, expecting others to meet all our needs can lead to frustration. Even "best friends" and spouses have limits to the amount of time they can spend with us.

Second, while we're feeling lonely, we need to recognize that we are treating God the same way we feel life is treating us. Just as we want someone in God's creation to return our affection, God wants us to return to Him the affection He pours out on us. Lonely days and cold winter evenings can depress us. But they also give us time to hear God's gentle voice—if we listen closely—which calls us to look into the eyes of the One who said, "I will never desert you, nor will I ever forsake you" (Hebrews 13:5).

Third, we need to return our mind and spirit to the Lord by praying something like this: "Lord, I know that You want all of my heart and soul and mind focused on You as the source of my life. I keep forgetting this and I continually try to make Your creation fill my cup. But at this very moment I look to You as my only God. You are my source of lasting life. Lord, You know how I desire to share my life with someone, either a good friend or a mate. I ask You to bring that person into my life, but I'm willing to wait however long is necessary to have Your best. And I only want to see this person as overflow, because I want You to continue to be my very best friend. In the meantime show me how to enrich my relationship with You and with those around me."

For some, loneliness may last longer than expected. Our prayer needs to persist as long as loneliness lasts. If it doesn't disappear quickly we may he tempted to rely on tranquilizers or other artificial means to counteract it, but depending on an aspect of creation will only allow loneliness to entrench itself more deeply. On the other hand, the more we recognize Christ as the source of life and the more we see His faithfulness, the sooner joy and peace will replace loneliness. Plus, reaching out to others increases our joy. One of the best ways to find meaningful friendships is to be the kind of friend to others that *we* would like to have.

This is not an exhaustive list of negative emotions. We could examine many others, but the principles for achieving victory are all very similar.

Knowing how to use natural negative emotions to strengthen our relationship with God has tremendous value, but think how great it would be if we could also use everyday trials, both small and great, to pull us closer to God. The next chapter uncovers one of the most exciting truths I have learned: how trials, hardships, and difficulties can be the doorway to a richer life, how they can lead us to live in God's will. Believe it or not, trials can make us more loving. And perhaps best of all, trials can even increase our sense of personal worth. Talk about an overflowing life—this is it!

7

Letting Trials Produce
Love and Self-worth

MONTE JOHNSON, AN eight-year veteran with the Oakland Raiders' professional football team, faced the most devastating crisis of his life. Would he be cut off from the team? Would he be traded? He had five months to worry.

Monte never started a game as an undergraduate at the University of Nebraska, but he attracted the attention of pro scouts in an all-star game, and Oakland drafted him. He went on to become a starting linebacker and played for the Super Bowl champions in 1977. Then tragedy struck. In a preseason game against the Washington Redskins, a teammate accidentally hit him on a kickoff return, destroying the ligaments and cartilage in Monte's knee. While his teammates went on to win the Super Bowl again that year, Monte worked diligently to rehabilitate his knee. But when I saw him the next year, he told me there was a real possibility he would never play football again. Training camp was five months away, but already his anxiety over the situation was straining all his relationships.

"I have no idea what I want to do after football," he told me. "I had planned to play at least two more years. Even my wife doesn't understand that my career may be over."

What good can possibly come from an injured knee? Or from flunking third grade? Or from losing several thousand dollars in a business deal? Or from being an abused child? Or from any other tragic circumstance? Although each of these situations was initially devastating to the victim, each eventually produced "gold" in the afflicted person.

Many of us have been tricked into believing the world's viewpoint that suffering is bad and to be avoided whenever possible. But the words of the apostle Paul say otherwise: "God causes all things to work together for good . . ." (Romans 8:28). How can any good be found in an illness or child abuse? Intellectually we believe the scriptural promise that *all things* work together for good, but most of us have wondered at one time or another what the *good* could possibly be.

I am convinced that the promise of Romans 8:28 is true in *every* case. In all my years of counseling and study, I have never found an exception, but it took me a long time to discover how to *find* the good in each trial. The concepts in this chapter have transformed my life and the lives of many others. I compare life to a treasure hunt because I know that in every negative situation God buries a valuable treasure that He wants us to have. Sometimes we have to search diligently for it. But if we search, we can find it.

I'm not implying that God causes all trials. I do not believe God was responsible for Judy's rape or for Jill's repeated sexual abuse by her uncle and brothers. Nor do I believe that God caused David's wife to take their children and desert him or that He caused Denise's parents to verbally and emotionally assault her. Judy, Jill, David, and Denise suffered years of emotional trauma from these trials until they learned how to treasure hunt. Buried in the debris of their tragedies were benefits as real as rubies and diamonds. As they dug into their tribulations and discovered the gems, their self-worth soared. They once considered themselves worthless; but when they learned the process of turning negatives into positives they saw the great value they possessed. It worked for Monte Johnson too.

I asked Monte to turn his injured knee and possible release from the Raiders into a benefit. First, we examined his options. One was to play football again for the Raiders. Another was to be traded to another team. The third was to retire and go into another line of work. I asked Monte to write down the benefits of all three possibilities. The first one was easy—playing for the Raiders—but it took a while for Monte to see the benefits of the other two options.

I saw Monte again a year later and he couldn't wait to tell me his experience. He had taken time to write down all the benefits he could think of for the two negative options—being traded or retiring from pro football. In both possibilities he saw ways to grow spiritually and to minister to other hurting people. He began getting ideas for developing a business. If he retired, he would have more time for his family. When he arrived at training camp, he was excited because he knew that whatever happened would be for his good. He saw an almost equal number of benefits in all three options.

At summer camp, after a thorough physical exam, the coach told Monte the bad news. His knee was not strong enough to handle the rigors of football; he would have to retire. The first words out of Monte's mouth shocked the coach. "I want to thank God for choosing you to be the instrument to help me discover what God wants me to do," Monte said. "Thank you for eight great years with the Raider organization."

Flabbergasted at such an unusual reaction from a player who had just been cut, the coach could think of nothing more to say. Monte gave him a hug and thanked him again for his years with the team.

Professional athletes dread retirement. Being told that their career is over at an age when most men are entering the prime of life devastates many of them. What made the difference for Monte was the time he'd spent treasure hunting. He uncovered the benefits and learned to see the experience as an opportunity rather than as a trial.

Several months after his release from the Raiders, Monte became involved in a financial counseling and management program to help athletes and other professionals plan for the future—a ministry that has helped hundreds of people.

Anyone can do what Monte did.

> Every problem—great or small—has in it a treasure waiting to be discovered. The secret to successful treasure hunting is understanding two life-changing words: faith and love.

FAITH

Christ's teaching on faith will show us its true meaning if we pay attention to how He helped distraught people through their trials. In one situation Jesus praised a Roman soldier for having "great faith." A few hours later, Jesus rebuked His disciples for exercising "little faith." Let's see if we can determine the difference.

Great Faith vs. Little Faith

In Matthew 8 a Roman officer came to Jesus and said, "Sir, my servant is lying paralyzed at home, suffering great pain." Even though the man made only a statement, not a request, Jesus answered, "'I will come and heal him.' But the centurion answered and said, 'Lord, I am not worthy for You to come under my roof, but just say the word, and my servant will be healed.'" Amazed by the centurion's faith, Christ said to the people around Him, "I have not found such *great faith* with anyone in Israel."

What prompted this response? In such a religious country how could there be so little faith? What about the Pharisees and religious leaders? No doubt they were irritated by Christ's words and proud of the actions that demonstrated their faith. And what about the disciples? Surely they had faith.

What the soldier said that so impressed Christ was "Lord, I am not worthy for You to come under my roof, but *just say the word,* and my servant will be healed. For I, too, am a man *under authority,* with soldiers under me; and I say to this one, 'Go!' and he goes, and to another, 'Come!' and he comes, and to my slave, 'Do this!' and he does it."

The reason Jesus called the centurion's faith great was because the man believed without question that Jesus could heal his servant. He could picture in his mind how Jesus could order the deed done in the same way he ordered his soldiers or slaves. Jesus was under the Father's authority just as the centurion was under the authority of the Roman government. People obeyed the centurion because the empire delegated power to him just as the God of the universe delegated power to Jesus. Jesus fulfilled the man's expectation "as you have believed," and his servant was healed that very hour.

The story of the centurion stands in stark contrast to a later event that illustrated the weak faith of the disciples. Jesus told them to get into their boat and to cross to the other side of the lake. Undoubtedly exhausted from an intense day of ministry, Jesus then fell sound asleep.

Halfway across the unpredictable sea, the boat nearly capsized when a fierce storm suddenly arose.

Waves crashed over the sides of the boat and the disciples panicked. In the fury of the wind and rain and waves, they could picture only one scene—a quick trip to the bottom of the lake! In desperation they roused Jesus, who in a word reduced the storm to a gently shimmering sea. Then he rebuked the disciples with these words. "Why are you timid, you men of *little faith?*"

Why did the disciples have little faith? How did their faith differ from that of the centurion? The difference was that in the midst of the storm, the disciples forgot that Jesus had said, "We're going to the other side." They pictured themselves drowning, not reaching the dry land of the far shore. They mistakenly assumed that if they were going to arrive safely on the other side that they would enjoy smooth sailing along the way. They didn't anticipate such fierce trouble en route to their destination.

Many of us make the same mistake. During difficult times we forget that God has promised to produce maturity, righteousness, and love through our trials. He has told us to "consider it all joy ... when you encounter various trials" (James 1:2) and that "we walk by faith, not by sight" (2 Corinthians 5:7). When waves threaten to capsize our boat, natural thinking takes over and we lose all hope of survival. People with inadequate faith say, "Those promises don't apply to me. God doesn't understand my situation. How can any good come out of all this suffering?" Years after a tragedy, they are lying helplessly at the bottom of the lake covered with barnacles of bitterness instead of walking on the sunny, sandy shore enjoying the fullness of God's blessing.

Many people I counsel suffer from a negative self-image because of the hardships they have endured. Discovering the treasure buried in our trials is the fastest way I know to raise self-worth. God wants us to think well of ourselves because He wants us to love others as we love ourselves. When we devalue ourselves, we hinder our love for others.

> Treasure hunting can raise self-worth, no matter what the circumstances.

Discovering Treasure in Trials

The following exercise is the one I use to discover the treasure in my personal trials. Perhaps it will work for you as well.

Divide a piece of paper into five columns and label the columns as follows: 1) What I like about myself; 2) My past trials; 3) Support people; 4) Benefits from trials; 5) Love in action. In the first column list at least three things you like about yourself.

In the second column list the things you don't like about yourself, the things that cause low self-worth. These are the painful experiences that cause anger, bitterness, and varying levels of grief. Some people have told me it's too painful to write down all their trials at one time, so you may prefer to focus on one or two for the moment and deal with others at another time.

In the third column list the people who have helped you through your more serious trials. Something in your past may have been so painful that you needed a professional counselor. Or perhaps you found a friend who prayed with you until you regained your strength after a particularly difficult experience.

In the fourth column list whatever benefits you can think of that came as a result of your trial. If you can't think of any at first, remember that for Christians all trials produce various aspects of love, so think of ways a trial has helped you to better love God, yourself, or others.

In the final column list ways in which the benefits of column four have changed your behavior. The purpose of trials is not just for our own self-worth, but so that we might love others as well. The two greatest commandments are that we love God and one another. So this final column shows how the value we've gained from trials can be used to help others.

You may still doubt that your own trials have any buried treasure, so let's look at some examples. I'll start with my own chart and illustrate how some of my painful experiences have turned into treasures. (See chart.)

TREASURE HUNT

What I Like About Myself	Past Trials	Support People	Benefits from Trials	Love in Action

Column One: What I Like About Myself

In the first column I wrote that I like my family life, some of my speaking skills, my concern for helping people, the fulfillment I've found in God's love and joy, and the overflow of ministering to others through seminars, books, and films. (This is a very personal list, so if you prefer to keep some things confidential use a numerical code as I have done.)

Column Two: Trials

In the next column, second only to my experience with Dale, I wrote flunking third grade. I've been embarrassed by that for years, and my kids still tease me about it. They wonder how anyone with half a brain could flunk third grade. But now I can smile about it because I've found the treasure in it. Another trial was the time I expected a $2,000 refund on my income taxes, only to learn that I owed $1,700 instead! List whatever *you* consider a trial, even though others may think it insignificant. (Again, you might want to use code.)

Column Three: Support People

During my trial with Dale my feelings were so intense that without the help of some close Christian friends my recovery would have taken much longer. So in column three I list the people God brought into my life to encourage and help me. Over a period of two years, much of that support came in my meetings with Jim and through the love of a small group of Christian friends.

Column Four: Benefits

Although extremely painful, I can say now that the benefits of my experience with Dale have been so great that I would go through it again for the treasures of love I discovered.

Empathy and compassion. Because of the rejection I felt, I now have tremendous empathy for couples going through a divorce. I understand the agony of rejection and separation when the situation is beyond control. My eyes often fill with tears when I listen to a man or woman in a painful relationship. I want so desperately to help them discover what I've learned. Compassion is another important part of love, and it's learned through trials (2 Corinthians 1:5-7). I also have a much better understanding of those in midlife crisis, which is probably what I was experiencing during those two years.

Renewed appreciation and love for Norma. Through all my trials, Norma held tightly to me and helped hold our family together.

A deeper sense of love and forgiveness. When I realized how selfish I had been and yet how my Lord and my family still forgave me, my love and forgiveness for others increased significantly.

Patience. Until my experience with Dale I always expected things to happen quickly. During this crisis I had no choice but to wait.

Wisdom. I learned what God's priorities for life really are—to love Him and others!

Love and acceptance. These have been the greatest benefits of all. My experience with Dale forced me to depend on Christ alone for love and acceptance. I hate to think of how many more years I might have wasted if I had continued to look to Dale or to any other person, possession, position, or place for fulfillment. Because I was humbled through this experience, I gained the greatest gift, an understanding of God's grace, which gives me the power to love others.

Humility was a benefit of flunking third grade. Not being promoted with my friends kept me humble for many years. To this day I am self-conscious about my spelling, especially if I have to write a note to one of my kid's teachers, because my atrocious spelling was one of the reasons I was held back. Even though my spelling has improved, I'm still embarrassed sometimes by words I carelessly misspell. I know, however, that being a better speller will not give me fulfillment. So whenever embarrassment strikes I thank God that His grace reflected in my weakness makes me a more loving person.

Flunking third grade also made it difficult for me to read aloud in front of people. One of my most embarrassing moments was being unable to finish reading a section of Scripture at my church when I was president of a large college group. That experience humbled me and gave me a deep concern for those struggling with dyslexia and other spelling and reading disorders. Also, because I was so embarrassed, I am extremely careful to not embarrass people who attend my marriage seminars. My embarrassment increased my sensitivity, a requirement for a loving person.

What about the benefits of owing the IRS $1,700 instead of it owing me $2,000? The first benefit was the reminder that money gives no fulfillment. Although we had to sacrifice to pay the extra money, I knew that neither the money nor anything we could buy with it could add anything to my knowledge of God. Second, we had to trust God to meet our needs. Third, the trial forced me to get professional help and learn to better manage our finances.

Column Five: Love in Action

The treasures I found through my problems with Dale gave me an opportunity to minister around the country. What I learned has been the basis for two books about marriage, a parenting book, a series of cassette tapes, the seminars I teach, a six-part film series, and many counseling opportunities.

The embarrassment of flunking third grade has made me more patient with my kids in regard to their schoolwork. Instead of reacting harshly if their grades aren't what I expect, I try to understand what caused the problem so I can help them succeed. Also, I'm more patient with those who struggle with low self-esteem, no matter what the reason.

I've often used the example of the tax miscalculations to encourage others to go to God alone as their source of life.

I could add many other trials to my list, but I don't want to leave the impression that this concept works only for me. Let's look at how it has worked in others' lives.

8

Thinking My Trial Is
an Exception

"THAT'S FINE FOR you," some may say, "but you don't know my problems. Surely there can't be any treasure in my situation."

Are there exceptions to this principle? After counseling with hundreds of individuals, I have yet to find a single one. Sometimes we have to dig deep, but the treasure is always there. Sometimes the treasure is coated with corrosion, but if we do some scraping we begin to see its value. And a glimpse of the first sparkle of gold keeps us scraping until the shiny nugget is free from its ugly coating. The best scraper is thanksgiving. Thanksgiving expresses our faith that God can indeed bring treasures out of our trials by producing love in us, and faith adds muscle to the scraping process, even in the worst of trials.

JILL—A SHATTERED LIFE MADE WHOLE

Jill was born into a wealthy family, but when she was three years old her father deserted the family, leaving her mother and brothers destitute. As a young girl she was raped by her uncle, then her brothers. As a teenager and young woman, she struggled through a number of relationships with males who took advantage of her sexually. She finally married, but the scars of her traumatic past remained.

In our first encounter, we spent two hours treasure hunting. When I asked Jill to state what she liked about herself, she couldn't think of a single thing. With some encouragement, she finally said she liked her blond hair, her loving husband, their pretty little daughter, and her col-

435

lege degree. Her trials were the repeated incidents of incest and rape and her father's rejection.

She particularly needed support concerning her father. She could not understand how someone so wealthy could reject his family and leave them penniless. Most of the time she took it personally, feeling that he had actually rejected her. She needed someone who could pray with her and help her talk through this trauma. She needed to see her father as a man with his own hurts and struggles, and ultimately she needed to forgive him. I assured her that forgiveness would come in time, but until then, she needed a friend or counselor to help her work toward that freedom.

We began to look for treasure in her trials. I had to prompt her at first, but gradually she began to see the love God had given her through what her family had done out of their own selfishness. She hated to see anyone misused, even on television, and she was extremely sensitive to injustice. Her deep empathy for others helped her raise her daughter. She was very careful who she used for baby-sitters and was doubly alert to even minor offenses toward her child.

Her sensitivity, which was highly refined because of the verbal abuse she received as a child, made her always careful to not hurt or mislead people with her words. She also had a realistic view of men, which she would use to educate her daughter. Even with her husband, who was a very gentle and caring man, she was alert to anything that might be interpreted as child abuse. Her cautiousness helped her husband be a more sensitive and loving mate and father. Jill also had an ability to spot abused women and children simply by the look on their faces. She was very aware of the social problems of incest and wife- and child-abuse.

The greatest benefit she received was her relationship with Jesus Christ. The repeated violation of her body had totally humiliated her and driven her into Christ's waiting arms. I reminded her that the greater our embarrassment from circumstances beyond our control, the more God's grace is available. "That's true!" she admitted. "Often I've gone running to Christ's arms and found great comfort there." She realized Christ understood how she felt, for He was physically and verbally abused and humiliated by His public beating and execution on a cross. Jill's dependency on Christ gave her supernatural grace to live and inner power that many never know.

God transformed Jill's trial into a treasure in a remarkable demonstration of love in action. Her painful past enables her to minister to teenage victims of incest and child abuse in a way few others can. They listen to her because they know she understands them. She emphasizes to the girls their great value, and gradually their self-worth rises as they witness her unconditional love and concern for them. From there she leads them on their own treasure hunt through their trials and on to a loving heavenly Father who gives them a blessing, not a curse.

Let me emphasize again that although good can *come out* of tragedy, that does not mean the tragic act is good. As Paul said in Romans 6, God's grace is applied to sin, but we do not sin that grace may abound. Woe to the man who would rape or abuse anyone (Luke 17:1). But when an evil act is committed against us, God's love is available for healing and growth.

Complete healing usually requires a grieving process. Immediately after a tragedy, the victim needs comfort from loving, sensitive people. Regret usually sets in next, followed by denial and an attempt to minimize the tragedy. Finally, after weeks or months, comes the willingness to treasure hunt. Although we can begin to treasure hunt immediately after a trial, and sometimes even during a trial, most of us need time to regain our strength before we begin the emotionally draining digging process.

DENISE—SELF-WORTH RESTORED

Treasure hunting is important because it can also build self-esteem. Seventeen-year-old Denise hadn't suffered any experiences as traumatic as Jill's, but constant conflict with her parents continually reinforced her poor self-image. Denise challenged me after a seminar, stating that she knew there were no benefits in the things she'd endured. "I'm always looking for the first exception," I said to her "Why don't we sit down and you tell me your problems."

I quickly learned from Denise that she hated four things about her life: she believed she was ugly, stupid, and overweight, and she was convinced her parents were unfair.

"Do you want God's best in your life?" I asked her.

"Yes," she answered.

"What do you think God's best is?"

"I really don't know."

"God's best and highest will is for us to love (value) Him with all our hearts, and to love (value) others as ourselves. Do you realize that you have everything you need to fulfill God's will and experience His best in your life?

"And just how can I find it?" she inquired.

We started with her problems concerning her physical appearance. I asked her if she wanted to be beautiful.

"Of course!" she snapped.

I explained that a humble attitude was the key to physical beauty because God gives His grace to the humble. I suggested that she pray a prayer like this: "Lord, thank You that through love You can give me spiritual beauty that will reflect on my physical appearance. Even though I think I'm unattractive now, thank You that as You teach me how to love You and others, people will begin to see Your beauty in me."

Then I suggested that perhaps God was using her appearance to protect her. She seemed puzzled, so I explained further. Because of her appearance, men would not be attracted to her for purely physical reasons, and she would not be tempted to use her appearance to manipulate people. So in any relationship, whether friendship or romance, she would know the person was attracted to her because of her inner, lasting qualities that only God could develop within her.

She smiled for the first time, and her smile revealed a pretty face. Simply relaxing her facial muscles immediately made her more attractive. When a person can thank God for the good they know is there but cannot yet see, facial expressions often change and others can see a new beauty and calm.

I went on to explain that self-hatred might be the cause of her overeating. If she started to relax and began to like herself, the compulsion to overeat might subside. But even if she could not lose weight, she could still find her fulfillment in God.

Denise's below-average intelligence also held a disguised benefit. Denise had never battled with God over theological issues. For her, a child-like faith was more natural. Although asking God difficult questions about our faith is not wrong, there is value in simple faith, as Jesus showed when He used a child as an example.

As we talked, Denise realized this was true. She told me of a number of times when students at her high school had sought her counsel because she was known for being trusting and for having above-average common sense.

We then considered Denise's relationship with her parents. Any support she received from them was based solely on her achievements, which were few. Denise believed they preferred her brother because he excelled in athletics and earned good grades in school. The concept of unconditional love and affection was foreign to the family. Her father traveled extensively, which Denise resented, and her mother complained about having to raise the kids without his help.

Each of these trials had its benefits. Because Denise felt unloved, her sensitivity to others from similar homes was unusually strong. I explained how that sensitivity could, if she would let it, enable her to reach out to others, to accept them as they are, and to understand their needs. Her parents' favoritism revealed the futility and frustration of expecting people to make her happy. Learning this could lead her into a closer relationship with Christ, who would never leave her or forsake her. And her father's frequent absences turned out to be the greatest benefit of all.

438

Her need for a father was the major factor that brought her to faith in Christ. And finally, her poor relationship with her parents could make her more sensitive to her own children when she married.

Denise skipped away from our meeting with a smile on her face. Several years after our meeting she sent me a letter telling me what good things God was continuing to do in her life. She had gone on to college, majored in sociology, and become a social worker helping the handicapped. Her trials, she said, produced the patience she needed for this kind of work, so now she too helps people discover treasure in their trials. *The more love she gives, the more her self-worth soars.*

The apostle Paul understood this mystery when he wrote his famous explanation of love: "Love is patient, love is kind, and is not jealous; love does not brag and is not arrogant, does not act unbecomingly; it does not seek its own, is not provoked, does not take into account a wrong suffered, does not rejoice in unrighteousness, but rejoices with the truth; *bears all things, believes all things, hopes all things, endures all things"* (1 Corinthians 13:4–7). These qualities of mature love are given to us through trials (see James 1:2; Hebrews 12:10–11).

DAVID—FROM REJECTION TO ACCEPTANCE

David was a successful real estate broker when his wife left him and moved with their two young daughters to a city 2,200 miles away. The emotional pain of rejection hurt so badly that David couldn't believe me when I told him we could find a benefit in his trial. We looked at Hebrews 12:11: "All discipline for the moment seems not to be joyful, but sorrowful; yet to those who have been *trained* by it [the discipline], afterwards it yields the peaceful fruit of righteousness." I explained to him how this trial could, if he was willing, make him more righteous, which meant he would be more Christlike, which meant he would also be more loving.

As we talked, David realized that his actions had caused his wife to leave him. His priority had been his career rather than his family, so he had neglected those he loved. David's new priorities were the first benefit of his trial. Next he realized his self-centeredness and how he had been caught up in attaining material wealth, which he knew could never give him a fulfilling life. His family wanted *him*, not more of his wealth. This experience forced Dave to see that no aspect of God's creation could give him lasting satisfaction.

Even though Dave failed to provide the love his family needed before they moved away, his concern for his daughters was genuine. He wondered how they would adjust to a new city, and particularly how their self-worth would be affected if they did not receive the love they needed. But it wasn't too late for Dave to start expressing his love. This trial showed him that he needed to communicate love to his wife and children. He started doing that in his phone conversations and letters, and he enlisted the help of an older Christian couple to help him learn practical ways of expressing love. The more he learned about how to love, and actually put that love into action, the more his self-worth improved.

BIBLICAL EXAMPLES OF TREASURE HUNTING

Scripture abounds with examples of good coming out of evil situations. We shudder at the injustice meted out to Jacob's son Joseph. Out of jealousy, his brothers sold him into slavery. Then, after he had risen to prominence in Potiphar's household, he was unjustly accused by Potiphar's wife and thrown in prison. But many years later Joseph was able to say to his repentant brothers, "*You meant evil against me, but God meant it for good* in order to bring about this present result, to preserve many people alive" (Genesis 50:20).

David was another victim of jealousy. King Saul, on hearing that David was to replace him as king, set out to destroy him and foil God's plan. Enraged, insane, and jealous, the king hunted his one-time friend and counselor for years through the wilderness. The experience, though bitter at the time, made David a better king.

Peter, although humiliated when he denied Christ three times, turned that distasteful experience into a powerful treasure that enabled him to follow Christ's command to "feed My sheep."

The greatest example of all is Jesus Christ Himself who suffered unjustly and was executed in one of the most humiliating manners ever devised. That tragedy has become the basis for our greatest joy—the hope of eternal life. The author of Hebrews expressed this truth when he wrote, "Although He was a Son, He learned obedience from the things which He suffered. And having been made perfect, He became to all those who obey Him the source of eternal salvation" (Hebrews 5:8-9) and "... fixing our eyes on Jesus, the author and perfecter of faith, who for the joy set before Him endured the cross, despising the shame..." (Hebrews 12:2).

Christ knew that after He suffered, we would enjoy the treasure of salvation.

We could look at many more examples of people who have found treasure in their hurts and suffering. Perhaps you're going through a problem right now and you can't find any treasure. Work through your own chart. If you still can't find it, thank God that it is there even though you don't see it yet. In fact, thanksgiving is one of the best ways to discover the benefits of a trial because it expresses our faith in God's promise that good can be found in all we suffer (see Isaiah 61:3).

Faith is trusting that God's Word is reliable. If He promises, "We are going to the other side," then we are going to the other side. Many promises in Scripture can sustain us in our trials. They are the equivalent of Christ's promise to the disciples. Here are some of God's promises that assure us we will get to the other side and find treasure.

"God causes all things to work together for *good* to those who love God, to those who are called according to His purpose [which is to love others]" (Romans 8:28). Almost every trial increases our love for others. So even though we may not immediately see any other good, we know of at least one—more love.

"In everything give thanks; for this is God's will for you in Christ Jesus" (1 Thessalonians 5:18). We can thank God *during* our painful circumstances because we know love is hidden in the pain.

"Consider it all joy, my brethren, when you encounter various trials; knowing that the testing of your faith produces endurance" (James 1:2-3). Trials are our friends because they produce maturity, eventually making us "complete, lacking in nothing."

"[God] disciplines us for our good, that we may share His holiness. All discipline for the moment seems not to be joyful, but sorrowful; yet to those who have been trained by it, afterwards it yields the peaceful fruit of righteousness" (Hebrews 12:10-11). Righteousness means right living and is summed up in loving God and others (Matthew 22:37-40).

"The goal of our instruction is love" (1 Timothy 1:5). Once again we see that love, life's highest purpose, is God's goal for us, and the Bible equates maturity with love (1 John 4:11-12).

You may be getting the impression that we can only learn to love through trials. Not true. We can short-circuit trials by humbling ourselves. Christ stated, "Whoever exalts himself shall be humbled; and whoever humbles himself shall be exalted" (Matthew 23:12). One reason the genuinely humble are lifted up is because God honors those who love. I prefer to humble myself and avoid trials and discipline whenever possible. Avoiding trials completely, however, is impossible.

No one likes trials, yet no one can escape them. We can let them ruin our lives—make us bitter, angry, and resentful—or we can look for the treasure that will let us love and serve others.

By allowing trials to draw us to God, our cups will not only be full but will be on the brink of overflow—the continual experience of those who know and do the greatest commandment: love God and others.

9

Gaining a Clear Purpose
in Life

TERRY NEVER ANTICIPATED that his boss, who was also his close friend, would lay him off after twenty-two years with the company. As vice president of one of America's largest truck-rental companies, Terry had just returned from an out-of-state training conference when he was told the shocking news.

"Why, God, did you let this happen?" Terry asked. His friends encouraged him to treasure-hunt, but the only benefit Terry could find was that he had a lot more time for his family. Within a month another national truck-rental firm hired him, only to release him six weeks later.

Most of us can relate to Terry's disappointment. We too wonder about God's plan and direction and how we can know if we are really in the center of His will.

God's Word addresses these questions directly. In fact, Scripture specifically states God's will for each of us. The power of this truth motivates and energizes us and adds creativity and excitement to any endeavor. It can pull us out of bed in the morning with renewed enthusiasm. It tells us when we're in the center of God's will, gives us a sense of purpose, and adds to our self-worth. It can even help us find, or live successfully with, our mate.

What is God's will? A lawyer once asked Jesus that same question. Jesus told him that God's highest will, the greatest commandment, was to "Love the Lord your God with all your heart, and with all your soul, and with all your mind" (Matthew 22:37–38). Then he added the second greatest commandment: "You shall love your neighbor as yourself." That pretty well covers it all; everything else required by God flows from these two commandments.

> Obedience to the first commandment fills us; obedience to the second makes us overflow with motivation, creativity, and excitement about life.

Seeing people renewed, healed, blessed, encouraged, and motivated by our love for them increases our self-worth, and that starts the overflow in our lives.

People frequently ask me how to find God's specific will about such things as who they should marry, what vocation they should pursue, whether or not they should change jobs or careers. For years I had similar questions. Since 1978, however, I've known God's will for me and have eagerly watched it materialize.

I believe God has something for each of us to accomplish. I've simplified the process of understanding and practicing God's will with a system I call the *FIVE M's*. If you or someone you know wants to "nail down" God's will, this simple five-point plan might help. Picture a circle with the word *Master* in the center. The words *Mission, Method, Maintenance,* and *Mate* surround it like four points on a compass.

The five M's illustrate both elements of God's will—loving God and loving others—by asking five questions. *Master* asks, "Who am I going to live for?" *Mission* asks, "What does God want me to do?" *Method* asks, "How will I fulfill my mission?" *Maintenance* asks, "How will I evaluate and adjust my methods?" And *Mate* asks, "Do we agree about our mission?"

Notice that Master is the first and most important aspect of God's will. The other four elements relate to God's second command. When all five parts work in harmony, we experience the overflowing life promised to those in the center of God's will.

MASTER—WHO AM I LIVING FOR?

The first M asks if I am living for my own self-centered desires or for God. We covered this in the first six chapters. Acknowledging God as the source of my life means that I treasure Him and His ways above all else. Phrased as a prayer it says: "God I love You. I commit my life to You one hundred percent. I understand that Your highest will for me is to love You and to love others as I love myself. You said that if we obey these commandments, we are fulfilling all the laws of Scripture (Matthew 22:40). I am committed to doing that, whatever it takes."

New Testament writers agree that loving God and loving others are the highest commandments, the royal decree, the law of God. Paul writes that one word—love—fulfills the whole law (Galatians 5:14). John says we prove our love for God by loving others (1 John 4:7-8). And James says we do well if we fulfill the royal law, "You shall love your neighbor as yourself" (James 2:8).

A basic principle about my own life can be summed up in one sentence: I realize I'm a "10" to God, but I choose to value God and others higher than I do myself (see Philippians 2:3-4). The highest position I can ever attain is to be a servant to God and others.

In the last chapter, we saw how God buries treasures in our trials. Through persistent digging we can find the gems of love, but using it for our own fulfillment and satisfaction is only part of the plan; the second half of God's law requires us to *invest* our newfound treasure in the lives of others.

MISSION—WHAT DOES GOD WANT ME TO DO?

Since God is our master, asking Him what He wants us to do in regard to loving people starts the process that uncovers our basic purpose for living. While Christ fills us, we are to search for ways to express His love to others, which is what it means to discover our mission.

Learning what people need and looking for creative ways to meet those needs unlocks the door to all successful relationships and enterprises. Those who learn the secret of serving people's real needs are the most successful. We can take this principle much deeper, however. Many people succeed in serving others, but for self-centered motives. We've already examined the futility of such efforts. Genuine fulfillment comes only through knowing and loving God first and then through serving others in response to His love.

It took two years to learn God's specific purpose for me after I stopped working for Dale. I used this four-point checklist to determine my mission in life.

I Consulted Scripture

As I read the Bible, passages about relationships jumped out at me as though God was drawing my attention to them. In Isaiah 58 I read phrases like "to let the oppressed go free" and to "break every yoke." The words "rebuild the ancient ruins" made me think immediately of how Christ could rebuild ruined families. I used this passage as a basis for many hours of prayer.

When I read Luke 4, where Jesus said He was the fulfillment of the prophecy in Isaiah 61, my heart leaped: "The Spirit of the Lord is upon Me, because He anointed Me to preach the gospel to the poor. He has sent Me to proclaim release to the captives, and recovery of sight to the blind, to set free those who are downtrodden." The words *release* and *set free* caught my attention. The Hebrew words from which they are translated are the basis of the word *forgiveness*, which means to untie someone so he can be restored. That's what I wanted to do—untie people from the knots that kept them from experiencing full and meaningful relationships.

I proceeded carefully in this process because I do not advocate pointing to isolated verses and stating, "This is God's verse for me." I went further by seeking God and waiting for His peace after I had checked as many facts in Scripture as possible.

While studying Scripture I also kept my eyes open to the world around me and saw that some of society's greatest needs were in family relationships. Experts confirmed my observations. Over and over they testified that family deterioration was one of the major problems in the United States.

I Prayed That I Would Have God's Desires

God has promised to give us the desires of our heart if we delight in Him (Psalm 37:4), so as I read passages about relationships I prayed, "Lord, is this Your heartbeat? Is this what You want me to do? I only want to follow Your plan."

As I prayed, read Scripture, and heard about the thousands of crumbling homes, I began to sense how God felt about this problem. With that understanding came a desire to help do something about it.

I Sought the Counsel of Friends

In addition to searching Scripture and praying, I quizzed others about what they imagined me doing for the rest of my life. I encouraged them to not limit their thinking to what they already knew about my knowledge and skills. Norma immediately responded by saying, "I see you doing something different than what you're doing today." Even while I was still working with Dale, she often told me she didn't think I was in the right spot because I was doing more administration than counseling, and counseling and speaking, she thought, were my strengths. I'm sad to have to admit that I ignored her input for many years.

One day a close friend stopped by my house to say he had been praying for me. He knew of my struggle to determine God's plan as to how I could demonstrate His love for people. When he said he felt impressed to read Isaiah 58 to me, I felt my eyes open wide. Of all the Scriptures he could have selected. "I see you releasing oppressed families and breaking every yoke that binds families in disharmony." Then he added, "I know this passage doesn't refer specifically to you, but when I read it I saw you jetting around the world, strengthened by the Lord with the heritage of Jacob."

Eventually all who knew me well reinforced what I was already learning from Scripture. Then one day my close friend Jim Stewart, a real estate broker and developer, drove me around town to see the various lots he was developing. As we rode, I summarized what I felt God was leading me to do.

"I've been praying about you and how I can help families through what I do," Jim said. "Much of my time is spent developing and selling commercial and residential buildings, so maybe what I can do is to help finance your work."

When our church personnel committee met to consider my future, their enthusiasm compounded my own. They even wanted to ask the church to help finance my mission. And so it went. Person after person corroborated what I sensed God was calling me to do.

Checking with all these people confirmed to me that my goal was not selfish, that I was not anxious for personal gain or loss. My relationship with Christ met all my needs for personal worth and achievement, so I prayed, "Lord, I'm already satisfied with You—You are filling my life. Now show me what You want me to do for others." Although I trusted God to reveal His plan in His time, the number of lives shattering around me countered my patience with a sense of urgency. So I kept saying, "Hurry up, Lord. But take Your time."

I Tested My Peace

A fourth test of knowing God's mission was His peace in my heart. When I was nearly certain that my desires matched what God wanted me to do, I thanked Him that He would be faithful to answer my request. I stood in His prayer line each day, knowing He would reveal His specific will for me. Then I waited for the peace of God that surpasses all comprehension (Philippians 4:7), which I knew would guard my heart and mind in the Lord and keep me from doubting, fretting, or continually questioning.

Sometimes I pretended I was teaching a conference. As I did, I examined myself to see if I had peace about it. Or I envisioned myself working in a counseling center, going through a whole week of appointments. What type of people would I see? Depressed and despairing parents? Misunderstood husbands and wives? Lonely singles? When I imagined myself helping husbands and wives find restoration with the Lord and harmony with each other, I had tremendous peace and excitement.

Finally I knew my mission: to mend broken relationships between people and between people and God. Specifically, I committed myself to love God and my family first, and on the basis of those relationships to teach others what I was learning and to help them discover their own mission and method. Today my mission statement is "to enthusiastically motivate others to highly value God, others, and themselves."

Unfortunately, many people make crucial decisions about the next step, method, which includes education and career, without stopping to determine their mission. I believe this is one reason for the proliferation of mid-life crises. It may also be a reason some people don't finish their education. College is a method, and a college education has much more value if we know our mission.

METHOD—HOW WILL I FULFILL MY MISSION?

Some people enjoy seeking God's will, but hesitate to move when He reveals it. But knowing our mission, although an imperative first step, is only the beginning. After testing it to be sure it's right, we need to move through open doors to fulfill it. First we need to evaluate the variety of possible methods to accomplish our mission. Here are some examples of missions and methods:

This is where the fun and adventure really begins. Part of the enjoyment of pursuing methods is realizing that our natural abilities are not the only criteria for determining whether or not to use a particular method. With enough study, time, and experience, and by drawing upon the power of the Holy Spirit, we can excel in almost any field.

Suppose a woman's mission is to relieve people of physical pain. She could do a variety of things to accomplish her mission: become a medical doctor or dentist, work for the Red Cross, raise money to send medical teams to third-world countries, do research to discover new pain-relieving drugs, become a paramedic, a nurse, or a physical therapist, etc.

MISSION (What I'll do in life)	METHOD (How I'll do it)
Relieve people of physical pain.	Doctor Dentist Nurse Physical therapist Hospital administrator Pharmacist Relief worker
Feed those who are hungry.	Restaurant (owner or worker) Missionary Grocery store (owner or worker) World hunger relief
Provide shelter for people.	Building contractor Remodeler Interior decorator Motel operator Builder of inexpensive homes for poor
Reach the unreached for Christ.	Missionary Airplane pilot Preacher Tract writer Crusade team member Film producer Evangelist

To carry out my mission of strengthening relationships I had an unlimited number of methods to choose from. I could teach seminars, counsel, become a pastor, disciple couples, become a psychologist or social worker, serve as a chaplain in a hospital, etc.

The process of eliminating methods is as difficult as thinking of them. One thing I did (which, incidentally, I continue to do to keep my skills sharp) was to ask experts how they thought I could accomplish my mission. For example, I talked with successful writers to learn what makes some books better than others; I studied popular speakers to learn what makes them effective; and I read books and periodicals to stay current on the latest insights in counseling. Throughout this process I tried not to rush God, but I didn't want to wait any longer than necessary to begin fulfilling His call.

Christian psychologist Dr. Henry Brandt strongly influenced my choice of methods. In 1978, while teaching a conference with him in the Virgin Islands, I told him what I believed God wanted me to do, and he gave me this fantastic advice: "Gary," he said, "I've used a lot of methods to help couples in my thirty years of ministry, and I've concluded that five of them are the best for ministering to people in difficult relationships. The first one helps the most people. The others follow in descending order of effectiveness."

1. Write a book. This method scared me. How could someone who has difficulty spelling ever write a book? But Dr. Brandt was emphatic. "You'll help more people more effectively by forcing yourself to clarify your message through the printed word," he said. "And you'll help people you'd never meet otherwise."

2. Record my messages on tape. This method offered a little more hope. By refining my messages and recording them on cassettes I could make them available all over the world.

3. Record my refined messages on film or videotape. The more specialized my message became, the more strongly he felt about my need to investigate this possibility. Initially I sensed that this too was something I could never do.

4. Speak in churches, conferences, and seminars. Although Dr. Brandt encouraged me to use this method, he warned me that I would help fewer people through this method than through the first three. He agreed, however, that there is tremendous power and effectiveness in preaching.

5. Counsel on a personal basis. This method, although highly effective, helps the least number of people. Dr. Brandt advised me to set up regular counseling sessions, however, because without contact with real people and real problems I'd soon have nothing to say through the other four methods.

In ways beyond my ability to imagine, God eventually opened all five of these doors for me. Within six years from the time I first began "standing in God's line," God began to supernaturally answer all five. At first I eliminated the thought of writing a book or making a movie. Considering my literary abilities and my financial resources, I felt these were out of the question. But the more I thought about how all things are possible through Christ who strengthens us (Philippians 4:13) and that it was God who wanted me to serve people, I concluded that my attitude limited God. The more I prayed about and studied the five methods Dr. Brandt suggested—books, tapes, movies, speaking, and counseling—the more I sensed a peace about using all five methods myself.

Norma was as excited about the five methods as I was, so together with our children and a few friends we began to pray that before I turned sixty God would allow me to write a book about helping couples stay in harmony. Like the widow in Luke 18, I started every morning in God's line, praying and hoping for the day I would see a book in print. Sometimes I walked into bookstores and imagined my book on the shelf, even though I knew my skills were still inadequate. I didn't expect God to answer my prayer for a number of years, but that didn't diminish my enthusiasm.

While I was standing in God's line many people tried to discourage me by reminding me of how many books have already been written about marriage and of how difficult it is to get a book published. Then they would say, "And almost none of them become bestsellers." They were right; the odds are slim that any one book will sell more than an average number of copies. They also tried to discourage me from doing a film series because of the popularity of the James Dobson films.

I countered their pessimism and my doubts with the assurance that God was leading me into this. Since He had a unique message to give me, it didn't matter how many books and films were already available. Besides, millions of people needed to be reached, so God could use as many people as He wanted to help.

I knew I needed a lot of preparation. Whatever your mission and whatever methods you choose to accomplish it, you must learn the necessary skills, even though it may take years. Don't limit yourself and God by dwelling on what you already know and can do. We learn best by doing—over and over and over—and if we are faithful in preparing, we will be ready when the opportunity comes. I wanted to be ready when the opportunity came. In other words, as a good friend of mine says, "If God promises you a horse, you'd better start learning to ride!"

Only six months after I started praying, God nearly knocked me off my feet with His reply. My friend Steve Scott called from Philadelphia and asked if I would let his company finance two books by me. He would help me write them and Pat Boone would endorse them in an advertisement on national television.

Ephesians 3:20 flashed through my mind: "Now to Him who is able to do exceeding abundantly *beyond* all that we ask or think . . ." I had prayed for one book, but God gave me an opportunity to write two. I had

453

dreamed of getting one title into bookstores, but God wanted to market my books to a much larger audience through television.

I accepted the opportunity enthusiastically, even though I still considered myself the least likely candidate to write a book. But God is not limited by our inabilities. He does his best work with people who are willing and available to carry out His will of loving others. Willingness is the key; knowledge and skills can be learned.

Although I was a willing student, I had no idea of the amount of time and effort learning required. That was especially true of my first two books. Each day I felt as if I were being whipped with a belt. Many times I wondered why I had allowed myself to get into such a pressurized situation—having to produce two books in only a short time. Many days I simply concluded, "God, since You opened this door, and because I know You're faithful to Your children, I believe You'll enable me to finish what You've started. But I want You to know that this is a miserable and painful experience."

While working on the two books, I continued to pray about the other four methods. Before I had finished writing, a producer from Hollywood, California, called to ask if he could send a film crew to Texas to make me part of a movie they were producing on strengthening families. In my busyness, I turned down the opportunity without really praying about it. Besides, I'd never heard of the featured pastor in the film, a man by the name of Charles Swindoll. The film, *Strike the Original Match,* as everyone knows by now, became an award winner that still ministers to thousands around the world. God had opened the door I was pounding on, and I had slammed it in His face.

That experience taught me an important lesson. From then on when I knocked, I kept my eyes on the door, expecting it to open any minute. I felt like the Christians in the Book of Acts must have felt when they failed to recognize answered prayer. They were so preoccupied with praying for Peter's release from prison that they didn't believe the servant who told them he was knocking on their door. Since turning down the opportunity to participate in "Strike the original Match," I've paid much more attention to open doors. For each opportunity I try to discern my "serving capacity" and God's will.

Other methods besides these five have also opened up, including opportunities on various television and radio programs. On some occasions I have felt such intense pressure that seconds before the program begins I can barely remember my name, much less the answers to any questions. In those final seconds, while listening to the director count down, I close my eyes and say, "Okay, Lord, here we go. I don't know how it will go, but I'm doing this to help people. If I embarrass anyone, including You, thank You ahead of time for the massive doses of grace I'll receive because of how humble I'll feel. I know Your grace will enable me to be a more loving person, which is Your ultimate will."

MAINTENANCE—ARE MY METHODS STILL EFFECTIVE?

Once we have recognized our mission and are actively pursuing several methods, we'll begin to see which methods are most effective and concentrate on those. In addition, we need to continually ask God to reveal any other methods He wants us to use to communicate the message He's given us. The first time I heard James Dobson's radio program "Focus on the Family," I realized it would be an effective vehicle to communicate the message God had given me. When I heard reports about the size of Dobson's audience throughout the world, I got in line before the Lord and asked Him for a chance to be a guest so I could share some of the principles of marriage I'd written in my two books.

The opportunity finally came through a parenting book I'd written, not the marriage books, but by this time God's unexpected tactics didn't surprise me as much as they did at first. I enjoyed the interaction with Gill Moegerle and Dr. Dobson and thought the interview went well—until I heard a recording of it. Hearing myself constantly interrupting Jim and Gill embarrassed me. The technique of "actively listening" that is so effective in individual encounters was an embarrassing liability on radio. Almost every time they spoke, I made a noise or comment. It was so noticeable that numerous friends from around the country pointed it out to me.

In humility I went back to God and thanked Him for the opportunity. I recommitted my dedication to Him and to serving people. I told Him that even if I was never on another show, my life would be full by knowing Him.

Shortly afterward, John Nieder, the host for Dr. Howard Hendrick's radio program, flew to Phoenix to tape some programs with me. John had heard my interview with Dobson and he lovingly and sensitively instructed me on how to correct my problem. I made a sign and placed it on my desk during our interview: DON'T TALK OR MAKE ANY NOISE WHILE JOHN IS SPEAKING. Keeping quiet was difficult, but the memory of my previous humiliation silenced me. I thanked God that He loved me enough to give me another opportunity to learn the skills I needed to communicate His message more effectively.

Soon after that I received the following letter:

> I'm writing to you to explain my changing feelings about you over the last several weeks. After I heard you on Dr. Dobson's program, I purposed that I would never listen to you again on radio because

you interrupted Dr. Dobson so many times. A friend of mine called me the other day and said you were on Dr. Hendrick's program and it was helping her and I ought to tune in. I told her I could not listen to Mr. Smalley any more but if she wanted to, that was fine. But my curiosity got the better of me and I finally turned on the radio. To my amazement, you did not interrupt Mr. Nieder one time. I decided that you must have learned your lesson and I'm looking forward to hearing you again.

Any relationship, vocation, or ministry, if it is to remain fresh and effective, needs continual evaluation. Churches that continually reevaluate the times they meet on Sunday, the programs they provide for people, and even the method of sermon delivery, all with the idea of better fulfilling their mission, usually have the most exciting ministries. Unfortunately, many get locked into a method and stay with it long after it's served it's usefulness, which may indicate they have either forgotten their mission or never knew it.

MATE—DO WE AGREE ABOUT OUR MISSION?

The last M depends on whether we're single or married. For singles, this fits nicely as the final piece in God's plan for life. Once we know our master, mission, and methods, we are much better prepared to decide what type of person we should spend the rest of our lives with. (Or perhaps we may be better prepared to understand why God is calling us to remain single.) I'm not suggesting that marriage partners must have exactly the same mission and methods, but Scripture convinces me that God wants us as equally yoked as possible. I am grateful for a pastor who encouraged me to look for a wife who was going the same direction I was. During our marriage, Norma and I have remained enthusiastic teammates in our efforts to follow the will of God.

This conclusion may seem obvious, but many people believe they can marry simply on the basis of being "in love" with each other. Later they discover that their mate has a mission and several methods that are counterproductive to their own mission and methods.

For those who are married the last M concerns entering into ONENESS with our mate. Part of becoming one in marriage is learning to be of one mind. Unfortunately, many Christians determine their mission as if they were still single, never considering the effect it will have on their mate and children. Choosing a mission or a method without consulting family members can destroy a family. I've met writers who feel compelled to write regardless of the resistance they feel from their spouse or children. Mission and methods must be determined with our spouse if we're married. The oneness we gain is a tremendous asset to help us fulfill God's will. Because Norma and my children were part of the praying and planning process, they support my work when I have to be away from home or when I'm under a deadline. And they have the freedom to tell me when I need to get away from my work to spend more time with them.

The importance of oneness in marriage was demonstrated recently when I wanted to hire three additional staff members for our organization. Norma was against hiring any new staff; she wanted to continue as a Mom and Pop operation. She was afraid that hiring more people would take more of my time away from home. This disagreement forced us to reexamine our ministry and our time together as a family. After considering the family's needs first and together planning how to keep our family life healthy with an increased staff, we were able to bring on our first two employees. But we agreed to some guidelines so that each of Norma's concerns about our relationship and our family would be protected. As she saw my commitment to oneness with her, she remained as committed as I was to our mission and methods.

The five M's have proved to be the final ingredients in my search for the fulfilling life. For many years, I sought fulfillment not only from people and things, but from doing good, spiritual activities. Though my work helped people, my motivation was wrong; I expected worthwhile activities to fill my life.

When I recognized that activities, no matter how noble, could never permanently satisfy me, I began to allow God to fill me with His joy and love. That's when my needs were met. Free to serve others in love, I began to experience overflow, and with few exceptions, my joy has spilled over ever since.

10

Uncovering Six Secrets of Answered Prayer

WHEN I FIRST thought about writing this book, I intended it to help people learn to deal with trials and to see how Jesus Christ fills our life. Now, looking back over the first nine chapters, I realize I've written a book about building a relationship with God through prayer.

In chapter two, when I began my search for the source of life, I expressed my desire in a prayer: "God teach me what I am missing..." When I took my two-day personal retreat, all the lessons I learned through Scripture related to prayer. I realized that persistence—getting in God's line every day—was the secret of experiencing the fulfilling life God promised. Next I recognized that my negative emotions were warning lights that showed me I was expecting to find life's meaning in God's creation rather than in the Creator. Prayer corrected each of those emotions. Trials motivated me to treasure hunt—through prayer. And my search to find and implement God's mission and methods for my life led me even deeper in prayer.

Perhaps some of us think of prayer only as words of thanks we mutter before eating, as a ritual performed during a Sunday morning worship service, as clichés spoken during family devotions, or as cries for help in the face of a major crisis. These are valid occasions for prayer, but there is so much more. Prayer is what connects us to the source of life that fills us and makes life overflow.

Is it that simple? Is prayer all we need to have a fulfilling life? In some ways, a prayer life is like a puzzle made for preschoolers: it contains only a few pieces. Some people, however, delight in cutting each piece into smaller pieces so that it takes years of education and experience to assemble the puzzle. Although understanding increases as we mature, newborn believers can experience through prayer the joy of an overflowing life just as those who have known God for many years.

Although we could never explore every aspect of prayer in one chapter, or even in an entire book, the following thoughts explain what I believe it means to pray effectively.

PRAYER—REHEARSING GOD'S WILL

As the Israelites prepared to enter the Promised Land, Moses warned them not to forget all that God had commanded. Since Canaan had no thriving religious book publishing industry to preserve the law in writing, the Israelites taught God's commands to their children from morning until night—as they sat in their homes, as they walked to and from work, as they went to sleep, and as they rose in the morning (Deuteronomy 6:1–9). Every day they reviewed and reminded each other of God's laws.

Like the Israelites who rehearsed God's law, I believe prayer is rehearsing God's will. Regularly reminding ourselves of God's will keeps us pointed toward His goal and helps us learn what it means to value Him and others. It makes us ask questions like "Who am I going to love today? Who will I encourage? Have I offended anyone from whom I need to ask forgiveness?" It points out my selfishness and reveals my need to continually turn away from my selfish ways and show compassion to those around me by becoming a channel of God's love.

Rehearsing God's will also requires that I keep my mission in front of me. All successful corporations set clearly defined objectives that determine their day-to-day business strategy. Christ taught this principle in His Sermon on the Mount: "But seek first His kingdom and His righteousness; and all these things shall be added to you" (Matthew 6:33). I allow God to set the goals that will further His kingdom, then I go to Him daily, praying for the opportunities and resources to reach those objectives.

The most important aspect of rehearsing God's will is making sure that I pray only for things that are consistent with 1 Timothy 6:3–4: "If anyone advocates a different doctrine, and does not agree with sound words, those of our Lord Jesus Christ, and with the doctrine conforming to godliness, he is conceited and understands nothing." This verse applies to false teachers, but I use it to double-check my prayer life. Is my prayer consistent with what Christ taught? Will what I am praying for lead to godliness?

But successful prayer requires more than knowing God's will. It also requires faith, and I have found that my faith works best when I mentally picture what I'm praying for.

PRAYER—PICTURING GOD'S DESIRES

In an earlier chapter I cited two examples of faith: the Roman soldier who exhibited great faith; and the disciples crossing the Sea of Galilee who exhibited little faith. When the storm raged around them they feared losing their lives, even though Jesus had told them they were going to the other side of the lake. The waves crashing over their boat washed away their vision of a safe arrival on the opposite shore. Great faith is knowing, even in the midst of a storm, that we will reach the destination God has given us. Great faith has confidence that it's only a matter of time—a few days, a few years—until we reach God's goals.

Having great faith is impossible without a picture of God's goal in our minds. We need to see how we should act with Christ in our life. All of us who know God personally should obey His commands to love Him, value ourselves, and be concerned for the welfare of others. God wants our lives to display the fruit of the Spirit (Galatians 5:22-23). How will we act when we are loving, full of joy, peaceful, patient, kind, good, faithful, gentle, and self-controlled?

We each need to ask ourselves who we know that exhibits the fruit of the Spirit? Can we say, "That person has life. That's what I want to be like." Though we must not place our expectations in humans, we need examples of men and women totally dedicated to God. The director of a powerful Christian ministry in Europe is a living example to me of how God can shine through us. He exudes life. His facial expressions, warm friendly greetings, and most of all his enthusiasm all convey his total love for Christ. He helps me *see* what Romans 8:29 means when it says that God's desire is for me to become like His Son Jesus Christ.

This also works with specific commands of Scripture. Just as we would use a movie camera to record an event so we could watch it as often as we wanted, our mental cameras can "record" an event that we can play back daily to help us understand how God may answer a prayer. For instance, using God's command to "encourage the fainthearted" (1 Thessalonians 5:14), I picture a scene in much the same way a movie camera would. I may see myself sitting in the living room with a husband and wife who are headed for divorce. They are "fainthearted" and want me to help. I imagine interacting with them, counseling them, and then seeing them emerge from our meeting with renewed hope. If the disciples had done this in Matthew 8, Jesus would have commended them for their great faith. Because they had not "filmed" their arrival on the other shore, they were not able to weather the storm.

God realizes that we need mental pictures in order to grasp His will. When God promised to make Abraham a great nation, He helped Abraham see the promise by showing him the stars of heaven. "So shall your descendants be," God promised (Genesis 15:5). Abraham believed God in spite of one major problem: He had no children. How could he have children as numerous as the stars if his wife couldn't become pregnant? His "storm" lasted for many years. When the fulfillment of that promise was delayed, Sarah tried to help God by having Abraham father a son by her servant Hagar, which proved to be a major disaster. We should beware of running ahead of God's plan and trying to "help" Him with our ideas of how to achieve the goal.

God, in His faithfulness, finally gave them a son when Sarah was ninety years old. But then, unexplainably, God told Abraham to sacrifice his only child. Abraham knew, however, what God had promised so he believed that even if he did kill his son, God could raise him up again. Abraham trusted God because he had pictured the fulfillment of all God had promised him.

This principle of prayer is so powerful that we must be careful how we use it. We might find ourselves receiving something we never really wanted. A classic illustration is the story of the Israelites who cried out for meat in the wilderness after God led them out of Egypt. I can almost hear them chanting, "We want meat! We want meat! We want meat!" It was not God's will for them to have meat; He had already provided manna. But in their stubborn persistence, visualizing the meat they'd had in Egypt, they were relentless. God gave them meat, but with it He sent leanness to their soul. Some translations say they vomited all over the desert.

A common meat-in-the-desert mental picture is lust. When our minds are filled with lustful visions and we imagine the pleasure of lying down with a person other than our spouse, we should be quick to remind ourselves and the Lord that we do not want this fulfilled. Certainly there is pleasure in sin, but only for a short time. Most of us do not realize the devastating effects of extramarital sexual relationships. I once heard a pastor say candidly, "Please, Lord, I never want this vision fulfilled. I do not want to trade the joy of a fulfilling life for the pain of sexual diseases, a calloused soul, a devastated wife, a ruined ministry, loss of self-control, and all the other consequences I don't even know right now. The price is too high."

To protect my prayers I refer again to Psalm 37:4: "Delight yourself in the Lord; and He will give you the desires of your heart." God is number one in my life. No person or thing is of more value to me than knowing Him. Consequently, the most important activity in my life is spending time with Him. As I get to know Him better, I've found that God, through His Spirit in me, gives me specific desires for expressing love to others. There are no limits to what He can do through those who are dedicated to Him.

God could have developed in me a desire to serve at a mission in Alaska or in an inner-city ministry. He could have called me to continue pastoring or to be a businessman who could support other ministries. The needs around the world are limitless, and God leads His children to love others through an incredible variety of helping ministries. Some serve through a full-time vocation, others through volunteer efforts, and still others give financial and prayer support. Through prayer, we commit to Him the specific desires He gives us. Once I'm convinced God is leading me toward a specific ministry, I begin to pray and picture how He might fulfill the desires He has given me.

Though we're eager to see our desires fulfilled, like Abraham, sometimes we have to wait to see the results of our faith. In the early 1980s, my desire to film my marriage seminar and make it available to families all over the world increased tremendously. I didn't read in Scripture, "Gary Smalley, thou shalt produce a film series." Over a period of several months, however, I asked God about this area and carefully considered if a film would put too much strain on my family or violate any section of Scripture. I also sought the counsel of several Christian leaders. When I finally felt a peaceful confidence that this project would honor God and help His children, I began standing in His prayer line each day.

That's when I started using my imagination, following the direction of Hebrews 11:1. "Now faith is the assurance of things hoped for,"—I hoped to see this film series helping families—"the conviction [or evidence] of things not seen"—I could not hold the film in my hand, but I could see the evidence in my mind. Hundreds of times, while I jogged early in the morning, I saw myself standing under hot lights as a camera crew filmed my marriage seminar. As I mentally lived those film sessions, I also prayed, "Lord, remove the peace if this isn't Your will. I only want to see this happen because I believe it will help Your people. But if it isn't Your will, I'll be glad to step out of line with this request."

Though I never had to step out of line, there were at least two false alarms. One film company wanted me and my board of directors to invest a large sum of money before they filmed. None of us had peace about that. On another occasion, a video company actually filmed my seminar. Apparently they either didn't like it or there were some technical difficulties because they never used it. When these opportunities did not materialize, I got right back into God's line. "Lord," I'd pray, "I really thought this was the answer to my prayer. But apparently it was a false alarm." Then I rethreaded the film in my mind and started running it again day after day, confident that we were going to reach "the other side of the shore." I always believed that before I turned sixty my seminar would be on film. But I always remembered, "Lord, I don't need this film to have fullness in You."

Then in the spring of 1984, the Zondervan Corporation flew one of their representatives to Phoenix. He offered me a contract to do a full, six-part film series. One of the most thrilling aspects of the offer was that without asking me what I had hoped for, he included everything I had already "photographed" in my mind. For instance, Zondervan wanted a follow-up program for the series and dramatic segments in each film, things the other two opportunities did not provide.

Those days were exciting, but they also required a great deal of work. The pressure was even greater than what I experienced with my first two books. I survived only by allowing God "to put His arms around me" and walk through it with me. Though I knew we'd make it to the other shore, there were times when I got so seasick from being tossed around that I could hardly wait for the storm to end.

Let me say that just because I see how God may answer a prayer doesn't mean He is obligated to do it my way. My mental images are only handles to help me grasp God's promises and His will. The actual fulfillment is God's responsibility and He often does it different—and much better—than I imagined. As I seek Him daily, however, making sure I have His desires and believe Him for those desires, I can be assured of one thing—God answers the persistent prayers of His children (see Luke 11:1-6).

Before we leave this section, let me suggest a few cautions. There is a form of mental picturing—some call it "visualization"—that could become an attempt to control our own lives independently from what God would want. As I have mentioned before, God's Word is what guides us at all times. My mental pictures in no way supersede Scripture. They simply do for me what Jesus' parables did for His disciples. They make God's promises as vivid and real as possible.

Today there is a need to biblically balance our understanding of what it means to "picture" something in prayer. On one hand, some leaders encourage us to picture ourselves as fabulously wealthy, promising that if we do we will be. Although the picture may come easily to mind, with all the biblical injunctions against piling up treasures on earth it is difficult to believe that such a goal could be from God.

On the other hand, some condemn as "psychologically based" and ultimately "satanic in origin" any form of picturing things in our minds. If this is taken too seriously it could frighten us away from using word pictures to strengthen our faith, a method that has encouraged believers—even King David—throughout history.

When David sought to capture God's presence during times of deepest trial, the Holy Spirit inspired him to use emotional word pictures. For thousands of years Christians have found comfort in picturing Psalm 23: "The Lord is my shepherd, I shall not want. He makes me lie down in green pastures; He leads me beside quiet waters." Is it wrong to "envision" God as our shepherd? How can a person read these verses and not do exactly that?

A picture paints a thousand words, we often say, and we have many pictures in Scripture to turn to. The Lord is pictured as our rock, our shield, our fortress, our counselor, our rear guard, our gate, and our shepherd, to name only a few. In Revelation 5, Christ Himself is pictured as both a lion and a lamb.

People can abuse mental pictures by either attributing too much power and significance to them or by denying their usefulness altogether. To forbid believers to picture the Lord as their shepherd is tragic and in error. We don't ever want to go beyond what God wills or expresses in His Word, but neither do we want to abandon a method of encouragement He has graciously provided.

Using word pictures or any other "magic formula" will not catapult us to instant spirituality. There is no substitute for a day-by-day, personal walk with Christ. Methods can be practical handles, but they can never solve all our problems. Only through persistent prayer and by spending time in His Word day by day, year by year, can we grow and develop in our love and understanding of God.

PRAYER—ANTICIPATING ANSWERS

Imagine a seven-year-old early Christmas morning. His parents sneak into his room and gently shake him awake so he can join the family in their Christmas celebration. His eyes open, but with a big yawn, he says, "Mom, since I was up so late last night can I sleep for another hour or two? You can open your gifts without me; I'll join you later."

Is this what usually happens? Of course not. The child has anticipated this moment for weeks. He's probably pulling his parents out of bed, impatient to find out what's in the packages under the tree. He has shaken them and examined their shapes, trying to guess what they might contain. He can hardly wait to tear through the wrapping paper.

For me, every day is a little like Christmas. I try to approach God in prayer like a seven-year-old on Christmas morning. I've prayed some of my prayers for years, yet each day I "get in line" with enthusiastic anticipation, asking, "Is today the day, Lord?" All day I wait to see if one or more prayers might be answered. And when they are, I often receive two packages when I only asked for one. But that only doubles the overflow, for my cup is being filled with Him every day, no matter how many packages I receive—one, two, or none.

Sometimes when I'm reviewing a "Scripture verse film" in my mind, the light bulb burns out or the projector malfunctions. Almost immediately a new film comes into focus showing that God will not be faithful to hear me again. This doubting film is so convincing that if I view it for long, I lose hope. Like when I think, "There's no way God can bring joy this time." I try to shut off the "doubt film" as soon as I recognize it, but sometimes it runs for several minutes no matter what I do.

And sometimes the off-switch fails to work at all. When this happens the only solution is to get up and walk out of the theater. Then later I reenter the theater of faith. And in this case, I'm big on reruns.

What is doubt? Put simply, it is negative faith. Doubt is allowing a film to run through our minds that says "This will never happen to me" or "God can't do this in my life" or "I don't deserve this." Doubt is stepping out of God's line. Doubt is Christ's disciples saying "We'll never make it to the other side." Doubt is the widow giving up and saying she will never receive justice. Imagine if she had gone before the judge for one hundred straight days and then given up hope. She would never have known that had she gone one more day the judge would have granted her request—just to get her out of his hair.

Faith, on the other hand, is the "assurance of things hoped for, the evidence of things not seen." In other words, it is believing that my film imagining the future God desires will eventually become reality. Scripture provides numerous examples. We've already seen how Abraham believed God's promise. Abel, Enoch, and Noah are three more in a long list. Their faith held firm even though God's promises were not fulfilled during their lifetimes. "All these people were still living by faith when they died. They did not receive the things promised; they only saw them [in their minds] and welcomed them from a distance" (Hebrews 11:13 NIV).

PRAYER—USING WORD PICTURES

Word pictures expand the boundaries of our language and thoughts and thereby increase our intimacy with God. They give us a better understanding of God as well as a new way of expressing to Him our thoughts and feelings. God's awesomeness is so far beyond our comprehension that we cannot begin to understand Him unless He expresses Himself in ways we can picture and in settings familiar to our experiences.

David was a master at expressing his relationship with God in word pictures. Look again at some of his visual thoughts: "The Lord is my shepherd.... He makes me lie down in green pastures.... He leads me beside quiet waters.... He prepares a table before me in the presence of my enemies.... My cup overflows." Picture with him what he saw when he wrote "You are my hiding place" (Psalm 32:7 NIV), "You are my rock and my fortress" (Psalm 31:3 NIV), and "Your righteousness is like the mighty mountains, your justice like the great deep" (Psalm 36:6 NIV).

Christ Himself helped us "see" who He is by using word pictures. He called Himself the bread of life, the living water, the way, the truth, the vine. And the list goes on and on.

Sometimes I make up my own word pictures: God is my lawyer; He defends me against unjust accusations. He is my architect; He designs a shelter that meets my needs. He is my best friend; I can tell Him anything without fear of rejection. He is my garden; He provides all the nutrients I need. He is my life preserver; He keeps me afloat during life's storms. He is my shelter; He protects me when battles rage. He is my bodyguard; He shields me from attacks.

Often I pray, "Lord, it seems as if all I've done this week is listen to people's burdens. My parched lips and dry, red eyes need Your living water. Let me drink deeply from Your well that never runs dry and splash Your living water over my face. Thank You that You continually satisfy my parched soul. I never cease to be amazed at how fresh You make me feel with so little effort on my part."

PRAYER—LISTENING TO GOD

Prayer is two-way communication. Just as true friendship requires equal participation from each member, so does our relationship with God. We cannot experience the fullness of Christ if we do all the expressing. We must also allow God to express His love, will, and truth to us. (He promised to teach us His knowledge through His Spirit [see Proverbs 1].) We can listen to Him in many ways, but the three I use most often are reading the Word, picturing it, and waiting for His peace.

His Word grabbed my attention one morning as I read James 3. It warned that God will judge teachers more strictly than others. God immediately had my attention. We all stumble in many ways, it said, but those who are able to control what they say are perfect, able to control their whole bodies. James used three word pictures to explain. First, the small bit put into a horse's mouth determines the direction the 2,000-pound animal will go. Second, a small rudder determines the course of a large ship. And third, a small spark can ignite a fire that consumes a whole forest. Our tongues are like the bit, the rudder, and the spark.

469

Verse eight confused me, however. No one can tame the tongue, it said. I wondered why God would say that those who control their tongues are mature and then say that no one can tame the tongue. I continued reading into chapter 4. In verses 6-10, God revealed the secret of tongue control. James writes that God gives His grace only to the humble—those who recognize their dependence upon Him and allow His power to control them—and that He opposes the proud. God's grace is power in us to control our tongue, but He only gives grace to the humble.

But that was only part of the equation. He continued by saying that if we humble ourselves in His presence, recognizing our complete dependence on Him, He will exalt us. In other words, He will lift us to maturity, which will be reflected in a controlled tongue.

Picturing God's Word in our minds, the second aspect of listening to God, familiarizes us with a verse, a passage, a chapter, even an entire book in the Bible. It is especially helpful when we don't have access to a Bible.

I try to picture God's Word when I'm running or have some idle time. One morning I read the story of how Jesus healed the woman who touched the hem of His garment. Later that day I imagined being at the scene, bringing it to life on my mental screen. I felt and smelled the people pressing around us. I heard the beggars shouting. I saw the lame pushing and shoving, trying to get through. I heard Christ ask who touched Him and I watched the woman tremble as she came forward. I heard Him speak to her: "Daughter, your faith has made you well; go in peace, and be healed of your affliction." Like the disciples, I wondered how Jesus felt one woman's touch among such a crowd. I glimpsed His sensitivity—He cared for someone I and the others had ignored. I saw faith and love first-hand.

Picturing God's Word also helps us apply Scripture. Recently Norma and I have tried to listen to God regarding painful swelling in her knees. Doctors cannot explain the problem. Many Christians have prayed for her, yet she continues to suffer. We can relate to Paul who three times asked God to relieve him of what many believe was a physical problem (2 Corinthians 12:7-10). His problem made him weak, and Norma feels a similar weakness. But Paul also listened. In verse 9 the Lord said, "My grace is sufficient for you, for power is perfected in weakness" and Paul responded, "Most gladly, therefore, I will rather boast about my weaknesses [rather than boast about himself], that the power of Christ may dwell in me. Therefore I am well content with weaknesses, with insults, with distresses, with persecutions, with difficulties, for Christ's sake; for when I am weak, then I am strong." Weakness humbles us and God's grace strengthens the humble.

470

In his weakness, Paul obtained God's strength—not just for his physical problem, but in numerous circumstances. Because of that truth, Norma and I are praying something like this: "Lord, we've asked You more than three times to heal Norma's knees. You've neither healed them nor given us direction as to how to continue praying. So we'll keep asking for direction. Like Paul we agree that Your grace is sufficient, for power is being perfected within Norma because of her weakness. We are, therefore, grateful for the weakness, knowing that the power of Christ is dwelling in us."

Another way to listen to God is to wait for His peace. One of the streets on which I jog passes a new development where each lot has a beautiful, panoramic view of Phoenix. A few years ago one lot caught my attention. It was expensive but I figured I could save for it.

Norma and I got in line, praying that God would allow us to purchase the lot so we could build our dream home. Although we never had complete peace about it, I continued to pray. Finally, when we had saved enough money, I checked with the owner and learned that the lot had tripled in price. This forced us to reevaluate God's will in our lives. We determined that His will for us at that time was to use our income in ministry, not in a new home. With that settled, we were free and at peace to stay where we were.

The peace of God should rule in our hearts (Philippians 4:7). One meaning of the Greek word translated *rule* is *to be the umpire*.

Peace, or lack of it, is one way God has of telling us whether we are out or safe, and whether a situation is fair or foul. This does not mean we can never make a decision until we feel some kind of mystical peace. Some people, by their very nature, would never make any decision if they had to wait until they felt peace about it. It means instead that we can be at peace about doing the things God's Word specifically says we should do. For instance, God says we should go to a brother or sister we've offended and ask forgiveness. Therefore we can have peace about doing it even though we feel anything but peaceful on the way over to do it.

As we experience God's peace, hear Him speak to us through Scripture, and see His answers to prayer, we will be motivated to worship and praise Him even more.

PRAYER—PRAISE AND WORSHIP

In the chapter on treasure hunting we discussed one aspect of praise—being grateful for trials—but praise and worship involve many other areas: for instance, singing praise songs, expressing gratitude for His love and generous gifts, and gathering together with fellow Christians for group expressions of love for God. Praise and worship recognize the magnitude of God's great worth. Praising God motivates us to be an expression of His love to others: "This is My commandment, that you love one another, just as I have loved you" (John 15:12).

Prayer undoubtedly encompasses many other areas, areas I am not confident to discuss today, areas that I may not experience until I reach old age. But my desire is for you to experience at least the degree of fullness I have in Christ, to know at least as much as I know of His love, and to experience at least the level of joy and peace He's given me. That will provide us with plenty of reasons to praise and worship our Creator God.

Many have far surpassed me. But for those who feel cheated by life or disillusioned in this relationship with God, I trust this book will be a freshly paved path leading you to a full and lasting relationship with the giver of life, our Lord Jesus Christ.

11

Putting Joy into Practice

YOU MAY WONDER how to implement all we've covered. Unfortunately, although seeing may be believing, reading is not necessarily doing. So I have a few suggestions to make it easier to remember and practice these important truths.

If all we've discussed could instantly become part of our lives, every day we would go to God and allow Him to fill us with His Holy Spirit. We would display His love and joy and peace. Our desires would be His desires. We would get in His line and pray expectantly about the many possibilities of serving others in love.

But it usually doesn't happen overnight. There are too many diversions: getting kids ready for school; hurrying to work; meeting demands from our employer; attending emergency meetings; making a once-in-a-lifetime sale; getting a broken car repaired; visiting a needy friend; resolving a misunderstanding with our spouse—the list is endless. Many of us jump out of bed in the morning, race through the day, and collapse exhausted in bed sixteen or eighteen hours later without giving God a thought, yet wondering all along why our lives are not fulfilled.

One reason we fail to follow through with our well-intentioned commitments is forgetfulness. If we talked about them every day and told others about them, we would be more likely to fulfill them. If everywhere we looked, we saw signs and posters and other tangible reminders, forgetting God's will would be less common.

God understands our forgetful human nature, so throughout the Bible He took great effort to make sure His people didn't forget Him or His commands. In fact, Moses' final instructions to the Israelites before they entered the Promised Land spoke to this issue: "These words, which I am commanding you today, shall be on your heart; and you shall teach them diligently to your sons and shall talk of them when you sit in your house and when you walk by the way and when you lie down and when you rise up. And you shall bind them as a sign on your hand and they shall be as frontals on your forehead. And you shall write them on the doorposts of your house and on your gates" Deuteronomy 6:6–9).

After several years of going to God daily and praying about how to meet the needs of others, the practice finally became a habit that carried on throughout the day, every day. I had my best time with God when I jogged, but sometimes a business trip or illness or unusually bad weather kept me off the streets, so I sometimes went several days without relating to God. I needed reminders to prompt me to return to Him, no matter what my circumstances. If I couldn't run, I could pray as I showered, drove to the office, sat in an airport or on a plane, took a coffee break, or did chores around the house. Time was available; I just had to concentrate and plan ahead to use it.

Most of us need tangible reminders to help us experience God's fullness. Here are a few ideas:

Buy a special mug to use in the office or your home for coffee breaks. Find one that's painted with a message like "Rejoice in the Lord" or "Love Never Fails" or "Get in God's Line." Each time you use it, take a moment to check the contents of your "internal cup."

Practice these principles with your spouse or a friend. Find someone who will agree to practice with you the ideas in this book for the next seven days or weeks. Check with each other once a day to see how you're progressing. At the end of the seven days you may want to continue your commitment, perhaps reviewing each other's progress once or twice a week instead of daily.

Form a small group that will study these principles. An accountability group will encourage you to go to the Lord for your needs and the needs of others. Report weekly on the progress you've made and reveal your plans for the next week. John Wesley, the founder of the Methodist church, understood this truth. Every day at noon he met with a group of men and reported what he had accomplished the previous twenty-four hours and what he planned to accomplish during the next twenty-four.

List on three-by-five cards the desires God has given you for loving others. Place each card where you will see it at least once a day: the bathroom mirror, by the phone, on the refrigerator, on the dashboard of your car, or on your office desk.

As a family project, make one or more banners or posters to decorate your house. Possible messages might be:
- Are you looking to the Creator or to His creation?
- What does your anger reveal?

- God's will is summed up in these words: Love God, and love your neighbor as yourself.

You might draw a large cup with a spigot over it, and under the drawing print:

- What's filling your cup today?

Memorize a simple prayer for restless nights. Instead of being frustrated when I awake too early in the morning, I thank the Lord that I'm awake and take the time to develop a closer friendship with Him.

Play the "Cup Game" at dinner. Invite family members to tell what God has done in their lives that day. You might include a warning light check. If anyone got angry or had hurt feelings, ask what that revealed. Take time to dream together about each family member's mission and brainstorm about methods that might fulfill the mission. If disappointment or a trial has entered anyone's life, you might want to help that person treasure hunt.

These few ideas will get you started. You might get together with family or friends some evening to come up with more ways to remind each other to walk with God on a daily basis.

I hope by now you have a clear picture of what it means to have a full cup:

- We know our cup is full when negative emotions such as anger, hurt feelings, lust, and worry no longer control our lives.
- We know our cup is full when our negative emotions are replaced by an inner contentment and love that comes only from God, through Christ.
- We know our cup is full when we recognize that no person or thing in this created world can substitute for the lasting joy of knowing the Creator Himself.
- We know our cup is full when we have learned how to use the painful trials of our lives as rich benefits to us and those around us.
- We know our cup is full and overflowing when we have a clearly defined mission from God to love and serve others.
- We know our cup is full and overflowing when we daily get in God's prayer line, waiting for Him to provide more methods for fulfilling His mission.

My desire is that every believer in Jesus Christ would realize that our joy and peace and fulfillment is not dependent on God's creation. Let's look to the Creator Himself, loving Him with all our heart, soul, mind, and strength. And as He meets our needs, let's look for ways to fulfill His command to love others.

There is no better way to experience lasting fulfillment. And it's open to any and all who *make a decision* to recognize and accept God as the source of JOY THAT LASTS.